In Search of Management Excellence Series - 2

FUNDAMENTALS OF HUMAN RESOURCES DEVELOPMENT

DR. WAZIR ALI KHAN

Dr. W.A. Khan, BSc, PhD (Eng.), FInstCES, MIHT, MIMgt
Engineering and Management Consultant

ISBN 0-9526436-0-X

Published by:

Dr. W.A. Khan, BSc, PhD (Eng.), FInstCES, MIHT, MIMgt
Engineering and Management Consultant
Bladon House, 95 Prior Road
Hastings, East Sussex TN34 3JG
ENGLAND, UNITED KINGDOM

Tel.: 0044 1424 752 726
Fax: 0044 1424 756446

British Library Cataloguing in Publication Data

Khan, Wazir Ali (b. 1943)
Fundamentals of Human Resources Development,
includes bibliographical references and index; -
(In Search of Management Excellence Series; no. 2)
1. Human Resources Development 2. Education
3. Personnel Management 4. Industrial Management
5. Manpower 6. Management of People
I. Title II. Author III. Series.
658.3

ISBN 0-9526436-0-X
£ 49.95

Fundamentals of Human Resources Development

OTHER BOOKS BY THE SAME AUTHOR IN THIS SERIES

Professional Manual on
Total Quality Management
ISBN 0-9526436-1-8

Applied Management for
Engineers and Technologists
ISBN 0-9526436-2-6

Fourthcoming Publications

Professional Manual on
Total Project Management (Volume 1: General Perspective)
ISBN 0-9526436-3-4

Professional Manual on
Total Project Management (Volume 2: Fiscal Perspective)
ISBN 0-9526436-4-2

Published by:

Dr. W.A. Khan, BSc, PhD (Eng.), FInstCES, MIHT, MIMgt
Engineering and Management Consultant
Bladon House, 95 Priory Road
Hastings, East Sussex: TN34 3JG
ENGLAND, UNITED KINGDOM
Tel.: 0044 1424 752 726
Fax: 0044 1424 756 446

TABLE OF CONTENTS

SECTION 2 : HUMAN RESOURCES DEVELOPMENT IN SCHOOL ENVIRONMENT

Foreword

In the Name of Allah, the Compassionate, the Merciful. Praise be to Allah, Lord of the Universe, and Peace and Prayer be upon His Final Prophet and Messenger.

It is for me a pleasant task to write this foreword and introduce Dr. Wazir Ali Khan, the author of this book, to you. This book takes you smoothly from the basic knowledge of human behavior and the effect of physical and chemical laws of nature to the human resources development during education stage to the continuing education through human resources development emanating from the process of learning and experience.

University degrees are the green light for holders of degrees to enter their respective fields of specialization. However, it is not the end of knowledge, but only the beginning as learning is a life long process. Prophet Mohammad (Peace Be Upon Him) has said "Learn from Birth to Death". We must, therefore, constantly engage ourselves with an open mind in acquiring further knowledge, ability and skills, vital for utilizing the scarce resources with maximum efficiency for the benefit of mankind, whilst keeping abreast with innovations and advancing technology.

Leadership is a skill and talent that is born with a human. Books of leadership and management are only to develop and improve such skills and talents. This does not, however, mean in any way that we should stop short of educating and developing ourselves. On the contrary, we must strive hard to learn and improve ourselves and develop the best and most effective ways of managing people to get the best out of them. Accordingly, We have to learn the proper way of motivating people to be satisfied with their jobs, to increase their productivity and to make them feel that they are useful members of our society. Motivation alone is, however, insufficient to get the best out of human beings as it must need to be complimented with individuals' willing obedience to render their best by striving hard, with discipline, conscientiousness and integrity together with making sacrifices necessary to overcome roadblocks in their routes to development and acquire the appropriate ability and skill which comes from untiring efforts and proper training. Accordingly, by learning new knowledge and skills and by applying known principles of management and leadership, we can effectively contribute not only toward our personal success but also toward the success of the organizations we work for.

Most Muslim countries have been grossly culpable for their insufficient emphasis in providing appropriate education, training and development and consequently could not make sufficient improvements in the quality of their human resources. The respective governments in these countries should realize that in order to help mobilize the large pools of talent and zeal that, by and large, remained untapped there is a dire need to concentrate on the development of their human resources. In the development of human resources, however, the moral dimension should not be undermined as Islam has a great potential for creating the key characteristics and qualities in people which are vital ingredients for the development of human character that in turn makes them feel more responsible before God as well as fellow human beings.

The author is a professional engineer a member of British Institute of Management, who has been actively participating, since 1982, in the management of major development programs and mega projects of the Kingdom of Saudi Arabia, primarily for the Ministry of Defense and Aviation including the General Directorate of Military Works (GDMW) of which I was the Director General at the time. The author has produced his book based on the acquired knowledge, experience and behavior concepts pertinent when embarking upon a program on human resources development, including formal training and self development.

Managing people, however, needs a thorough understanding of the basics of human resources development and in this respect this book is a useful resource and aide-memorie. This book is an excellent peace of work that covers a wide range of basic knowledge and provides guidelines for the benefit of newly developing managers, tyro teachers/instructors and all professionals involved in managing people, i.e. the most important asset, and the author deserves our felicitation for this contribution. May Allah Almighty bestow His Blessings upon his plans for the future. Ameen!

Brig. General (Rtd) Dr. Eng. Abdulaziz T Al-Otaishan
Chairman of Otaishan Engineering Office
Chairman of the Board of Saudi Projacs; Program & Construction Managers
Larry Miles Foundation Trustee
Former Director General of Military Works - Ministry of Defence & Aviation - Kingdom of Saudi Arabia

Preface

The purpose of this Book is to provide guidelines; to new and developing managers, technologists, instructors and all other professionals involved in directing, developing and managing people; in understanding the basis of human resources development within a practical framework of both the school and the work environments. In the Book the importance of concepts and practices that can bring about improvement in human resources development is stressed. The Book may be particularly useful as a resource for all those professionals who are pursuing their own self development.

However, this Book is not intended to be the last word but to provide impetus to the realization of certain definite ends in the search of excellence in the Human Resources Development. Each chapter of the Book is intended to stand alone so that the reader can refer to the chapter which deals with his or her specific area of interest, hence some repetition occurs. A Bibliography in the form of references and recommended reading' is appended at the end of each chapter arranged in author's name is alphabetical orders. The Book is divided into 4 sections.

Section 1 is of an introductory nature and consists of two chapters. Chapter 1 is aimed at providing a general introduction of the concept of human resources development whilst chapter 2 to provide a broad outlook of the role of the dynamics of human being in Human Resources Development.

Section 2 consists of eight chapters covering the salient aspects of the human development which is expected to take place in the school environment through the processes and programs of teaching and learning. This section is designed around the traditional approach commonly applied in the school environment and hence far from comprehensive, if looked upon in the light of the development in teaching technology, methods and concepts such as: the concept of Total Quality Management (TQM) in the classroom, the transformational leadership, control theory in the classroom, computer based learning, etc.

Section 3 consists of seven chapters covering the important aspects of human development in the work environment. This section too is far from comprehensive if looked upon quality and management learning and training practices.

If the reader wishes to gain a comprehensive knowledge and deep understanding of the subject matter, he or she is directed to consult the author's further work consisting of two companion books, namely; (I) Professional manual on TQM and (ii) Applied Management for Engineers and Technologists.

Section 4 consists of a useful information in the form of a directory of leading organizations offering services in training and development of human resources.

With the Kind permission of the American Association of Colleges for Teacher Education (AACTE), under chapter 5 a paper entitled ' A conceptual Model of Instruction by B Strasser', has been included which is the reprint from the Journal of Teacher Education, 18 1 (1967) pp. 63 - 74. The author found this paper an excellent piece of contribution and therefore, sincerely extends his appreciation and felicitation to both B. Strasser and AACTE. The author feels great pleasure in acknowledging his gratitude to all the authors and publishers of scholastic work listed under 'references and recommended reading' which have been consulted and quoted in the text. I also feel great pleasure in extending my thanks to my daughter Freda, who has provided me moral support and encouragement and also kept me motivated to complete the manuscript.

I earnestly hope that the matter raised in this book will help all those professionals, including managers, technologists, instructors and tyro-teachers alike, who are striving towards the development of human resources for the benefit of our society.

The readers and users of this Book are cordially invited to point out errors and mistakes and also forward their comments and/or suggestions which may bring about improvement to the next edition of this publication.

Dr. Wazir Ali Khan
Engineering and Management Consultant
Hastings, East Sussex
England
UNITED KINGDOM

SECTION: 1

INTRODUCTION

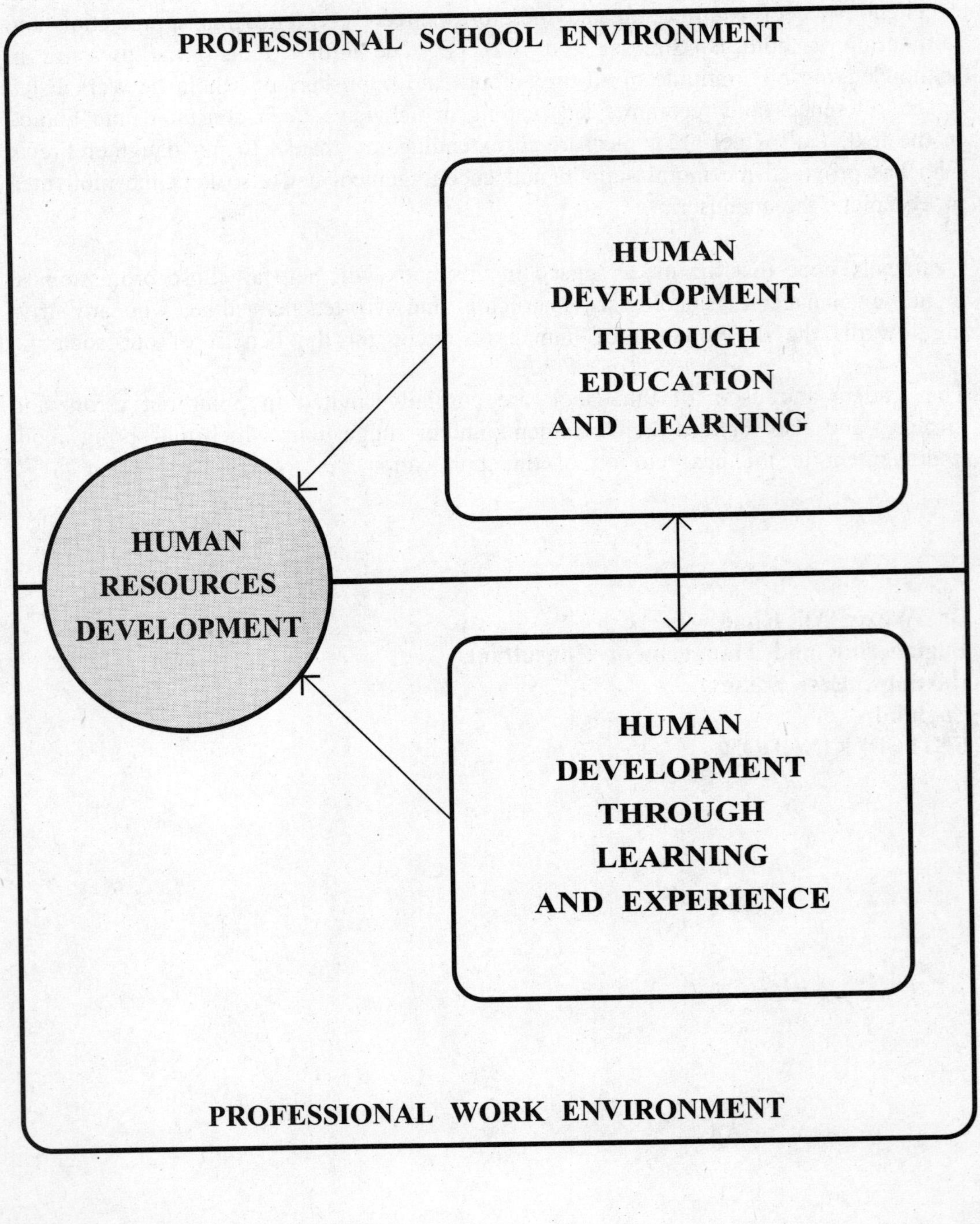

INTRODUCTION TO THE CONCEPT OF HUMAN RESOURCES DEVELOPMENT

CHAPTER 1

INTRODUCTION

Human development is important for the individual, for the organization, for the country and even for the humanity at large. A society that is to grow and develop must have within it people who grow and develop. In today's highly competitive environment workers need a higher quality of education and training to win and hold down technically oriented jobs.

By and large, basic education/training is acquired in the school environment through an education system and learning process which in turn gives a certain level of ability and competence. When a person leaves school he (or she) is generally equipped with basic education and training needed to enter into the work environment.

Learning commences at the birth of a child and as Margaret Mead puts it "it must go on not only at special times and in special places, but all through production and consumption"[5]. It is, therefore, wrong to assume that learning stops when people leave school. We must keep on learning and developing ourselves, if we are to remain effective in our contribution to our personal welfare, to our employers and to our society. We know very well that in this fast changing environment even to keep us in the same place, we need all the running we can do. Therefore, learning never stops but in fact, it continues as a life long process.

In many organizations the management begins with the new employees' present level of development and provides additional training and development as deemed necessary. In this term of reference, it is, however, important to understand the distinction between training and development. Training, by and large, is associated with attainment of specific, detailed and routine job skills, methods and techniques, whereas development is associated with broader spectrums of promotion and enhancement of abilities, attitudes and other personality traits.

On effective utilization of human resources, it is appropriate to appreciate the following remarks made by Dr. Edwards Deming.

"Everyone might well ask himself every day what he has done this day to advance his learning and skill on this job, and how he has advanced his education for greater satisfaction in life"[2]

From the above remarks of Deming, it can be deduced that improvement in skill, education and learning should effect constantly. In other words, for human resources development, development in school environment and development in work environment are equally important requisites. Accordingly, for effective development of human resources it is vital to institute a vigorous program of education as well as of self improvement.

The other important aspect of effective human resources development is building up of courage to strive for high achievement through high targets and high sights. In this respect remarks made by John R. Noe are cited hereunder:

"The great enemy of courage is not cowardice, but conformity. The vast majority of people yield to the necessary pressures of conformity because it is safe. It is unconventional to set your sights high, to climb out of ruts. That takes courage"[6]

Another important aspect of effective human resources development is implementation of quality concept in both development in school environment as well as work environment, as a real test of achieving objective is the quality of end results. In this term of reference the following remarks made by Crosby and Deming are noteworthy;

Crosby opins:
"If we make our profit goals, but don't pay our bills, then we have not met our profit goals. If we deliver on time, but the product has defects, we have not delivered on time. If we meet our safety objectives, but damage somebody, we have not met our safety objectives"[1].

Crosby further opins:
"Satisfy the customer, first, last, and always"[1]

Deming opins:
"Poor quality begets poor quality and lowers productivity all along the

line, and some of the faulty product goes out the door, into the hands of the customer"[2]

Deming further opins:
"Quality comes not from inspection but from improvement of the production process"[2]

The above Crosby and Deming concepts of quality are equally applicable in both school as well as in work environment.

Yet another important aspect of effective human resources development is enthusiasm as Ralph Walds Emerson puts it:

"Nothing great was ever achieved without enthusiasm. And true enthusiasm comes from giving ourselves to a purpose".

In this reference it is important to remember that the dominating force behind our purpose is our actions as Leo Buscaglia puts it:

"Each of our acts makes a statement as to our purpose".

From the above discussion we may conclude that a human resources development process or program imposes some fundamental human development requisites in both school environment as well as in work environment. Accordingly, it is important for us to develop our conceptual understanding of human resources development activities in both of these environments.

REFERENCES AND RECOMMENDED READING

1. Crosby Philip. - 'Let's Talk Quality'/New York: Mc-Graw-Hill Book Co., 1989.
2. Deming, W. Edwards - 'Out of Crisis'/Cambridge, MA: Productivity Press, Washington DC., 1982.
3. Hunt, David M. and Carol Michael. - *'Mentioning; A career Training and Development Tool'*/Academy of Management Review 8, July 1983, pp. 475-485.
4. McGregor D. - 'The Humanside of Enterprise'/New York: McGraw Hill, 1960.
5. Mead, Margaret. - *'Thinking Ahead: Why is Education Obsolete?'*/Havard Business Review 36, Nov-Dec. 1958, pp. 34.
6. Noe, John R. - 'Peak Performance Principles for High Achievers'/New York: The Berkley Publishing GMP, 1986.
7. Tichy, Noel M. and Mary Anne Devanna. - *'The Transformational Leader'*/Training and Development Journal, July 1986.
8. United States Department of Education. - *'America 2000: An Education Strategy'*/ Washington DC: US Department of Education, 1991.

THE ROLE OF THE DYNAMICS OF HUMAN BEING IN HUMAN RESOURCES DEVELOPMENT

CHAPTER 2

INTRODUCTION

Individual personality is a dynamic organization and it requires a continuous adjustment and development. It is therefore, imperative that key characteristics of an individual are studied, such as attention & memory, perception, attitude, emotion, personality etc.

In any human activity nothing of any consequence happens until an individual wants to act and any accomplishment depends, to a large extent, on how much and why one wants to act. There is a famous proverb "you can lead a horse to water, but you cannot make him drink". This implies that an individual's will to work is more akined to need or desire and is something different from his or her capacity to work.

Since one can buy man's time (i.e. his physical efforts) but not his initiative, enthusiasm or loyalty, therefore, how to get the maximum efforts and contribution remained a major problem in modern organizations. Individuals differ in many aspects such as physical characteristics, intelligence, personality, appearance, attitude, intellectual aptitude, character, temperament, interests, training, knowledge, education, skills etc. Such differences should need to be identified and measured so that the right individuals are placed on right jobs and proper training and development is arranged accordingly. Since individual behavior is a function of such internal forces as personality and motivations, therefore it can be used as a tool to attain better performance on the job.

A person soon after birth is affected by his or her environment and consequently his or her inherited characteristics are modified by learning experience thus enabling him or her to develop into a complete personality. Through the learning process, which involves stimulus-response patterns, a person's habits, knowledge, values and other personality characteristics are acquired. From a study of inherited human characteristics and human traits of learning, perception, emotion, attitude, and other complexes, one can gain a better understanding of actions of human beings.

WORKING OF HUMAN MIND

The first systematic exposition of Psychological facts about human mind was made by Aristotle (384-322BC) which was later augmented by Clandius Galen (130-200 AD) a Roman physician and naturalist. Clandius Galen conducted experiments on animal and tried to prove that the brain is the organ of sensation and thinking in which mental processes such as consciousness, perception, conception, emotion, volition etc., exist.

The power of human consciousness allows man to gain insight indirectly, through thinking which cannot be cognized through sensation. The development of psychology enabled the study of various manifestations and aspects of human consciousness (e.g. Perception, attention, emotion, thinking, memory and the will).

Cognitive Process

The mental process that enables us to know and judge objects, their quality characteristics and relations with the environment are called cognitions or cognitive process. Cognition without the aid of memory would be limited to a sensing of present object only, but it is able to link the present object with some past experience when the co-operation of memory images of the past experience is available. Accordingly cognition develops confidence in its perceptions of the object.

Cognitive processes by and large, accompany such different nervous processes which receive their excitation from the sense-cells in the sense organs each of which appears receptive to only selective stimuli form its environment. This is why at time the sense organs particularly the sensory cells are called receptors. The receptors then transform the environmental stimuli into nerve excitations.

There are three components to human psyche which develop and relate to the three general regions of the brain (see Fig. 2.1). The functional relationship between these three components suggest a view of man.

ATTENTION AND MEMORY

Attention

Attention is a selectivity of cognitive response and is conveniently

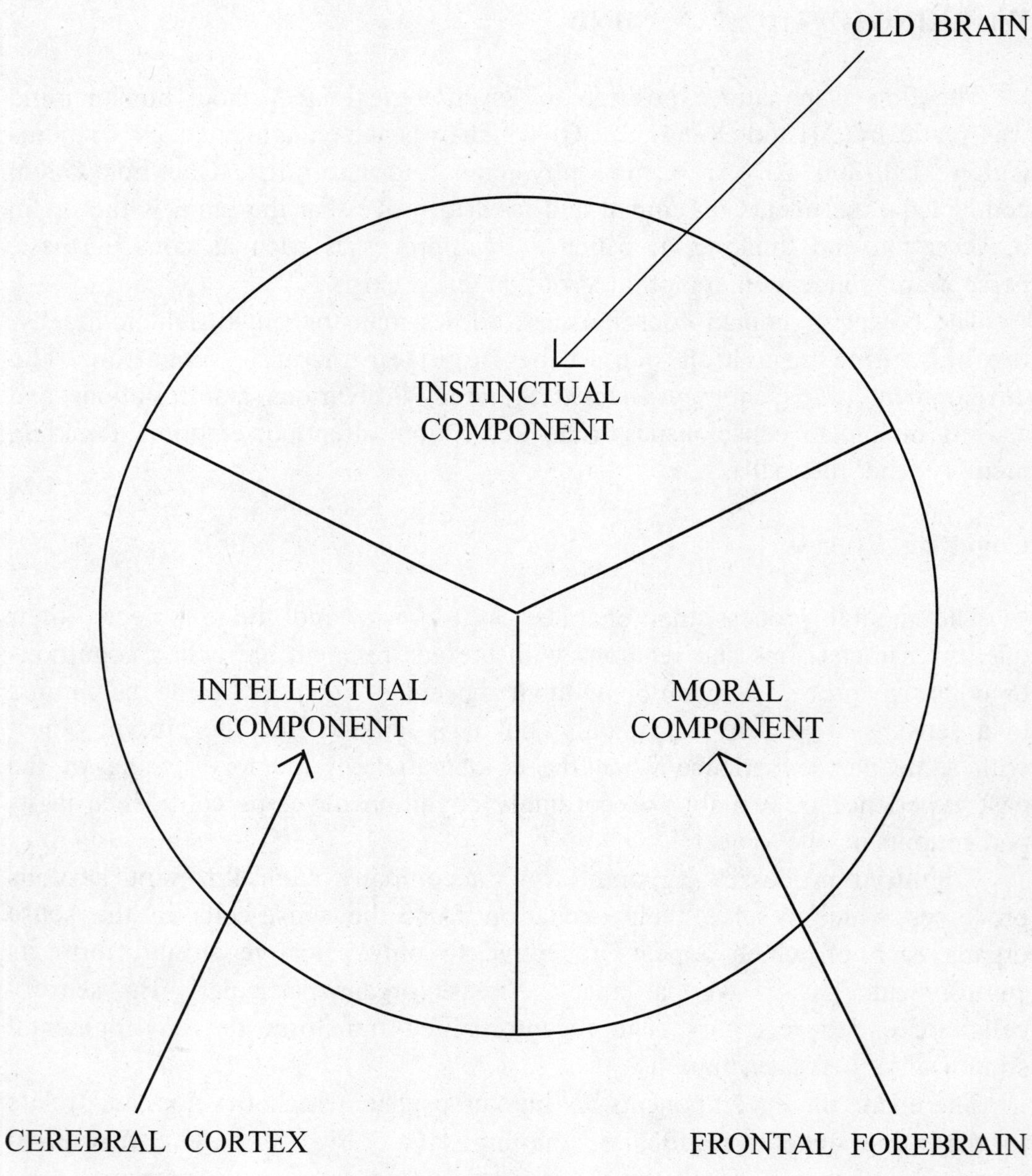

FIG. 2.1 : COMPONENTS OF HUMAN PSYCHE

considered as a function of mind which is supposed to be controlled, guided or directed. It relates the subject with the object in experiences of 'conation' and 'cognition'. In other words, it is concentration of the consciousness on some perceived or called objects with its distraction from other objects, it manifests itself in an individual's facial expressions, general behavior and gestures. Attention is some kind of force on energy which operates in accordance with the quantitative principles of cognition. A person must learn to direct his or her attention purposefully and voluntarily at a definite object without allowing an external stimuli to distract him or her. Anythging that turns a person's attention away from the task in hand is called a distraction and when the distracting stimulus is intrinsic, it leads to a certain loss of output. Like other human traits, attention can also be sharpened. However, the training in switching one's attention from one thing to another must proceed on the lines such as (a) training in actual and quick switching (i.e., training in elaboration of perception) and (b) training in the ability to single out the most important things from those having secondary importance.

Memory

Memory is the mental capacity of retaining reviving impressions or recalling/recognizing previous experience and is a result of formation of sufficiently strong temporary connections in the cerebral cortex. Researches have shown that memory is a storehouse of mind having many positions and it is therefore, necessary to store everything in its proper place.

Memory can be developed and improved. Improvement of memorizing appears to be entirely due to the development of suitable cognitive dispositions do not due to any improvement in the sense organs. Memory is often ascribed to the phenomena which result from the retentive and reproductive functions of the individual's mind, whilst conscious memory implies that any sensory experience tends to leave behind it an impression. Such impressions or their traces are somehow observed and retained and may be reproduced in the absence of the original stimulus complex.

PERCEPTION

It is believed that the human being has five senses namely: vision, hearing, taste, smell and touch (See Fig. 2.2) through which images of the original sensory impressions are formed. Herbert (1816) suggested that each sensory

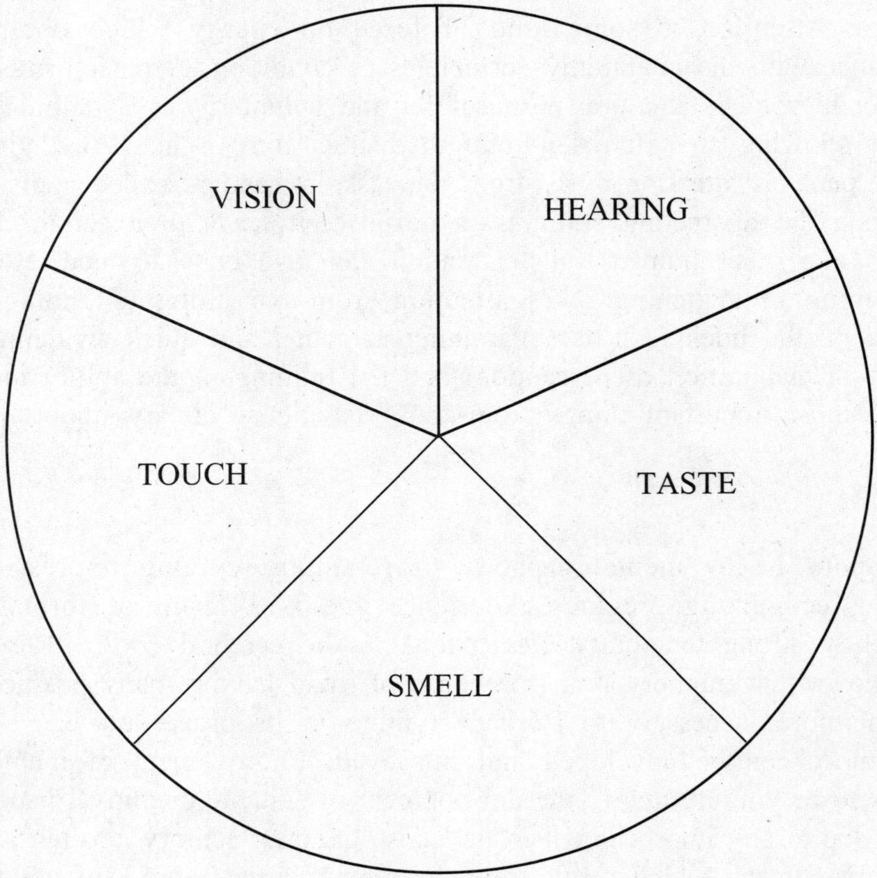

NOTE

Under poetic impression sixth sense is often referred which is known as 'the sense of beauty and intuition.'

FIG. 2.2: SENSES OF HUMAN BEINGS

impression leaves traces that continue, active in forming connection with other such traces (i.e., influencing other sensory experiences). However, the existence of activity of these traces is not consciously noticed by the individual. But nevertheless it would be the past experience (i.e., organized activity of past experiences) that would be generally emphasized in the process of perceiving objects.

Much earlier another renewed researcher, Locke (1617) proposed a very simple explanation of perception which states that all knowledge (i.e., all perception of objects) is a structure of ideas of sensation and reflection which are described in modern terms as sensations and images. The mind has power to repeat, compare and combine all sort of simple ideas into complex ideas whilst images are essentially the results of reproductive function of the mind. The images and sensations may have the quality of familiarity or memorial attribute in common (i.e., a back reference to the individual past), but the number of qualities reproduced in images is smaller than those reproduced in sensations. In the case of complication and perception the simplest experience of images are found and in case of distance receptors, the anticipatory images are quite common.

When perception is inadequate it is called illusion (i.e., false perception) and it is produced due to peculiar conditions of the sense-organs. There is no single theory that covers all kinds of illusions, as one set of reasons produces one illusion, whilst other set of reasons produces another.

Making an arbitrary judgment based on illusions should be avoided and instead in making a judgment, accuracy in one's self perception based on reliable evidence, should be sought.

Perception is the complicated process by which we make selection, organize, and give meaning to the environment around us. Experience is a major influencing factor on what we tend to perceive, as the different experiences account for the varied interpretations of communication events and actions in addition to personal characteristics such as needs, desires, interests, motives etc. In other words, we recognize things by what experience we have had with them and perceive what is in accordance with our needs, desires, motives and interests. We sometimes even distort things so that they will fit the situation we want.

A road accident is a typical example to illustrate this point. Suppose people who have witnessed a road accident include: a policeman, a doctor and an automobile mechanic. After the interview, if we ask these people what they saw, most probably we will get the answers which are related to their particular field of experience. The doctor would probably have seen the conditions of the people involved in the accident and whether they need medical help. The policeman would have probably seen who violated traffic rules and who was responsible for the accident. The automobile mechanic would have probably seen the condition of the vehicles and how much damage was done. The above example implies that because of their particular field of experience, each one would have probably noticed certain things about the accident, which stand out for him.

We also notice that people are more likely to pay attention to those aspects of the situation which they expect or anticipate rather than those they do not expect or anticipate. This situation can best be illustrated by citing an example about 'No Parking' notice. In London, once a man outside his house door painted a road marking in blue color to read "Polite Notice: do not park" and he succeeded to keep clear his door front. The reason being the people perceived this notice as "Police Notice: do not park" and because of fear of breaking a traffic regulation did not park in this area. This implies that people tend to anticipate or expect what they are familiar with.

There are situations when the emotional state of the perceiver is influenced, to a large extent, by the perception of others. It has been observed that people high in such traits as disorder and obstinacy tend to rate others much higher on these traits, than those who are low in these undesirable traits. To overcome such a situation a defensive mechanism (i.e. projection mechanism) available to an individual is the projection technique which influences the perceptual process. This perceptual defense offers an excellent work that enables the perceiver to distort the data (consisted of inconsistent facts) in such a way as to climate inconsistency.

The other influencing factor of perception is the visibility, as we are more accurate in judging people who like us than those who dislike us and we often make mistakes in judging and listening to those people who we dislike as we have perceived opinions about them. Such a situation is dangerous and require a careful attention.

The characteristics of perceiver and the person being perceived also bring some problems in perception. For the perceiver to know himself makes it easier for him to perceive others accurately and his own characteristics will affect the characteristics he will see in others. The status of the person who is being perceived has a variable influencing judgment about his behavior.

It is advisable to widen our range of vision in seeing others, as if we look at them in this style there is a less likelihood of being negative or critical about them. Our ability to perceive others accurately depends on how sensitive we are to the differences among people and to the norms for judging them. Furthermore, there is a great need for greater cohesion between our style traits and other aspects of our personality.

ATTITUDE

Attitude Defined

The generic definition of attitude is "a mental position with regards to a fact or state". Accordingly it may be considered as a bent of mind and predisposition to a certain action. In organizational terms we may define attitude as a process by which individuals learn as a result of experience to orient themselves towards goals and objects. Attitude can also be defined as readiness to act i.e., guide for conduct, convictions, desires, fears, mental postures, etc. It is a precondition of behavior in various degrees of readiness, or a process of individual consciousness or a frame of reference that influence behavior.

In Psychological terms attitude is the detailed direction of human behavior and a state of sensitiveness and proneness to act, which is associated with a physical neural state, verbal opinion, ideologies and an integrated philosophy of life.

In social terms, according to Bernard "social attitudes are individual attitudes which are directed towards social objects and individual attitudes strongly inter-conditioned by collective or groups contact".

In general terms, Allport defines common attitude as "those attitudes which are uniform oweing to the operation of similar environmental and cultural conditions upon similar constituted beings". Allport further defines the Attitude as "a mental and neural state of readiness organized through experience exerting a dynamic influence upon the individual's response to all situations and objects with which it is related."

Concept of Attitude

The concept of attitude is a hypothetical postulate which implies a broad-based behavior tendency in an individual towards a Psycho-Social object. However, human behavior is a four phase phenomenon (see Fig. 2.3), as Lapiere has suggested; and since a convert phase of behavior cannot be

*** PHASES OF HUMAN BEHAVIOR**

PHASE 1

OVERT SYMBOLIC

- SPEAKING
- WRITING, etc.

PHASE 2

OVERT NON-SYMBOLIC

- DIRECT MUSCULAR ACT LIKE RUNNING, JUMPING, SWIMMING, CLOSING A WINDOW, etc.

PHASE 3

COVERT SYMBOLIC

- THOUGHT

PHASE 4

COVERT NON-SYMBOLIC

- FEELINGS
- EMOTIONS

NOTE

Phase 1 and Phase 2 can be analysed but Phases 3 and 4 cannot be measured (only guessed)

(*Adapted from the work of Lapiere)

FIG. 2.3: PHASES OF HUMAN BEHAVIOR

measured, therefore, much controversy as to the nature and measurability of genuine behavior tendencies (i.e., attitudes) has arisen. Accordingly, the concept of attitudes proceeds an overt behavior.

Attitudes are formed through experience which means that they are learnt and can be improved. However, once an attitude is formed (whether based on strong emotional bias or rational considerations), its impact on the person's thinking or behavior will be very little.

Structure and Formation of Attitude

Attitudes are not alike in their structures but differ from one another in a number of characteristics such as: (a) attitudes are developed in the process of need satisfaction, (b) an individual develops favorable attitudes, towards objects and beliefs that satisfy his (or her) wants, (c) an individual develops unfavourable attitude to objects and persons that impede (or block) the achievement of his or her goal, (d) an individual's attitude is shared by information to which the individual is exposed and may lack validity if the information is deficient, (e) an individual may develop an irregular attitude by inventing facts by himself or herself in case he or she is unable to find facts from his or her first hand information, or authorities or expertise. When an individual is placed in a group his or her attitudes tend to reflect the norms, values or benefits of the group. To maintain his or her attitude the individual is liable to have the support of like minded person(s). This implies that a group helps individuals in the formation of attitudes.

However, the research findings have revealed that in the work situation, productivity and job satisfaction do not necessarily go together as there can be circumstances when work situation may not provide strong motivation to a high level of job performance. A renowned behaviorist H Wilensky have identified certain variables which account for these differences. These variables include the nature of work incentives, economic, social, cultural, technological, and leadership, etc.

By and large, attitudes are associated with likes and dislikes and consequently have an emotional content i.e. an individual's mode (having emotional reactions) can influence the attitudes. This explains why unfavorable reactions to groups are most common during periods of tension.

In the determination of the type of attitude, personality differences (in born and acquired) are highly important in a general sense and other differences such as decisiveness, social dependability, emotionality, sex, and intelligence, in a specific sense. These factors can give rise to emotionally unfavorable attitudes which are not easily changeable. Therefore, changing the attitude and developing a desirable attitude is the biggest challenge in human resources development, as attitudes are not simply changed by telling, advising, showing or even by the process of training, but only by education i.e., counselling. Researches have shown that strong attitude develops strong reactions and wrong information/knowledge creates adverse reactions.

Relationship Between Job, Attitude and Behavior

Behavior is a function of attitude but at times attitude is based on behavior (i.e. action, activities and communication which just do not happen but are caused). However, in the group generally the behavior is governed by group pressure, irrespective of the individual's attitude. Therefore, behavior is not merely nature of the individual but instead it is the product of the nature of the individual and situation of the individual.

The researches have shown that perception, conception attitude and defensive mechanism i.e., withdrawal, regression, compensation, aggression, fantasy, rationalization, etc. are the basis of behavior. Both perception and conception are elements of a cognitive process. Perception gives rise to understand the situation whereas conception gives the power of constructive thoughts and calls for vision and imagination, anticipates trends, prepares for eventualities and leads to creativity. Attitude on the other hand is a pre-disposited state of mind characterized by consistency and definite direction and is a function of environment, organization system and group pressure.

In a job situation if an individual does not like a thing, then even motivated, he behaves indifferently. Therefore in an organizational environment it is vital to be able to modify the attitudes of an individual in order to acquire autonomy and maturity and remain near to reality. The most commonly used methods for changing the attitudes or personality traits include. (a) role playing, (b) management games, (c) case studies (methods), (d) sensitivity training.

An effective management (or executive) development program should only work on modifying the behavior which also includes self evaluation (examination) and self awareness in an executive. Transaction analysis operates on self, others, individual roles, and also on group dynamics. Whereas, sensitivity training brings improvements in self realization and self evaluation. It is a fact that changing one's attitude can have a profound effect on an organization and its employees. Therefore, organization should not restrict counselling to any special time or place but must consider it a long range educational process. Accordingly, each manager within the organizational structure should use every opportunity to counsel and encourage his subordinates to develop better insight into the respective organizational matters.

EMOTIONS AND TRAITS

Emotions

A fact of a human being is often an index of his emotions and its effect is also influenced by the tone of the voice. However, the bodily processes need not be identified with the emotion, though they are very important in facilitating the experience of emotions or reinforcing the emotion. During emotion, the more complex and intense experience of affection is found with varying behavior. Moods, stubbornness, beauty and temperaments are manifestations of emotion. Mood is the largest and at the same time weakest manifestation of emotions. Stubbornness is inexpediently persistent which makes a persons behavior absurd. Beauty is an emotional state that bring joy at man's creative ability. A temperament is the most general characteristic of each individual person that leaves a certain imprint on all the activities of each individual and it manifests itself in the general wake-up of personality. The more common types of emotions are: fear, joy, sorrow, anger, etc. Emotions play a very important role in man's life. According to V.L. Lenin "without human emotions there has never been, nor can there be a human quest for truth".

Feelings

According to Woodworth "feelings are a reactive attitude of the organism". The simplest stimulus for a feeling is sensation. Mira, by basing on his profound theory of the mental life as a whole, regards "feeling as the source of all our experience and is essence of what we call mind". The experience of feeling carry the attributes of intensity, duration and quality of affection. We often come across situations in which some parts arose a pleasant affection whilst others gave rise to unpleasant feelings i.e. a mixture of partly pleasant and partly unpleasant feelings, thus equating the total experience to a simple algebraic sum of the different feelings for various parts in a given situation. Psychologists deny this experience of mixed feeling as according to them any psychosis as a whole is either pleasant or unpleasant and cannot be a mixture or fusion of the two mutually exclusive affections. However, they do admit that some situations may give rise to a complex experience in which there is a rapid oscillation in affection being at one moment pleasant and another moment unpleasant.

Determinants of Emotions

These include curiosity, facial expression and suicide. Curiosity is a pleasant and valuable emotional state that enables the executive to discover new meanings and broaden his or her field of interests and activities.

The facial expression shows an executive's feelings about himself and his environment more than his actions. Since love is deep, tender and rewarding, and, deprivation of love results in emotional starvation, therefore, deprivation of any emotion of love is especially damaging. In organizational terms an overmothered executive may become conservative and start showing lack of self confidence, aggressiveness and leadership qualities. A balance needs to be struck between excess of love and deprivation to bring better adjustment and greater happiness. Loneliness or isolation can degenerate endogeneous depression or persistent depression which in turn can cause people to commit suicide. Such depression requires timely professional treatment.

Traits

Traits are the characteristics of an individual and his learned tendencies to react to the environmental stimuli. Traits are based on hereditary foundations and include trustworthiness, generosity, honesty, rudeness, egocentreism and cruelty. The traits are often the result of integration of several specific habits acquired from social learning in a particularly cultural setting. According to some experts every trait has three characteristics namely: uniqueness, degree of likeliness and consistency. Traits can be either expressive (a group of traits consisting of regular habitual responses of individual i.e., Physical, movement, perceptual, style, age, sex, etc.) or of a performance type (i.e. intellectual abilities, special aptitude/abilities, physical performance; non intellectual traits such as interests, temperament, character, schema, motives, etc.).

PERSONALITY

Formation of Personality

Personality is a dynamic organization within the individual that determines his characteristics, thoughts and behavior. It is the totality of a man i.e. combination of body and mind and represents what a man really is. We may say that personality is the sum total of various tendencies of the individual inherited and acquired by experience such as traits, attitudes etc., held together and influenced by a central core called the concept of self. When we say man we imply not merely a person as an organism but also his personality. Personality is neither exclusively physical nor exclusively mental but is a function of body and mind in unity.

According to some behaviorial scientists there are four very closely interconnected aspects that determine a human personality namely: (a) moral qualities (the social aspects of personality) (b) Temperament (the biological basis of personality, (c) individual characteristics of Psychic process (sensations, perceptions, emotion, volition, thinking, attention, memory, etc.) and (d) learning/schooling (i.e. knowledge and skills). The personality pattern is unique. Researchers have found that the process of human production involves a total of forty-six (46) chromosomes (23 from the mother + 23 from the father), which appear in the newly formed cell and develop into a new human being containing around 30,000 genes or carriers of individual traits.

Personality is formed from inter-action of father, mother and siblings with the child who brings to interaction certain biological constituents such as: needs, intellectual capacities and drives etc. The various factors that contribute to the formation of personality is shown in Fig. 2.4. However, the core of personality is made up of attitudes and beliefs towards self. Major factors which contribute in determining the development of personality include: individual heredity, experiences and the important events outside the family environment. It is a fact that every child is a unique personality.

Major problems in today's organizations are related to the optimization of the efforts and contribution of individuals which in turn demand a thorough study of an individual and how to develop personal characteristics and introduce operative effectiveness among its members.

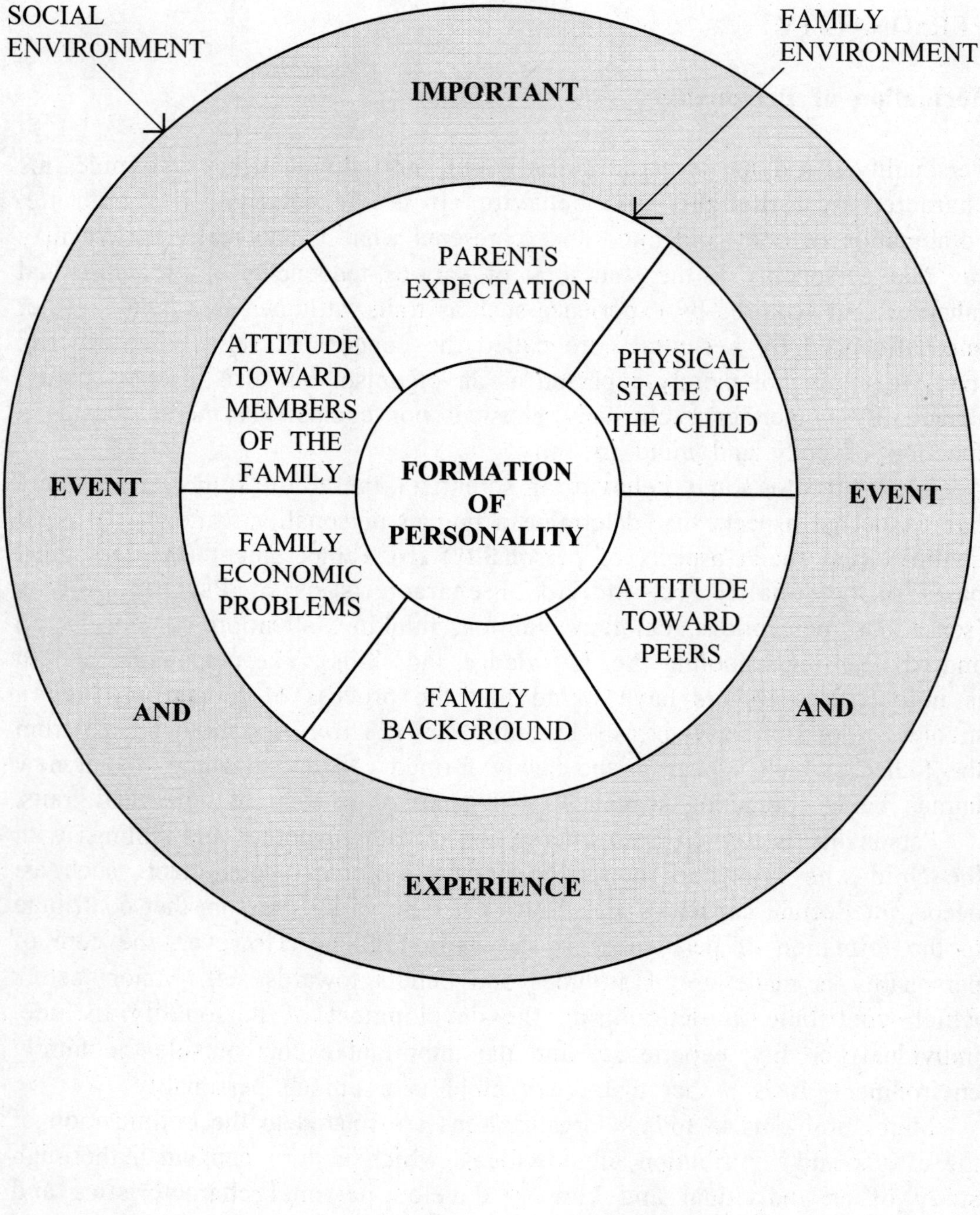

FIG. 2.4: A GENERAL PRECURSOR OF PERSONALITY FORMATION

Human Nature

The term human nature refers to the characteristics of mankind which, by and large, distinguish human being from animals. Human nature, though vary enormously, can be said, as the set of mental & emotional capacities, motives, and psychic mechanisms common to human being i.e. human needs, drives, tendencies, predispositions, behavior, and propensities etc. Human nature can be described in terms of norms, dialects, levels, innateness and learning. However, the sociological and psychological perspective treats human nature as a source of systematic variance in behavior. But the Greek philosophers have described human nature as a rational principle governing human being in an almost law-like manner.

Human nature can be 'law-bound' (when it is caused by, or emerging from or the result of something external to mankind) or 'self-bound' (when it is the result of something internal to mankind). If nature is 'law-bound' then human characteristics can be predicted, explained, accounted for, and controlled by reference to biological, historical, social, metaphysical, or environmental forces. When it is self-bound then it emerges out of sense making or purposiveness rather than in response to external law. Human nature has been studied by various theorists and researchers and the deeply embedded belief structures of organization life have been characterized by four theories of human nature, namely 'Democratic Man'; 'Modern Man'; Totalitarian Man'; and 'Hermeneutic Man'. These theories influence organization structuring and guide managerial behavior.

'Democratic Man' perspective views human nature as compelling human to seek perfection by freely pursuing their individual self-interests and it has emerged out of the work of Thomas Jefferson (US political thinker), Roursean (French Philosopher), and English thinkers (including Adam Smith, Locke, Shaftesbury, and Hume). This perspective is not being considered as dominant today, yet organizational theorists occasionally base their ideas on this model.

'Modern Man' perspective encompasses most management theories (i.e. Theory 'X', parts of theory 'Y', Theory 'Z', contemporary theory, theories of learning, human resources and human relations etc.). This perspective stresses that mankind has a nature which is bound by rules and laws in such a loose manner as to make human being almost infinitely malleable. This model could be used to develop ways to influence the process to attain desired behavior. In the view of Scott and Hart, the renowned theorists, modern organizational values are replacing traditional values based on individual rights to dignity, freedom, and the pursuit of happiness.

'Totalitarian Man' perspective view human nature as compelling human beings to provide self-interest and drift into totalitarianism.

'Hermeneutical Man' model is based on the self-bound and malleable elements of human nature. It has its roots in the work of G.H. Mead (1934) who opins that human interactions create a reality which gives us norms and moulds our nature. Some organization theorists (Feldman & March, 1981, Weick, 1979) have stressed the importance of interactions, myths, stories, signs, rituals, and symbols, etc. as embodiment of reality for organization members.

Developing and Improving Personality

Researchers have found that personality is a function of feelings, thoughts, sensation and infusion. It also reveals introvert and extrovert attitudes. Both introversion and extroversion are marked traits which should be recognized by an effective manager to help him to choose a matching leadership style. The introvert has inward orientation (i.e. attending more to his inner life), whereas the extrovert tends to be in touch with the world and is open and eager to interact with his surroundings. Introverts are over conscious, pessimistic, unsociable, often lack confidence, shy, quiet, difficult to understand, and prefer reflection to activity. On the other hand, extroverts are sociable, confident in uneven situations, active, helpful, tend to be optimistic and enthusiastic, interested in activities/events/people influenced by the environment and above all they want to be with the people and would prefer to work through the people.

In an organizational setting for introverts the high task low relationship or low task, low relationship style of leadership can be more effective whereas for extroverts high task high relationship or low task-high relationship leadership style is more appropriate. Accordingly, extroverts are best in line positions where there are high inter-relationships with others.

In shaping personality an individual should overcome the feelings of inferiority complex which are rooted in the human conditions by facing the situation in such a way that he is not afraid of making mistakes, admitting and developing courage to work on mistakes. It must be remembered that for an effective executive persistence motivation/efforts, self confidence, purposefulness, freedom from informal feelings, strength or force of character are important traits for success. For the improvement of personality, the following guidelines should be followed:

* An executive should conduct a study of himself to get an insight into the reasons leading to lack of confidence and thereby releasing the depressed emotions, if any. This is a fundamental step forward to self development.

* An executive should guide himself by replacing the fear by the confidence generated with the help of suggestions by others.

* An executive should imagine himself becoming what he wants to be by using his own will power, his power of imagination, and by creating a self scheme (i.e. a mental picture of oneself plus the desired change).

* An executive should concentrate on one thing at a time as improvement in personality i.e. sum total of habits, physical traits, mental and emotional determinants, etc. require the needs to be broken down into specific habits, traits or opportunities which need to be developed.

* An executive must continually develop and improve self confidence as it is the basic element to success and a stepping stone towards the process of self development.

* Since social activities are the channel for expression of personality, an executive should always look for infinite varieties of inter-personal relationships which will no doubt provide him with ample opportunities for social satisfaction.

* Since apart from self awareness and self development polymerizing the individual's skill and abilities are equally important to build a cohesive force in an organization. An executive must establish a bond with others, multiply/generate power to create, to produce or to build, keeping in mind that only the human resources appreciate with time, if motivated.

* An executive should strive toward developing a matured personality by seeking improvement to the elements such as accepting responsibility, developing tolerance and self motivation, taking order without becoming obstinate, withstanding criticism, saying 'no' to one's self, putting extra

efforts when needed, and above all weening from dependence.

* An executive should develop in himself, depending upon his particular level and a particular situation, a combination of various skills such as: conceptual, perceptual, human relation and technical.

* An executive should understand, appreciate and use transactional analysis as a tool to know himself and gain a more conscious control of his interactions with other people.

CONCLUDING REMARKS

The human system tends to maintain itself and grow & function in accordance with its inherent potential in which human beings are bound to obey physical and chemical laws of nature. However, within these bonds an almost infinite range of human behavior and attitude is possible. Lapiere mentions four phases of totality of human behavior namely: (i) Overt symbolic (speaking, writing etc.) (ii) Overt non-symbolic (direct muscular action), (iii) Covert symbolic (thought), and (iv) Covert non-symbolic (feeling and emotions). As we have already discussed, covert phases of behavior are not measurable which has caused so much controversy as to the nature and measurability of genuine behavior tendencies (attitudes).

Accordingly, attitude cannot be directly observed and has to be analyzed in the light of the broad based pattern of real life situations to which they are related. However, a knowledge of attitudes (which should be continually improved) greatly contributes to an understanding of the people. But to determine the type of attitude, the knowledge of personality differences is highly important. To what extent personality differences are inborn and to what extent they are acquired is not known, though some of these differences must be attributed to heredity.

Human beings are basically keen to be motivated and the development of this perspective can be seen in Maslow's work on motivation theory which pre-supposes that humans are bound to make efforts to satisfy their basic physiological needs. When these needs emerge, they are sensed as an imbalance thus effecting motivation which in turn leads to intentions and behavior to undo the imbalance. This motivation theory was extended to include a whole range of other needs such as: achievement, affiliation, consistency, etc. by Maslow, David McClelland and other researchers. The researchers have proved that, given the right manipulation, almost any kind of behavior can be elicited.

We may conclude this discussion by emphasizing that people differ in their experiences and also vary in degree to which they possess the necessary ability and intelligence to learn from experience. Therefore, performance of an executive on the job is considered as a function of two different variables namely: (a) the ability or skill of the individual to perform the job and (b) his motivation to use his ability or skill in actual performance of the job. This implies that performance of an individual is the product of individual ability and motivation and not the sum total of these variables.

REFERENCES AND RECOMMENDED READING

1. Argyris, Chyris. - 'Personality and Organization'/New York: Harper & Brothers, 1957.
2. Armstrong, Michael. - 'A Handbook of Human Resources Management'/Kogan page, 1987.
3. Campbell, John P. - 'Managerial Behavior Performance and Effectiveness'/McGraw-Hill, 1970.
4. Davis, Keith. - 'Human Behavior at Work'/New York: McGraw-Hill, 1977.
5. Likert Rensis. - *'Human Resources Accounting', Building and Assessing Productive Organization'*/Personnel, May-June 1973, pp. 8-24.
6. Marting, Dermond D., and Richord L. Shell. - 'What Every Engineer Should Know About Human Resources Management'/New York: Marcel Dekker, Inc. 1980.
7. McCelelland D.C. - *'That Urge to Achieve'*/Think vol. 32, No. 6, Nov. - December 1966, pp. 19-23.
8. Sayles, leonard R., and George Strass - 'Human Behavior in Organizations'/Cliffs, N.J: Practivce-Hall Englewood, 1966.
9. Schnake, Mel. E.M. Dumler, D.P. Cochran and T.M. Barnett - *'Effect of Differences in Superior and Subordinate Perception of Superiors'*/Communication Practices, Journals of Business Communication 27, Winter 1990, pp. 37-49.
10. Torrance, E.P. - 'Education and the Creative Potential'/Mianeapolies: University of Minnesota press, 1963.

SECTION: 2

HUMAN RESOURCES DEVELOPMENT IN SCHOOL ENVIRONMENT

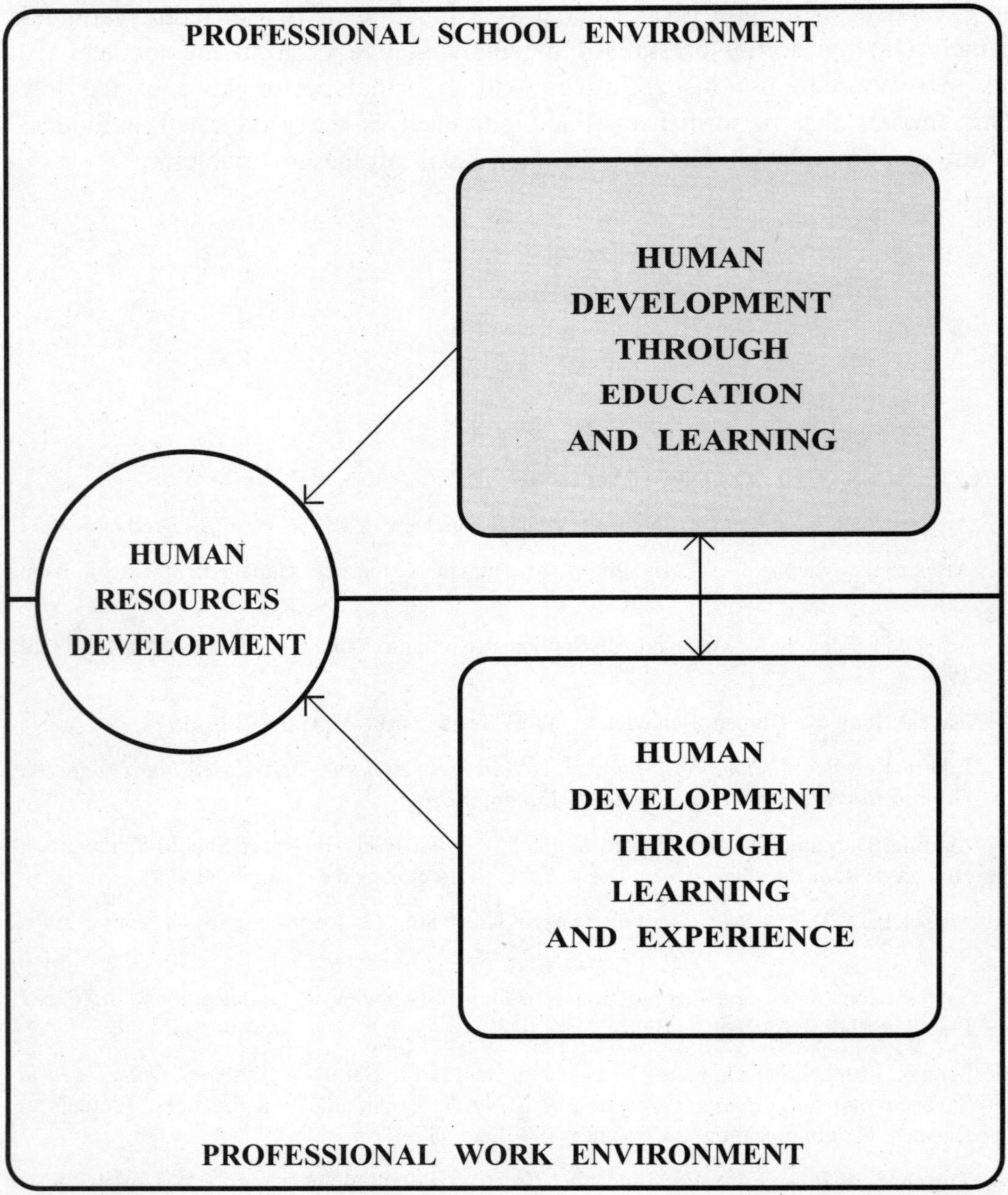

CHAPTER 3

LEARNING AND EDUCATION IN A SCHOOL ENVIRONMENT

INTRODUCTION

Children are continually engaged in some learning activity or another. They, for example, learn a great deal and great many things even though they may have no particular intention of doing so, nor need there be intention on anyone else's part. No stage managing is necessary for the proverbial child to find out about fire and learn to avoid it. The essential features of this situation are interaction between learner and environment, and subsequent change in the pattern of his behavior. However, if the circumstances have been deliberately engineered to bring about such a change, of course we would notice it and label it as a learning situation. Therefore, to consider learning is to consider how the interaction between an individual and his environment brings about changes in the way in which he intends to behave. Teaching on the other hand is an intentional activity, an intention being simply to bring about learning. In teaching the teacher must mark out, present, display, indicate or in some way exhibit what is to be learned. This marking out can of course be done in a general variety of ways, e.g., by questioning, demonstrating, explaining, instructing and so on.

Before we come to classroom interaction it is important to explain what is a school environment. A school by its definition is a special place with special purposes. It is a place which has been specially arranged and intended so that pupils may learn things under the direction, guidance and authority of teachers. In other words emphasis is on teachers teaching the children to learn. Interaction between teachers and pupils depends not only on a deliberate policy adopted by the teachers to encourage pupils to communicate with them and with their peers, but also upon factors implicit in the situation which impinges upon social behavior. Some of the most important factors influencing the nature of interaction are the physical setting, rules, rituals and routine of the classroom; interpersonal judgements and mode of communication, both verbal and non-verbal. Interaction in most classrooms is supported by some kind of routine or ritual which provides a structure or framework for the pupils and gives support to teachers.

Judging others or forming impressions of them is an integral part of all social interaction. Forming judgements of children is an inevitable part of any teacher's task. What a teacher says about his pupil, either in informal staffroom conversation or on a more formal written record, may shape that pupil's future more than a teacher can imagine. It is particularly vital that teachers must be aware of the effects their judgements may have on pupils. They must also gain some understanding of how their opinions might be influenced by external factors as well as their own personality make up. They can then try to ensure that the judgements they make are fair, unbiased and as objective as possible.

Education is a social process. When children come to school, they do not simply learn a given body of knowledge which they carry away in neat packages, rather they learn from other people, both teachers and peers, by sharing their knowledge and experiences, by seeing the world through their eyes and by developing an understanding of what others consider important and worthwhile. Their learning is not only cognitive but also social, emotional and moral. In other words, children are not only developing their intellectual abilities by mastering concepts and retaining facts relating to various curriculum areas, but are at the same time learning to communicate with others, to form judgements and eventually to develop autonomy both intellectually and morally.

In formulating the aims of basic education in a primary school the questions such as the following should be raised:

What should the pupils in our primary schools be learning?

What, in general terms, should we be aiming at?

What kind of upbringing do children need if they are to be able to take their place in society as responsible citizens?

How much social learning is necessary to bring self confidence in children?

What is success and what is failure in the way of learning in a primary school?

Furthermore, it is important to note that at the primary stage, the future is more open and children are as generous and as tolerant as they ever will be towards attempting to evoke their wider interest. The primary school attitude should, therefore, be one of widening opportunities, rather than of preparing for a particular role.

With the above consideration in mind the following most important aims of education in school environment should be formulated and practiced.

a) Children should be cheerful, happy and well balanced.

b) Children should enjoy school work and find satisfaction in their achievements.

c) Moral values should be taught as a basis of behavior.

d) Individuals should be encouraged to develop in their own ways.

e) Children should be taught to respect property.

f) Children should be taught courtesy and good behavior.

g) Children should be taught to read fluently and accurately.

h) Children should read appropriate material with understanding.

i) Society's legitimate interest in moral behavior and in making an economic contribution must be related to the individual's claims to having a life of his own and extended capacity for choice.

PRACTICAL IMPLICATIONS

Judgements made by teachers on their pupils may have a longlasting effect. They are not usually formally recorded; and undoubtedly open to various kinds of bias. But since they form part of an interaction process, they can constantly be modified according to the way in which pupils react, develop and change.

On a rather different level are those judgements which are formally documented for specific purposes and are usually on permanent written record for others to consult and use. Once they are written down, they are not open to modification unless further material is added at a later stage. The main purposes of such record keeping are to assess what a child has achieved in the past and to show his general rate of progress. His achievement in specific curriculum areas is noted so that any serious academic weakness requiring remedial work can be spotted and dealt with before it is too late and the child perceives himself as a failure.

Teachers need to know whether creative promises can be discovered in children and whether creative talents can be promoted in schools. Teachers should discover what creativity means to them and what could count as a creative response in any particular sphere of children's activities and learning. Although we cannot teach children to be creative, we can provide conditions in which creative ability can develop, by ensuring that teaching, like play, does not stifle children's imagination by its rigidity and inflexibility.

In order to make pupils increasingly independent, educational weaning could begin much earlier, indeed the whole system might be designed, from the earliest beginnings in primary school, to place an increasing emphasis on learning by child rather than on instruction by the teacher.

Teachers should be respectful of children's unusual questions and ideas, showing them that these ideas have value. They should provide opportunities for self-initiated learning and for periods of non evalued practice, indicating that whatever children do may be of some value and is not constantly going to be assessed by some absolute criterion of correctness set up by the teacher. This emphasizes not only the need to value children in their own terms, by acknowledging the worth of common sense knowledge they bring with them into the classroom, but also acknowledges the importance of freedom and flexibility to develop and grow. These seem to be not only the cornerstone of both cognitive and creative development but also part of what is meant by education.

CONCLUDING REMARKS

Many people, thinking back over their educational experience, may trace their interest in a particular subject or even more generally in the activity of learning or to the personal influence of individual teachers or to a kind of contagious transmission of enthusiasm. It should not be impossible to analyse the type of behavior that brings about such a result as a step towards making it an explicit objective of teachers training.

Increasing emphasis on the subject matter, as a preparation for teaching at more senior levels, should be paralleled by even greater concentration on the learning process by those who intend to teach in primary schools. Given that the latter are responsible for laying the foundations for later achievements, their relatively low status within the educational hierarchy, coupled with low training requirements, is one of the most serious shortcomings of our educational system. However, investment in better schools and better learning processes is likely to produce return on a compound interest basis, and an administration prepared to take the long-term view could lay the basis for a significant break through in education in our schools.

REFERENCES AND RECOMMENDED READING

1. Adams, R.S. and D.J. Biddle. - 'Realities of Teaching'/New York: Holt, Rinechart & Winston, 1970.
2. Allport, G. - 'Personality - A Psychological Interpretation'/New York: Holt, 1937.
3. Archambault, R.D. (ED). - 'Philosophical Analysis and Education'/London: Routledge and KeganPaul, 1965.
4. Argyle, M. - 'The Psychology of Interpersonal Behavior'/Harmondsworth: Penguin, 1967.
5. Ashton, P. Kneen, P and F. Davies. - 'Aims into Practice in the Primary School'/London: University of London Press, 1975.
6. Ashton, P. - 'The Aims of Primary Education: A Study of Teacher's Opinions'/London: Macmillan, 1975.
7. Ball, C. and M. Ball. - 'Education for a Change'/Harmondsworth: Penguin, 1973.
8. Bandura, A. and Walter, R.H. - 'Social Learning and Personality Development'/New York: Holt, Rinehart & Winston, 1970.
9. Banks, O. - 'The Sociology of Education'/London: Batsford, 1968.
10. Bigge, M.L. and M.P. Hunt. - 'Psychological Foundations of Education'/New York: Harper and Row, 1962.
11. Britton, J. - 'Language and Learning'/Harmondsworth: Penguin, 1970.
12. Cashdan, A., and Z. Whitehead. - 'Personality Theory and Learning'/London: Routledge and Kegan Paul, 1971.
13. Dearden, R.F. - 'Philosophy of Primary Education'/London: Routledge & Kegan Paul, 1968.
14. Delamont, S. - 'Interaction in the Classroom'/London: Methuen, 1976.
15. Dewey, J. - 'Experience and Education'/London: Macmillan, 1938.
16. Downey, M.E. - 'Interpersonal Judgements in Education'/London: Harper & Row, 1977.

17. Elliott, R.K. - 'The Concept of Creativity in Proceedings of the Philosophy of Education'/ Society of Great Britain, 1971.

18. Getzels, J.W. and P.W: Jackson. - 'Creativity and Intelligence'/New York: Wiley, 1962.

19. Hargreaves, D.H. - 'Interpersonal Relation in Educatio'/London: Routledge & Kegan Paul, 1972.

20. Hollins, T.H.B. - 'Aims in Education: The Philosophic Approach'/Manchester: Manchester University Press, 1964.

21. Kagan, J. - 'Child Development and Personality'/London: Harper & Row, 1967.

22. O'Connor, D.J. - 'An Introduction to the Philosophy of Education'/London: Routledge & Kegan Paul, 1957.

23. Page, E.B. - *'Teacher Comments and Student Performance'*/Journal of Educational Psychology, 1958.

24. Parry, M. - 'Pre-school Education'/London: Macmillan, 1975.

25. Peel, E.A. - *'Understanding School Material'*/Educational Review, 1972.

26. Peters, R.S. - 'Ethics and Education'/London: Allen and Unwin, 1966.

27. Peters, R.S. (ED): - 'Aims of Education: A Conceptual Inquiry in the Philosophy of Education'/London: Oxford University Press, 1973.

28. Piaget, J. - 'The Origins of Intelligence in Children'/New York: International Universities Press, 1952.

29. Piaget, J. - 'The Psychology of Intelligence'/New York: Harcourt Brace, 1950.

30. Skinner, B.F. - 'The Technology of Teaching'/New York: Appleton-Century Crofts, 1968.

31. Thompson, K.B. - 'Education and Philosophy'/London: Blackwell, 1972.

32. Whitehead, A.N. - 'The Aims of Education'/Williams and Norgate, 1932.

33. Wittgestein, L. - 'Philosophical Investigations'/Oxford: Blackwell, 1953.

34. Watrock, M.C. and D.E: Wiley. - 'The Evaluation of Instruction: Issues and Problems'/ New York: Holt Renehart & Winston, 1970.

IS TEACHING AN ART OR A SCIENCE?

CHAPTER 4

INTRODUCTION

There have been two approaches to teaching practice. The first, and most widely held approach is 'Model the Master Teacher'. In this approach teaching practice is viewed as a process of initiation in which the student acquires from the master teacher teaching skills, performance, attitude and personality, through imitation, observation and practice. However, there are some disadvantages to this approach. Firstly, a master teacher, however versatile, can offer a student only a limited set of skills, attitudes and personality traits. Secondly, it does not allow the student to go beyond the teaching that is observed. Thirdly, there is a practical difficulty of finding sufficient master teachers in the right places to go round. The final and most important disadvantage is that it stands for imitation rather than critical analysis, and therefore, it puts obstacles in the way of understanding the teaching processes. L.M. Stolurow points out: "However, neither the observation of master teachers nor that of a large number of effective teachers has led to findings that are either substantial or sufficient for the understanding of teaching as a process. Thus, an alternative approach is needed." (15, 1965).

The second approach is known as 'Master the Teaching Model'. This approach to practical experience makes possible, and necessary, the integration of theory and practice. Unlike the first approach, this approach offers practical, usable help to all students irrespective of their personality traits, abilities and attitudes. Akin to the first approach is the view that it is impossible to teach anyone how to teach. Teaching like poetry or painting is an art. Any creative teaching act although can be facilitated by teaching, cannot itself be taught.

A quite contrary, but akin to second approach is adopted by those who regard teaching as a part of behavior sciences. Teaching is behaving in a social context and is, therefore, amenable to scientific observation and analysis. This teaching behavior is modifiable by feeding back to the tyro teacher data about lesson learnt and his or her ongoing behavior in the classroom and likewise, the result of his teaching in terms of the student behavior and learning. This approach necessitated the theory of teaching.

Without a coherent theory of teaching, to which the student's teaching is linked, improvement in teaching is going to be a very haphazard affair. This theory has already made contributions in five major areas:

a) Educational objectives and goals.

b) The teacher's and pupil's verbal behaviors in the classroom.

c) Techniques and strategies for producing cognitive growth in pupils.

d) Classroom and group management.

e) Teacher's personality tracts and their relations to both teachers' and pupils; behavior.

THEORY OF TEACHING

Since by learning theories the desired behavior in students is rewarded; likewise the teachers' teaching is understandable and controllable in terms of theories of teaching. Teaching practice must be organised so that the students can have a clear grasp of the teaching objectives, and as a result can achieve necessary learning. In the words of B.O. Smith: "Teaching is a system of actions intended to produce learning." He further says: "Learning does not necessarily issue from teaching, that teaching is one thing and learning is quite another, is significant for pedagogical research. It enables us to analyse the concept of teaching without becoming entangled in the web of arguments about the processes and conditions of learning: In short to carry on investigation of teaching in its own right. What is needed for a scientific enquiry is a concept which recognizes teaching as a distinctive phenomenon general enough to embrace normative definitions as well as special cases." (10, 1961). Therefore, both learning and teaching processes are distinctive from each other, but both these processes must be adopted to each other so as to get the best possible combination of procedures to achieve optimum conditions of learning. Gage confirms this as: "We need not consider learning to be an immutable, fixed, given process to which teaching must be adopted. Instead we should conceive of a teaching-learning process, both of whose parts can be changed to make learning more effective;" (17, 1964). This view of teaching which is a prescriptive and theoretical approach, will not appeal to those who view teaching as an art. But on the other hand this approach seems to offer a great prospect of valuable and interesting developments in the teaching field and a great potential of becoming the applied science of teaching for the days that lie ahead.

It is a pity that this theory was long denied by the people in the profession, which resulted in a great disadvantage not only to theorists but also to the teachers. Popper points out as: "Theories are nets cast to catch what we call 'the world', to rationalize, to explain, and to master it. We endeavour to make the mesh ever finer and finer." (8, 1959). Like scientific development, if teaching development is aimed then we must not throw this net away from the classrooms but instead we should work towards making the mesh of theory of teaching ever finer and finer. In order to achieve optimum learning it is essential to be concerned with the conceptions, theories and methods of teaching.

Smith details this approach in these words: "A theory of teaching will consist of (a) statement of variables comprising teaching behavior, (b) formation of the possible relations among these variables, (c) hypotheses about the relations between the variables comprising teaching behavior and the variables descriptive of the Psychological and social conditions within which teaching behavior occurs." (12, 1963). This was further expanded by the (American) Commission on Instructional Theory in 1968 by proposing that a theory of instruction should: (a) include a set of postulates and definitions of terms involved in these postulates; (b) should make explicit the boundaries of its concern and the limitations under which it is proposed; (c) must have internal consistency; a logical set of relationship; (d) should be congruent with empirical data; (e) must be capable of generating hypotheses; (f) must contain generalizations which go beyond the data; (g) must be verifiable; (h) must be stated in such a way that it is possible to collect data to disapprove it; (i) must not only explain past events but must also be capable of predicting future events; (j) at the present time, instructional theories may be expected to represent qualitative synthesis." (5, 1968). However, it is the fact that this theory is not situational-specific as specific teaching activities may be derived from a body of general principles. This is probably the reason which leads most critics of theory to deny its use in the practical teaching situation. Smith provides argument against this criticism by saying: "One of the chief differences between a teacher who is theoretically trained and one who is not, is that the theoretically trained teacher will perform with a set of sophisticated concepts taken from the underlying disciplines of pedagogy as well as from the pedagogical field itself. The teacher who is not theoretically trained will interpret events and objects in terms of common sense concepts that have come from the experience of the race permeated with outmoded ideas about human behavior." He further says: "What should be the theoretical content of an introductory program of teacher education? To answer this is to identify concepts such as motivation, feedback and explanation, which are needed to interpret situations the teacher most frequently encounters." (13, 1969). Smith's statement seems to offer a great promise for the future development of the theory of teaching.

TEACHING VARIABLE MODEL

If we wish to relate this theory to the practice of teaching, it is necessary to identify key variables which will assist the Tyro teacher to perceive the outline of teaching model and subsequently by studying of methods of controlling the variables will directly influence his classroom practice. Central to any consideration of the variables in a teaching situation is the question of teaching objectives. Starting from these objectives in the behaviorial term the teacher will sharpen his perceptions of the way in which the variables are likely to apply in specific teaching situations. These variables may be classified in three important phases: (a) belonging to a diagnostic phase; (b) belonging to a prescriptive or 'treatment' phase; and (c) belonging to an evaluation phase, (See Fig. 4.1).

All these three phases require specific abilities, skills and expertise and competence of the teacher. Therefore, the problems of classroom performance by a teacher may be viewed in the context of three phases in teaching outlined in the above model. Although our main concern is with phase 2, however, we must regard all three phases as different elements in one process rather than three different types of activity; and also we should not overlook that the activities occur simultaneously or cyclically rather than linearly. Strasser proposed a conceptual model (Chapter 5) representing various teaching activities in the above light and considers teaching as ".... a dynamic, and, over a period of time, self correcting, continually redirected, influenced/ influencing, interactive process." (14, 1967). However, there are some specific variables in the teaching situation, out of which the key global variable is the teacher's personality. Personality characteristics influence teaching, but rather the proposals that will help teachers to develop their personalities along lines computed to improve their teaching. This aspect may be associated with

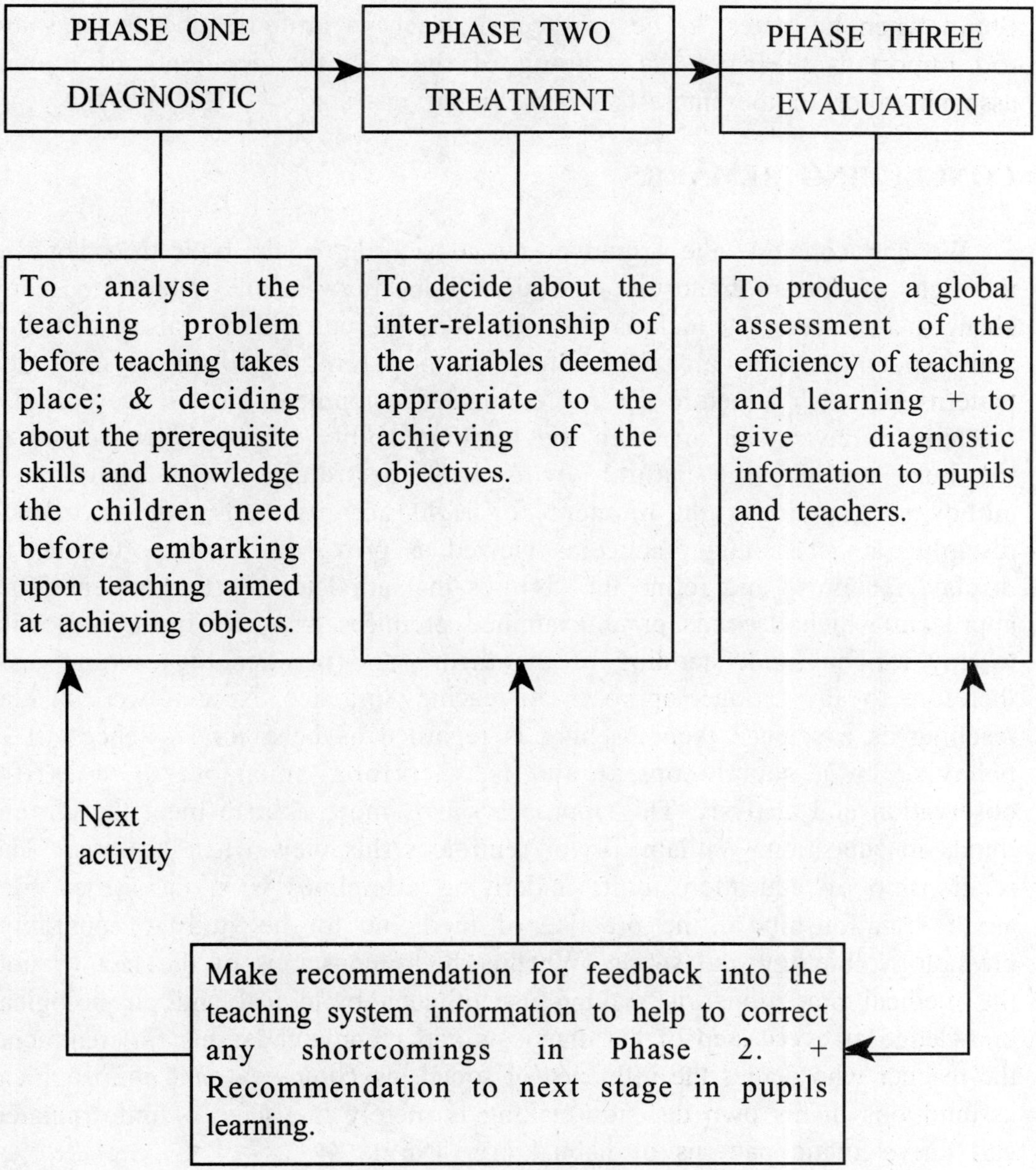

FIG. 4.1: TEACHING VARIABLES MODEL

Smith when he states " The prospective teacher's attitudes and feelings are too important to leave the shaping of them to the accidents of human association or to the interests of individual instructors." (13, 1969).

CONCLUDING REMARKS

We can conclude the argument by considering again both the views in the light of current trends in education. Education is now subject to many changes and pressures including a new form of curriculum, raised demands and expectations, greater accountability to parents and society and new patterns of career structure and professional development. Now if we consider teaching purely as an art, then the teaching ability largely being innate in the born teacher, the natural owing little to training, with charismatic authority, knowing right moment for right activity and being a natural disciplinarian. Teaching practice is viewed as providing the opportunities to display, recognise and refine the abilities that are latent in the student. This approach, which depends on unexamined premises and half truth, is hostile to any rational understanding of the theory and practice of teaching and, therefore to any rational approach to teaching practice. Now if we consider teaching as a science then teaching is regarded as behavioral sciences. It is behaving in a social context and is, therefore, amenable to scientific observation and analysis. This approach seems more akin to meet the current trends in education. William Taylor reinforces this view when he says: "The relationship of 'education' to its underlying disciplines is in the same order as the relationship of the practice of medicine to the study of anatomy, physiology, biology and so on. Whether he is conscious of the fact or not, the medical practitioner is making use of such biological and physiological knowledge at every step of his diagnosis and recommendations for treatment; the teacher who denies the influence of social, psychological and philosophical assumptions in his own decision-making is merely the slave of unformulated and unsystematic patterns of habit." (16, 1969).

REFERENCES AND RECOMMEND READING

1. Adams, R.S. and B.J. Biddle. - 'Realities of Teaching'/New York: Holt, Reinehart & Winston, 1970.

2. Amidon, E.J. and N.A. Flanders. - 'The Role of Teacher in the Classroom' Association for Productive Teaching, 1967.

3. Bayles, E.E. - *'General Teaching Theory'*/Journal of Teacher Education, 21, 3, pp. 403-416, 1970.

4. Clarke, S.C.T. - *'Theories of Learning and Classroom Methods'* - Theory into Practice, 5. 71-76, 1966.

5. Gordon, J. - 'Systems for Evaluating Videotaped Instruction'/Paper presented at the Annual Conference of the American Educational Research Association, Oregon State System of Higher Education (MIMEO), 1968.

6. Maddox, H. - *'A Descriptive Study of Teaching Practice'*/Educational Review, 20, 3, pp. 177-90, 1968.

7. National Union of Teachers, Teacher Education - 'The Way Ahead'/London: 1970.

8. Popper, K.R. - 'The Logic of Scientific Discovery'/London: Hutchinson, 1959.

9. Pounds, R.L. - *'Educational Values and Classroom Methods'*/Theory into Practice, 5, pp. 63/6, 1966.

10. Smith, B.O. - 'A Concept of Teaching' - Language and Concepts in Education, Chicago: Rand pp. 86-101, 1961.

11. Smith, B.O. And M.O. Meux - 'A study of the Logic of Teaching'/University of Illinois, 1962.

12. Smith, B.O. - *'Toward a Theory of Teaching'* - Theory and Research in Teaching,/New York: Teachers College Press, Columbia University, PP. 1-10, 1963.

13. Smith B.O., S.B. Cohen, and A. Perl - 'Teachers for the Real World'/Washington, D.C.: American Association of Colleges For Teacher Education, 1969.

14. Strasser, B. - *'A Conceptual Model of Instruction'*/(American) Journal of Teacher Education 18, 1, 1967. pp. 63-74.

15. Stolurow, L.M. - *'Model the Master Teacher or Master the Teaching Model'*: Learning and the Educational Process/Chicago: Rand McNally, pp. 223-47, 1965.

16. Taylor, W. - 'Society and the Education of Teachers'/London: Faber & Faber, 1969.

17. Gage, N.L. - *'Toward a cognitive theory of teaching'*/Teachers College Record, 65, 1965, pp. 408-12.

A CONCEPTUAL MODEL OF INSTRUCTION

B. STRASSER

CHAPTER 5

The motivation that led to the evolution of the Conceptual Model of Instruction is common to all who are in education: a desire to understand more of what teaching is all about.

A point of departure for this work was the notion of teaching strategies and tactics as evolved by Taba (Taba and Elzey 1964, Taba 1963). To what aspect of instruction does the term teaching strategy refer? What activities of the teacher can be described as tactics? What do the learners do while a teacher is engaged in such activities? And finally, how does this notion of strategies, tactics and learners' responses interrelate in a picture of instruction?

To begin with, a series of lessons ranging in grade level from first grade through college was studied in an attempt to identify various tactics and strategies of teachers in order to evolve an operational definition of each of the terms. As a frame of reference for his observations and reflections, the author accepted a definition of teaching by B. Othanel Smith (1963), which he outlined as follows: 'Teaching is a system of action involving an agent, an end in view, and a situation including two sets of factors — those over which the agent has no control (class size, size of classroom, physical characteristics of pupils, etc.) and those that he can modify (ways of asking questions about instruction and ways of structuring information or ideas gleaned).'

Smith points out that it is by means of the set of factors the agent can control that the particular end in view is reached. It might be concluded, then, that the dimension of the instructional situation that includes those factors the agent can modify is, in sum, the strategies and tactics of the teacher. This definition of teaching is also of aid in identifying those elements of teaching over which teachers have little or no control, thus helping one to be consciously aware of the limitation of the model, that it focuses only on factors over which the teacher has control.

Some assumptions about instruction used as a basis for observations

1. What the teacher does is a critical factor in determining what the pupil learns.

Implied in this assumption is the notion that teachers have to display some behavior so that the learners will know what is expected of them: what goals they are to work towards, what they are expected to do, and how they are to do it.

James Gallagher (1963), in reporting his study of productive thinking, stated, 'The teacher is the key in the initiation and stimulation of productive thinking in the classroom.'

2. Children can set goals in the instructional situation; teacher behavior determines if they will.

3. Children can do productive thinking in the instructional situation; teacher behavior determines if they will.

4. Some aspects of learner behavior in an instructional situation may be directly related to specific units of teacher behavior; that is, learner behavior is influenced by the behavior of the teacher.

   In a meeting at the Manhattan Beach Unified School District in 1965, Marie Hughes stated, 'There is a syndrome of teaching acts that will (1) lead to good order and management in the classroom, and (2) lead to the development by the learners of higher mental processes; and there is also a syndrome of acts that will lead to involvement and self-commitment on the part of the learners.'

5. Some aspects of teacher behavior in an instructional situation may be directly related to learner behavior; that is, teacher behavior is influenced by the behavior of the learners.

6. Other factors being equal, certain units of teacher behavior (tactics) generally elicit learner behavior within a given range.

   This is not to imply that all teachers need do is to behave in a certain way and the learners will respond accordingly. Certainly teaching is not so simple. But with students of our culture, our range of socio-economic backgrounds and kinds of past experiences, the responses of the learners in a given learning situation are generally predictable. The work of J.

Richard Suchman in the Illinois Studies in Inquiry Training is interpreted as evidence in support of this assumption. When a teacher creates a certain kind of structure (conditions for enquiry among the structural factors), learners usually do enquire — and in a more or less predictable fashion.*

Strategies and Tactics

From the observation and analysis of forty-nine tape recorded lessons, the following operational definitions of strategy and tactic, as these terms apply to instruction, were developed:

Strategy: A generalized plan for a lesson(s) which includes structure, desired learner behavior in terms of the goals of instruction, and an outline of planned tactics necessary to implement the strategy. The lesson strategy is part of a larger development scheme — the curriculum.

Strategies are, in a sense, the 'why' of specific teacher behavior. Some are a function of more explicit 'now' goals, or 'one-lesson-accessible' strategies; others, which take more than one lesson to develop and usually continue over a period of several lessons, are referred to as 'overtime' strategies.

Either one-lesson-accessible or overtime strategies may be changed, modified or discontinued (with another substituted perhaps) as a lesson proceeds and the teacher interprets feedback from the students. One factor which may give rise to such change in a lesson strategy is the nature of that strategy in relation to the hypothesized and real readiness and rate of progress of the unique group of students (pupils).

Strategy planning is done at a time other than that at which the teacher is teaching; however, this is not to deny that the teacher may get some ideas for future strategies while in the process of teaching.

Tactic: Goal-linked influenced/influencing behavior of the teacher — the way a teacher behaves in the instructional situation in working towards the development of the strategy; units of teacher behavior through which the teacher fulfils his various instructional roles with the students of his class from moment to moment; the components of teacher behavior through which the teacher, the students and the subject matter interact.

A tactic may range from no overt teacher behavior (e.g. using silence for a specific purpose) to one question or statement to a complex of verbal or purposeful non-verbal teacher behavior interlaced with student behaviors.

* This assumption is drawn from the author's experience in Inquiry Training during the last five years and from many discussions with Dr. Suchman.

In the lessons observed, it was found that one lesson may vary from one tactic for the whole lesson to a highly complex inter-weaving of several different tactics. In some cases, while using one tactic with an entire class, a teacher may employ several different tactics at different times or at the same time with different individuals within the total group. Some tactics may be directed towards one child and some towards a group of children; some may be in the form of one teacher behavior directed towards one learner response, while others are more complex and dependent upon a sequence of teacher—student interactions; still others may be directed to learner responses at some time in the future.

It also became evident that a given lesson may illustrate two different kinds of teacher tactics, planned tactics and responsive tactics. The difference between the two is that planned tactics are those a teacher decides to use to implement his strategy; they are planned before the lesson takes place. Then, as the teacher uses these tactics with the class, certain responses by the children may clue him to apply a different tactic with a particular child in terms of the goals established or in order to enhance the child's self-concept. In this case, the teacher draws from his tactic repertory, or he may consciously or subconsciously invent a new (new to the teacher) tactic to meet the specific situation.

Instruction

After an operational definition of tactics and strategies had been built, attention was turned to searching for the ways in which tactics and strategies fit into the total picture of instruction; that is, an attempt was made to seek relationships among tactics, strategies, teacher behavior, goals of education and the learners.

Smith provided the idea that led to the development of the Conceptual Model of Instruction:

> Everyone knows that the teacher not only influences student behavior, but that he is also influenced by student behavior. The teacher is constantly observing the student and modifying his own behavior in terms of his observations.... We may therefore say that instructional behavior consists of a chain of three links — observing, diagnosing, acting. (Smith 1963, p. 296).

The idea of influencing/influenced teacher behavior seemed most intriguing, as was the picture of the teacher as behavior, observers and diagnoser. By applying these two ideas, the following four aspects of instruction were identified:

1. Teacher planning — in terms of what the teacher knows of the learner, the curriculum, the situation.
2. Teacher behavior, initiatory — to create a focus for thinking and working, what the teacher does to get things started.
3. Teacher observation, interpretation and diagnosis of learner behavior — in terms of the situation, knowledge of prior experiences of the learner, prior observations of learners' behaviors, enhancement of child's self-concept, the curriculum (affective, cognitive and action dimensions).
4. Teacher behavior, influenced/influencing — influenced by the observations, interpretations and diagnosis of learner behavior and influencing to the degree that teacher behavior stimulates further learner behavior.

Consideration of the flow of those aspects during the process of instruction led to the development of the Conceptual Model of Instruction (Fig. 5.1), from which it can be seen that the potential lesson takes shape as the teacher, making decisions about goals, structure and planned tactics, begins the development of the strategy. Teacher planning (I) is completed.

Teacher behavior, initiatory (2) is a tactic(s) that creates the focus for the lesson and sets the appropriate structure. As a result of the teacher behavior, initiatory, the children become aware of some of the goals that will direct their activity as well as their evolving responsibilities in the specific instructional situation. The lesson begins to unfold.

At the same moment the initiatory tactic takes place, teacher observation, interpretation and diagnosis of learner behavior (3) take place. The teacher observes the consequences of his influencing behavior. Some observations may be singular in nature, leading directly to influenced teacher behavior; some may take place for a longer period of time over a more complex series of learner-teacher behaviors as related to the purpose of the tactic; some may yield information about the learners that is not directly related to following the teacher behavior. For example, while a group of third grade children were working to make a compass, one said, "The north part of one magnet will attract the north part of another magnet." Rather than stop the lesson to attempt to correct this misconception, the teacher made a mental note of the response, which became information to act on in the future (3a) and possibly the basis of planning for a future lesson. In this case, the observation, interpretation and diagnosis of the learner behavior did not lead to influenced teacher behavior — at that particular moment.

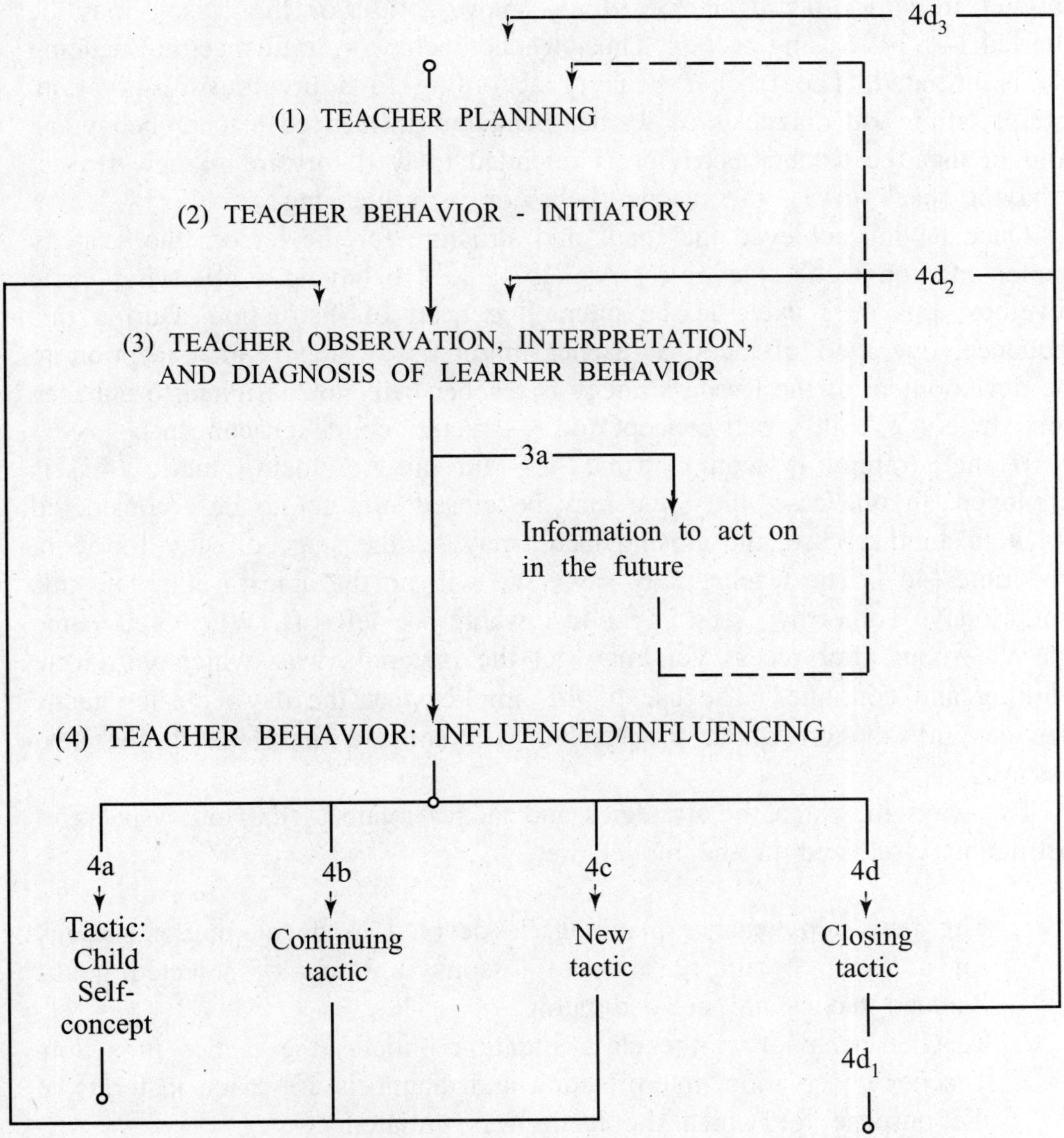

FIG. 5.1: A CONCEPTUAL MODEL OF INSTRUCTION

As the lesson continues, the teacher's observation and interpretation may lead to the diagnosis that the initiatory tactic is developing according to plan, and the tactic is therefore continued (4b) — continuing tactic). It may be, however, that the initiatory tactic is not achieving the intended purpose, and the planned teacher behavior is consequently modified or discontinued and another initiatory tactic started (4c — new tactic); or the lesson may be aborted (4d — closing tactic). Thus, teacher behavior, influenced/influencing (4) is initiated. The teacher behaves according to a previous observation, interpretation and diagnosis of learner behavior (influenced teacher behavior). And in that the teacher behavior is intended to feed forward to new learner behavior (back to 3), the teacher behavior is influencing.

Once having achieved the focus and structure for the lesson, the strategy implementation tactic(s) evolves. A4, 3, 4, 3 ... behaving - observing cycle develops; this 4, 3 cycle is the interactive heart of instruction. During this sequence, one kind of tactic a teacher might use which is an exception to the development of the lesson strategy is teacher behavior designed to enhance immediately a child's self-concept (4a — tactic: child self-concept).

If the strategy is won or time has run out, a closing tactic (4d) is employed. In one case, the topic may be closed off, not to be reconsidered ($4d_1$); in another case, the closing tactic may set the stage directly for work next time ($4d_2$). The teacher may say, "We will not be able to complete this work today. Tomorrow, let's begin just where we left off. When you come into the room after recess you may get the materials with which you were working and continue." The use of $4d_3$ implies that the day's closing tactic provides information which the teacher will consider in planning the next lesson.

The ways in which the strategies and tactics relate to the four aspects of instruction visualized in the model are:

1. The first step, teacher planning, is devoted to developing a strategy for a lesson or for a series of lessons in terms of selected goals. Planned tactics are decided upon.
2. Teacher behavior in the class situation initiates the tactics in action.
3. Teacher observation, interpretation and diagnosis are made in terms of the purpose for which the tactic was initiated.
4. Teacher behavior proceeds with tactic as planned or the tactic is modified as a result of prior observation, interpretation and diagnosis. In reaction to students' interactions, teacher may draw on responsive

tactics to pull certain students into class interaction, to take advantage of problems, questions, etc., which arise.

It may be concluded, therefore, that the central directive element of instruction is the lesson strategy, and the essence of classroom interactions, the lesson tactic(s).

Tactical Elements

As attention is turned to classroom interaction, all tactics, whether they are directed towards a convergent behavior such as interpreting a contour map or more divergent behavior such as setting the stage so that the students can

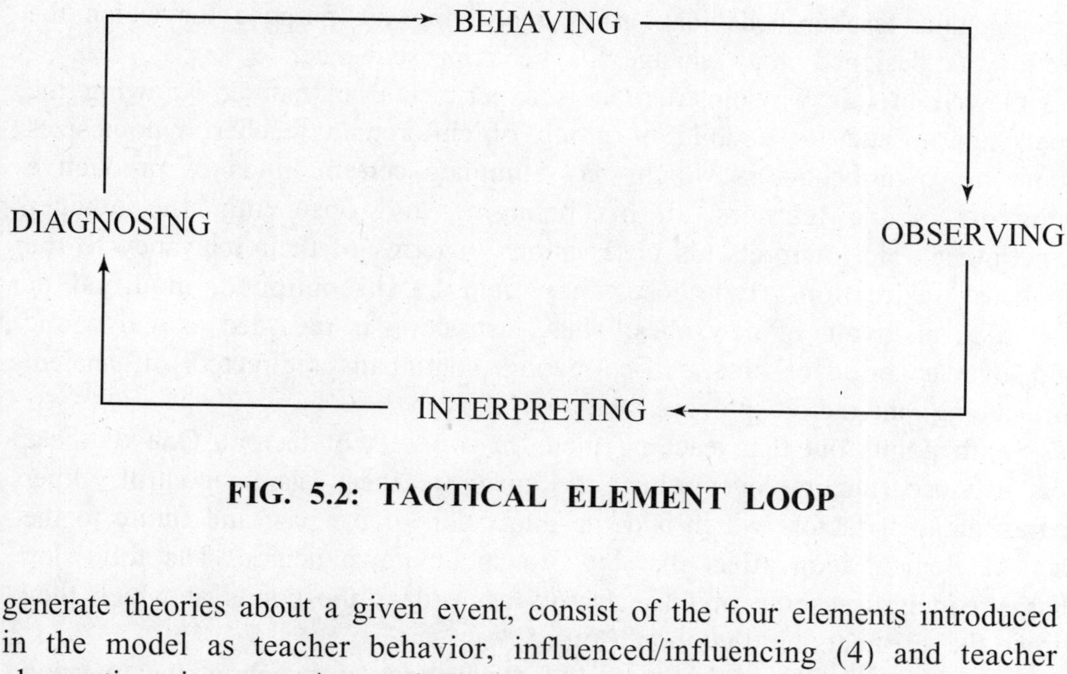

FIG. 5.2: TACTICAL ELEMENT LOOP

generate theories about a given event, consist of the four elements introduced in the model as teacher behavior, influenced/influencing (4) and teacher observation, interpretation and diagnosis (3). A behaving—observing cycle develops.

In the light of some previous diagnoses and in terms of explicit goals, a teacher behaves. Simultaneously, he observes the students. Such observations are interpreted in terms of the purposes of the tactic. With this information, diagnoses about continuing or new teacher behaviors are made which lead to continuing behaving. Thus, a tactical element loop takes shape which involves diagnosing, behaving, observing and interpreting by the teacher.

Teaching as Experimenting

In making a diagnosis, the teacher generates a hypothesis about a relationship between his potential behavior and its effect upon the students. In effect, he is saying, 'If I ..., then the learners will ...'

Following the formulation of such a hypothesis, the teacher experiments: he behaves and observes the responses of the students, viewing such responses largely as a consequence of his behavior. These observations are then interpreted in terms of the purposes that motivated his behavior in the first place. Thus, if a tactic does not seem to be successful in helping the learners move towards the purposes for which it was hypothetically designed, the teacher, either by drawing on his repertory of tactics, by creating a new tactic (spontaneous teacher behavior), or by modifying the purpose for which the tactic was designed, may change his behavior sequence.

Viewed in this way, instruction is experimental in nature. Knowing the goals appropriate for a child or group of children, a teacher hypothesizes about his own behaviors which may stimulate certain kinds of productive behavior of the learners. In his behaving and observing, the teacher experiments. He interprets his observations in terms of their relevancy to the goals of instruction. Hypotheses may then be discontinued, modified or discarded in favour of new ones. Thus, instruction is regarded as a dynamic and, over a period of time, self-correcting, continually redirected, influenced/influencing, interactive process.

Smith points out that teaching includes two sets of factors. One of these sets is those (factors) over which the agent (teacher) has no control. Other extrasituational factors which add the dimension of the past and future to the tactical element loop affect that loop to an unknown degree. The following diagram identifies some of these factors as well as the points at which they affect the elements of the loop (Fig. 5.3).

As attention is directed to some of the 'knowns' instruction, the question of relative uncertainty about instruction arises. One group of such knowns is those factors which Smith defines as being modifiable by the teacher; another is the body of educational goals which motivate teacher behavior. As the teacher interacts with the students, a third group of knowns — the teacher's past experience (strategy and tactic repertory) and present awareness — is marshalled in directed effort. To what degree, however, are all of these

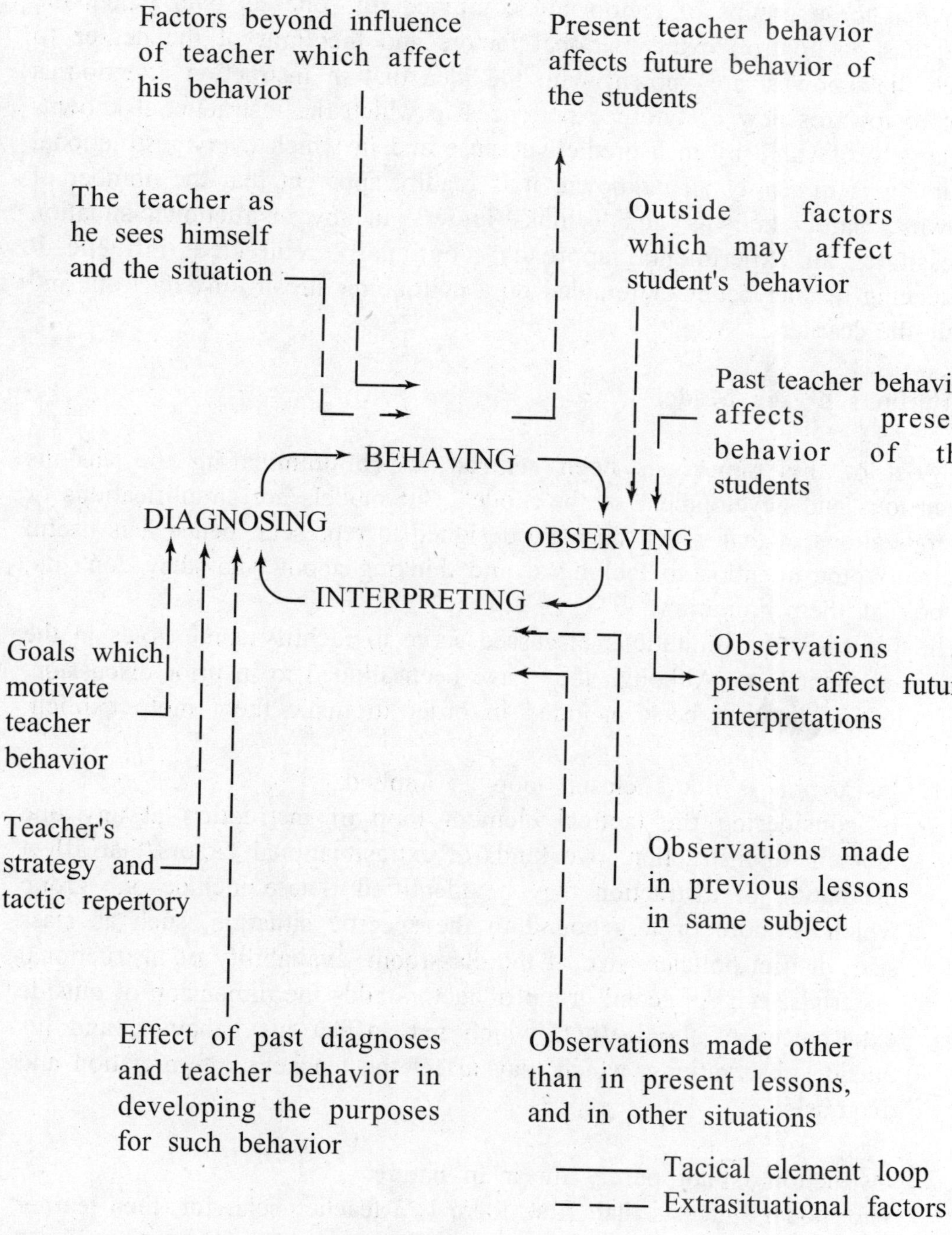

FIG. 5.3: SOME EXTRASITUATIONAL FACTORS THAT AFFECT THE NATURE OF INSTRUCTION.

knowns in instruction operationally known?

When these groups of factors are combined (the one set over which the agent has no control, extrasituational factors and the limit of the degree to which the 'knowns' are known) with the idea that in instruction attention is directed towards new or future experiences in which the instructional knowns are largely of value by in a predictive sense and in which every instructional excursion is in reality an unknown, it is readily apparent that the number of 'knowns', 'barely knowns' and 'I-think-I-know's' in any instructional situation necessitates an experimental approach: continually redirected, influenced/ influencing teacher behavior founded on a continuing stream of data from and about the learners.

Limitations of the Model

Most of this paper has been centred on communicating the various dimensions and development of the model. But models are simplifications or generalizations of that which they are designed to represent; hence it is useful to direct some attention to looking at and thinking about what they don't do, to look at their limitations.

In this case, the limitations discussed serve to identify some holes in the tactical element loop. Although they have been alluded to in prior discussion, the following list has been included in order to make them more explicit.

1. Instruction is not a closed loop as implied.
   In considering the tactical element loop of instruction at any one moment of instruction, two kinds of extrasituational factors that affect the nature of instruction may be identified. These include one group which is more or less bound to the specific situation, such as class size, district policies, size of the classroom, availability of instructional materials, etc. A second group of factors adds the dimension of outside experiences of the learner, which may affect his behavior, and his outside observations, which may affect the teacher's interpretation and diagnosis.

2. Instruction is not purely linear in nature.
   The model suggests that, first, there is a teacher behavior, then learner behavior, then teacher behavior, then learner ... This, however, is not necessarily the case. A kind of feed forward and feedback exists. That

is, teacher behavior in previous situations and on previous days may affect the present behavior of the learners, and present teacher behavior may affect the future behavior of the learners in like manner. In addition, a present observation of a learner may provide the key through which prior observations may be more clearly understood.

3. Observing, interpreting, diagnosing and behaving are cumulative.
   The longer a teacher works with a given group of children the more data he brings to each observation, interpretation and diagnosis; thus, hopefully, the more rational is his behavior.

4. The behavior of a learner at any one moment is the result of a complex of affective factors, rather than of teacher behavior alone as implied.

5. The behavior of one student in a class may affect the behavior of another student(s).
   The effect of the behavior of one child on another is not discussed as a factor of the instructional situation. It is recognized, however, that such influence may be significant in some classes in some instructional situations.

6. Tactical elements may occur simultaneously.
   Human behavior is such that a teacher may be behaving and at the same time observing the effects of that behavior, interpreting it, and forming diagnosis. Thus, teacher behavior may appear to be continuous even though the discrete tactical elements are aspects of that continuous teacher behavior.

Implications for Instruction

After a look at the Conceptual Model of Instruction and consideration of some of its more apparent limitations, attention is turned to what this model implies about instruction, how it ties together past experiences and opens up some new hypotheses for further consideration.

1. Instruction is viewed as a two-way situation.
   In one case, students are growing towards the stated curricular goals:

in the other, teachers are learning about the children or their classes, the effect of their behavior upon a specific group of students, ways to behave in terms of certain goals, and the limitations of present instructional goals: students grow towards curricular goals and teachers' tactic and strategy repertoire is empirically extended.

2. One relationship between learner behavior and ongoing instruction is indicated.
   The tactical element loop illustrates the role of the learner behaviors in instruction and identifies some specific points at which learner behaviors affect the nature of instruction.

3. The necessity for continuous feedback (completing the tactical element cycle) in shaping instruction is highlighted.
   According to the model, it may be predicted that if part of the tactical element loop were eliminated the effectiveness of instruction would become limited. When the loop of tactical elements is destroyed, effectiveness is diminished and the cumulative learning effect of instruction for both teacher and student is impeded.

4. Use of the model provides one basis from which some aspects of instruction may be observed, discussed and experimented with.
   The notion of tactics and strategies provides one useful organizer for observing, classifying and experimenting with teacher—learner behavior.

5. Implicit in the model is the goal-directed behavior of the teacher; the control points at which goals affect the behavior of those involved in instruction are suggested.
   The model indicates the specific points at which goals affect the instructional process — as the bases for strategy decisions, as planned tactics are decided upon, as responsive tactics come into the situation, and as the tactical element loop proceeds from moment to moment during instruction.

6. Evaluation in instruction is not something unique to the instructional situation; rather, it is a part of the tactical element loop.
   Viewed from the perspective of the tactical element loop, instructional

evaluation proceeds while the students learn, during instruction rather than apart from it (although it is recognized that for some purposes some evaluation takes place apart from instruction).

7. One route to increasing teacher effectiveness is through a purposeful experimental approach to instruction.
   Implied is a relationship between a teacher's tactic repertory (both planned and responsive) and the variety of instructional goals accessible through his behavior. Thus, one route to extending one's tactic repertory may be through reflecting on his spontaneous behavior as well as purposeful experimenting to discover the real effect of a certain hypothesized tactic upon the students.

8. The model provides a unifying element through which some of the studies about various aspects of instruction may be related.
   The model may serve to place goals, curriculum, pedagogy, teacher, students, materials, etc., in perspective so that increased understanding of what such factors are and how or where they relate to the total picture of instruction may be further hypothesized.

In summary, perhaps the essential implication of the model about teaching is that teaching is enquiring and invites a teacher's thinking and behaving in terms of certain goals or enduring purposes. In another sense, teaching is viewed as learning — learning about the learners; learning about the effect of one's behavior on the learners, based on a continuing stream of feedback from and about the learners; and learning as the teacher extends the goals which direct his activity.

A Model for What Purpose?

The model is an attempt to make sense out of experience. It may serve to facilitate educational dialogue about the topic, that is, a way to talk and think about instruction. Models also suggest what is to be observed and imply the meanings ascribed to such observations. They also outline ways certain facts may be organized, classified and interrelated. Furthermore, models usually stimulate the derivation of hypotheses and/or new questions which may serve to substantiate the relationship postulated or suggested a new model.

In Theories of Instruction, Ryans (Macdonald and Leeper 1965) indicates that the chief function of theory (a model) is to serve as a framework for observation and analysis rather than a once-and-for-all description of how certain kinds of phenomena operate.

The criterion by which a model is judged is its usefulness in tying together past experience and ideas and in opening new doors for continuing research. At this time, the Conceptual Model of Instruction provides some basis for looking at and thinking about instruction: the limitations pointed out illuminate several paths for reflection and the ideas generated suggest inviting explorations. As it now stands, the model is incomplete; it represents only a point on the time line of our growing understanding of the nature and essence of instruction. Hopefully, many new questions about instruction may arise which will demand our attention and lead to the extension of our awareness. If so, this model will have served us well.

REFERENCES

1. Amidon, E. and A. Simon. - *'Teacher-pupil reaction'*/Review of educational research, 35, 1965, pp 130-9.
2. Amidon, E. and M. Giammatteo. - *'The verbal behavior of superior teachers'*/Elementary school journal, 65, 1965, pp 283-5.
3. Bellack, A.A. (ed.) - 'Theory and research in teaching'/New York: Bureau of Publications, Teachers College, 1963.
4. Cyphert, F.R. and K. Openshaw. - *'Research in teacher education: practices and promises'*/Theory into practice, 1964, pp 1-.3.
5. Eisner, E. W. - *'Instruction, teaching and learning: an attempt at differentiation'* Elementary school journal, 65, 1964, pp 115-19.
6. Flanders, N.A. - *'Intent, action and feedback: a preparation for teaching'*/The journal of teacher education, 14, 1963, pp 251-60.
7. Gage, N.L. - *'Toward a cognitive theory of teaching'*/Teachers college record, 65, 1964, pp 408-12.
8. Gallagher, J. - 'Problems in stimulating productive thinking of the gifted'/A presentation made at the California Teachers Association in Los Angeles, 1963.
9. Hughes, M.M. - *'What is teaching? One viewpoint'*/Educational leadership, 19, 1962, pp 251-9.
10. Macdonald, J.B. and R.R. Leeper, (eds.) - 'Theories of instruction'/Washington, D.C.: Association for Supervision and Curriculum Development, 1965.
11. Scheffler, 1. - *'Philosophical models of teaching'*/Harvard educational review, 35, 1965, pp 131-43.

12. Smith, B.O. - *'A conceptual analysis of instructional behavior'*/The journal of teacher education, 14, 1963, pp 294-8.

13. Taba, H. - *'Teaching strategy and learning'*/California journal for instructional improvement, December, 1963, pp 3-12.

14. Taba, H. - *'Strategy for learning'*/Science and children, 1965, pp 3, 21-4.

15. Taba, H. and Elzey, F.F. - *'Teaching strategies and thought processes'*/Teachers college record, 65, 1964, pp 524-34.

16. Taba, H., Levine, S. and F.F. Elzey - 'Thinking in elementary school children'/San Francisco State College, 1964.

17. Withall, J. - *'Mental health teacher education research project'*/The journal of teacher education, 14, 1963, pp 318-25.

RATIONAL CONSTRUCTION AND DEVELOPMENT OF A CURRICULUM

CHAPTER 6

INTRODUCTION

Curriculum is a term that is often used to denote of subjects on a school's program or even sometimes the content that is taught within any one of those subjects. This is only a narrow concept as it also denotes timetables, prospectus and syllabus and therefore covers the totality of the provision that an educational institution tries to make for its students. In this wider sense the best definition we must take is that of John Kerr who defines it as "all the learning which is planned and guided by the school, whether it is carried on in groups or individually, inside or outside the school" (21).

Curriculum has four elements, content and methods on horizontal axis; and objectives and evaluations on vertical axis. All these four elements have a very close relationship and links. Curriculum is subject to development and changes are generally taking place with content and method although objectives are implicit in these changes.

For rational construction of a curriculum the following four general principles should be considered:

i. A first principle might simply be that of 'Preparation of Life'.

ii. A second principle is that of contributing to a balanced general education.

iii. A third principle is that importance should be attached to the 'rational aims' which are especially concerned with the cultivation or encouragement of certain attitudes, e.g., interest; individual choice and expression; more autonomous, in the sense of being more willing and able to think and act for themselves, etc.

iv. The school continues to be conceived as being a special place with special purposes, and should not be regarded as being just a general child-minding institution.

Briefly speaking, before finalizing the construction of curriculum, on the proposal the following four questions should be asked:

a) Does it provide a useful preparation for subsequent life?

b) Does it provide a worthwhile contribution to achieving a balanced general education?

c) Does it provide opportunities to cultivate educationally the important attitude towards one's learning?

d) Does it merit high enough priority to gain a place in a school?

To ensure that curriculum planning achieves an adequate balance between the needs of the pupil, the need of society and the demands of knowledge itself, we must not lose sight of the dangers of imprisoning pupils in their own culture and of failing to broaden their horizons by not offering them adequate opportunities for experiencing many things they may come to value which are beyond their immediate environment.

There is an essential moral dimension to all education, that in a sense all education is moral education. The moral education we offer to pupils will only be fully effective if it is the result of a concerted effort to ensure that all the experiences the pupils have in school have a morally educative effect. This means that we must begin by acknowledging that, like language education, moral education goes right across the Curriculum.

Secondly, we must recognize the role the total organisation of the school has to play in promoting moral education. We should try to organize the school in such a way as to ensure that these effects forward that purpose of moral education. In other words, we must try to create a climate in school of such a kind which does not hinder but contributes to the moral education of pupils. This means we must look very closely at such features of the organisation of the school as the ways in which pupils are grouped, the teacher-pupils relationship, the system of rules and patterns of authority within the school, the form and purpose of any school council we might set up for the discussion of problems and many others; all recognizing that these are not just administrative devices but parts of the total program of moral education.

There is another important factor to consider whilst constructing the curriculum and that is social education for the children. To cultivate children socially rather than merely socializing them must mean that we must try to nurture in them social autonomy, that is the ability to think for themselves on social issues. Furthermore, social education in the real sense must teach pupils the value of social responsibility and the worthwhileness of the social behavior they choose to adopt. Thus students need to care about what they are doing rather than take a merely instrumental view about their social behavior. It must be appreciated that to care about one's behavior towards other people so that to bring about social change for the good of the community, involves the effective dimension of social education and therefore, this aspect too must go right across the curriculum.

OBJECTIVES

It is important that the objectives that teachers set for their pupils in their classroom activities should be consistent with the overall aims of the school. A distinction shall be drawn between objectives and aims of education. The latter being very broad goals or purposes, the former quite precise and specific intentions derived from such broad aims. Thus educational objectives are seen as highly specific teaching goals. Some writers have in fact suggested that there should be at least three levels of specificity for our teaching goals, 'ultimate', 'mediate' and 'proximate' goals (33), and it is the last of these that are most properly described as objectives. Secondly these objectives are seen as being behavioral. They are 'intended learning outcomes' defined in terms of behavior the pupil is intended to display in his thought, actions or feelings (Bloom, pg. 56). Thirdly, system of objectives are seen as hierarchically organized and involving close interlocking and interrelationships of objectives, on the following lines:

It is felt that groups of objectives can be divided into families of 'domains' and classification of objectives into cognitive, affective and psychomotor domains by Benjamin Bloom (1956), and the division into those related to intellectual, physical, spiritual/religious, aesthetic, emotional/personal, and social/moral development.

It is also claimed that within these domains they can be arranged hierarchically according to levels of complexity. With the cognitive domain, for example, it is selected (Bloom, 1956) that there is material progression from knowledge of 'specifics to classification' to 'comprehension to application' to 'analysis to synthesis' and so to making of evaluative judgements. Within the affective domain, from 'receiving to responding, valuing, organisation and characterisation by value complex'.

The relation of objectives to aims, or of 'proximate to mediate to ultimate goals', is characterized by a logical link, the proximate goals being derived or deduced in some way from the mediate and likewise mediate from ultimate. In general, objectives are seen as forming a network on both horizontal and vertical axes.

Lastly, these systems of objectives are value-neutral, and left to the best judgement of the person using the model.

The ideal position is for educators to have a fairly wide range of objectives which are clearly and precisely expressed. These can then be used to plan the learning opportunities of the pupils and to devise means of evaluation and assessment. Teachers must have a clear idea of where they are going in order to have a rational basis to guide and direct the activities in the classrooms. Equally will they need to know the extent to which these intentions have been successful.

Sources of Objectives

1. **Pupils:** Central to the situation are the pupils themselves. Diagnosis of their strengths and weaknesses, their abilities and interests and their approach to learning will indicate their needs which will in turn indicate to the teacher many suitable objectives for his pupils to pursue.

2. **Local Environment:** A study of the local environment, including the pupil's homes, might give the educator further ideas for possible specific objectives.

3. **School:** The school itself will have an influence on what the teachers in it are able to achieve. The practical curriculum in action is a controlled interaction between pupils, teachers, space, materials, equipment, content, time and other activities. This influence will have some effect on the objectives teachers set for their pupils and ought to take into account in the curriculum planning.

4. **School Climate:** The school climate, the cumulative effect of the attitudes of the teachers and attitudes of people and teachers-pupils relationship, could well be, in practice, the greatest single influence on the curriculum.

The other influences are school's general aims, priorities of importance and attainment objectives.

5. **Teacher:** Linked up in this network is the teacher's own philosophy of education, the ideas which he has about the priorities of education as he sees fit and concerned with.

Short-term and Long-term Objectives

It is obvious that some objectives could be achieved in a fairly short period of time, at least by some pupils, while others could be very long-term objectives, even covering the allocated period of education. For example, name in German of all equipment and articles of common use in the classroom, is a short term objective whereas, learning to show increasing sensitivity towards other people, is a long-term objective.

Specific and General Objectives

Specific objectives are those which are related to a particular area of the curriculum whereas, the general objectives are those which are not related to any subject area at all but related to school-wide aims and aspirations.

We must keep in our minds that the objectives are there to the selection of their elements of the curriculum viz., content, materials and methods, and must be referred to constantly when decisions about these are being made.

CURRICULUM CONTENT

In a teaching activity one must teach something to someone. The someone being the pupil, whereas something the content. Such areas as Mathematics, Physical Sciences, History, Literature, Human Sciences and Fine Arts; and others, i.e., Morals, Religion, and Philosophy are said to be logically distinct from one another. The central concern of education should be to initiate pupils into all of them. If central concern is with the principle of rationality, autonomy, and understanding; then these are to be attained by involving pupils in all of these forms of knowledge or understanding.

The analysis of the concept of education reveals that the content of education must be seen as being intrinsically valuable, that it cannot be something whose justification is to be found outside itself and it must consist of that which is valued for itself. The educational content of the curriculum must be justifiable entirely in terms of one kind of approach or the other. There is plenty of scope in the time table for a number of different kinds of activities, some involving a great deal of pupils choice, others perhaps far less. If we are to include certain elements in the time table on ground of their social or vocational usefulness, there is no reason why we should not also have both interest-based activities and compulsory studies and also offer scope of a whole range of activities to meet a variety of purposes.

INTEGRATED STUDIES

Whatever view is taken of the overall curriculum pattern and of content, it is usually acknowledged that there is far more to be learned than is possible during the period of school education and so some kind of flexibility is required. It is not a matter of having to go all about for one approach or the other. There are many advantages in including a number of different elements, activities or approaches in our curriculum and there is nothing inconsistent in engaging pupils for part of the week in integrated studies and other times in the 'straight' study of the subjects. This approach indeed makes very good sense, since not only does it lead to much needed variety for the pupils, it also ensures that a number of competing interests can be attained too. The curriculum must, therefore, be looked at the competing demands of the society and of the individual pupil.

CRITERION OF VALIDITY

It is important that content should meet the criterion of validity, i.e., it must be authentic or true. Due to rapid advancement of knowledge nowadays, subject matter used in school can quickly become obsolete. Teachers in all kinds of schools need to be aware of this problem and to exercise great caution in the choice of content, and must keep themselves abreast of changes in their particular fields. There is another aspect of validity, which applies to both content as well as method and that the content (or method) is valid if it is possible for the objectives to be achieved through its use.

CRITERION OF INTEREST

Pupil's interest is important in the selection of content, but nevertheless, it is necessary to apply this criterion with caution because to devise a curriculum solely on the basis of pupils' interests, is likely to be found in restrictive learning, whereas to ignore pupils' interests is to lose a strong motivational force and to run the risk of little or no learning taking place. The well balanced approach might be to give pupils' interests priority when new learning is introduced, in order to form an immediate link between the pupils and the curriculum.

CRITERION OF SIGNIFICANCE

Another important consideration in the selection of content is that of significance. This criterion is often overlooked in many countries' educational system, in particular, the third world countries' schools are frequently concerned that people should learn large bodies of facts without realizing that facts are least significant and only important when they contribute to the understanding of basic ideas, concept and principles of subjects.

This criterion is linked with the matter of the horizontal and vertical dimensions of the curriculum, i.e., of breadth of coverage and depth of understanding. It is important to seek an appropriate balance between these two, to achieve desired learning objectives.

CRITERION OF LEARNABILITY

The criterion of learnability is not always satisfied, though it seems obvious to say that what is included in the curriculum should be learnable by the pupils. The main problem is that of adjustment to the abilities of the pupils' content must be available in forms which are appropriate to the pupils, and these of course, be different for different pupils. This suggests the need for variety in the ways in which content of the curriculum is made available and in the manner in which pupils are expected to learn it. But in practice to meet this criterion is very difficult, due to lower teacher-pupils ratio and limited resources available for school education.

Ideally, content selected for inclusion in the curriculum should satisfy all the above criteria; certainly no one criterion should be applied in isolation or carried to an extreme, although some criteria may carry more weight than others under different circumstances. Content must be considered in relation to the objectives teachers have set and methods to be used for the achievement of the objectives; as we know that these three elements, together with evaluation, constitute the curriculum.

METHODS OR PROCEDURE

Education involves interaction of a number of forces, the pupils, the teachers, society, knowledge and so on. Therefore, to plan a curriculum from the point of view of any one of these is to create a caricature of the real thing. This is equally true for the methods we adopt. Any approach that is based on a consideration of one or two of these forces will be distorted and, as a result, vulnerable to criticism. It is very difficult to fully understand which methods are best suited to achieve particular objectives. What we do in selecting one or more methods for use is to put forward a hypothesis to be tested and only at the evaluation stage may we know if the hypothesis holds good. A common belief about method is that one particular method is the 'best' or right one. Some people may claim to 'believe' in activity methods, progressive methods, discovery methods formal methods or informal methods. But this is a long way from the position that there is a best or right method. This is indeed a very difficult task as no method is the best one to meet the very complex educational objectives and appropriate for pupils of varying abilities; therefore in the selection of methods more variety, flexibility and choice are required.

ROLE OF THE TEACHER

The role of teacher varies with different methods of teaching for different learning situations. If a teacher has been accustomed to the task in which the class teaching has been the main approach then he has been in a central position, teaching the content, directing, leading and controlling most of classroom activities. On the other hand if discovery methods of learning are used, the role of the teacher here is very different. He is no longer in a central position, i.e., the focal point. He no longer comes directly between the pupils and the subject matter to be learnt; he is not the interpreter, director or total controller. Instead he might act as an adviser, a consultant, a questioner or a guide. If, in order to achieve objectives concerned, say, with the learning of certain concepts, with ability to study independently in co-operation with others, then the teacher acts as a planner of learning opportunities in which pupils have to work individually. The teacher has a changing role in relation to different methods and it is important that the teacher should get accustomed to such change and variety.

ORGANISATION OF LEARNING OPPORTUNITIES

Organizing a learning opportunity to suit the desired objectives is one of the crucial tasks in curriculum development. Learning being a slow process it is, therefore, to be more effective in the long run, learning opportunities must be arranged in such a way that they support and reinforce each other. In order to do this, learning opportunities must be related in certain ways. For example what is learnt in Mathematics in the first year must be related to what is to be learnt in the second year and this is described as a vertical relationship. Similarly what is learnt in the first year may be related, in some appropriate ways, to what is learnt in Physics in the same year, and this is referred to as a horizontal relationship.

In the case of vertical relationships the methods used in a learning opportunity must make provision for pupils to learn the behavior indicated in the objectives. On the other hand horizontal relationships are concerned with objectives which are being pursued in two or more areas of the curriculum. These may be knowledge objectives concerned with the development of certain concepts, or they may be intellectual skills such as analysis, synthesis and evaluation. Horizontal relationships are usually termed integration, which in practice often means putting two or more subjects together. A view of integration presented here is that the objectives can serve as integrating elements in the curriculum and that integration does not refer only to knowledge but may be related to attitudes, skills, and values which are being developed in more than one area of the curriculum.

Remember the objectives are one factor, the content another, the pupils, teacher, school, facilities and all the other elements in the total situation are others. They all have a bearing on the suitability of proposed methods. It is, therefore, obvious that objectives, content and methods are so closely interwoven that it is very difficult to achieve a coherent examination of any one of them in isolation from the others. Curriculum development must be an ongoing open-ended process of a kind that will allow for continuous adoptation and development at all three levels.

EVALUATION

Parents give considerable importance to the progress their children are making in schools. Teachers give both formal and informal attention to the progress of their pupils. Formal attention might be regarded as the tests and examinations which are given, and informal attention as the general observation and judgements that are made. The outcome of both these attentions are recorded frequently in reports which are sent to parents. School tests and examinations tend to be concerned with attainment in particular subjects. The implication of this kind of assessment is that each pupil is being compared with others in his class, that attention is only given to intellectual attainment and the marks recorded are absolute measures. The teacher also makes informal assessment and remarks on pupil's attitude to the subject, sometime on his progress or lack of it and sometime on his efforts or lack of it. Underlining most assessment undertaken in schools is the assumption that the curriculum is 'right'. But curriculum development is concerned with the planning of learning opportunities which will give pupils the chance to make progress towards stated objectives considered desirable. This approach suggests that the curriculum can be improved and that pupils' progress towards the objectives is the main criterion for determining the success of the curriculum. This leads to determining the success of the curriculum. This leads to a most important question, viz., who should do the evaluation that is 'democratic' rather than 'autocratic' or 'bureaucratic'?; since its main concern is to provide information for teachers and others in the interest of forwarding curriculum development.

SOME PRACTICAL CONSIDERATIONS

All the four elements of the curriculum described in this text are built into a continuous cycle of activities which constitute a process of curriculum development:

a) Analysis of the situation
b) Selection of objectives
c) Selection and organisation of content
d) Selection and organisation of methods
e) Assessment and evaluation.

Although this sequence seems logical to adopt in practice, but due to very close relationships and the elements of the curriculum there is a necessity to move backwards and forwards through the cycle. Another important consideration related to the sequence is that of a starting-point. If teachers are planning a completely new course, or where a new school is being opened then the most logical starting-point is 'analysis of the situation'. However, if teachers have a particular interest or orientation, say towards methods or content, then there is no reason why these should not provide a starting point. There are some practical problems which act as inhibitors of curriculum development. Some of these are:

i) A narrow view of education
ii) Non-availability of time
iii) Headmaster imposing his views
iv) Teachers who do not question
v) Teachers who are unwilling to see another view point
vi) Unwillingness to co-operate with others.

A headmaster who is inclined to impose his strong views on his staff and see himself as the sole source of educational ideas and innovation will tend to act as a strong deterrent to the development of a balanced curriculum in his school. The ideal situation is one in which all the staff including the headmaster are willing to work together to decide what is the best course of action and work accordingly. Such a situation requires much goodwill, effort, energy and co-operation and support from the top management.

CONCLUDING REMARKS

Curriculum development is a dynamic process, a task which has no beginning and no end as it is suggested by its cyclic nature. The changing nature of society, schools and pupils needs, support the view of curriculum development as a never-ending activity. A school which is standing still in terms of its curriculum is in fact going backwards. To undertake curriculum development in the way suggested in this text is not an easy task, but then nothing concerned with teaching is easy. It is a challenge which all the teachers and educators must accept. It is a truism that quality of the education received by children depends on the quality of their teachers. If pupils are to receive an adequate education then the teachers must carry the major responsibility for the development of the curriculum and consequently for the education itself. It is, therefore, vital that we raise the quality of teachers to the highest possible level and maintain that level by continuous support and in-service training.

REFERENCES AND RECOMMENDED READING

1. Barnes, D. - 'From Communication to Curriculum'/Harmondsworth: Penguin, 1971.
2. Bennett, S.N. - 'Teaching Styules and Pupil Progress'/London: Open Books, 1976.
3. Bernstein, B. - Class, Code and Control'/London: Routledge & Kegan Paul, 1971.
4. Bloom, B.S. (ED) - 'A Taxonomy of Educational Objectives'/London: Longman, 1956.
5. Bobbitt, F. - 'The Curriculum'/Bolston: Houghton Mifflin, 1918.
6. Charters, W.W. - 'Curriculum Construction'/New York: MacMillan, 1918.
7. Cronbach, L. - 'Course Improvement Through Education'/Teacher's College Record, 1963.
8. Crossland, A. - 'Some Thoughts on English Education'/Encounter, 1961.
9. Dewey, J. - *'Experience and Education'*/London: MacMillan, 1938.
10. Haddon, F.A. and H. Lytton. - *'Teaching Approach and the Development of Divergent Thinking Abilities in Primary Schools'*/British Journal of Educational Psychology, 1968.
11. Hamilton, D. - 'Curriculum Evaluation'/London: Open Books, 1976.
12. Harris, A. Lawn, M. and W. Prescott. (Eds) - 'Curriculum Innovation'/London: Croom Helm, 1975.
13. Hirst, P.H. - 'The Curriculum and its Objectives — A Defence of Piecemeal National Planning in Studies in Education — 2, The Curriculum' /London: University of London Press, 1975.
14. Hirst, P.H. - *'The Logic of the Curriculum'*/Journal of Curriculum Studies, 1969.
15. Hogben, D. - *'The Behavioral Objectives Approach: Some Problems and Some Dangers'*/ Journal of Curriculum Studies, 1972.
16. Hollins, T.H.B. (ED) - 'Aims in Education: The Philosophic Approach'/Manchester: Manchester University Press, 1964.
17. Holly, D. - 'Beyond Curriculum'/St. Albans: Hart David Mac Gibbon, 1973.
18. Hooper, R. (ED) - 'The Curriculum: Context, Design and Development'/Edinburgh: Oliver and Boyd with Oxofrd University Press, 1971.
19. Hoyle, E. - *'How Does the Curriculum Change? A Proposal for Enquiries'*/Journal of Curriculum Studies, 1969.
20. Kelly, A.V. - 'The Curriculum: Theory and Practice'/London: Harper & Row 1977.
21. Kerr, J.F. (ED) - 'Changing the Curriculum'/London: University of London Press, 1968.
22. Lawton, D. - 'Class, Culture and the Curriculum'/London: Routledge & Kegan Paul, 1975.
23. MacDonald, B and Walker, R. - 'Changing the Curriculum' - London: Open Books, 1976.
24. Marland, M. - 'Language Across the Curriculum'/London: Heinemann, 1977.

25. Musgrove, F. - *'Power and the Integrated Curriculum'*/Journal of Curriculum Studies, 1973.
26. Schools Council - 'Education in Curriculum Development: Twelve Case Studies'/London: Macmillan, 1973.
27. Socket, H. - 'Designing the Curriculum'/London: Open Books, 1976.
28. Stenhouse, L. - 'An Introduction to Curriculum Research and Development'/London: Heinemann, 1975.
29. Taba, H. - 'Curriculum Development: Theory and Practice'/New York: Harcourt Brace Jovanovich, 1962.
30. Tawney, D. (ED) - 'Curriculum Evaluation Today: Trends and Implications'/Schools Council Research Studies, London: Macmillan, 1975.
31. Tawney, D. - 'Evaluation and Curriculum Development in Schools'/School Council, 1973.
32. Taylor, P.H. - 'Curriculum Planning For Compensatory Education: A Suggested Procedure'/London: School Council, 1970.
33. Tyler, R.W. - 'Basic Principles of Curriculum and Instruction'/Chicago: University of Chicago Press, 1949.
34. Wheeler, D.K. - 'Curriculum Process'/London: London University Press, 1967.
35. White J.P. - *'The concept of Curriculum Evaluation'*/Journal of Curriculum Studies, 1971.
36. White, J.P. - 'Towards a Compulsory Curriculum'/London: Routledge & Kegan Paul, 1973.

SOME CLASSROOM PRESENTATION STRATEGIES AND TACTICS

CHAPTER 7

INTRODUCTION

It is difficult to determine what type of educational goal can best be attained by any particular teaching technique. Lectures, television, programmed learning, visual aid, integrated study and large group instruction are usually best suited for presenting information to pupils, but they are equally useful to motivate and initiate thinking. However, discussions and other group processes are perhaps more useful for deep-rooted ideas and changing attitudes. Pupils are different in a number of ways and to be really successful in teaching, teachers should devise strategies that will accommodate much differences. Among the techniques that the teacher could incorporate in these strategies are programmed instruction; individualise reading and instruction; and small group work. Strategies for assessment and evaluation have to be devised for specific purposes to be compatible, with specific teaching goals. Classroom teaching includes both strategies and tactics. In the words of B. Othenel Smith "Strategies are large-scale maneuver", and "Tactics are the means by which the subject matter of instruction is manipulated and controlled from moment to moment." The teaching theories in the past have centred on teaching strategies and now there is a greater need to place increasing emphasis on teaching tactics in the classroom environment. Professional teachers must adopt the proper teaching strategies and use skilfully the appropriate teaching tactics to achieve the educational goals they are aiming at. In choosing their tactics teachers must consider not, only teaching objectives but also pupils, subject matter and other classroom variables. In practice these choices present difficulties for which many teachers are often ill prepared.

PLANNING

Planning is essential for the development of any kind of strategy because strategy itself is a plan. Although each teacher is responsible for contribution in the planning of the entire school curriculum, but his own personal planning responsibility is limited to three types: Planning the course; Planning the units or topics that make up the course and Planning lessons that make up each unit or topic. In course planning it is necessary to use work breakdown structure. Break the course into topics or units and allocate the amount of time to be spent on each one keeping in mind their relative importance; and then to determine what the major assignments and approaches will be. Then each unit is broken down into lessons. Lesson plans are plans for a single day's instruction in a course.

AN EFFECTIVE DAILY LESSON PLAN

The type of format one uses can vary, but however some things are required to be remembered in each lesson plan. Such as: write down objectives for the day; outline the procedure clearly and logically in detail so that you can follow it as you are teaching; write down the assignment you plan to give to your pupils; list material and equipment you need for the class for that particular lesson; and note down any remarks you may have on content, subject-matter, references or anything else you may want to remember. Lesson plan should be simple, flexible and clearly written and adequate, i.e., neither too brief nor too lengthy. It should be comprehensive, logical and on a systematic form, so that any teacher can follow without any difficulty the daily lesson, in case the regular teacher is absent at the last minute!

The following general rules may form a set of criteria against which to judge a lesson plan:

The teacher should be able to teach from it; including anyone qualified in that subject area; and it should be useful, if it is taught again sometimes in the future.

A standard form sometimes proves a very useful and effective lesson plan, logically organised for any teacher to follow without difficulty. This form should include the sections on: Date: Subject: Teacher's name: Topic: Educational objectives/ goals: Content to be considered: Procedure or method to be used: Evaluation techniques: Assignments, class, individuals: Pupil to see: Things to do: Notes, etc. This is only a proposal and every teacher must develop it to suit his own idea of lesson plan. The proposed daily lesson plan form as shown in Fig. 7.1 may be adopted.

Many teachers may feel that this type of lesson plan asks too much from them, as it demands a great deal of time consuming planning. This is true, but a perfect, complete lesson each day is not expected during the first year the form is used. In the span of two or three years, however, by building on previous plans a teacher can develop a fairly satisfactory set of daily lessons.

CLASSROOM PROBLEM SOLVING AND CREATIVE THINKING

The first responsibility of the school is to teach pupils how to think and to give them tools to think with. Thinking and creativity are much akin. Analysis, research, original criticism, painting, composition and invention are creative processes. The objective of such teaching seem to be to allow pupils some opportunity for free thoughts and expression.

CLASSROOM DISCUSSION

Teachers talk too much which is no doubt an education fault and must be altered with classroom discussions. A good classroom discussion should be a conversation in which the pupils freely and openly air their views and must not be teacher dominated. Discussions should give pupils an opportunity to share and examine their thinking, and give the teacher a nice problem of how to give pupils enough freedom to allow them to think freely and at the same time structuring the discussion enough to provide impetus and direction toward the learning objectives. Conducting discussion successfully, requires considerable skill and planning. Inexperienced teachers find it especially difficult to plan and guide intelligent and rewarding discussion activities. Skilfully conducted group discussions, however, can be an effective means of influencing pupil's attitudes, clarifying their concepts and generating ideas. Therefore, there are many dangers in classroom discussions which must be avoided, such as: Inexperienced teachers conducting discussions: The teacher may actually and directly inhibit creating thinking by over-planning: Over-emotionality in the classroom: Etc. If these dangers are avoided then the classroom discussion will, no doubt, foster critical, independent thinking in our students.

ROLE-PLAYING

Role-playing is a dramatic technique in which people attempt to portray a situation by putting themselves in the role of the participants. Role-playing

Name of Teacher: ________________ Date: ________

Subject: ____________________ Lesson No. ________

Objectives/Goals: ______________________________

____

Unit/Topic: ___________________________________

____

Content to be considered: _______________________

____

____

____

Procedures/Methods to be used: ___________________

____

____

Evaluation Techniques and/or Questions to be posed: ________

____

____

____

Assignments:

Class: ____

Individuals: ___________________________________

____

Pupils to see: __________________________________

Things to do: __________________________________

Notes/Remarks/Feedback: _________________________

____

____

FIG. 7.1: PROPOSED DAILY LESSON PLAN

requires, courage, love and skill. With the technique of this teaching method, one may move anywhere in time or space, past or present, out of reality into fantasy of dreams. A teacher who can work well with pupils in a group has sufficient skill to do some role-playing. Role-playing is a difficult technique to use and it often fails. One who has sincerely 'role-played' the issue of the day in school should find the transition from school life to real life and role taking much easier.

QUESTION & ANSWER EXERCISE

The teacher should ask the type of question which trigger thinking, depending on the goals he wishes to achieve. Asking questions — in class discussions or assignments and tests — is one of the basic ways by which the teacher stimulates pupils thinking and learning. From this questions and answer exercise the teacher measures and evaluates the learning and thinking progress of his pupils and consequently stimulates possible four main types of thinking abilities viz., remembering; reasoning; evaluating or judging, and creative thinking.

To design a good classroom question, the teacher should begin by analysing and planning the kind of thinking objective and then phrase the question to achieve that objective. This skill is very important for the teacher because it helps young minds to grow.

PROBLEM SOLVING TECHNIQUE

This technique requires higher visibility coupled with a systematic approach. The following steps need to be taken:

Feeling a need; defining the problem; guessing the hypothesis; testing the hypothesis on the basis of available evidence and finally arriving at the conclusions. Research is a best form of problem solving technique that can be used in schools. If it is to be profitable to the pupil in a school, research should consist of a real problem whose solution would provide the researcher with some new knowledge and information which was not available to him before. For this technique the following elements of importance need to be considered:

a) organization in problem objective
b) open-mindedness in the research

c) dedication to seeking the truth
d) accurate recording of observations
e) control in the experiment
f) reporting the completed work

Since research is a complex of deliberation involved in the pursuit of knowledge or information, it can, emphatically, be done in schools provided it is aided by the proper guidance; selection and interpretation of information, knowledge and ideas. However in practice there are many limitations.

EVALUATION

In schoolwork evaluation is used for two major purposes: a) to diagnose the condition of learning as a basis for the next steps and b) to mark or rate pupils' work. If the first is more important, the second is more prevalent. Evaluation in schools is based upon some form of measurement and perhaps the most common measuring device used is the teacher-built test, but there are many other devices available. None of them is very accurate, which one should be used depends upon the learning situation. The teacher needs to choose the correct strategy for measuring the learning quality. In some instance, object tests may be best; in others essay tests may be best; or a rating scale; or a check list; or analysis of written work; or it may be best to depend upon observation of performance or some other device. In the long run, an evaluation is usually best based on a mixture of several measurements of various kinds.

In order to assess the multiple learning of children in schools, the teachers and supervisors should plan for comprehensive evaluation of major objectives. For this purpose some of the formal evaluation methods will be standardised and administered periodically whereas other informal methods will be used daily by the teacher as a part of an instructional process.

MATERIALS AND TOOLS

Instructional technology constitutes not only on methods and techniques of teaching but also tools and materials to be used in teaching. Obviously, teachers must choose their strategies and tactics partially on the basis of materials and tools available. Imaginative teachers will take steps to incorporate the available tools and materials into their teaching strategies and consequently make their teaching more effective and efficient.

CONCLUDING REMARKS

Classroom strategies and tactics equip teachers to emphasize the necessity for good classroom atmosphere and to show that teaching is a process of interaction and the relationships between teacher and pupil must be friendly, co-operative, and conductive to give and take in classroom work. They help to understand both teachers and pupils that learning to teach consists of learning to integrate pupils, to enlist them in activities, and to co-operate in ventures jointly worked out. They also guide the beginner teacher that to learn to teach, one must also learn to be alert to situations challenging to pupils and he must learn to use materials to frame situations that involve his pupils. A point to remember is that one must pick up the strategies and tactics most likely to accomplish the desired objectives.

REFERENCES AND RECOMMENDED READING

1. Billett, Roy O. - 'Fundamental of Secondary School Teaching'/Boston: Houghton Miffin Company, 1940.
2. Bowman, Clude C. - *'Role Playing and The Development Insight'*/Social Forces 28:2, Dec. 1949.
3. Dunham, J. - 'Appropriate Leadership Pattern'/Educational Research, 1964.
4. Gahagan, D.M. and Gahagan, G.A. - 'Talk Reform'/London: Routledge & Kegan Paul, 1970.
5. Gleeson, D. and Whitty, G. - 'Development in Social Studies Teaching'/London: Open Book, 1976.
6. Gordon, Mitchell - *'Roll Playing'*/The Wall Journal 149, March 15, 1957.
7. Gross, R.E. and Zeleny, L.D. - 'Educating Citizens for Democracy'/New York: Oxford University Press, 1958.
8. Hargreaves, D.S. - 'Interpersonal Relations in Education'/London: Routledge & Kegan Paul, 1972.
9. Hebb, D.O. - 'The Organisation of Behavior'/New York: Wiley, 1949.
10. Holt, J. - 'How Chioldren Fail'/Harmondworth: Penguin, 1964.
11. Jennings, H., Hendry, C.E., Lippitt, R. and Zander, A - 'Reality Practice as an Educational Method'/New York: Beacon House Inc., 1947.
12. Kahl, J. - *'Some Measurements of Achievement Orientation'*/American Journal of Sociology, 1965.

13. Klein, S.S. - 'Student Influence on Teacher Behavior'/American Education Research Journal, 1971.

14. Linton, R. - 'The Cultural Background of Personality'/New York: Appleton Century, 1945.

15. Mead, G.H. - 'Mind, Self and Society'/Chicago: University of Chicago Press, 1934.

16. Nash, R. - 'Classroom Observed'/London: Routledge & Kegan Paul, 1963.

17. Walker, R. - 'A Guide to Classroom Observation'/London: Methven, 1975.

MOTIVATION, DISCIPLINE AND AUTHORITY

CHAPTER 8

INTRODUCTION

If learning in schools is to be effective, classes must be orderly. Therefore, it is most important that pupils must learn to be well behaved in class, no matter how much they dislike it. The teacher must be in control at all times, but nevertheless the class should be free enough from the fears to allow pupils to think independently. In other words the teacher has the right directly to structure orderly the learning situation, however subtly, intelligently or inconspicuously he may do this, but of course he has no right to coerce understanding. But this freedom must be limited and controlled, as pupils should never be free to follow their every whim. Even when they are given some freedom their freedom must be limited to activities compatible with the goals of the particular lesson, or part of it.

Discipline is a universal cultural phenomenon which generally serves four important functions in the training of young children. First it is necessary for socialization. Secondly, it is necessary for normal personality development, i.e., for acquiring such traits as dependability, self control, self reliance, persistence and ability to tolerate frustration. Thirdly, it is necessary for the development of conscience. Lastly, discipline is necessary for children's emotional security. Therefore, discipline is a complex phenomenon and is not free of problems. The main problem of discipline in the classroom is a problem of motivation and establishment of values and standard of behavior, and key to good discipline is a well motivated class. When an experienced teacher is faced with a child who apparently doesn't learn and doesn't want to learn, he calls upon his knowledge of human behavior and his experience to motivate the child. He finds that success is a propellant for achievement. He knows that the teacher who 'accents the positive' in recognizing the basic need of each child for security, status and a feeling of accomplishment, is working effectively to change the unmotivated child into a well motivated adult.

The progress that children make at school will not depend only on the views that teachers hold about such things as intelligence, motivation and the judgements that they are thus led to make of their pupils, but it will depend equally, if not more conclusively, on the kind of relationship the teacher develops with his pupils. The approach he takes to classroom control, and the kind of atmosphere that is generated by the view he takes of the competing demands of freedom and authority.

The authority necessary to teaching is manifest in such activities: as setting tasks; pointing out pupils' needs; correcting errors; making critical judgements; identifying dangers and pitfalls; specifying what to do next; and directing attention and interest and asking for sample performance and so on. Therefore, the teacher's authority is necessary to keep order in the classroom, to direct the movement of pupils, to give or with-hold permission and to administer punishment should that become necessary, and so on.

Professional teachers must know that constructive positive teacher's authority, attitudes and methods play an important part in building pride in scholastic achievement. The teachers in our school must therefore accept a major responsibility to work with other educators in enlarging and vitalizing the total school program including curricular and extracurricular.

PRACTICAL CONSIDERATIONS

The teachers must keep this in mind that in the long run, a positive, permissive atmosphere will be more effective than a negative, repressive one in motivating pupils. Although there are many other considerations present, the central problem for teachers remain to be the need for adequate motivation at all levels of ability in their classrooms. The teacher who faces thirty or more individuals within the confines of a classroom, must know the individual pupils if he is to do best in motivating the whole class. He needs to have a classroom memorandum on each student to enable him to know the members of a class more quickly.

Experienced teachers always wish and enjoy teaching in those schools which have 'spirit' or high morale, because they know from their experiences that students in such schools are alert to their academic responsibilities, and react positively to the future challenges in their practical lives. Student morale is characterized by strong inner motivation. Such teachers know that strong, lively and positive leadership among teachers and pupils is necessary to maintain good morale. They provide good leadership in their classrooms by using positive motivational procedures and encourage a high sense of achievement from participation in curricular and extracurricular activities. They create a unity of purpose by adopting the procedures which include: giving clear, short range goals; assigning projects, allowing student participation in setting class standards of behavior and performance; insisting on the observance of the amenities of courtesy and behavior; placing explicit value on contributions to problems under study. Such teachers know, also, that intellectually oriented extracurricular activities focus students' attention on immediate, attainable, satisfying experience in scholastic activities. They believe that constructive, positive teacher's attitudes and methods play an important part in building pride in scholastic achievement and consequently accept responsibility to work with other teachers and administrators in vitalizing and developing the total school curriculum including curricular and extracurricular programs.

Many teachers have a narrow approach to their role and seem to think that their principal role is to find mistakes and correct them, without realizing that reward is a superb motivation, and praise can be the best reward of all. As pupils need encouragement and too often, emphasis on correcting faults causes discouragement. Teachers should, therefore, follow the wise policy, whenever possible, to accentuate the positive even in correcting themes and papers.

Teachers sometimes make poor assignments which lead to inefficient studying. Since the assignment sets the direction and scope of pupils' task, therefore, the assignment must be aiming at worthwhile learning activities that will lead the pupils to the instructional goals set by the teacher. A teacher sometimes by giving greater care to his assignments and assignment procedures can avoid the frustrations of poorly done work and the disciplinary problems that may result from ill prepared, unmotivated pupils.

The classroom discipline and standards of behavior must be maintained for effective teaching in schools. Sometimes beginners in the profession forget this truism. Sometimes they seem to feel that to demand pupils to live up to certain standards will warp their psyches. This belief is a distortion of the ideal of permissive or democratic classrooms. The proponents of democratic classroom discipline believe in imposing minimum degree of external control necessary for socialization, personality maturation, conscience development, and the emotional security of the child, but it must not condone licence in pupil behavior. The miscreant must suffer from the results of his misdeeds; and misbehavior must result in punishment. Democratic discipline always aims at being as rational, bilateral and nonarbitrary as possible. It provides explanations, permits discussion, and invites the participation of children in the setting of standards whenever they are qualified to do so. It implies respect for the dignity of the individual and avoid exaggerated emphasis on status difference and hence it repudiates harsh, abusive and vindictive forms of punishment; and the use of intimidation, ridicule, and sarcasm. Nevertheless, democratic school discipline does not imply freedom from all external constraints, standards and directions and must not presuppose the eradication of all distinction between pupil and teacher roles as to make the final decision in the classroom always rests with the teacher.

Since 'prevention is better than cure', likewise prevention of discipline problems is more important than remedial action once a discipline problem has arisen. The following procedure will prove helpful, particularly to the beginning teacher, in keeping classroom discipline:

a) **Learn names:** Whenever possible, be familiar with the names of pupils in your class.

b) **Look over the Permanent Records:** The records will give your clues on students' social history and prepare you for special teaching needs for pupils with social problems or physical ailments.

c) **Plan the lesson:** Plan the lesson in advance. It will save time and also avoid any possible embarrassment.

d) **Watch seating:** Place pupils with defective vision or hearing near you and insure that all pupils are in your sight and line of vision.

e) **Learn symptoms of illness:** Sometimes misconduct has a physiological bases, i.e. skin rash, watering eyes or flushed face, so be guarded.

f) **Practice marginal vision:** Learn to see out of corners of your eyes.

g) **Deal with individuals:** Save the time of others and embarrassment of the offender, reprimand him outside class in a private meeting.

h) **Mind your manners:** A teacher's good or bad manners reflect on student behavior, so be guarded.

i) **Don't stay glued to your desk:** It is important to move about in the classroom to supervise the learning activities of the pupils.

j) **Insure class is not distracted:** Let the business of the class go on and use short code to maintain discipline, i.e., for talking or whispering, a finger on your closed lips may be enough.

k) **Use a bit of ritual:** Use person to person reminder by sign language with humour.

l) **Relate learning to life plans:** Your early knowing the career plans, interests and hobbies of your pupils, will assist you in directing all their energies into constructive channels.

m) **Be yourself:** Pick up good ideas and teaching practices wherever you can, but be original and teach in the way that is right for you.

CONCLUDING REMARKS

Motivation is in many ways difficult to assess because there is no easy way of objectifying children's actions. However, it is not only an individual process, but also influenced by organizational and social factors within the school. The judgements and expectations which teachers hold can indirectly affect pupil's motivation and aspiration by having a long lasting effect on their self-concept or self-image. Teachers can and should encourage a child more positively by bolstering his self-esteem by helping him to see himself in a more favourable light. It is important, therefore, that all teachers should be aware of the impact that the methods they adopt in organizing their schools and their classes and in handling their pupils will have on many aspects of the development of these pupils. They should recognize that their central concern as educators is to set about these tasks in such a way as to develop the kind of authority and the kinds of relationship that will lead their pupils at a proper pace towards the stage where they can exercise self discipline and self control and take responsibility for their own behavior and learning. Therefore, the exercise of authority by the teacher can only be justified when it is shown to be conductive to the achievements of educational objectives or the agreed goals of both teachers and pupils. When this is not the case, it becomes authoritarianism, an abuse of authority, which is unacceptable to both pupils and parents.

REFERENCES AND RECOMMENDED READING

1. Adorno, T.W. - 'The Authoritarian Personality'/New York: Harder and Row, 1960.
2. Aristotle: Politics.
3. Asch, S.E. - *'Forming Impressions of Personality'*/Journal of Abnormal and Social Psychology, 1946.
4. Benn, S.I. and Peters, R.S. - 'Social Principles and the Democratic State'/London: Allen and Unwin, 1959.
5. Berger, P.L. and Luckman, T. - 'The Social Construction of Reality'/London: Penguin, 1967.
6. Bloom, B.S. - 'Stability and Change in Human Characteristics'/New York: Wiley, 1960.
7. Bull, N. - 'Moral Judgement from Childhood to Adolescence'/London: Routledge & Kegan Paul, 1967.
8. Couthard, M. - *'A Discussion of Restricted and Elaborated Codes'*/Educational Review, 1969.
9. Daniels, J.C. - *'The Effects of Streaming in the Primary School: What Teachers Believe'*/ British Journal of Educational Psychology, 1961.
10. Dunham, J. - 'Appropriate Leadership Pattern'/Educational Research, 1964.
11. Easthope, G. - 'Community, Hierarchy And Open Education'/London: Routledge & Kegan Paul, 1975.
12. Elkind, D. - 'Childrfen and Adolescents'/London: Oxford University Press, 1970.
13. Elliott, J. and Pring, R. - 'Social Education and Social Understanding'/London: University of London Press, 1975.
14. Flanders, N.A. - 'Analysing Teacher Behavior'/New York: Addison-Wisley, 1970.
15. Flew, A. - *'The Justification of Punishment'* Philosophy, 1954.
16. Fromm, E. - 'The Fear of Freedom'/London: Routledge & Kegan Paul, 1942.
17. Goffman, E. - 'The Presentation of Self in Every Day Life'/Harmondsworth: Penguin, 1959.
18. Hargreaves, D.H. - 'Social Relations in a Secondary School'/London: Routledge & Kegan Paul, 1967.
19. Jones, R.M. - 'Fantasy and Feeling in Education'/Harmondsworth: Penguin, 1972.
20. Kelly, A.V. - 'Mixed Ability Grouping: Theory and Practice'/London: Harper & Row, 1978.
21. Kelly, G.A. - 'The Psychology of Personal Constructs'/New York: Norton, 1955.
22. Maslow, A.H. - 'Motivation and Personality'/New York: Harper & Row, 1954.

23. Merrett, F. and K. Wheldall. - *'Play the Game: A Behavioral Approach to Classroom Management in the Junior School'*/Educational Review, 1978.

24. Nash, R. - 'Classroom Observed'/London: Routledge & Kegan Paul, 1973.

25. Peters, R.S. - 'Authority, Responsibility and Education'/London: Allen and Unwin, 1959.

26. Piaget, J. - 'The Moral Judgement of the Child'/London: Routledge & Kegan Paul, 1960.

27. Rosenthal, R. and L. Jacobson. - 'Pygmalion in the Classroom'/New York: Holt, Rinehart & Winston, 1968.

28. Sugarman, N. - 'The School and Moral Development'/London: Croom Helm, 1973.

29. Walker, R. - 'A Guide to Classroom Observation'/London: Methuen, 1975.

30. White, J.P. - *'Instruction in Obedience'*/New Society, 1968.

31. White R.K. and Lippitt, R. - 'Autocracy and Democracy: An Experimental Enquiry'/New York: Harper & Row, 1960.

32. Williams, R. - 'Culture and Society 1780-1950'/London: Chatto and Windus, 1958.

33. Wilson, J. - 'Practical Problems in Moral Education'/London: Heinemann, 1973.

34. Wilson, P.S. - 'Interest and Discipline in Education'/London: Routledge & Kegan Paul, 1971.

AN APPROACH TO THE ACHIEVEMENT OF TEACHING OBJECTIVES

CHAPTER 9

INTRODUCTION

What does it mean to teach? According to Edgar Dale: "To teach is to transform by informing, to develop a zest for lifelong learning, to help pupils become students — mature independent learners, architects of an exciting, challenging future . . . a kind of communication, a meeting and emerging of minds." (5, p4). A less complex definition could be, to teach is to help or guide someone's learning. It is not just telling or hearing lessons as its forms are myraid. There are numbers of kinds of strategies and tactics in the pedagogical repertory and one of the principle tasks is to pick the right strategies and tactics for the particular classroom situation he faces.

Teaching is now becoming more and more professional and therefore it is a time demand that teachers must acquire certain skill and knowledge that distinguish them from the crowd and make them professionals. With these skills and knowledge, the teacher can carry out his peculiar functions, which are to make and carry out decisions that will result in the most effective, efficient teaching of his pupils possible. These skills and knowledge make up educational method.

Educational method is made up of strategies and tactics in this context, a strategy refers to the overall approach to teaching whereas a tactic is a specific operation and in multiple makes up a strategy. It must be remembered that in a teaching situation, method includes content, whereas the subject to be taught is part of the strategy or tactic.

The core of educational methodology is decision making or selection. The teacher must decide what goals it would be best to teach for under a given situation and what strategy and tactics are best suited for reaching these goals. In deciding what strategy to use, one crucial factor is to decide what subject matters to include.

Although the specific strategies and tactics suitable for particular situations are contingent on many variables, such as, the objectives, the pupils, nature of subject matter, technology available, the environment surrounding of school, the teacher himself, etc., one general pattern does seem desirable in most teaching situations which usually consist of the following five steps:

i) Diagnosis
ii) Preparation
iii) Guiding learning
iv) Evaluating the results of learning
v) Follow up or follow through.

Diagnosis is the step in which the teacher determines what should be done. Preparation refers to the teacher's getting himself ready to teach; motivating the pupils and planning. Guiding learning includes the preparation, discussion or whatever is done. Evaluating the result of learning includes the teacher's attempts to assess the success of his teaching by finding out how much the pupils have learned. Follow up or follow through is the process of filling in the spots that pupils seem to have missed, reteaching if necessary or build on what the pupils have learned.

The key step in this pattern is, of course, diagnosis, since without good diagnosis one does not have an adequate basis on which to make a selection of strategy or tactics. Obviously, a good diagnosis depends upon an analysis of as many of the variables, in the particular teaching-learning situation, as possible.

The ultimate objective in teaching methodology should be to develop an arrangement that will allow each teacher in the team to make the most of his capabilities of assistants and teaching devices to the utmost. In other words he should try to pick the best techniques, content, material, equipment to do the specific task required in a particular situation, under the given circumstances.

COMMUNICATION PROBLEMS IN TEACHING

From the definition of teaching by Edgar Dale described in the beginning of this chapter, the most important point emerges that communication theory has a direct bearing on educational theory because the heart of teaching is communication. As good teaching is good communication, therefore, the teaching strategies and tactics should be consistent with good communication techniques.

However, there are many communication problems in schools, the most important ones are administrative communication problems and problems of communication in classroom. Some school administrators need to be told that they have communication problems. Some school executives go through their career with a pervasive and vague sense of being misunderstood; others get awoken suddenly, to the realisation that communication has broken down when they face a crisis in their school system. They must realise that the most important part of their work is communication, therefore, they must learn to explain, persuade, strive to understand, keep their ears turned to faint signals. When the communication problems are looked in the classroom, they are indeed very complex, as receivers in the classroom vary greatly one from another. Hence in theory it requires different messages and also in a group teaching situation not very often teachers achieve the degree of "in-tune-ness" which really good communication requires. Furthermore, the teacher is dealing with a functional group or series of groups so that all communication within the classroom must have reference not only to individual needs and interests, but also to group norms and group dynamics. These classroom communication problems are not easy to solve except that the teacher should be on the lookout for certain danger signals of insufficient communication. There are other communication problems in teaching, such as, communication aid to teaching of poor qualities, the test as communication channel and the world outside over which the school has no control. These are some of the communication problems as our task here has not been to make an exhaustive list of problems; rather to discuss some of the areas in which an educator must go forward with an open mind and take appropriate remedial measures.

PSYCHOLOGICAL ENGINEERING IN TEACHING

It is important that teachers pay careful attention to the engineering concepts, as the role of psychology of teaching can be described in terms of engineering concepts. The following approach could lead to the use of Psychological Engineering in teaching.

Define Your Objectives

This is the first task of a teacher as he studies the broad aims of education, the courses of study, and the parts of the curriculum for which he is responsible.

Modify Objectives to Reach Attainable Goals

This is done in part by allocations of curricular, knowing the status of one's pupils and by studying the phenomena of readiness as the status of the class changes from day to day sessions.

Make Decision on Strategy

The strategies of teaching can be derived directly from the strategies of public relation, which include, timing, forbearance, teaching techniques, participation and association.

Set up Themes and Appeals

This is the most important factor as it acts as a reinforcer for educational motivation. This could include appeals to the pupils desires for good health, achieving good grades, vocational choice and learning how to get along with peers.

Prepare Educational Planning

This is a dual approach. One is to capitalize on pupil skills and interest to carry out democratic participation in student activities and academic work. The other is to chart the daily and monthly lesson plans including audio-visual aid, library resources, laboratory and field activities.

Chart the Plan for Timing and Tactics

This could include the sequence of studies, the successive skills and knowledge to be acquired and the techniques used to evaluate progress and communication tactics, such as lectures, discussion, demonstration, testing, etc.

Carry out Tactics

Here the problem is one of adjusting the above points to the exigencies of the moment and put a trust in the cumulative effect. Since education is a slow process, therefore, faith in sound planning and sound techniques must be maintained at all times.

Continuous monitoring and close examination of the above points will reveal that teaching efforts can become more effective when carefully engineered.

TEACHING STRATEGIES AND TACTICS

Strategies and tactics have been defined by B. Othanel Smith in the following words:

"Strategies are the large-scale maneuvers by which the teacher frames the general direction of student behavior", and "Tactics are the means by which the subject matter of instruction is manipulated and controlled from moment to moment." (12, PP 98-105).

The teachers need to place an increasing emphasis on teaching tactics and must adopt the proper teaching strategies for the goals at which they are aiming. In choosing his tactics, the teacher must consider not only his teaching goals but also the pupils, the subject matter and other classroom variables.

THE TEACHER'S ROLE IN DIAGNOSIS LEARNING

The teacher must learn to be flexible and adjust their tactics and strategies to the teaching situation if he wants to be sure of a greater degree of success in raising his pupils to intellectual excellence. But in order to know which strategies and tactics to choose, he must diagnose the situation under the given circumstances. Diagnosis gives teachers the basic data he needs in order to work with individuals. Without it the teacher does not know what is likely to motivate the various individuals in the class and which subject matter is likely to meet their immediate educational needs or whether a particular reading is too hard or too easy. Although many teachers are unaware of it, but the need for diagnosis is most vital and self evident.

A pattern common to good teaching, consists of 'diagnosis', 'preparing the setting for learning', 'guiding the learning', and 'follow up or follow through'. Of these steps of teaching pattern, diagnosis is the key. Without it the teacher has nothing to indicate the strategy and tactics he should use in a particular situation. In other words he has no information to use as a basis for choosing the content and teaching methods for his classes. Therefore, diagnosis must be treated as an intrinsic part of teaching act for all learners.

Out of such diagnosis, educational prescriptions are created and are later filled from the pharmacy consisting of the repertoire of competencies of the teacher and alternative offered by the school.

We must identify and design the appropriate diagnostic questions and then seek instruments whose validity and precision and reliability give us confidence in the accuracy of assessment on which diagnosis is based. Each datum and standard we use in the diagnostic procedure should pass the screen of contributing to the answers of the following diagnostic questions:

a) What objective is appropriate for this learner?

b) What is his present status in relation to that objective?

c) What is the next learning step to attain that objective?

d) What can the teacher do to help the learner to take that step efficiently and economically? (based on data about this particular learner)

e) Was he successful?

f) If so, what is the next appropriate step?

g) If not, what changes should be made?

Questions a, b & c are content based; question d, is learner based and questions e f & g are evaluation based. Question d, above is most important as it is concerned with the use of data about the learner that will guide use in planning the learning opportunity and teaching strategy to help him accomplish his task.

Our estimate of the correct answers to all the diagnostic questions become the revised or adjusted prescription which would be filled from the Pharmacy of Teaching Competency and alternative offered by the school. Diagnosis must lead to action, as a mere intellectual exercise it is useless. Therefore, we must take action to the best of our judgement. If all goes well we would proceed to the next learning task and if not, we will reassess our answers to each of the questions, revise our diagnosis and prescription and try again.

PROGRAMMED LEARNING

The advent of programmed learning is likely to be one of the major landmarks in the development of education practice. If the teaching program is to be prepared in advance in such a way as to incorporate and make allowance for the student's responses at the many test points of the program, it is necessary to make some predictions about those responses. Is this ever possible? If the construction of a detailed and predetermined learning program is possible — the size and sequence of steps being adjusted to produce either a virtually 100% correct response, or allowing for various degrees of branching — it follows that the instructional process may be mechanised. Although the whole topic of programmed learning is usually associated first and foremost with teaching machines, because they are in fact conceptually quite incidental, however great their practical importance may be or eventually become, the essence of programmed learning is in the program — the nature of information provided, the size of information unit and the sequence of presentation in relation to different possible responses.

Programmed learning may enable pupils to pass tests, but how will they be able to cope with the more varied developments that may be made upon their knowledge subsequently, is a question which yet remained to be answered. However, some evaluative studies have been carried out in the U.K. which showed that program learning, especially with the use of teaching machines, can be highly efficient in terms of retention.

We must now turn to some of the objections to the whole concept of programmed learning, particularly in connection with teaching machines. The idea of machine in education is sometimes regarded as an affront to the dignity of man; particularly that of teaching man. What becomes of the role of the teacher? Is he to be replaced by a machine? The answer is quite clear. There is little sign of people being replaced by machines. It is what many people do, or expected to do, which can sometimes be taken over by machines. The teaching machines can only carry out programmes; they can neither discover the information that is to be presented, nor structure it in such a way that it is effectively learnt. The explanations that a program provides are rigid and severely limited; as teacher has much flexibility.

However, man-machine system approach is best for the teaching profession. This approach need not be as frightening to prospective teachers as it might seem. Basically a man-machine system is a teaching team in which machines as well as people, are given a role, and each person and machine is allowed to do the type of work he or it can do best. If it works as it should, the systems approach should result in more efficient and effective learning, with teachers giving pupils much more personal attention than they have in any period since the advent of mass education.

LEARNING BY DISCOVERY

Learning by discovery is not envisaged as something that just happens. It is designed to happen, as a result of a definite teaching method or strategy. At least five different strategies can be distinguished.

Type 'A': For the most part, the teacher is a mute presence. His task is to 'structure the environment', or to provide 'structured apparatus'. The children are then left to learn the relevant concept or principle, in the course of self-chosen activities.

Type 'B': Here the teacher supplements the self-chosen activity with his own seemingly casual commentary on it. He asks questions about what is being done, supplies information, suggests further activities, and draws attention to certain feature, such as, outside visits to places of interest.

Type 'C': Research activity by children is carried out. This principally is concerned with books or more broadly with textual resources.

Type 'D': With this variation a task is set or proposed by the teacher. But the task requires independent activity for its completion.

Type 'E': The teacher hints, provokes, asks leading questions, components the learner with the implications of what he thinks, or prods him to framing some hypothesis. The object is to stimulate active, searching thinking in some specific direction but always to stop short of actually telling anything.

CONCLUDING REMARKS

Although the foundation of method described in this text will lead to the achievements of teaching objectives, however, there are other areas which are also important, such as, physical layout adopted by the teacher and pupils, his personal image, interpersonal judgements made by the teacher and pupils of one another and other wide discretionary areas where teachers are free to adopt their own style for the betterment of education, regardless of the type of school in which they teach or the age group of children with whom they are concerned.

REFERENCES AND RECOMMENDED READING

1. Amidon, E.J. and N.A. Flanders. - 'Research On Teacher Behavior'/Minneapolis, Minn: Paul S. Amidon And Associates, 1963.
2. Bennett, S.N. - 'Teaching Styles And Pupil Progress'/London: Open Books, 1976.
3. Bernard, H.W. - 'Psychology of Learning and Teaching'/New York: McGraw Hill, 1965.
4. Bruner, J. - 'The Process of Education'/New York: Vintage Books, 1960.
5. Dale, Edgar - *'What Does It Mean To Teach'/*USA, The News Letter, Volume 30, March 1965.
6. Flanders, N.A. - 'Analysing Teacher Behavior'/New York: Addison-Wesley, 1970.
7. Hamblin, D. - 'The Teacher And Counselling'/Oxford: Blackwell, 1974.
8. Holt, J. - 'How Children Fail'/Harmondsworth: Penguin, 1964.
9. Hunter, M. - *'Educational Leadership'/*USA, Association For Supervision And Curriculum Devel,opment, Vol. 23, 1966.
10. Midwinter, E. - 'Priority Education'/Harmondsworth: Penguin, 1972.
11. Musgrove, F. and Taylor, P.H. - 'Society And The Teacher Role'/London: Routledge & Kegan Paul, 1969.
12. Smith, B.O. - *'The Bulletin Of The National Association Of Secondary School Principals'/* NASSP, Vol. 47, April 1963.
13. Taylor, P.H. - *'Children's Evaluations Of The Characteristics of The Good Teacher'/* British Journal Of Educational Psychology, 1962.

CHARACTERISTICS OF A GOOD TEACHER

CHAPTER 10

INTRODUCTION

Teaching is a high responsibility and must be taken seriously. Classroom interaction is affected not only by what goes on inside the classroom but also by outside influences impinging upon the teacher's interpretation of what is significant and upon his relationship with others. Therefore, a teacher who wishes to make a real impact on the teaching profession must respect and care for himself, for his colleagues, and for his pupils as persons.

SOME CHARACTERISTICS OF A GOOD TEACHER

Some of the characteristics of a good teacher are listed as follows:

A good teacher is one who has attained working knowledge of the History of Education, Teaching Methods and Educational Psychology and Sociology. William Taylor forcefully points out: "The relationship of 'Education' to its underlying disciplines is in the same order as the relationship of the Practice of Medicine to the study of anatomy, physiology, biology and so on. Whether he is conscious of the fact or not, the Medical Practitioner is making use of such biological and physiological knowledge at every step of his diagnosis and recommendations for treatment; the teacher who denies the influence of social, psychological and philosophical assumptions in his own decision-making is merely the slave of unformulated and unsystematic patterns of habit." (29, 1969).

A good teacher is one who can exercise such skills as: ability to state objectively a point of view; ability to accept, clarify and use ideas; ability to relate accurately the ideas of others; ability to summarize ideas presented in group discussions; ability to accept and clarify emotional expression and relate them to ideas; ability to use criticism without offending the recipient and ability to communicate encouragement and so on. E.J. Amidon rightly points out: "The key to developing more effective classroom verbal behavior is the opportunity to experiment with and practice desired communication skills." (2, 1963, P.3).

A good teacher is one who cares about himself, about helping pupils develop healthy self-concepts, about democracy, about making content meaningful in the lives of pupils, and other teaching objectives. He cares for him by viewing himself in a positive way and appreciating and respecting worth of others. He cares about helping pupils to develop healthy self-concepts by appreciating that to care about young adolescents, one must understand them in their cultural setting. As Eric Hoffer puts it: "The reasonable approach is to assume that the adolescent's behavior is induced largely by his mode of existence, by the situation in which he finds himself. This would imply that adults, too, when placed in a similar situation, would behave more or less like Juveniles." (19, 1965, p.1). Therefore, a good teacher realises that values and self-concepts are almost inseparable. He cherishes differences and helps pupils clarify their own values and respect the values of others.

He cares about democracy by appreciating psychologists view that the most effective learning and personality development takes place in democratic settings and having faith in others. Adlia Stevenson says so well: ". . . I would\. . . emphasize first that any discussion of education cannot be cast in terms of national needs . . . For education serves the ends of democratic society only as it meets those of the individual human being. The essential condition of the system of free choice between conflicting ideas and leaders, which we call democracy, is that it be made up of all different kinds of people — which means that what we demand most of education is the development of informed people who are at the same time unique, different, unpatterned individuals." (28, 1958, pp. 155-156). A good teacher cares about making content meaningful in the lives of pupils by fully understanding that for content to be meaningful to pupils, he must see his importance to them, and in order for pupils to learn knowledge and skills most effectively he must need to direct where they are going.

A good teacher must make distinction between the task of learning and the feelings, purposes and problems of the learner. Huston Smith says so well: "It would be good if we could add that education should be permeated with an accepting attitude towards students. Such acceptance has nothing to do with softness-leniency toward work carelessly done, laxity with regard to academic standards, or indulgence toward foolish ideas. Doubtless teachers should be infinitely patient in helping students to bring their ideas to birth, but they should stand ever prepared to apply euthanasia to those that turn out to be monsters. Acceptance has nothing to do with indulgence; it is compatible with the most forthright criticism." (27, 1955, pp. 97).

A good teacher involves pupils in the teaching processes, and by so doing he can avoid the temptations to self-centred teaching and thereby make teaching effective. Richard L. Loughlin has drawn up a list of ten do's and don'ts for teachers and a good teacher would do well to follow his lead. These are: "(1) Encourage student-instructor planning, execution, and evaluation of the lesson. (2) Lead students to suggest possible avenues of approach to and applications of the subject matter. (3) Keep the entire group in the picture, even when working with individuals. (4) Make the group a circle not a triangle. (Do not dominate, judge, or 'steel the show', nor permit a student to do so.) (5) Varied activities (dramatization, panel discussion, audio-visual aids, oral reports, blackboard work, student lectures, committee work, guests). (6) Stimulate socialization, critical listening, and inter-criticism by referring one student's reply to another student for comment or additional information. ("What is your reaction to that, (name)?" Then, have the respondent ask another why he agrees or disagrees.) (7) Don't exploit "star" pupils or volunteers; the diffident need encouragement and are often more profound. Involve all in a creative, co-operative, and courteous enterprise to learn. (8) Student errors in fact or in oral or written English should be corrected obtrusively (merely supplying the correction, without stopping the recitation), unless the mistake is typical enough to require concentrated drill. (9) Cultivate an audience situation by changing your position; e.g., moving to or towards the rear of the room; by insisting on audibility; by using hand signals to get the speaker to stand, face the class, and speak up; by discouraging calling out or chorus answers; or by insisting on group courtesy to a student, chairman, or speaker. (At the end of the period, the instructor — not the bell — should dismiss the class.) (10) Students' questions, animated responses, evident enjoyment, rapt attention, and an unwillingness to leave the room at the end of the lesson usually indicate that the instructor has inculcated self-direction — the first step in self-improvement. (21, 1962, pp. 35-36).

A good teacher should be familiar with the role of the teacher as a counsellor such as: (a) The teacher-counsellor works earnestly with his children by taking them more seriously than the subject he teaches. He spends much of his time in trying to determine just how the subject matter may have some meaning for each of the children in his class. (b) The teacher-counsellor prepares a Memorandum on each child so that he can establish individual differences and adjust his teaching goals and methods accordingly. (c) The teacher-counsellor tries to allocate some time out of his full-time load for student surgery in which individual consultation with some of the children can take place. (d) The teacher-counsellor tries to develop in the class an atmosphere, a climate, a relationship, so that learning of positive nature should occur, rather than dispensing knowledge or teaching an isolated skill.

PRACTICAL ROADBLOCKS

However, there are many practical problems to achieve this role in a system of mass educational schools. Such as: (a) Some teachers may feel that their concern is with teaching a subject and not to function as a counsellor. Such teachers fail to appreciate that there is little evidence to indicate that concentration on a subject has much positive effect on the learning of that subject, but on the contrary there is much evidence to indicate that learning is directly related to the teacher's concentration on the learner, rather than on what is being learned. (b) Some teachers may feel that for some of the attributes, the teacher's normal attitudes are not desirable for a counsellor; such as: most teachers are at various times, the judges, the evaluators, the disciplinarians and at time they may have to step into a punitive role; whereas a counsellor is neither a judge nor a disciplinarian. This is clearly a very difficult area to reconcile, but however, the best the teacher-counsellor can do is to develop the sort of classroom situation where the children have achieved an inner self-discipline so that the teacher rarely has to function as a disciplinarian. (c) A teacher who teaches several different classes may have contact with several hundred students and he obviously cannot get to know all of them; and in this situation to function as a teacher-counsellor effectively is almost an impossible task. To do full justice he has neither got the time nor physical facilities.

Although it seems that, with the improved resources, these problems can be overcome or limited but nevertheless, under the present mass educational systems this role of teacher-counsellor remains to be an ideal and perhaps a long term objective for the days that lie ahead.

CONCLUDING REMARKS

Some of the characteristics of a good teacher have been outlined in this chapter for the guidance of relatively less experienced teachers, in particular for tyro & beginner teachers. However, in no way, is this a comprehensive list and therefore, needs to be developed with time, research, experiences, innovation and future advancements and expectations of the teaching profession.

The readers who are more experienced teachers should enhance this listing by including more characteristics of a good teacher as they see appropriate. This exercise should be treated as a system which needs continuous development and like curriculum development can be considered as a cyclic process.

REFERENCES AND RECOMMENDED READING

1. Adams, R.S. and D.J. Biddle - 'Realities of Teaching'/New York: Holt, Rinehart & Winston, 1970.
2. Amidon, E.J. and N.A. Flanders - 'The Roll of the Teacher in the classroom: A manual for Understanding and Improving Teachers' Classroom Behavior'/Minneapolis: Paul S. Amidson & Associates, 1963.
3. Anderson, H.H. and Brewer, H.M. - 'Studies of Teachers' Classroom Personalities'/ Applied Psychological Monographs of the American Association For Applied Psychology, Calif, Stanford, University Press, 1946.
4. Arbuckle, D.S. - *'The Teacher as a Counsellor'/*the High School Journal, Vol. 40, Chapel Hill N.C.: The University of North Carloina Press, May 1957.
5. Bennett, S.N. - 'Teaching Styles and Pupil Progress'/London: Open Book, 1976.
6. Berlyne, D.E. - 'Conflict, Arousal and Curiosity'/New York: McGraw-Hill, 1960.
7. Bernstein, B. - 'Class, Codes and Control'/London: Routledge & Kegan Paul, 1971.
8. Bloom, B.S. (ED) - 'A Taxonomy of Educational Objectives'/London: Longman, 1964, Vol. 1 (1956), Vol. 2 (1964).
9. Brady, E.H. - *'Education'/*Leadership, Vol. 18, The Association for Supervision and Curriculum Development, March 1961.
10. Chanan, G. and S. Delamont - 'Frontiers of Classroom Research'/F.E.R., 1975.
11. Cope E. - 'School Experience in Teacher Education: A Study of School Practice in Two Colleges of Education' University of Bristol, 1971.
12. Elliott, J. and C. Adelman - 'Innovation in Teaching and Action-research'/Norwich Centre of Applied Research in Education, 1974.
13. Epstein, H.T. - *'An Experiment in Education'/*Nature, Vol. 235 (28 January, 1972), pp. 203-5.
14. Flanders, N.A. - 'Analysing Teacher Behavior'/New York: Addison-Wesley, 1970.
15. Goldacre, E. - 'Teachers and Their Pupils' Home Background,/NFER, 1968.

16. Green, T.E. - 'The Activities of Teaching'/New York: McGraw-Hill, 1971.

17. Gurrey, P. - 'Education and the Training of Teachers'/London: Longmans, 1963.

18. Hilsum, S. - 'The Teacher at work'/Slough: National Foundation for Education Research in England and Wales, 1972.

19. Hoffer, Eric - *'A Time of Juveniles'*/Harper's Magazine, June, 1965.

20. Hoyle, E. - 'The Role of the Teacher'/London: Routledge & Kegan Paul, 1969.

21. MacMunn, N. - 'The Child's Path to Freedom'/London: Bell, 1921.

22. Mac Murray, J - 'Reason and Emotion' - London: Feber & Feber, 1935.

23. Morrison, A. and D. Mcintyre - 'Teachers and Teaching'/Penguin, 1969.

24. Moustakas, C.E. - 'The Teacher and the Child: Personal Interaction in the Classroom'/ New York: McGraw-Hill, 1956.

25. Prescott, D.A. - 'Emotion and The Educative Process: The Committee on the Relation of Emotion to the Educative Process'/Washington D.C: the American Council on Education, 1938.

26. Smith H. - 'The Purposes of Higher Education'/New York: Harper & Row, 1955.

27. Stephenson, A.E. - 'As Quoted from Louise parrish and Yvonne Waskin, Teacher-Pupil Planning'/New York: Harper & Row, 1958.

28. Taylor, W. - 'Society, and the Education of Teachers'/London: Faber & Faber, 1969.

29. Tropp, A. - 'The School Teachers'/London: Heinemann, 1957.

30. Warr, P.B. - 'Tought and Personality'/Harmondsowrth: Penguin, 1970.

31. Woods, P. and Hammersley, M. (EDS) - 'School Experience'/London: Croom Helm, 1971.

SECTION : 3

HUMAN RESOURCES DEVELOPMENT IN WORK ENVIRONMENT

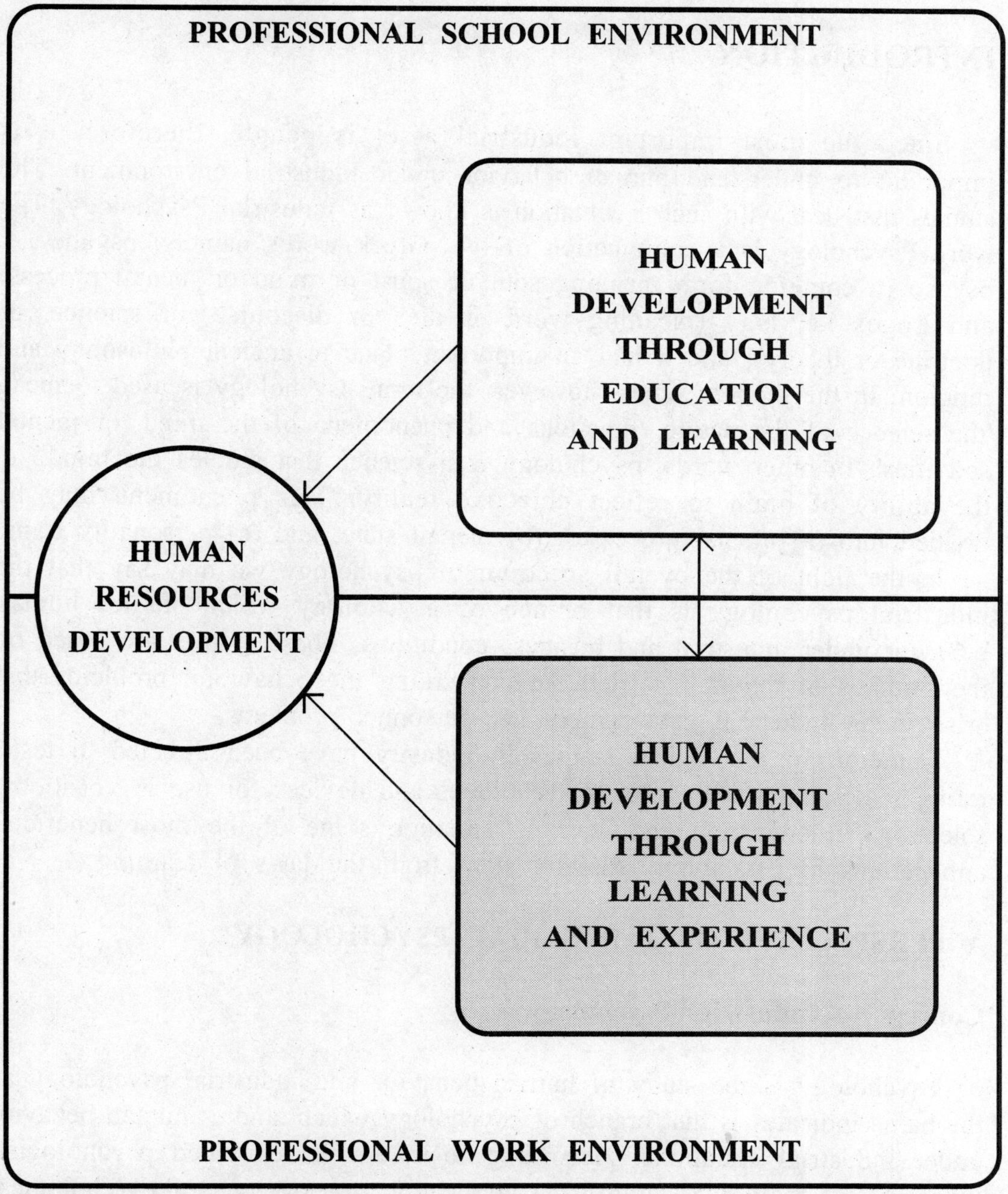

HUMAN BEHAVIOR IN INDUSTRIAL ENVIRONMENT: A PSYCHOLOGICAL PERSPECTIVE

CHAPTER 11

INTRODUCTION

Since the most important industrial asset is people, therefore, it is important to understand human behavior under industrial environment. The studies that deal with such a situation is known as industrial Psychology. The word Psychology is a combination of two Greek words namely: psykhe i.e. psycho (a combing form meaning soul or spirit or mind or mental process) and Logos i.e. logy (meaning word or idea or discourse, or science, or doctrine or theory); and it had an important place in ancient philosophy and religion. In the modern times, however, the term psychology is used to mean 'the science of the nature, functions and phenomena of the mind, or mental activities'. In other words, psychology is a science that studies the mind i.e. the ability of brain to reflect objective reality. This phenomena may be divided into (a) mental processes, (b) mental state, and (c) personality traits.

In the light of the overall spectrum of psychology we may say that the industrial psychology is that branch of psychology which studies human behavior under industrial and business conditions. These studies are based on the findings of research carried out concerning the behavioral problems that arise in an industrial environment i.e. personnel problems.

Numerous psychological studies in industry have been directed to tests, rating scales, interviews, etc. as techniques and devices for use in vocational selection. In education and learning situation some of the most beneficial applications of psychology directly stem from the laws of learning.

A PERSPECTIVE ON INDUSTRIAL PSYCHOLOGY

Concept of Industrial Psychology

Psychology is the study of human behavior and industrial psychology as the name indicates is that branch of psychology which studies human behavior under industrial situations. According to Bhum, a renowned psychologist, industrial psychology is simply the application or extension of psychological principles and facts to the problem concerning human relations in business and industry. Smith, another renowned psychologist, defined industrial psychology as the study of conduct of those who exchange the work of their hands and brain for the mean to live.

We can say that industrial psychology is concerned firstly with the study and discovery of information relating to human behavior and secondly, with the application of information about human behavior to the various problems of human life. It is, therefore, the professional aspect of psychology.

The Aim of Industrial Psychology

The aim of industrial psychology is to make provisions for the industrial worker with greater physical and mental ease at his work through research. This research takes the form of investigation, in an unbiased manner, the ways in which psychological problems are handled at present; development of new improved methods and formulation of certain principles which will help in the solution of new problems.

The Scope of Industrial Psychology

The scope of industrial psychology is limited to a material and social environment to which an individual adapts himself while he is at work and by which his attitude is modified. The main premises of the scope of industrial psychology are shown in Fig. 11.1. Industrial Psychology, addresses the following:

* It studies the economic, social & physical aspects of the industry and physical aspect of work environment;

* It studies aptitude and motives. These are major influential factors on human behavior in the industrial environment as behavior changes with changes in stimuli. It is, therefore, necessary to study the rules pertaining to correct attitude and motive, the importance of which can be highlighted by the Hawthorne study i.e. study conducted by Hawthorne Works Western Electric Company into the effect of the attitude of worker upon production.

* It studies human relations (i.e. human behavior in an industrial context)

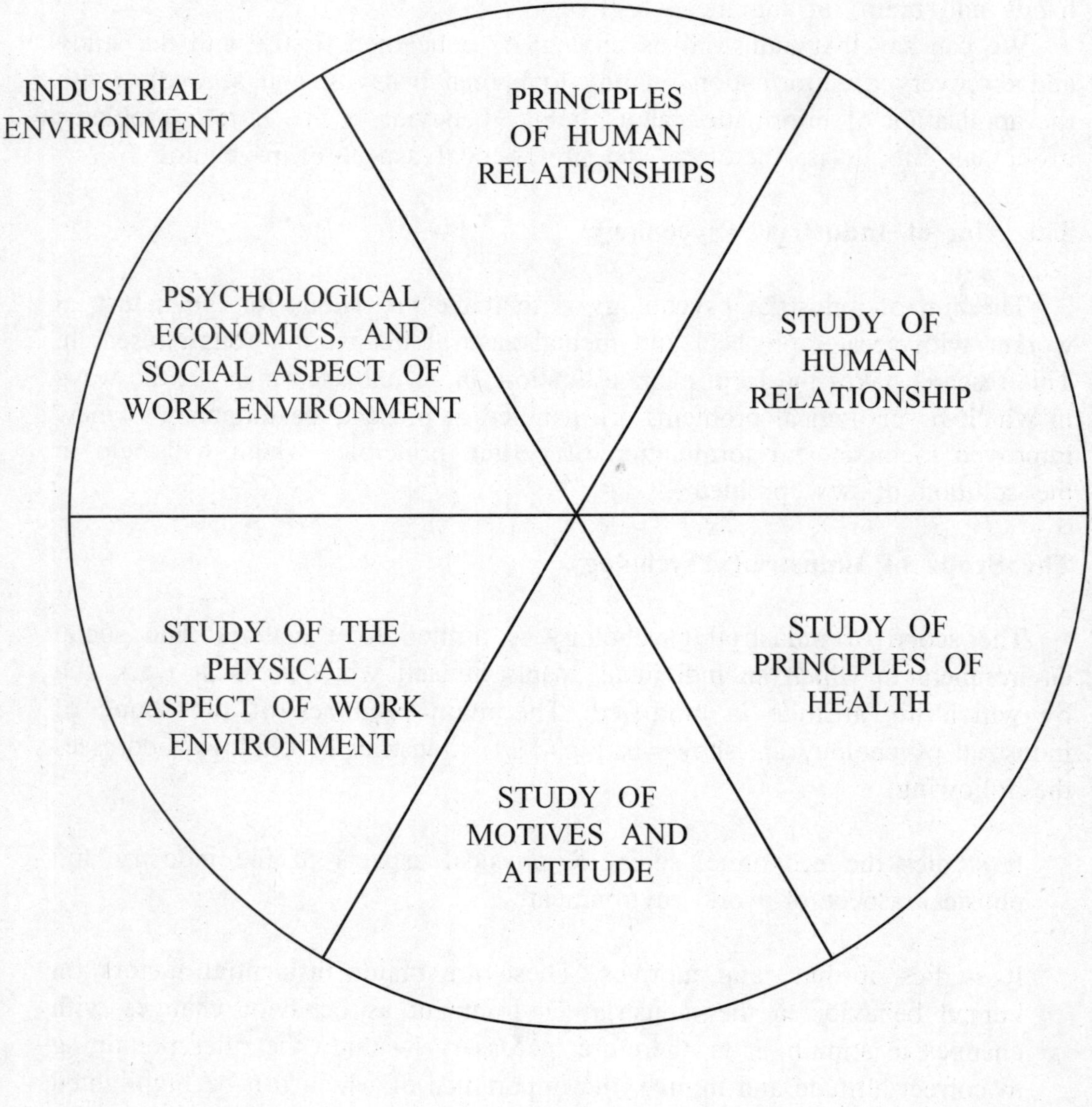

FIG. 11.1: SCOPE OF INDUSTRIAL PSYCHOLOGY

and discovers principles for improving human relationship in an industrial environment.

* It studies the factors that influence the mental health of workers, discovers principles for maintaining their mental health, and gives suggestions for improving the mental health of those who are suffering from mental diseases.

Since industrial psychology is the study of people at work and is concerned with an entire spectrum of human behavior, its scope is free from administrative details, but covers the entire process of management's dealing with people at work.

Objectives & Applications of Industrial Psychology

Industrial Psychology being applied psychology has many objectives, some of these are shown in Fig. 11.2.

The findings, principles and techniques of industrial psychology may be applied to provide benefits to the areas of management such as the following:

* Selection and placement of personnel, motivation and public relation research; worker attitude and morale.

* Workers training, development of human resources including executive development and counselling.

* Human Engineering (designing and laying out equipment in order to get the greatest efficiency of man-machine system).

* Organization Behavior: The research findings on organization behavior helps a great deal in creating a team spirit in the organization and re-organizing their organization structures and policies. In this context it is worth mentioning the remarks of USA Industrialists Carnegic & Andrew: 'Take away our factories, our trade, our money, leave us with nothing but organization and in four years we shall have established ourselves'.

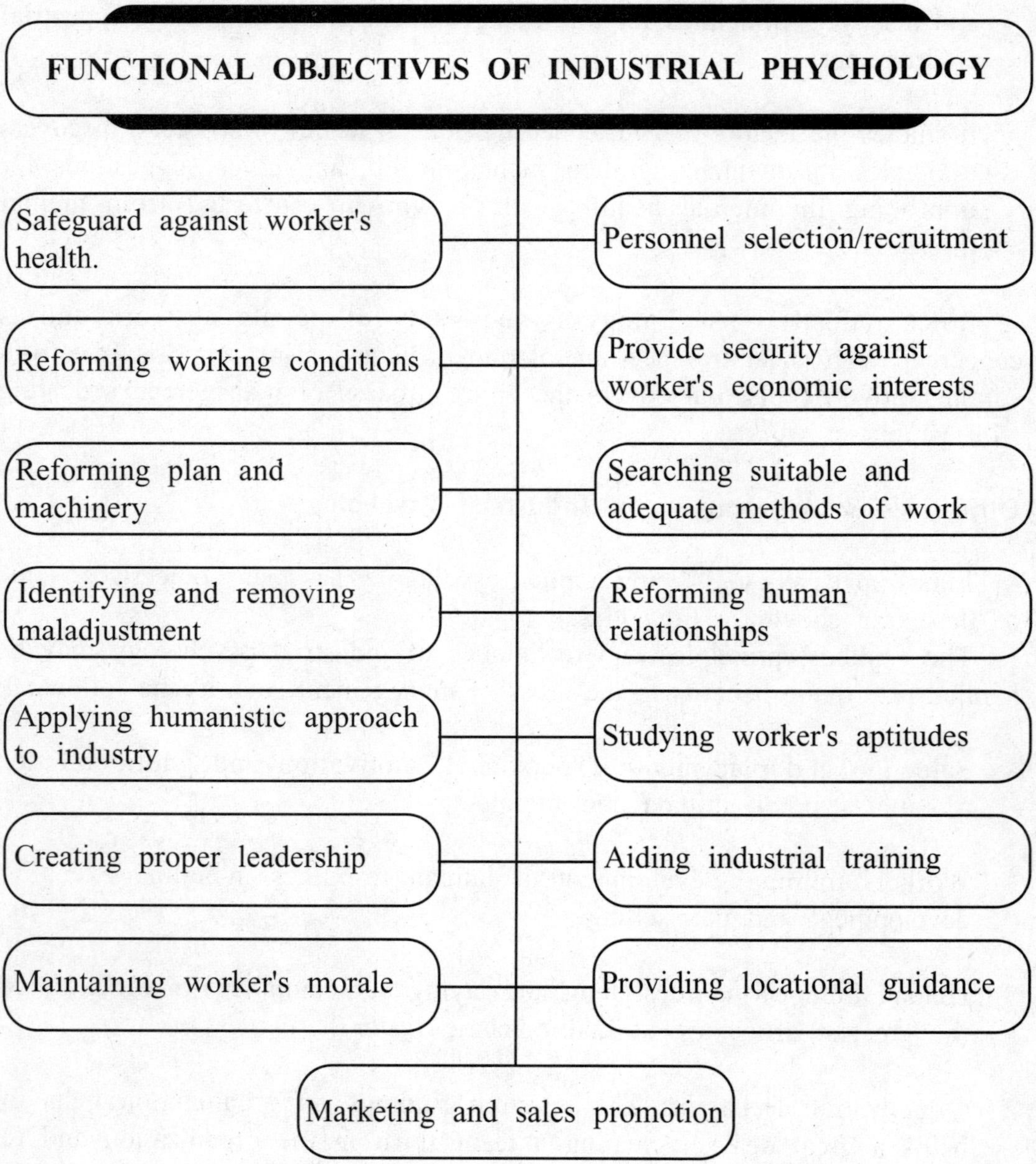

FIG. 11.2: OBJECTIVES OF INDUSTRIAL PSYCHOLOGY

Phases of Totality of Human Behavior

Laprer, a well renowned Psychologist, has postulated four phases of totality of human behavior as follows:

Phase '1' Overt Symbolic (speaking, writing, etc.).

Phase '2' Overt non-symbolic (direct muscular act like jumping, playing, running, etc.).

Phase '3' Covert Symbolic (thinking).

Phase '4' Covert non-symbolic (feeling and emotions).

However covert phases i.e. phases 3 & 4 i.e. what any man is actually feeling and thinking, cannot be measured in abstract terms and psychologists have to rely on guesses which has caused so much controversy as to the nature and measurability of genuine behavioral tendencies.

Causes of Human Behavior

Human behavior is caused by needs as when a need arises, the individual person feels that there is a lack of something which makes him dissatisfied and he, through certain responses and actions, seeks to satisfy his needs, which constitutes his behavior. Maslow's model of the hierarchy of human needs is shown in Fig. 11.3. However, Maslow's suggested steps do not always have to be fulfilled in sequence and there are certain exceptions. For example a starving artist may sacrifice first level needs in pursuit of a higher level of creativity. But, by and large, Maslow's model is a useful reminder for a manager/supervisor to evaluate the needs of his subordinates as an individual basis and then give them suitable assignments in which they can become motivated by satisfying their needs.

Since behavior is directed towards the fulfilment or satisfaction of certain needs, therefore, process of motivation begins with the needs and ends with the satisfaction of the need. In other words satisfied needs no longer motivate workers. Industrial psychologists study human behavior by analysing the people's needs to provide them with appropriate motivation to contribute fully to the objective of their respective enterprise and suggest the types of

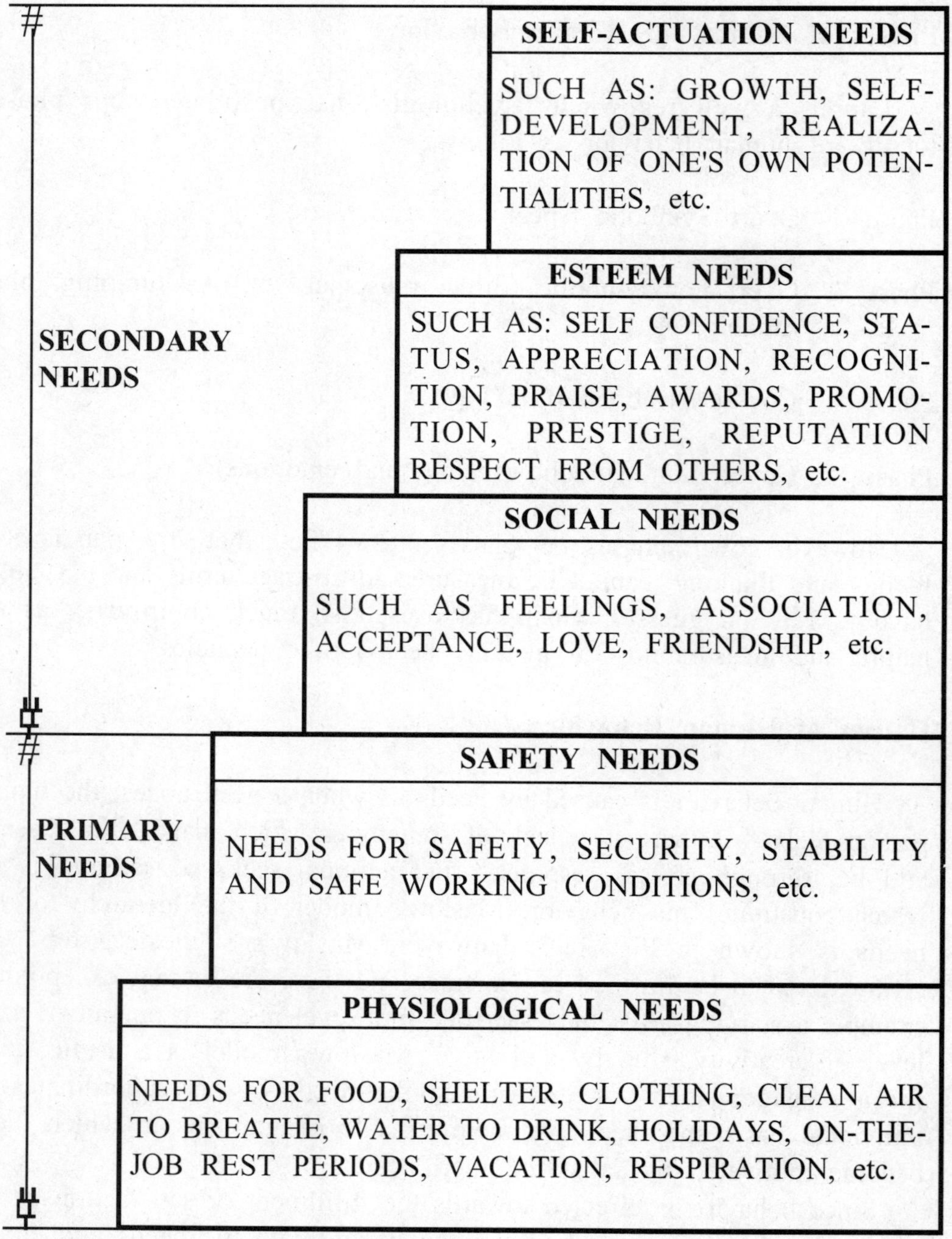

FIG. 11.3: MASLOW'S HIERARCHY OF NEEDS

incentives to be provided to different types of personnel. They have also developed certain techniques whereby individual differences in psychological factors can be identified and measured to help the management to place the right man on the right job and to arrange proper training for each person.

Industrial Psychology and Personnel Management Distinguished

Both industrial psychology and personnel management basically deals with various aspects of management's dealing with people at work. However, Industrial Psychology places more emphasis on the scientific and research aspects of people at work and omits many of the routine administrative details, whilst personnel management deals with the execution aspect and with the help of principles of industrial psychology makes selection of right person on right jobs on right times and at right costs.

INDIVIDUAL BEHAVIOR

Individual Behavior Defined

The action of an individual towards others is called individual behavior. Individual behavior is a function of such internal forces as attitude, personality and motivation, as an individual thinks for himself and acts on his own himself. The branch of psychology that deals with individual behavior is called human psychology. Among various factors that influence an individuals behavior is the influence of others.

Since behavior is viewed as being conditioned solely by external forces, therefore by controlling environmental variables and through a set of techniques called behavior modification it is possible to replace undesirable behavior with desired behavior.

Individual Differences

Differences in individual behavior have a great importance in the industrial environment, since in an industry different individuals with different abilities and qualities are required to perform various functions. If an individual gives a better performance he can be taken to be superior to the average and if he gives less performance can be classified inferior. Studies of individual differences help the managers/supervisors in planning, scheduling and distributing the work among their subordinates and also assigning tasks according to capacities of each worker. Some major courses of individual differences are shown in Fig. 11.4. Such differences have their important impact in industry as they affect the job behavior of people. The behavior of any individual does not just happen but instead it is caused by the continuous interaction between the individual and environment.

The individual differences has a wide application in the section, placement and designing of training needs and also to know how to motivate individuals and to understand the behavior of subordinates. The environment, on the other hand, has a great influence on human nature, traits, habits and characteristics. Therefore, by educating and training the workers and by changing their work environment, the management can change the behavior of the individuals.

When we study behavior of an individual towards his job, we come to a conclusion that this behavior is dependent upon not only individual variables i.e. interests, personality, age & sex, education, experience, physical characteristics etc. but also situational variables i.e. methods of work, work space, type of training, social and physical environment, characteristics of organization, etc. The situational variables can be classified into two categories, namely: organizational and social variables and physical and job variables. A graphic representation of individual and situational variables associated with job performance is shown in Fig. 11.5.

The importance of placing individuals on jobs which they can perform at a satisfactory level, by and large, stems from at least four considerations, namely: (a) personal considerations (b) social considerations, (c) economic considerations, and (d) legal and contractual considerations (see Fig. 11.6).

In the direction of effective utilization of human potential, the efforts to provide education and training opportunities to individuals who are potentially capable, is a major step forward. Modern industry, by and large, seeks ways and means to facilitate individuals to grab the opportunities to work on jobs that are compatible with their potentialities.

In an industrial environment individual difference plays a vital role in the following context:

— In terms of job potential (difference between individuals)
— Effect of training (upon individual differences); and
— Job performance (difference even after training)
— Employees evaluation

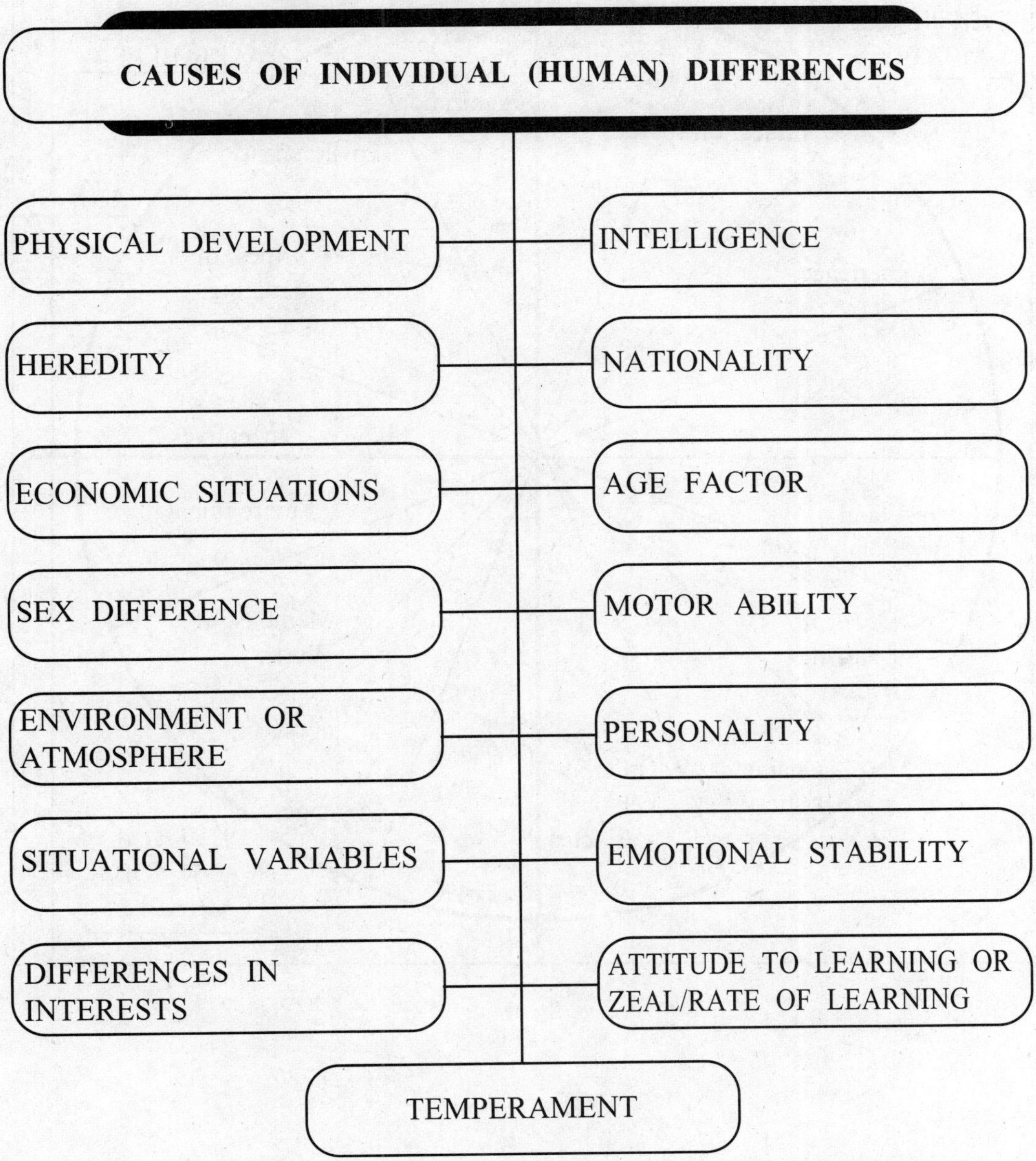

FIG. 11.4: SOME MAJOR CAUSES OF INDIVIDUAL DIFFERENCES

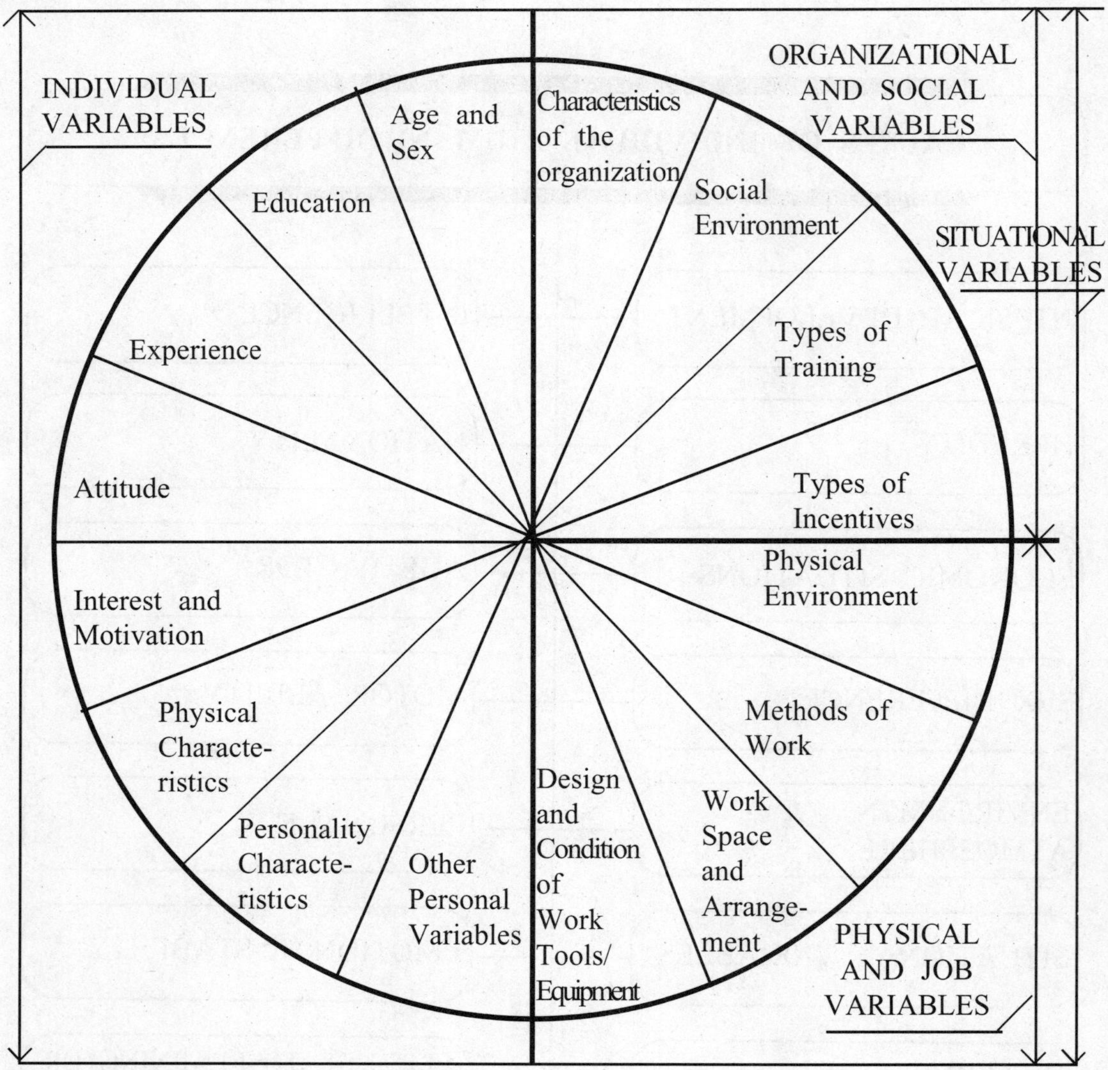

FIG. 11.5: A MODEL OF INDIVIDUAL AND SITUATIONAL VARIABLES ASSOCIATED WITH JOB PERFORMANCE

CONSIDERATIONS FOR INDIVIDUAL JOB PERFORMANCE

ECONOMIC CONSIDERATIONS

Emphasis is placed on efficient use of resources. Employee is selected who performs at the desired level of performance

PERSONAL CONSIDERATIONS

Ability to perform the assigned job. This is a basic consideration.

SOCIAL CONSIDERATIONS

Emphasis is placed on the effective use of resources (including human and non-human). Individual differences play an important part on aspects such as:

- difference in terms of job potential
- effect of training upon individual difference
- difference in job performance even after training

CONTRACTUAL AND LEGAL CONSIDERATIONS

Emphasis is placed on the employment of individual who will be expected to give satisfactory performance on the job. Contract may provide that the individual cannot be removed (after the probationary period) without a definite cause

FIG. 11.6: FUNDAMENTAL CONSIDERATIONS FOR SATISFACTORY INDIVIDUAL JOB PERFORMANCE

Behavior Modification

As we said earlier that through a set of techniques called 'behavior modification', it is possible to replace undesirable behavior with desired behavior. But this necessitates the control of environmental variables. In an organizational context, a manager, in increasing the frequency of desired response among his subordinates, uses operating conditions and the process of learning through reinforcement.

To implement behavior modifications techniques in an organization, a six stepped approach as shown in Fig. 11.7 should be adopted. Behavior modification can be applied in many areas of an organizational set up. It is particularly relevant in the training and human resources development, since it provides encouragement to people to learn tasks accurately and quickly. It can also be used effectively in job design, group dynamics, management by objectives, organizational development, supervisory training, basic skills training and leadership training etc.

GROUP BEHAVIOR

Characteristics of Group Behavior

A group enables an individual to achieve results not otherwise open to him, helps to make sense of the world around him, and gives him emotional support. Group behavior has many characteristics some of these are listed below.

* Every group has its unique characteristics and cultural pattern to which the individual must conform if he is to remain a member of that group.

* A group, by and large, influences and changes the attitude and behavior of an individual towards work and also the organization as a whole.

* In a group an individual is no longer guided by his will. It has been observed that an individual has a mind, and individuality and a will consciousness of his own; and that the behavior of an individual in a group is different from his behavior when he acts alone.

* Group behavior may prove good as well as bad for the management

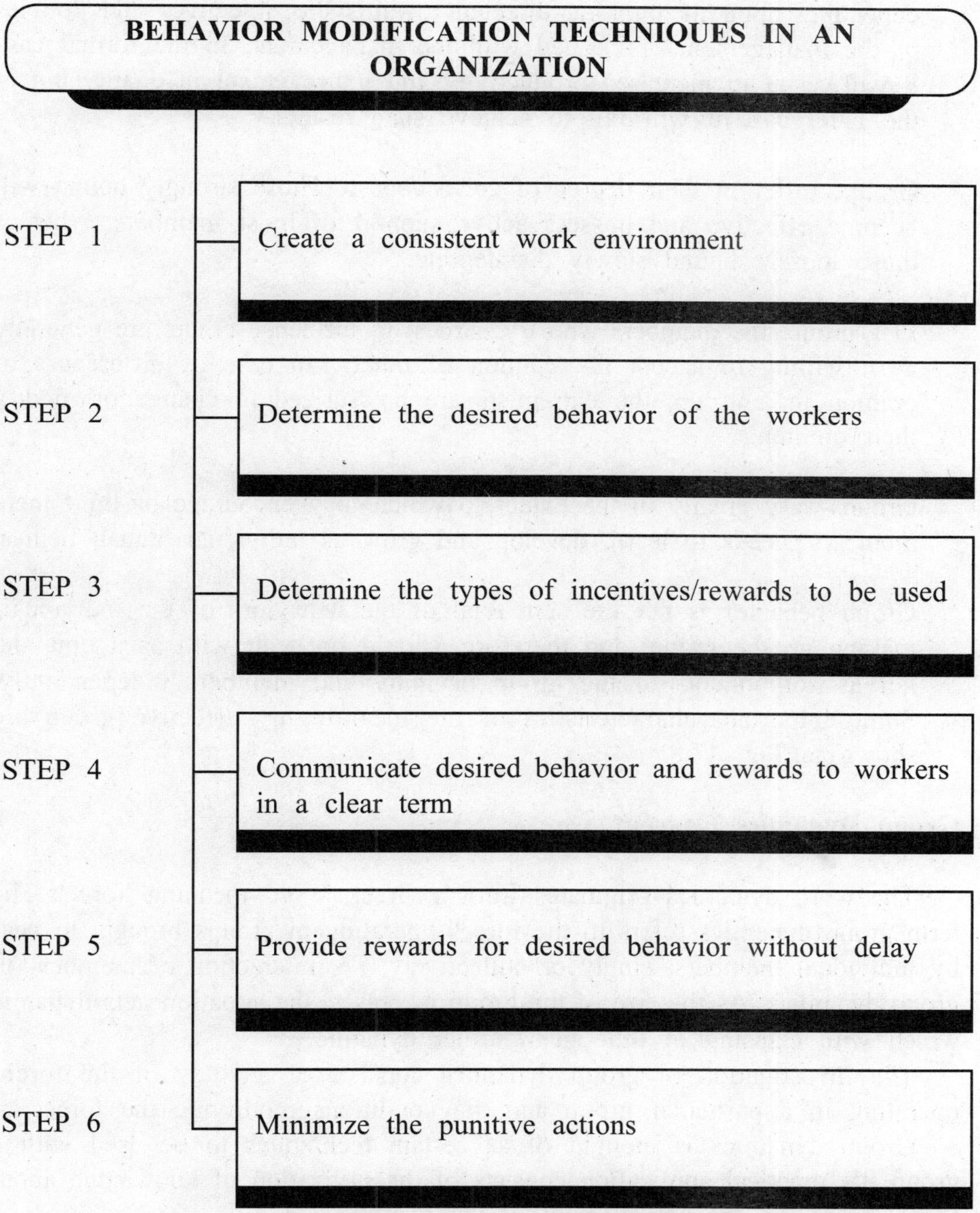

FIG. 11.7: SIX STEPPED APPROACH TO IMPLEMENT BEHAVIOR MODIFICATION TECHNIQUES IN AN ORGANIZATION

depending upon its thinking directed towards the objectives and policies of the management or clashed with the management. In the formal case it will result in increased productivity and improvement in quality but in the latter case it will fail to achieve such results.

* Groups differ in their degree of cohesiveness. Those strongly bound will become effective and possess active support of most members, whereas those loosely bound slowly disintegrate.

* In a group, the members who try hardest to influence others are generally most willing to accept the opinion of others. In case of differences of opinion in a group, the extremists are pressurized to change or modify their opinion.

* Groups vary greatly in the extent to which they encourage or limit there members' needs to learn, develop and grow as individual human beings.

* Group behavior is not the sum total of the behaviors of the individuals making up the group, and therefore, should be dealt with as a unit and not as components of the group or individual members independently. Some important characteristics of the ideal highly effective group are shown in Fig. 11.8.

Group Dynamics Concept

The word dynamics originates from a Greek Word meaning 'force'. The term group dynamics refers to the forces operating in groups brought to bear by individual members, singly or collectively, i.e. interaction of members in group dynamics. As the size of the group increases, the situation gets dynamic which with elapsing of time gets further dynamic.

The investigation of group dynamics consists of a study of the forces operating in a particular group and the conditions modifying the forces.

Group dynamics is thought of as certain techniques to be used with a group. Its practical application consists of the utilization of knowledge about these forces for the achievement of some purpose.

Since modern jobs involve greater independence between workers and their departments and demand close co-operation among all parties, the workers, in order to fulfill their social needs, form small group on the job itself and

CHARACTERISTICS OF THE IDEAL HIGHLY EFFECTIVE GROUP

- The members of the group are cohesive in their approach and are loyal to each other and their leader
- The members are skilled in various leadership and membership roles and functions which are important for interaction between the leader and members and among the members
- The members and leader have a high degree of trust and confidence in each other
- There is a strong motivation to receive communications as each member is interested in any information on any relevant matter that each member can provide
- The leader of each work group, by his leadership principles and practices, exerts a major influence in establishing the tone and atmosphere of the work group
- There is a high motivation in the group to use the communication process effectively so that it best serves interests and goals of the work group
- The group knows the value of constructive conformity and also knows when to use it and for what purposes
- There is a strong motivation on the part of each member to communicate fully and frankly all the information to the group, which is relevant and of value to the group activities
- The values and goals of the group and the relevant values and needs of the members are satisfactorily integrated and expressed
- The group is eager to help each member to develop to his (or her) full potential
- There is a strong motivation among members to influence other members as well as to be receptive to influence them with regards to all the group's activities, technical matters, methods, organizational problems, interpersonal relationships and group process
- Individual members feel secure in making decisions (which seems appropriate to them) because the goals and philosophy of operation are clearly understood by each member and provide him with a solid base for his decisions
- The group has been in existence sufficiently long to have developed a well established and relaxed working relationship among all its members
- Suggestions, comments, ideas and informations are offered with a helpful orientation. Interaction, problem solving, and decision making activities of the group occur in a supportive atmosphere

FIG. 11.8: SOME IMPORTANT CHARACTERISTICS OF THE IDEAL HIGHLY EFFECTIVE GROUP

their membership in a group helps to shape their attitude and work behavior toward the job and the organization. The greater the strength of the group attachment, the greater the power of the group to compel conformity to its ideas, to the extent that it may exercise stronger control over its members than the management.

For the management, a thorough study of group dynamics is very essential to avoid any negative consequences generated by the work groups.

Group Dynamics Defined

Group dynamics may be defined as the social process by which people interact face to face in small groups. In other words group dynamics is concerned with the dynamic interaction of individuals in a face to face relationship. Group dynamics focuses a team work wherein members are constantly in touch with each other and effectively provide their contribution to accomplish a common task.

Importance of Group Dynamics

Due to the size and complexity of modern industry, the management depends more and more upon the effectiveness of group efforts. The days are long gone when an employee worked more by himself and his productivity was often dependent upon his efforts alone. In those days, by and large, jobs were unskilled which are now taken over by automation. In modern industry jobs involve greater independence between workmen and between departments and demand class co-operation among all parties.

To a manager, the importance of group dynamics lies in the fact that many people tend to act differently, as individuals than as members of a group. Therefore he must study both individuals as well as groups as interrelated elements of a motivational situation. It is appropriate to quote Likert's (a renowned industrial psychologist) statement. "An organization will function best when its personnel function is not as individuals but as members of highly effective work groups with high performance goals." This implies that a manager should look into a series of interlocking groups with himself as the link between such groups and not as an organization structure in the normal individually oriented manner. He should see himself simultaneously the leader and the participating member of his own group.

Group activities are vastly different than the sum total of activities of the individual members. Group activities provide useful norms and guidelines for behavior and teach new employee how to behave Group activities help the individual to assign meanings to things (not properly understood) and thus help him in his work environment. Group activities also support the individual socially and psychologically on areas where he may feel powerless or exposed.

Groups provide security for individual members and an identity to achieve a feeling of belonging from which he derives recognition, status and esteem.

There are many other merits of group dynamics far too numerous to list here. To sum up the importance of group dynamics, we may say that the group is better geared to develop its clear goals, better resourced to accomplish its goal, and better furnished to provide very useful suggestions in goal achievements.

INDIVIDUAL VERSUS GROUP BEHAVIOR

Individual behavior as discussed in great detail above, is the action of a person or an individual towards others as he thinks for himself and acts on his own himself.

In an industrial environment individuals have to act together in many situations in a group i.e. a sort of collective mind where thinking of every member contributes something and resultant actions are considered as group behavior.

Human psychology deals with individual behavior, where as social psychology deals with group behavior. Group behavior is an outcome of action and motivation of individuals in a group and is not to be seen as characteristics of any single person belonging to the group.

WORK GROUP BEHAVIOR

Types of Work Groups

In organizations, two types of group are found namely: Formal and informal. Formal groups are those prescribed, established or found deliberately by the organization. Informal groups evolve out of the formal organization but are not formed by management nor appear in the organization structure. These are friendship groups that enjoy discussion on general and social issues over coffee or lunch break etc.

Formal groups consist of those groups who are structurally independent and those who are functionally and operationally independent. Functional groups consist of team groups, task groups and technical groups. A schematic structure of work groups is shown in Fig. 11.9.

Group Cohesiveness

The team feeling and mutual liking in a group is called group cohesiveness. Frequency of communication and size of group plays a major part in the cohesiveness of a group. The concern on overall goals, plans/processes to achieve those goals enhances group cohesiveness. Factors that determine group cohesiveness are shown in Fig. 11.10.

Group Development

B.W. Tuckman has developed a model of small group development that encompasses four stages of group development[40], which has also basically been followed by Heinen and Jacobson[12]. These stages of development include:

Stage 1: Forming: (forming first impression and role expectation)

Stage 2: Storming: (period of conflict arising over leadership, goals and task behavior etc.)

Stage 3: Norming: (team development, information sharing, creation of openness of communication and group cohesion etc.)

Stage 4: Performing: (efficient and effective performance of the group to achieve its goals)

The above stages of group development are not mutually exclusive and some overlap between the stages do exist. This necessitates shifting back to the earlier stage to resolve unsettled issues.

Psychological Functioning of a Group

Groups can provide (with or without the conscious knowledge of its

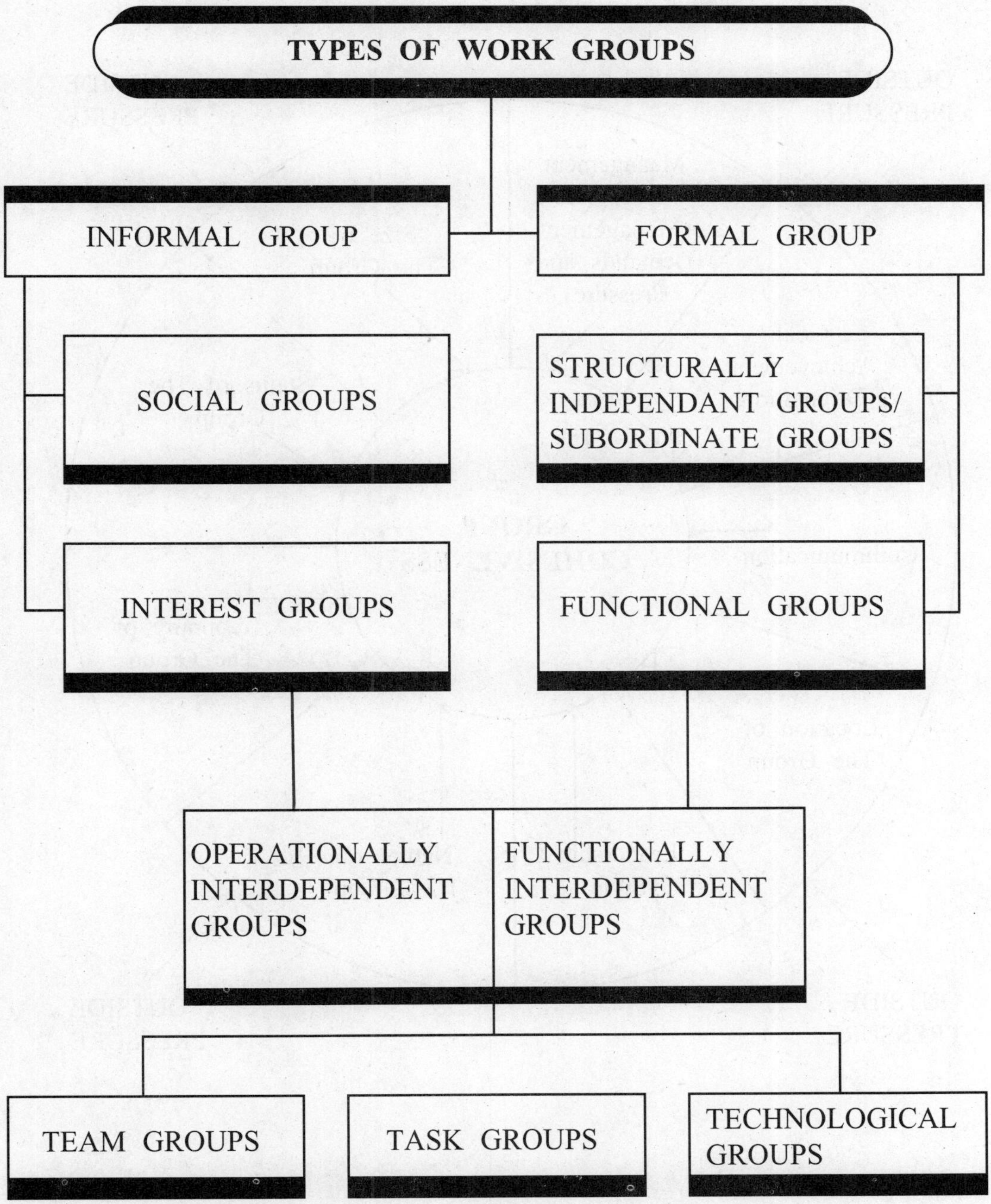

FIG. 11.9: TYPES OF WORK GROUPS

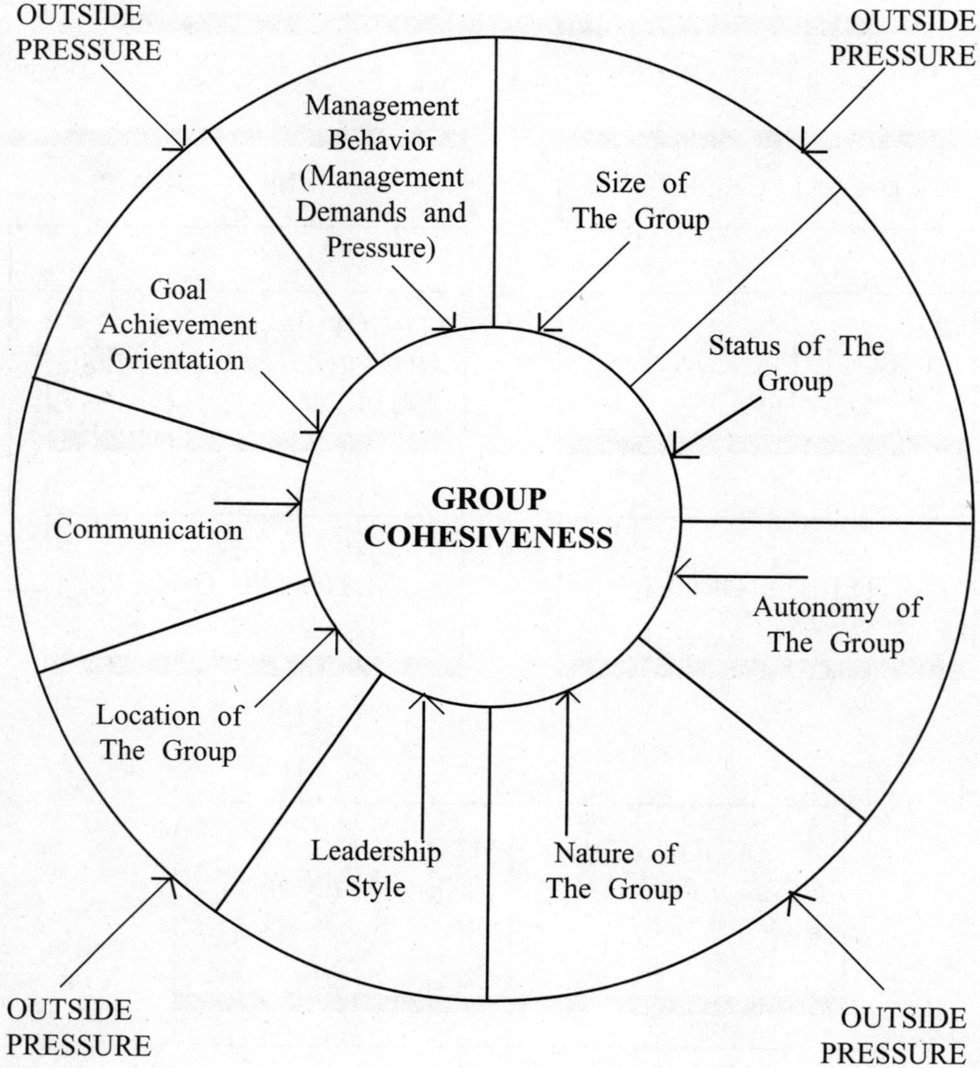

FIG. 11.10: GENERAL PRECURSOR OF GROUP COHESIVENESS (FACTORS THAT DETERMINE GROUP COHESIVENESS)

constituent members) a means of fulfilling many of the needs of individuals. A model of psychological functioning of a group is shown in Fig. 11.11. Principal needs met by the group include: affiliative, egoistic, cognitive, and instrumental.

Group Behavior Mechanism

People when work together develop some ways of thinking and behaving differently. Sometimes, this emergent behavior assists in the more effective performance whilst at other times, it may hinder it. In order to understand and predict work group behavior it is important to look at different elements. Mechanism of work group behavior is shown in Fig. 11.12. Major elements of work group behavior include activities, sentiment and interaction.

Sentiment may be defined as belief, feelings, or idea about the work and others involved in the work activities. Sentiment can be classified into two types i.e. 'required sentiment' and 'given sentiment'. 'Required Sentiment' is a belief or feeling which a worker must have in order to perform the assigned task, whereas 'given sentiment' is a belief or feeling which a worker brings with him into a group because of his personal background and life outside the work environment. When 'given sentiments' pertain to aspirations and ideals which are desirable, then they become 'values'. Thus we may define a 'value' as an unlimited idea of what is desirable,' such as: good pay and working conditions, freedom from being pushed around or belief in fair treatment etc. In contrast to a 'value' when idea of what is desirable is limited, it is called a 'norm'. Norms developed serve to define how a member of a team should behave in relation to outsiders, the job, and other members. They develop in any group with greater or lesser degree of consensus. The extent to which such norms are upheld by a member helps in defining his social standing and internal rank within the group.

The determination of 'given behavior' as well as 'required behavior', to a large extent, is influenced by the 'background factors' such as: job design and technology; management policies and practices; the assumptions and behavior of immediate supervisor; individual characteristics; workers' background and outside environments (i.e. social and economic influence), etc. For example, two identical jobs within the same technology can differ in achieving required activities, due to the fact that management may have used different assumptions with regard to how much individuals should be allowed to contribute and how the work activities should be performed.

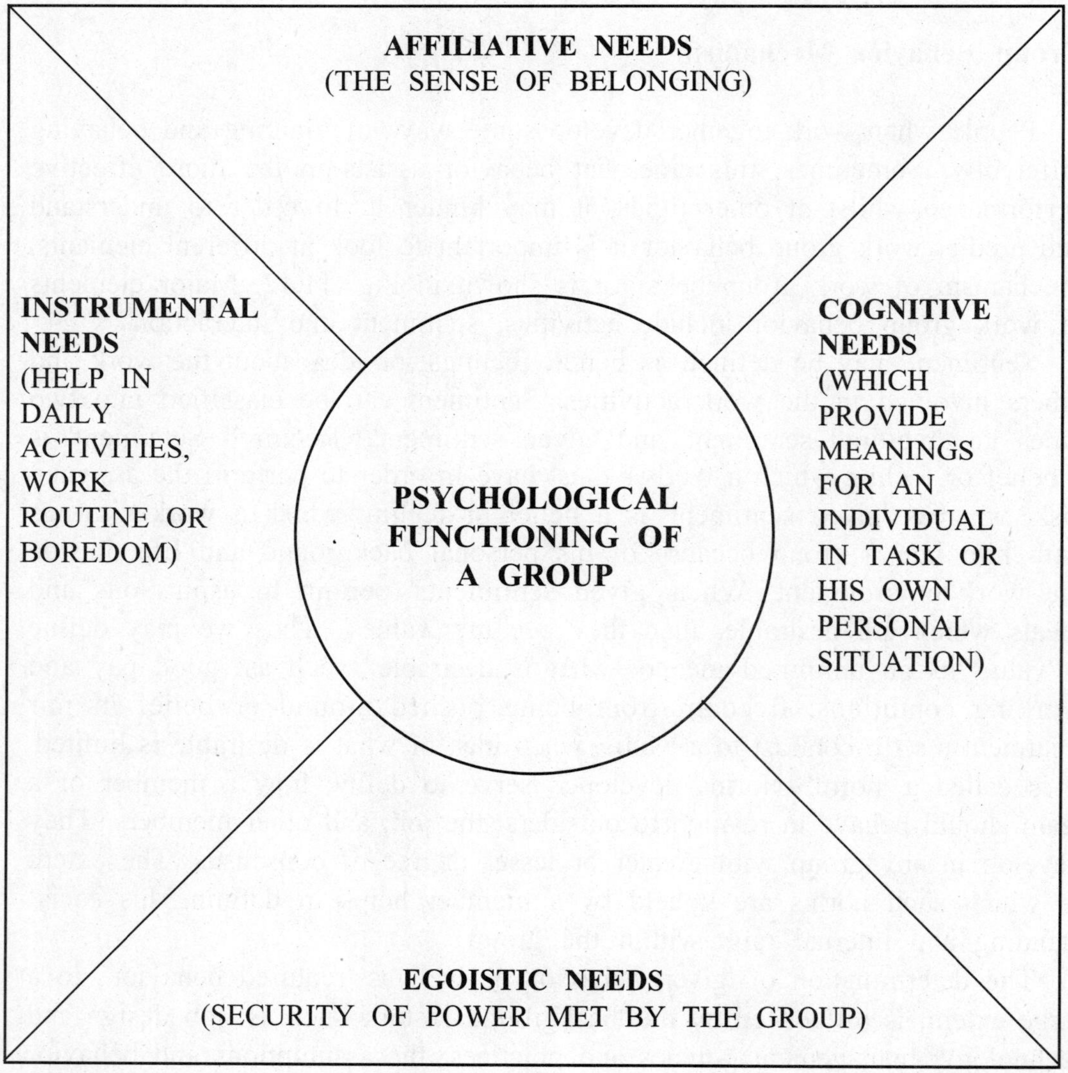

FIG. 11.11: A MODEL OF PSYCHOLOGICAL FUNCTIONING OF A GROUP

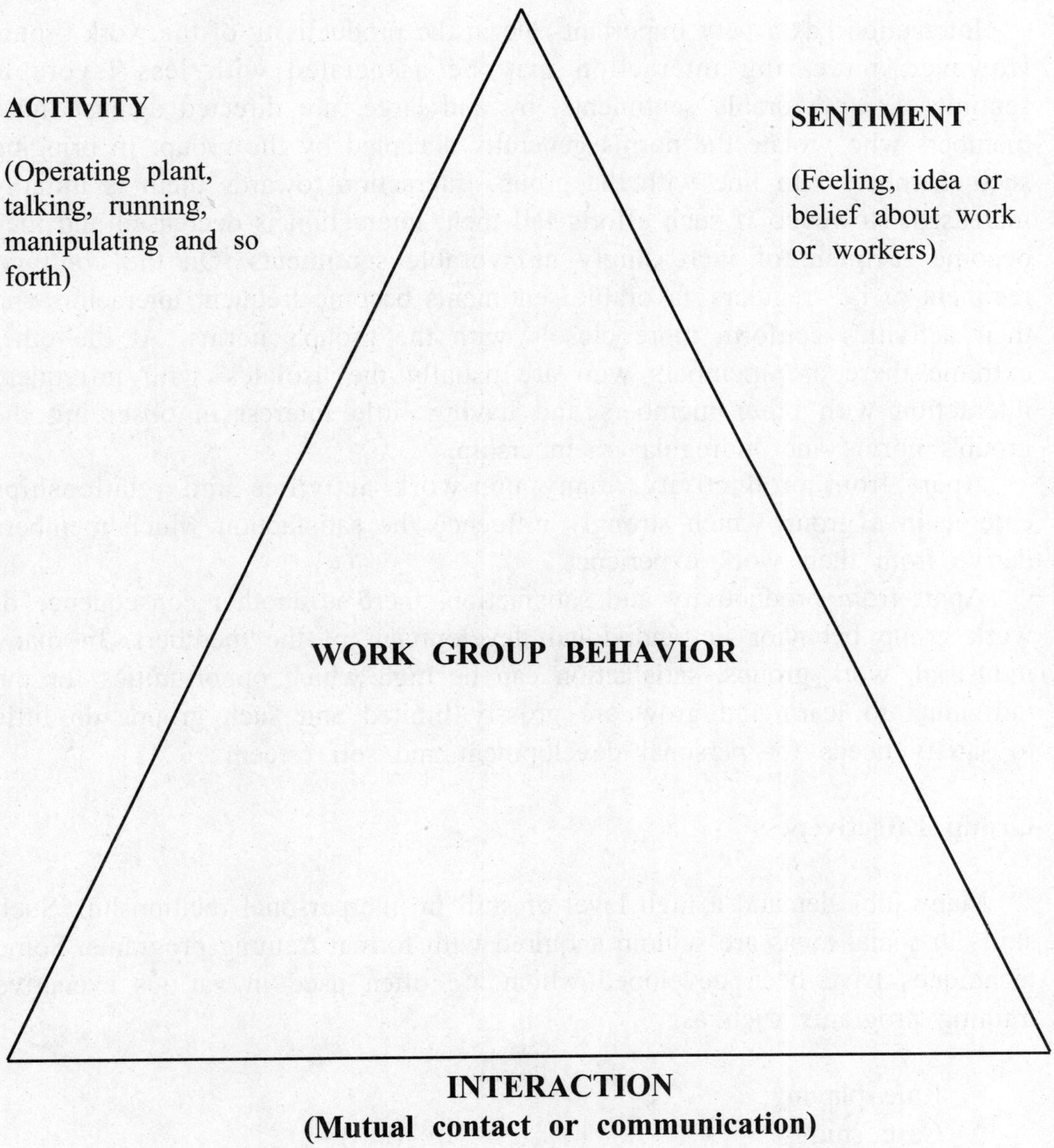

FIG. 11.12: MECHANISM OF GROUP BEHAVIOR

Interaction has a very important role in the productivity of the work group. However, increasing interaction may be associated with less favorable sentiments. Unfavorable sentiments, by and large, are directed against those members who violate the norms generally accepted by the group. In bringing such members into line with the group, interaction towards them is initially increased. However, if such efforts fail then, interaction is decreased and they become recipient of increasingly unfavorable sentiments. On the contrary, recipient of i.e. 'regulars' favorable sentiments become frequent interactors and their activities conform more closely with the group's norms. At the other extreme there are members who are usually the 'isolates' with infrequent interaction with other members and having little interest in observing the group's norms and in regular membership.

Apart from productivity, many non-work activities and relationships emerge in a group which strongly influence the satisfaction which members derive from their work experience.

Apart from productivity and satisfaction, there is another consequence of work group behavior i.e. individual development of the members. In many industrial, work groups, satisfaction can be high which opportunities for the individual to learn and grow are grossly limited and such groups do little to satisfy needs for personal development and self esteem.

Group Effectiveness

Many jobs demand a high level of skill in interpersonal relationship. Such skills in social areas are seldom acquired with formal training programs. Some techniques have been developed which are often used in various executive training programs such as:

* Role playing;
* Case study;
* Management Games;
* Multiple Management;
* Conference Training.

In such executive development program groups are formed with like minded individuals having integrative and structural characteristics and who operate in similar social environments. Such groups possess cohesiveness, morale, norms and ideologies.

Cohesiveness has a major influence on group effectiveness as higher the cohesiveness lesser the variation in resultant productivity among the members. However, the anxiety of group members have a major affect on the cohesiveness of the group. (See Fig. 11.13).

In a broader sense we may say that group effectiveness is determined by group size, member composition and rules, group cohesiveness and norm ideologies. In a narrow sense, the readers should consult the characteristics of the highly effective group discussed earlier.

MOB BEHAVIOR

Mob Psychology

People in large numbers who are unrelated to each other socially, culturally or organizationally and come together by chance for a particular activity is called a mob. Workers on industrial action, a crowd of students on strike throwing stones on public properties, are examples of mob behavior. Mob is temporary, and large without a formal recognized leader, and people in a mob generally follow the action of a particular type of persons. Mobs may be classified into various types such as:

* Welcoming mobs (the mobs who gather for the purpose of welcoming some renowned personality or a national heroic team i.e. Foreign head of the state, the national support champion team etc.)

* Aggressive mobs (crowds whose aims are injuring people, and/or damaging properties etc.)

* Acquisitive mobs (crowds gathered for getting something not readily available in market, etc.)

* Fear driven mobs (crowds escaped in panic which may be created due to fire, accident, flood, etc.)

Characteristics of Mob Behavior

Mob behavior has many characteristics, some important ones are:

* Strong emotions (such as: violent/furious, panicky, hilarious, etc.)

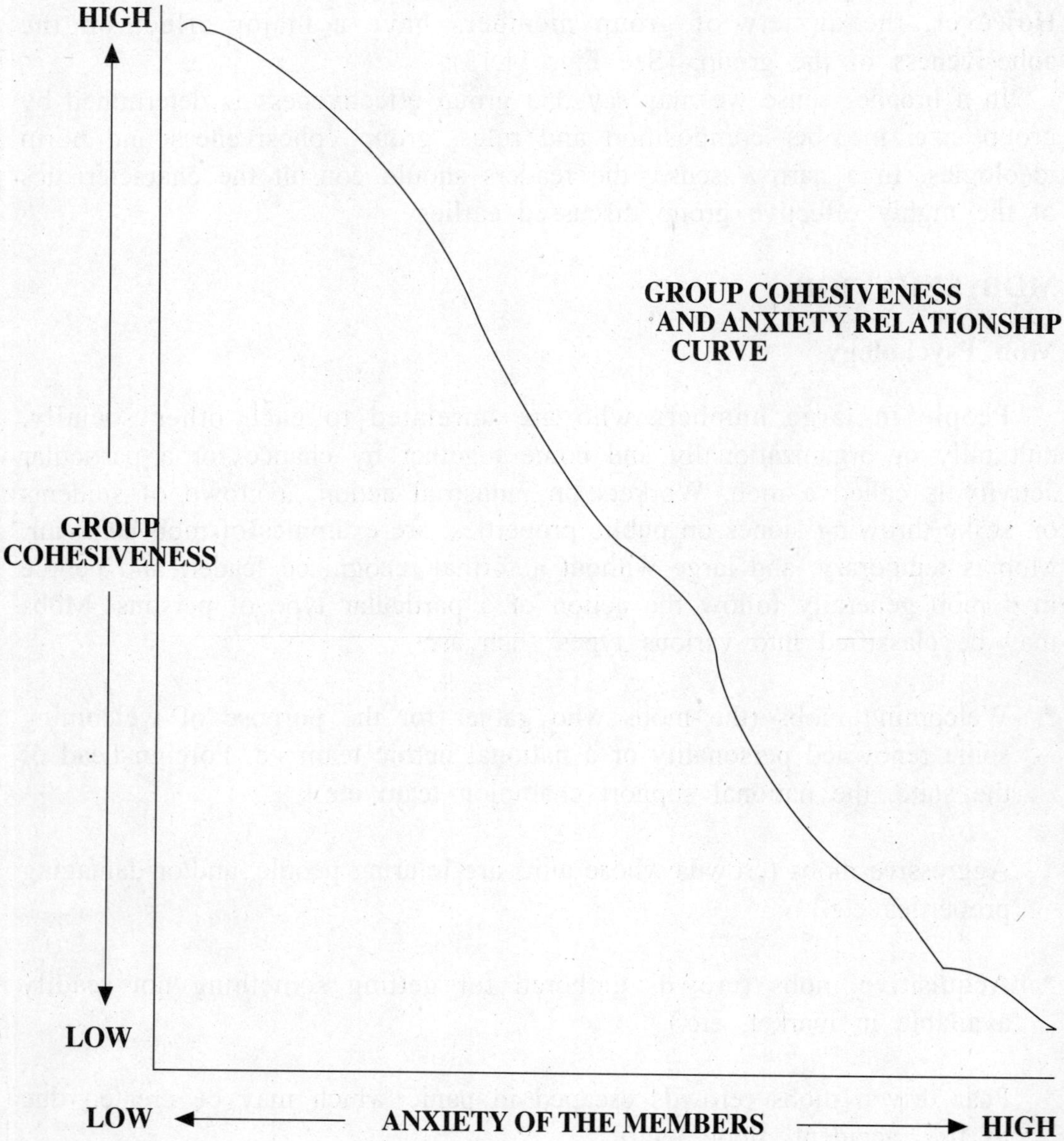

Fig. 11.13: GROUP COHESIVENESS VERSUS ANXIETY

* Irresponsible (by and large, the behavior of a mob is irresponsible and decency/morality is generally isolated by mobs).

* Irrational (the actions of mobs are without much reasons and thinking on what is right and what is wrong)

* No personal inter-relation (members generally unrelated to each other)

* Security in anonymity (individual identity cannot be found out and his behavior remains unknown)

* Possess mental homogeneity (generally common ideas, feeling and actions exist in a mob)

ADMINISTRATIVE BEHAVIOR

Human Relations

Executives, administrators and managers need to develop a high level of human relations skill in them to enable them to 'get along' with people in their respective work environment. Many executives believe that human relation skill is innate and therefore cannot be developed. Such beliefs and skepticism stands in the way of improving human relations skill. It is true that many competent administrator have developed a high level of human relations skill without training and that everyone has some degree of innate human relations skill, but it is equally true that human relations skill can be sharpened through training in human relations and continuously developed through conscious efforts.

By and large, every problem in human relations stems from a difference in perception (two or more people viewing the same situation in different ways). This perception tends to be distorted by the values, which an individual brings to a situation in question, stemming from previous experience, his attitude about himself, his sentiments, his likes and dislikes, his ideals, his objectives and goals, the obligations he feels toward others, and so on. Through training and development in the techniques self-awareness, observation and analysis, communication, and decision making considerable improvement can be achieved in public relations. In decision making as Robert L. Kasty puts it all previous techniques are combined and put into practice, both in the form of human skill alone, and in combination with the other skills that are essential to the administrative process[17]. To achieve success in training deep understanding and conscious effort is required not only on the part of the trainee, but also on the part of the instructor.

Dynamics of Leadership Dilemmas

Effective leadership lies not only in securing the desired behavior among the subordinates but also in creating a sense of satisfaction among them whilst following the instruction of the leader.

Leadership depends upon a proper understanding of the opinions and needs of the subordinates, the context in which it occurs, and good training. Researchers have proved that some of the most effective leaders have been those who were able to release anti-social behavior in others, through more than their fair shares of psychopathic traits. Their secret in doing so is that by setting an example they open a walkway that is normally inhibited thus giving pleasure to their followers, and receiving reinforcement in their leadership.

The leaders are often required to fulfill incompatible roles and show, initiative, yet governed by regulations and constraints. They must be aggressive yet never insubordinate. In caring for their followers, they must be assiduous yet maintain an enormous social distance. They must know everything about everything yet never appear intellectuals. The exercise of power and authority, by and large vested in the leader, poses the dilemmas i.e. conflicts, the dynamics and the different form of which are open to us for their resolution. In this respect Martiam Zaleznik highlighted two main points: (a) that the main source for the dilemmas leaders face can be found within themselves (within their own conflicts) and (b) effective dealing, with naughty decisions and inevitable conflict of interests among the employees, presupposes that the executives, at least successful ones, are able to resolve or manage their inner conflicts and make effective decisions i.e. not constantly making and undoing decisions[46].

Two distinct roles of a leader have been identified through research findings, namely: (a) 'Task specialist' and (b) 'Social specialist'. As a 'task specialist', the prime concern of a leader is to achieve the ostensible goal of the group (i.e. defeating the enemy in a war). For such a role, the principal trait of a leader being more active and being likable is less important. As a 'social specialist', the prime function of a leader is to preserve a good personal relationship within the group and maintain morale intact i.e. reduce discretion, absenteeism, sickness, crime and prevent meeting (in military milieu). In this case the principal trait is being liked and other traits such as task ability and efficiency are secondary and less important.

In industrial milieu, an effective leader is a competent individual who influences his followers in such a manner to achieve not only high productivity but also high morale; better training and development; less accidents on the job sites; and low turnover etc. It is generally believed that, whatever the other causes, organizational incompetency implies a failure in leadership as a leader serves important organizational functions namely, to guide and motivate employees and also to be a recipient of information and responses from the subordinates, that modify behavior and corporate future plans.

The principal prerequisites to effective leadership include: providing clearing organization structure; providing communication channel; providing control system and matching man and job. The principal leadership activities include: developing co-operation, directing and disciplinary subordinates and maintaining a two-way communication. The principal leadership functions include: to guide and motivate subordinates and understand their problems and difficulties. Because of leadership importance of various kinds highlighted above, leadership calls for certain essential qualities, though it is highly difficult to classify these in a standard form. However, Ordway Tead has suggested some vital qualities that a successful leader must possess. These are shown diagramatically in Fig. 11.14.

Training oneself to act and react in modern industrial environment is the basic necessity for leaders to overcome the sense of inertia to which they are susceptible from time to time. The most elementary step, though sounds puritanical, is necessary for achieving a mature orientation and a leader is to assume responsibility for one's own development to enable him to march successfully on the high need towards experiencing leadership and adventure in human development.

CONCLUDING REMARKS

In an organizational milieu people are the most important asset that need to be effectively managed as the core of all activities in business the world is the human activity. In any human activity nothing of any consequence happens until an individual wants to act. The productivity depends to a greater

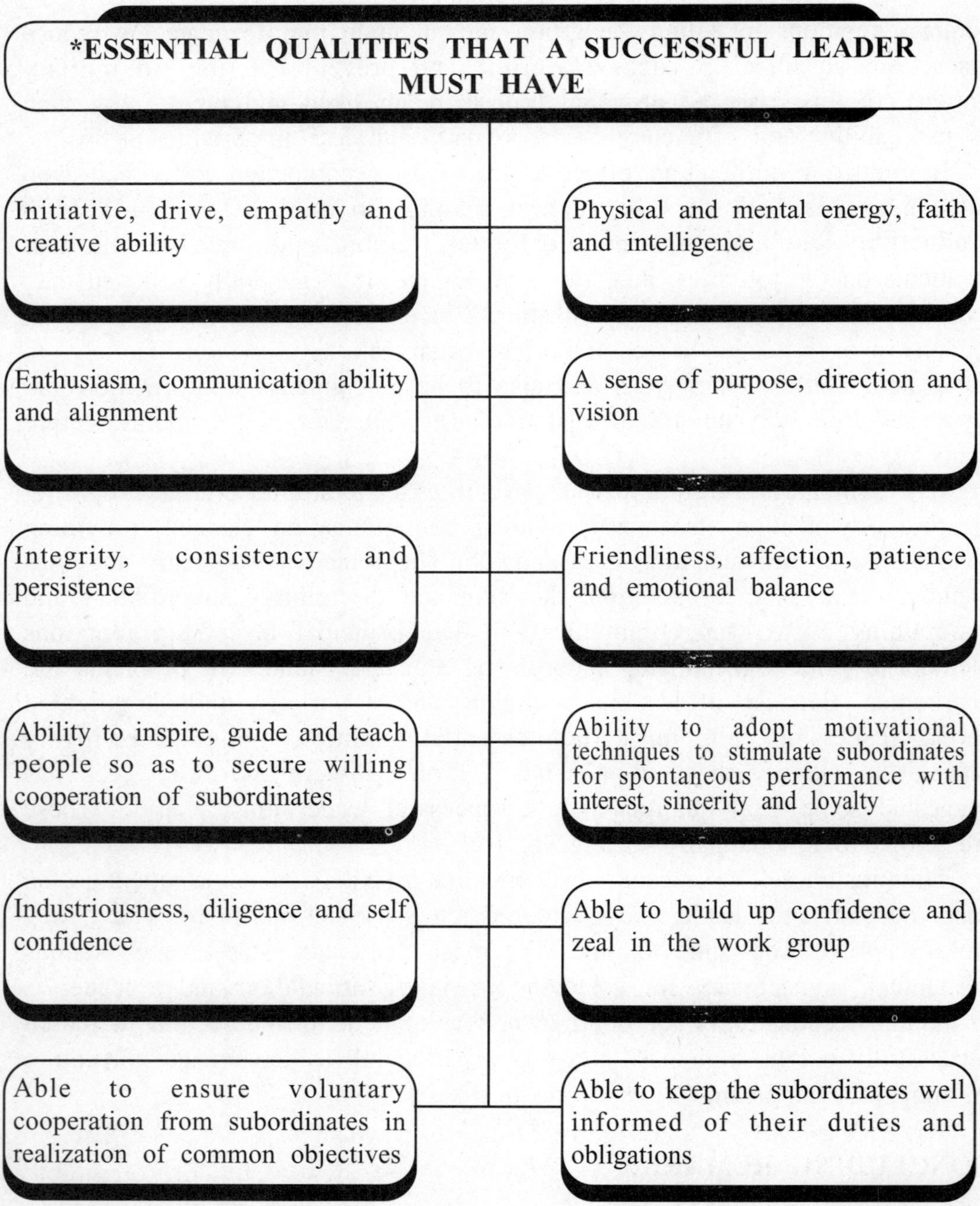

*Adapted from the suggestions made by Ordway Tead in his book "The Art of Leadership"

FIG. 11.14: ESSENTIAL QUALITIES FOR AN EFFECTIVE LEADERSHIP

extent on how much and why one wants to act as an employer can buy man's time and his physical efforts but not his loyalty, initiative or enthusiasm. Major problems that exist in today's organizations are to find ways and means to get maximum efforts and contribution of individuals as the individuals will to work is something different from his capacity to work, individuals needs and desires. However, the conflict between individuals needs and the achievement of organizational objectives do exist which has been a major concern to management. To understand these problems, it is absolutely essential to study the human behavior i.e., the individual under different roles.

Individual personality in the dynamic organization requires continuous adjustment and development as according to the Peter Principle every employee tends to rise to his level of incompetency by progressing through super competent and competent stages. An employee may be as competent as a supervisor and reaches level of incompetence as a manager. Therefore the Peter's Principle demands an individual to develop himself through the process of development to mach the changing needs of the organization.

To conclude this discussion we may say that study and understanding of human behavior is an essential requisite for the manager not only for his self development but for organizing human resources and polymerizing the individuals (in his respective organization) to achieve a cohesive and enormous force for the benefit of mankind.

REFERENCES AND RECOMMENDED READING

1. Andrews, Kenneth, R. - *'Executive Training by the Case Method'*/HBR Sept. 1951, pp. 58.

2. Baer, M., R.A. Eisenstat, and B. Spector - *'Why Change Programs don't produce Change'*/HBR Nov-Dec. 1990, pp. 158.

3. Bradford, D.L. and A.R. Cohen - 'Managing for Excellence'/John Wiley & Sons, 1984.

4. Carlsen, Brown - 'Listening Comprehension test'/World Book, company.

5. Carrol, Bonnie - 'Job satisfaction'/Industrial Gerontology, 4, Winter 1970.

6. Coach, Lester and John R.P. French Jr. - *'Overcoming Resistance to change'*/Human Relation, Vol. 1, No. 4, 1948, pp. 512.

7. Doyal, Ishwar - 'Role Analysis Techniques in job description'/California Management Review, Summer 1969, pp. 47.

8. Flanagan, John C. - *'The Critical Incident Techniques'*/Psychology Balletin, 51: pp. 327, 1954.

9. Flanagan, John C, and Robert K. Burns. - *'The Employee Performance Record: A new Approisal and Development Toll'*/HBR September-October 1955, pp. 95.

10. Gabarro, John J. - *'Socialization at the Top: How CEO's and their Subordinates develop interpersonal contacts'*/Organizational Dynamics, Winter 1979.

11. Gibson, Gerge W. - *'The Filmed case in Management Training'*/HBR May-June 1957, pp. 123.

12. Heimen, F.S., and Eugine Jacobson - *'A model of taste group development in complex organization and a strategy for implementation'*/Academy of Management Review 1, Oct. 1976, pp. 98-111.

13. Hevinson, Harry - *'Management by Whose Objectives'*/HBR July-August 1970, pp. 125.

14. Hunt, John W. and Peter N. Saul - *'The Relationship of Age, Tenure and Job Satisfaction in Males and Females'*/Academy of Management Journal, 20, 1975, pp. 690.

15. Jacobson, Eugene and Stanley E. Seashore - *'Communication Practices in Complex Organization'*/the Journal of social users, vol. VII, No. 3, 1951, pp. 37.

16. Johnson, Wendell, *'The Fateful Process of Mr. A. Talking to Mr. B'*/HBR, Jan. - Feb. 1953, pp. 49.

17. Katz, Robert L. - *'Skills of an Effective Administrator'*/HBR, Jan. - Feb. 1955, pp. 33.

18. Kotter, John P. - 'Power in Management'/AMACOM, 1979.

19. Kouzer, J.M., and B.Z. Poster - 'The Leadership Challenge: How to Get Extraordinary Things Done in Organization'/San Francisco: Josey-Bas, 1980.

20. Lasagna, John B. - *'Make your MBO Pragnatic'*/HBR, Nov-Dec., 1971, pp. 64.

21. Laurence, P.R. - *'How to deal with Resistence to Change'*/HBR, May-June 1954.

22. Learned, Edmand P., David H. Ulrich, and Donald R. Booz - 'Executive Action'/Boston: Division of Research Havard Business school 1952.

23. Levinson, Harry - 'The Exceptional Executive, Cambridge'/Havard University Press, 1968.

24. Mace, Myles L. - 'The Growth and Development of Executives'/Boston: Division of Research, Havand Business School, 1950.

25. Meyer, Herbert H. Ermanual Kay and John R.P. French Jr. - *'Split Roles in Performance Appraisal'*/HBR, Jan-Feb. 1965, pp. 123.

26. Orsburn, J.D. - 'Self-Directed Work Team: The New American Challenge'/Homewood Illinois: Business One Irwin, 1990.

27. Ouchi, W.G. - 'Theory Z: How American Business Can Meet the Japanese Challenge'/ Reading Massachusatts: Addison-Worley Publishing Co., 1981.

28. Roethlisberger, F.J - 'Management and Morale'/Cambridge, Havard University Press, 1950.

29. Roethlasberger, F.J. - *'Training Supervisors in Human Relation'*/HBR, Sept. 1951, pp. 47.

30. Rogers, C.A. - 'A way of Being'/Boston: Houghtons Miffin Co., 1980.

31. Ronken, Harriet O., and Paul R. Lawrance - 'Administering Changes'/Boston: Havard Business School, 1952.

32. Schwab, Donald P., Herbert G. Heneman and Thomas A. DeCotis - *'Behaviorally Anchored Rating Scale: A Review of the Literature'*/Personnel Psychology, 28: 549, 1975.

33. Shartle, Carrol L. - *'Leadership and Executive Performance'*/Personnel, March 1949, pp. 377-378.

34. Sirota, David, and Alam D. Wolfsons - *'Job Enrichment: what are the Obstacles'*/ Personnel, May-June 1972.

35. Sirota, David and Alam D. Wolfson - *'Job Enrichment Surmounting the Obstacles'*/ Personnel, July-August 1972.

36. Styayer, R - *'How I Learned to let my Workers Lead'*/HBR, Nov.-Dec. 1990, pp. 66.

37. Stryker, Perrin - *'The Growing Pains of Executive Development'*/Advanced Management, August, 1954, pp.15.

38. Thompsons, Paul H., and Gene W. Dalton - *'Performance Approisal: Managers beware'*/ HBR Jan-Feb 1970, pp. 149.

39. Todryk, L. - *'The Project Manager as Team Builder: Creating the Effective Team*/Project Management Journal December 1990 pp. 17.

40. Tuckman B.W. - *'Development Sequence in Small Groups'*/Psychological Bulletin, May 1965, PP. 384-399.

41. Vromn, Victor H. and Bernd Pahl - *'Age and Risk Taking Among Managers'*/Journal of Applied Psychology 12, 1971, pp. 22.

42. Welford, A.T. - *'Twenty years of Psychological Research on Age and work*/Journal of Occupational Psychology, 49, 1979, pp. 129.

43. Whyte, William H. Jr. - *'The Fallacies of Personality Testing'*/Fortune, Sept. 1954, pp. 117.

44. Winn, A - *'Training in administration and human relation'*/Personnel, Sept. 1953, pp. 139.

45. Zalezik, A. Forman - 'Training in a Growing Enterprize'/Boston: Havard Business School, 1951.

46. Zalezik, A. Forman - 'The Human Dilemas of Leadership'/Boston: Havard Business School, 1951.

BINDING EFFECT AT THE INTERACTIONS OF HUMAN ELEMENTS

CHAPTER 12

INTRODUCTION

Human organizations are organic in nature with various elements, though independent, but having strong interactions with each other. Furthermore, modern organizations have become more complex, powerful and pervasive institutions which not only influence the individuals, groups or organizations but also national interests. It is, therefore imperative for management to understand the binding effect at the interactions of human elements involved in organizations such as communications, motivation, socialization, human relations and morale etc. and be able to predict the impact of technology and human reaction to work.

We all know that communication among human beings has always been problematic and there is a dire need to create a situation in which each of different parties, in any organization, should be able to understand each others point of view. Other elements of human interactions namely: motivation, socialization, public relation and morale building also play an important role in human resources development and achieving a successful operation of organizations. In this context it is appropriate to quote John W. Vongoethe as saying "treat people as if they were what they ought to be and you help them to become what they are capable of being". The objective of this discussion is to develop an understanding of the binding effects at the interaction of each of the human elements mentioned above.

EFFECTIVE COMMUNICATION IN ORGANIZATIONS

WHAT IS COMMUNICATION?

Communication is the process of transferring meaning between persons (in the form of ideas, information, facts, viewpoints, etc.) placed in different positions to achieve understanding. With the beginning of behavioral approach to management, communication became one of management's chief concerns, as nothing happens in management until communication takes place. Success of a manager depends more on his ability to communicate than any other skill. Communication process involves listening, speaking, writing and non verbal communication. Communication is our greatest power and the most significant characteristic of mankind. Research has shown that we spent (on average) 80 to 90% of our working time in communicating with others, of which around 60% is spent in verbal communication (talking & listening) and the rest in written communication (reading & writing). Despite the most widely recognized importance of communication, it remains a number one problem of management as it is not being handled effectively in organizations.

HOW THE COMMUNICATION PROCESS OPERATES

Let us examine the interpersonal communication model shown in Fig. 12.1. One of the most important decisions the source has to make is to determine the appropriate channel for transmitting a given message. In addition to speed, oral (person-to-person) communication has further advantages in providing opportunity for interaction between source and receiver (feedback). Written communication (may be transmitted by Memos, Letters, Reports, Bulletin Board Notices, Company Manuals and Newsletters etc.) has the advantage of providing a record for future reference.

TYPES OF COMMUNICATION

Communication process involves following types of communication:

* Listening,
* Speaking,
* Non-verbal communication,
* Communicating electronically,
* Writing,
* Formal communication,
* Informal communication.

EFFECTIVE LISTENING

Listening is the finest art and an extremely important skill required for effective management, yet many managers possess some poor listening habits such as the following:

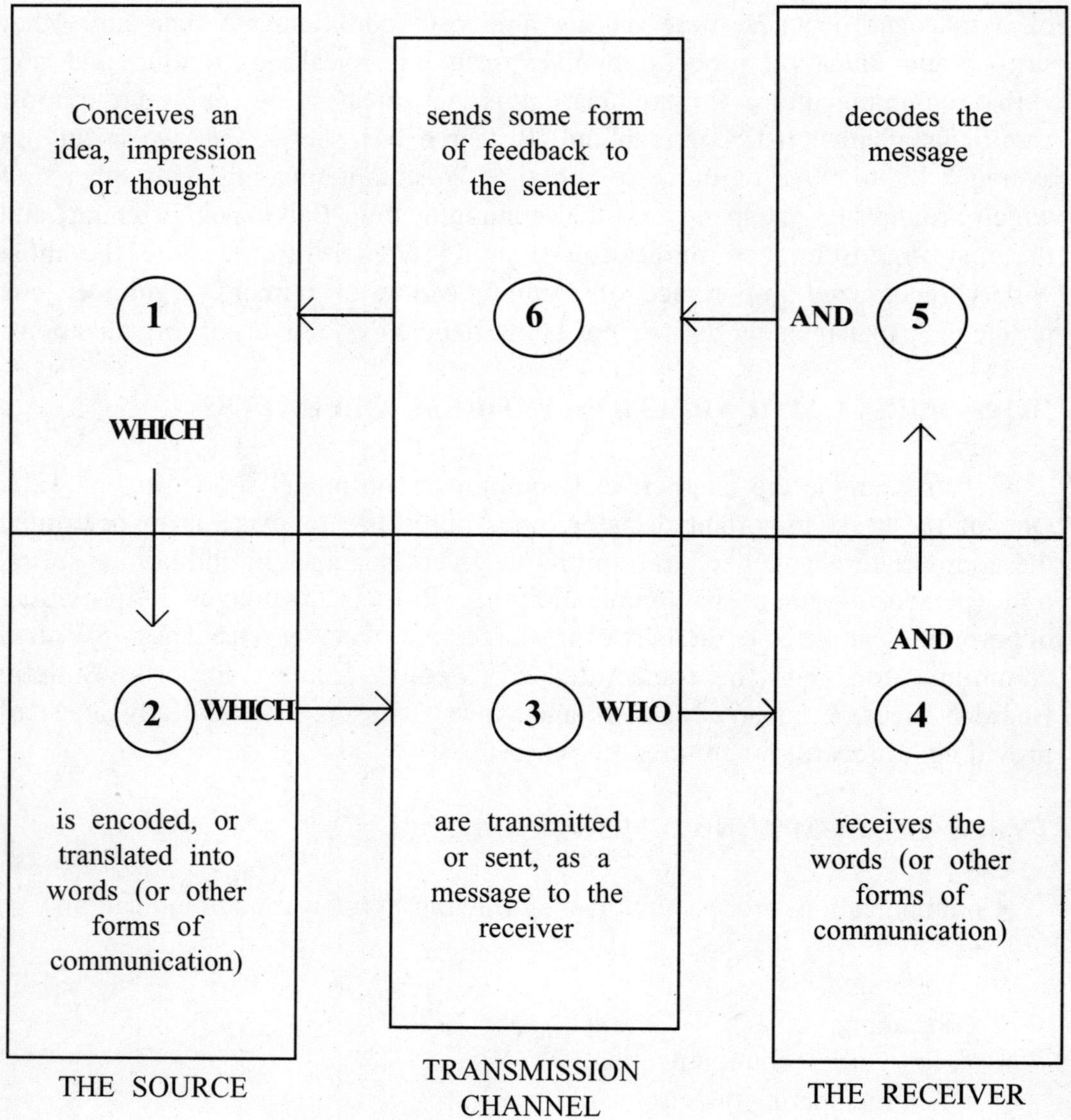

FIG. 12.1: AN EXAMPLE OF A COMMUNICATION PROCESS

* Failing to understand the frame of reference of the speaker.

* Giving the impression of eagerness to end the conversation.

* Listening only at the surface, with no serious consideration to what the other person is saying.

* Showing sign of distress or annoyance over the subject matter.

To be a good manager, one should be a good listener. To be a good listener one must adopt the following habits:

* To concentrate and work at listening.

* To understand and weigh what is being said.

* To listen between the lines.

* To review listening habits from time to time.

Remember if managers don't listen, how can they know what others are thinking and know their needs, ideas, wants and wishes. Furthermore, the span of control of managers should not be too large to impede their listening opportunities.

Note: The attitude of managers towards listening should be positive with willingness to spend some time with employees.

Some Guidelines for Effective Listening

I Look for the main ideas and facts and avoid being distracted by unnecessary details.

II Tune yourself into the speaker by trying to understand other person's view point.

III Encourage others to speak freely by showing your lively curiosity and genuine concern.

IV Listen to the whole message before planning your response and always avoid jumping to conclusions.

V Remember pre-judgement can shut out new messages, therefore, give the other person the benefit of doubt and never enter into conversation with an already made up mind (at least partially) based on past experience.

VI To make certain you are listening, get feed back at intervals.

VII Work at listening as hearing is passive whereas listening is active and takes mental effort and attention requiring our nervous system to do the work.

VIII Since each of us listen differently, therefore monitor your own feelings and point of view with mindfulness of the fact that our emotions and convictions filter (even distort) what we hear.

EFFECTIVE SPEAKING

Effective speaking is another essential skill for effective management. A manager's attitude to what he has to say, to whom he has to say, where he has to say, when he has to say, and how he has to say, makes all the difference.

Research has shown that only 10% of the impact of speech is of words, 50% of speaker's gesture and non-verbal communication and the remaining 40% of the way the words are expressed.

To be a good speaker, A manager/executive should ask himself the following questions:-

* Am I clear in my mind what I want to say?

* Is the topic, tone, volume, pitch, different than the words I use?

* Is my choice of words and expressions clearly presented?

* Am I using too much jargons, or high sounding words?

* Am I too technical in style?

* Am I specific to the point I want to express?

Some Key Points in an Effective Speech

The following points should be remembered in making a speech:

* The speaker should know his subject, collect ideas and sufficient supporting material on the subject matter.

* The speaker should prepare an outline of the topic.

* The speaker should practice out loudly without trying to memorize.

* The speaker should survey his audience before starting the speech.

* The speaker should use a good attention-focusing opening and specify the approximate time he will take.

* The speaker should use humor and eloquence when appropriate.

* The speaker should not deviate from the main theme of the subject matter.

* The speech must not be too long and boring.

* The speaker should close with recap of the salient points or a brief summary of the speech.

ROLE OF NON-VERBAL COMMUNICATION

Non-verbal communication is the term used for transmitting meaning without the use of words but other means such as: through tone of voice, body movements, facial expressions, postures, clothes, and loudly or subtly transmitted messages etc. Even how we sit, stand, walk, smile conveys messages to others. In fact, nonverbal messages cannot be as readily disguised or controlled as verbal ones because eyes and (for most people) even their faces don't lie. It is not the words but expressions that leads us to perceive different types of people such as: confident type; nervous type; grumpy type; forgetful type; or indifferent type.

Research has shown that as much as 55% of the content of a message is transmitted by body posture, and facial expression, 38% is derived from tone of voice; and only 7% of the meaning is derived from the words themselves.

Therefore, managers should be conscious that non-verbal communication plays an important role in the communication, particularly so in interaction with people from other cultures.

The principal forms of non verbal communication include:

* Sign language (traffic signals and road signals, military salute, a nod of head etc.)

* Object language (graphs, charts, clothes, furniture, art, etc.)

* Action language (rising and walking towards exit indicates readiness to terminate a conversation, walking quickly indicates someone in a hurry, etc.)

COMMUNICATING ELECTRONICALLY

With the emergence of advanced computer techniques with space-age telecommunication technologies, it has become possible to communicate electronically by using various information processing techniques such as the following:

* Computer Networking: (access to common data base and usage of shared programs and exchange information).

* Personal Computer: (many applications assist communication).

* Electronic Mail: (transmission of information to other users by means of a computer and appropriate software).

* Tele-computing: (telefax, and extensive use of computers through telephone line).

* Teleconferencing: (audio conferencing & video conferencing).

Note: The above techniques if properly used can facilitate to make more rapid managerial decisions and contribute a great deal in the organizational effectiveness and efficiency.

ROLE OF FORMAL COMMUNICATION

Formal communication channels are the prescribed means by which messages flow inside an organization. These include: upward communication, downward communication, horizontal/lateral communication (with peers), horizontal/lateral communication (with other departments). See Fig. 12.2.

ROLE OF INFORMAL COMMUNICATION

Informal communication is the communication which flows through channels other than formal channels. It serves a variety of purposes such as:

* Countering the effects of monotony or boredom.

* Some job-related information not available through formal channels may be provided through this source.

* Attempting to influence the behavior of others.

* Satisfying personal needs i.e. friendship etc.

The best known type of informal communication is Grapevine, (transmission of information by word of mouth without regard for organizational level i.e. outside official network), which like its namesake, is tangled, twisted and hard to follow, but functions selectively, rapidly, and effectively. A manager cannot eliminate grape-vine even if he tries, but instead he may use this to his advantage in following three ways:

I In scotch false rumors (present correct facts and information well in time on matters which bother people most).

II In predicting employee's behavior. It provides the manager with a tool to

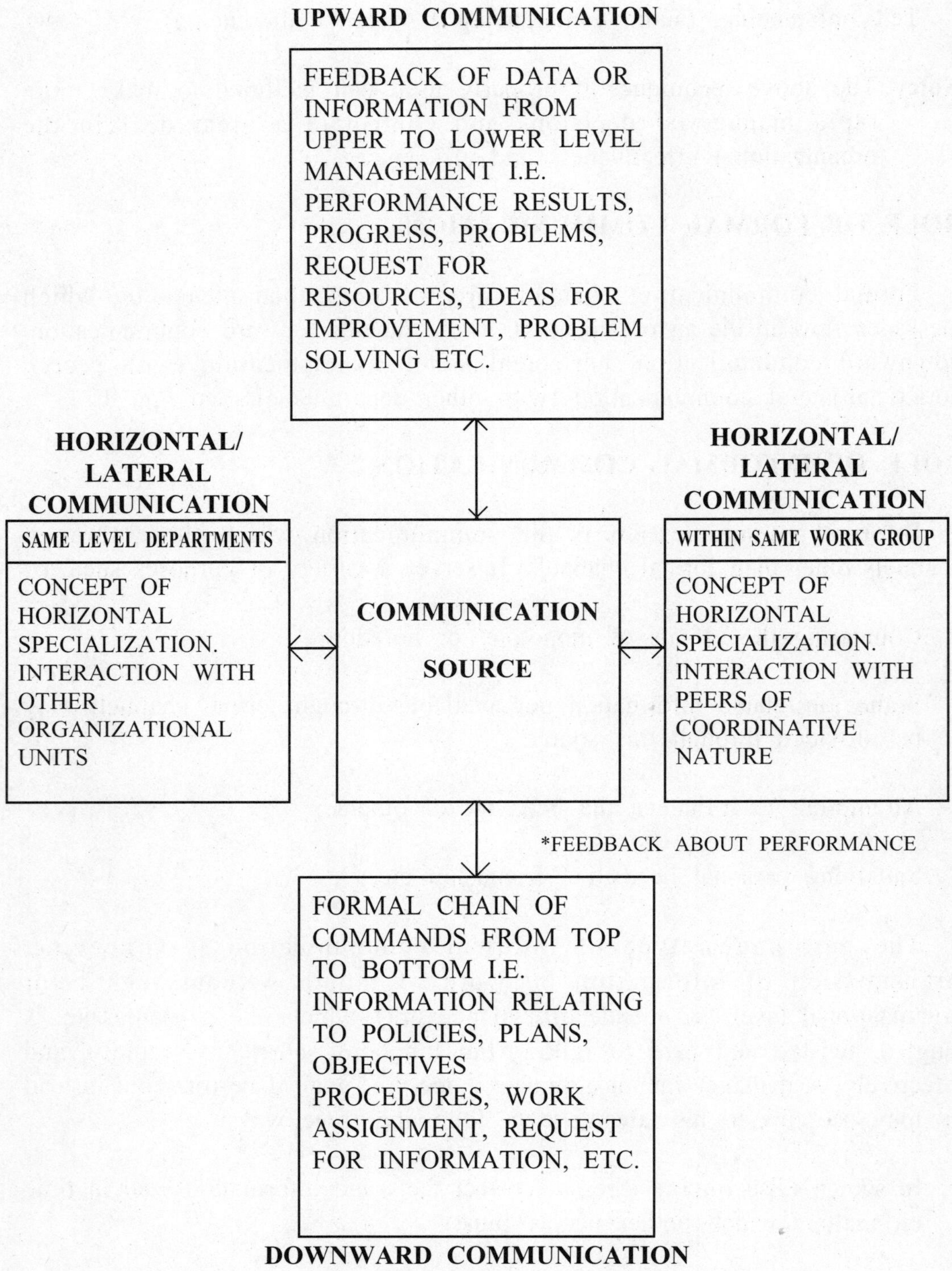

FIG. 12.2: ROLE OF FORMAL COMMUNICATION

know what employees believe, and to assist him in predicting their behavior.

III In spreading information informally (Grape-vine acts as a good and speedy carrier).

EFFECTIVE WRITING

Writing well is an art which does not come easily. It requires extensive study, experience and observation. The tense and tone of a written communication can change the communicated message drastically, even when essentially the same words are used. Often trouble with writing is poor diction. Therefore a careful choice of words should be made when communicating in writing.

Whenever we begin to write we should keep in the forefront of our minds Carl Goeller's (a specialist in business writing in New York) one essential 'Do' and one essential 'Don't'.

'Do' "write to communicate. Your first and foremost mission is to tell somebody something".

'Don't' "try to impress with your writing. The harder you try, the more transparent you are, and more difficult your writing is to read".

Remember! "A good business write-up is clear, crisp, businesslike as it makes its point and says good-bye" as some one has quite rightly said.

SOME GUIDELINES FOR EFFECTIVE WRITING

The following guidelines will prove extremely helpful if carefully observed:

1. Write simply by using simple sentences. Whenever possible keep sentences short.

2. Write in clear and concise sentences.

3. Avoid over-use of adjectives and adverbs and do not use flowery language.

4. Be sure that you know what your correspondent is asking before you begin to answer him.

5. Limit letters and memos to a simple topic and avoid writing long letters. Lengthy back-up should become an attachment rather than be included in the body of the letter.

6. Do not say more than is necessary.

7. Read correspondence out loud to yourself. Your ear will hear what your eyes don't see.

8. Explain technical terms in simple words.

9. Be courteous and tactful as well as honest and diligent.

10. If two words convey your meaning equally well, use the common one rather than the less common.

11. Double check for all reference numbers and spellings in the text.

Some Useful Suggestions for Effective Writing

I. Avoid Unnecessary Jargon

Jargon can be good or bad. In its good sense, it refers to the specialized technical language of a profession (Medicine, Law, Engineering). Jargons are unclear, either because the audience is unfamiliar with them or because new meanings are attached to them by the writer, and should be avoided as far as possible. If the use of professional jargon is unavoidable, then the meanings should be explained in bracket against each term.

II. Replace Cloudy Long Words with More Precise Short Words

Some writers often use cloudy long words (to cloud their meanings) to impress the reader, rather than to inform him. Since big words tend to mislead, therefore as far as possible, these should be replaced with small substitutes.

III. Prune The Deadwood

Some writers use a class of words known as deadwood which add nothing to the meaning of a passage (being empty and lifeless) but only make longer sentences longer and detract from the meaning of other words. Such words should be pruned. For example in 'round in shape', 'two miles in distance', 'red in color' have, 'in shape', 'in distance', 'in color' as dead branches of a tree.

Writing Letters & Memos

There is no hard and fast rule for writing effective business letter, but it is a general belief among the writing experts that shortness, simplicity, strength and sincerity are the essentials of a good business letter. According to Carl Goeller the first principle of effective letter-writing is "I am writing to communicate — not impress".

In examining the final draft, the writer should ask the following questions to himself:

* Does the letter (regardless of its contents) sound courteous?
* Does the letter reflect the kind of organization image it should?
* Has the letter accomplished what it intended to accomplish?
* Will the letter help to improve the writer's image.
* Does the language of the letter appear dignified (not arrogant) and forthright not (blunt).
* Does the letter appear neat, accurate and consistent with the official style.

Writing Reports

Management styles, philosophies of business, and personal idiosyncrasies dictate the type and style of report writing.

The first step towards more effective report writing is to establish the purpose and understanding of the basic types of reports such as the following:

* **Periodic Reports:** (basically informatory types reporting status of organization on regular intervals i.e. product report, tax report).

* **Examination Reports:** (containing data/information obtained from first hand knowledge of the subject such as financial status, evaluation reports etc.).

* **Progress Reports:** (providing information on progress status of some project or activity).

* **Technical Reports:** (engineering, scientific or research and development reporting about 'how of process or product, etc.).

* **Recommendation Reports:** (reports used as a basis for decision and actions).

* **Research Reports:** (scientific or engineering reports about systems, processes or products based on findings of research activities).

Five Stepped Approach to an Effective Report

Step I: **Preparation:** (After brainstorming a rough outline of the report should be prepared. Preparation is a first step to an effective report).

Step II: **Research:** (Relevant data needs to be collated. Remember effective research cannot be done unless adequate preparation is already made).

Step III: **Organization:** (Material should be organized to build the type and style of the report. Remember organization of material cannot be done adequately unless the research is completed).

Step IV: **Writing:** (Follow the guidelines for effective writing. Remember effective organization cannot adequately be produced without solid organization.

Step V: Revision: (For revising successfully a good and detailed attempt at the writing at the first draft is a must).

Some Guidelines for Report Writing

I Write in simple, concise, short sentences, short paragraph and the way you talk.

II Don't be afraid of using the first person, particularly if your report depends upon your personal observation.

III Avoid abstraction whenever possible.

IV Use contraction (a report need not be stuffily in tone or manner).

V Quote in the report what you have read.

VI Quote in the report what people have told you.

VII Anticipate questions and cover the answers in the report.

VIII During final revision, make your writing as easy to read as possible (put yourself in the reader's place), as simple as possible, and as direct as possible.

IX Plan a beginning, middle, and end.

X Your approach should be from the familiar to the new or from the rule to the exception.

XI Be brief, to the point, but not too brief as the report should include sufficient detail, illustrations and all necessary information/data and explanations. The detail should be prudently selected and should be clear and convincing.

XII Avoid catalogues of facts that don't make a point and be absolutely sure about reasoning for every fact included in the report.

XIII Be specific, use illustrations, case studies and examples as appropriate.

XIV Underline or highlight for emphasis (specific point, fact or idea, requiring special attention, should be underlined or highlighted to indicate to the reader what is important).

XV Use familiar combinations of words. Once a speech writer for President Frankline D. Roosevelt wrote "we are endearing to construct a more inclusive society." President Roosevelt changed it (quite rightly), "we are going to make a country in which no one is left out".

XVI Make your report look its best.

Effective Press Releases

The press release should (with rare exceptions) follow the universal formula of a new story, giving the 'who', 'what', 'where', 'why (or 'how') as directly and succinctly as possible.

The standard release is organized in pyramid fashion. All important facts are placed in the beginning with background detail following in order of importance to facilitate the editor to cut some text (usually for space reasons) from last paragraph upward without eliminating the important facts.

The media (trade press, newspapers, magazines, radio, and television etc.) receives many more releases than they can possibly publish. Therefore, press releases should be written with dominating interest of media rather than organization.

SOME GUIDELINES FOR GOOD COMMUNICATION

The manager should create a climate of trust and confidence by considering the following guidelines:

I The executive should clarify his idea before communication. He should plan ahead and begin to think before talking.

II The executive should examine the purpose of each communication. What needs to be accomplished from communication must be known to him and understood by him before hand).

III The executive should create an atmosphere of openness and confidence. The executive should expose himself to people and encourage cordial and informal relations and appreciation of jobs well done. He should try to understand the problems of his subordinates and be sympathetic and responsive towards them.

IV The executive should be mindful while communicating and not make promises that cannot be fulfilled. Refusal to discuss is not the correct approach.

V The executive should convey something of value to the receiver.

Note: Remember good communication is a flux which binds the people together, and is the life blood of an organization.

SOME BARRIERS TO EFFECTIVE COMMUNICATION

Effective communication is a flash of lightening (illuminating) as it enables us to make ourselves seen and known and see others. Fig. 12.3 shows a system for effective communication. The role of effective communication in the management process is vital as good managers are, generally speaking, good communicators and poor managers are usually the opposite. Due to poor communication, managers often fail to achieve their intended objectives. There are many barriers to effective communication, including organizational barriers and interpersonal barriers. Most important ones are as follows:

Organizational Barriers

1. **Organizational Levels:** (Each level in the communication chain can modify, add to, take from or completely change the intent of a given message i.e. it takes longer to reach its destination and also tends to be distorted along the way).

2. **Managerial Authority:** (Some superiors may not fully admit conditions, problems or results that may make them look weak. On the other hand many subordinates who withhold unfavorable information, are distort to look more favorable on matters such as: job problems, disagreement with the managerial policies, sub-standard work, frustrations etc.).

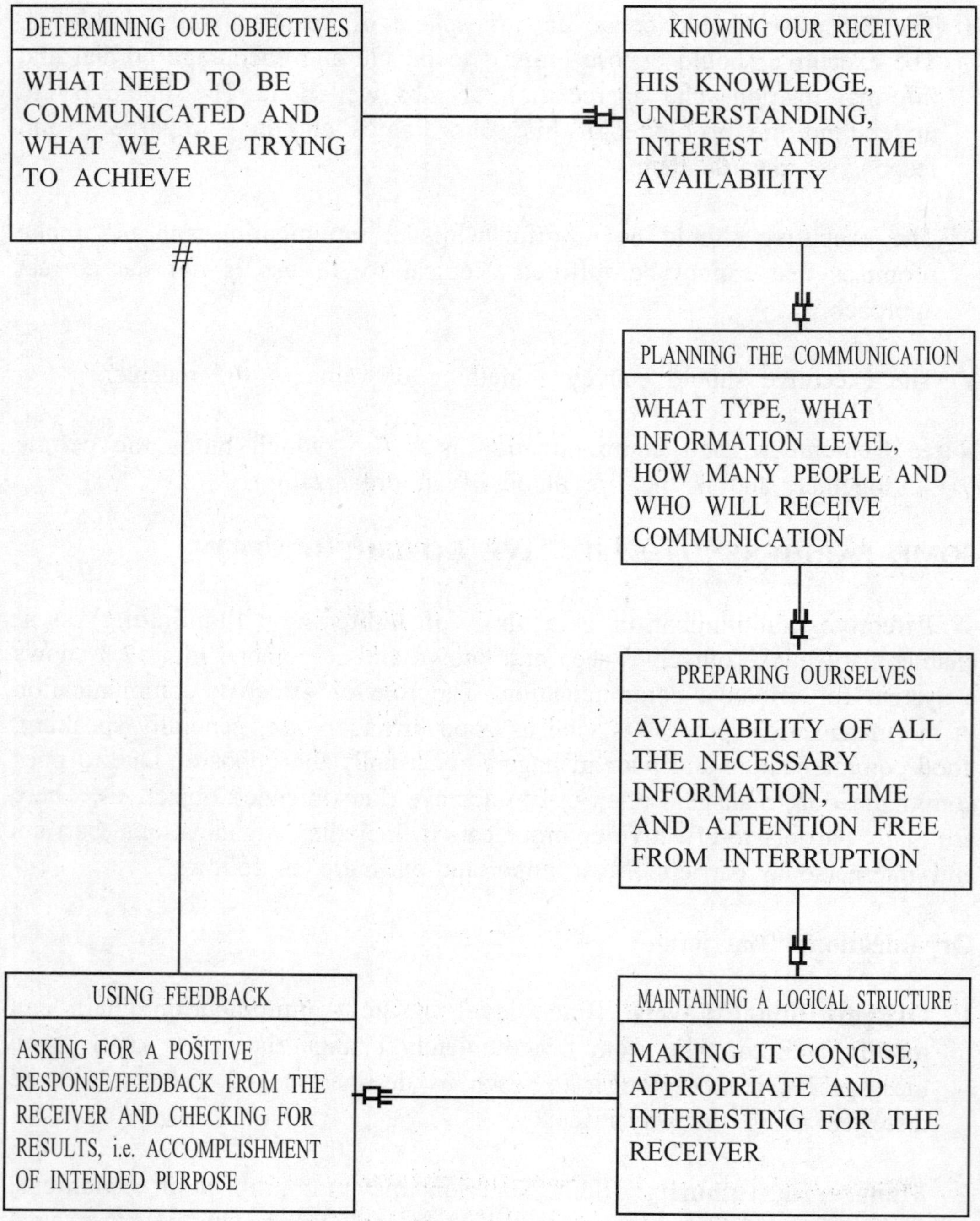

FIG. 12.3: A SYSTEM FOR EFFECTIVE COMMUNICATION

3. **Specialization:** (The jargons or technical vocabulary used by specialists causes communication problems).

4. **Information Overload:** (As a result of information overload, the recipient gets confused and uncertain and this, contrary to some manager's assumption, i.e. "make communication is better communication" can lead to inaction).

Inter-Personal Barriers

1. **Inattention (Poor Listening):** (Attention guided by self interest and also the manager's attitude towards listening is influenced by availability of managerial time. Managers must learn to listen effectively as inattention leads to break in communication and resultant inefficiency).

2. **Status of the Communicator:** (Since when subordinates perceive the manager as having a high credibility they are more likely to accept their messages, therefore the lack of trust in the manager is greatly handicapped against effective communication).

3. **Closed Mindedness:** (Some managers' attitude that they know everything makes them dogmatic and rigid and in the case of closed mindedness of such managers, the communication often breaks and subordinates lose the initiative to put forward some new ideas or discuss some personal issues).

4. **Resistance to Change:** (Human beings generally tend to maintain status-quo. Therefore the resistance to change is an important obstacle to effective communication).

5. **Highlighted Emotions:** (These have a great influence on effective communication, the matured manager remains cool when the atmosphere is charged with high emotion).

6. **Vague Viewpoints, Feelings or Assumptions:** (We may be sending unclear messages, being not fully aware of our own assumptions, viewpoints or feelings. Likewise we may not be aware of the assumptions, viewpoints of feelings of the others with whom we seek to communicate, thus both sides may misinterpret each others messages).

7. **Failure to Evaluate the Effectiveness of our Communication:**

8. **Failure to Give Recognition to the Ideas of Others:**

9. **Talking Too Much and Listening Too Little:**

10. **Failure to Differentiate Between Inference and Fact:**

11. **Communication at Higher Than Desired Level:** (We may be speaking or writing above the comprehension of the people with whom we are communicating).

12. **Failure to Realize and Recognize the Importance of the Communication Process and Effective Communication:**

13. **Adopting Attitude that can Hinder Communication:** (For example the disease of know-it-allness i.e. which leads to arrogance and freeze up/stop the observation process is a serious impediment to communication).

SOME ESSENTIALS OF EFFECTIVE COMMUNICATION

1. To get better acquainted with yourself take 15 to 20 minutes in quiet each day to study yourself, your purpose, your relationship to your fellowmen and the organization as a whole.

2. What is said on the job, is the most important part of communication in business and industry. Intelligence, honesty, living with what is said, acting with cooperation as well as talking about it, are other essentials in developing good communication within an organisation.

3. When listening, look for what the speaker intends, not just what he says.

4. When talking, think in terms of the total impression you create, and not just the words used and also consider every indication of the listeners.

5. Overcome your feeling, tendency to evaluate pass judgment, to agree or disagree with statements before finding out what they meant.

6. Where difficulties have arisen, try to keep the talk centered on the problem, rather than on personalities.

7. Ask more questions, to see whether your listeners have understood what you intended.

8. Do not abruptly disapprove someone's statement, and do not directly contradict. Disapprove indirectly, preserving the other individual's ego in the process.

9. Recognize that during discussions, disagreement is normal and inevitable. Accept it, prepare for it, use it to the best of your advantage obtaining greater awareness of the various aspects of the problem at hand.

10. Control your own natural ego and the desire to get the upper hand and to show up weaknesses in other fellow's point of view. Do reveal the weaknesses when they are important, but do it, in a way that levels the other fellow's ego intact and take every honest opportunity to make the other person feel better or more important.

11. The tone of voice is more important than what we think. Consider what impressions you are conveying with your voice.

12. When talking, pause more often, to think about what you are about to-say.

13. Be direct, as if your listeners were very important.

14. Body movements give clues to feelings and meanings. Consider what is being communicated by your action.

ROLE OF MOTIVATION IN ORGANIZATIONS

WHAT IS MOTIVATION?

Motivation is a key determinant of an individual's behavior. It is the action that impels or urges him to assume an attitude generally favorable towards his work, which in turn will lead him to perform satisfactorily. Motivation concerns the study, of impulses, desires, urges, preferences, aspiration, etc. of people at work, and if satisfied will tend to promote and maintain high morale and consequently improve productivity. In this context it is appropriate to quote Douglas McGregor as saying "Many managers would agree that the effectiveness of their organizations would be at least doubled if they could discover how to tap the unrealized potential present in their human resources"[24].

Motivation is, therefore, a productivity factor which concerns itself with the will to work by creating a need and desire on the part of a worker to improve his present performance. In other words motivation means instigating and inspiring workers with a zeal to do work (more efficiently and effectively) for the accomplishment of objectives of the organization. Accordingly, the management must pay more attention towards motivation of employees and should carefully apply behavioral science techniques to motivate and influence the workers so that they will strive willingly, to a large extent, towards achieving organizational objective. The importance of motivation in management functions is emphasized by Koontz, O'Donnel, and Wuchrich in the following words:

"Because managing involves the creation and maintenance of an environment for the performance of individuals working in groups toward the accomplishment of a common objective, it is obvious that a manager cannot do this job without knowing what motivates people. The necessity of building motivating factors into organizational roles, the staffing of these roles, and the entire process of directing and leading people must be built on a knowledge of motivation"[18].

MOTIVATION DEFINED

Motivation has been defined in numerous ways since, the first systematic studies of human motivation occurred in the year 1800, during the industrial revolution when competition necessitated the need to develop more efficient methods of producing high quality of products more efficiently and cost effectively. Some of these definitions more commonly understood are as follows.

Megginson, Mosely & Pietri have defined motivation as: "The process of inducing a person or a group of people, each with distinctive needs and personality, to achieve the organization's objectives, while also working to achieve his or her own objectives"[25].

Motivation may be defined as "an action that stimulates an individual to take a course of action which will result in the attainment of same goals and at the same time the satisfaction of certain material or needs of the individual himself".

Motivation has also been defined as "the complex of forces inspiring or motivating a person at work in an organization to intensify his desire and willingness to use his potentialities for the achievement of oganizational objectives".

In a more general term, we may define motivation as "the process or the reaction which takes place in the memory of the individuals and may be viewed as a combination of motives maintaining human activity". Harry Levinson have captured the essence of employee motivation in his observation as follows:

"The highest point of self-motivation arises when there is a complementary conjunction of the individual's needs and the organization's requirements. The requirements of both mesh, interrelate, and become synergistic. The energies of the individual and the organization are pooled for mutual advantage"[18].

According to Dalton E. McFarland: "the concept of motivation is mainly psychological. It relates to those forces operating within the individual employee or subordinate which impels him to act or not act in certain ways".

Michael J. Jucius opines: "Motivation is the act of stimulating someone or oneself to get a desired course of action and to push the right button to get the desired action".

CHARACTERISTICS OF MOTIVATION

some important characteristics of motivation are:

* Motivation is created from aims, goals or objectives.
* A person as a whole is motivated and not just a part of him.
* Motivation is a psychological concept (inherent in every person).
* Motivation is different from mental strength as motivation is the strength that instigates an individual to perform an act whilst mental strength is the desire to perform an act oneself which is strengthened by motivation.

* Motivation is that strength which leads to perform or not to perform an act and also to instigate to perform work in the same specific direction.

* Motivation is an unending process as man's needs are unending and needs instigate to motivation.

KINDS OF MOTIVATION

There are two basic kinds of motivation, namely: (a) positive motivation and (b) negative motivation.

Positive motivation means instigating workers by injecting incentives and inducements which may be financial or non financial. Negative motivation is based on punitive action such as punishment or fines if workers are not encouraged for work.

An effective manager should use both these kinds of motivation according to the situation. At times good performance should be rewarded and bad performance should be punished.

VARIOUS STUDIES ON MOTIVATION

A number of competing conceptions have been studied since the industrial revolution by the behavioral scientists including Frederic Winslow Taylor (1856-1915) the pioneer of the scientific management movement who has noted in his book "Principles of Scientific Management" that all employees are fundamentally the same and all workers are uniformly motivated by a desire for money and other motives.

The other relatively new studies by leading behavioral scientists include: Kurt Goldstein (1939), Erich Formem (1941), Donald Syngg and Arthur Combs (1949), Karen Horney (1950), David Reisman (1950), Carl Rogers (1951), Rollo May (1953), Abramam Maslow (1953), Gordon Allport (1955), Frederick Herzbug (1957), McGregor (1960), Black and Mouton (1964), Myers (1964), Rensis Likert (1967), Bennis 91967), Fieller (1967), Litwin and Stringer (1968), Livingstone (1969), Reddin (1970), Hersey and Blachard (1972), Hunt and Larson (1974) and Brown (1976).

There is no universal study or system that can explain the factors that influence motives which control man's behavior at any particular point of time. By and large, different motives operate, at different times amongst different individuals thereby influencing their behavior. This explains why the concept of motivation has been numerously identified as an unquestionable fact of human experience (or an indisputable fact of behavior) and a merely explanatory fiction. However, the common and unifying element in the above noted diverse, conception, as pointed out by Bolles in his theory of motivation, is that motivation is a hypothetical cause of behavior.

CLASSIFICATION OF THE STUDIES ON MOTIVATION

Various important studies on motivation can be classified as follows:

- Likert, Black Mouton, McGregor, Livingston

The studies under this grouping suggested various tasks of supportive management, participative systems of organizations and positive expectations to motivation i.e. a positive approach on the part of management and the need for a new concept of man, a new concept of power and a new concept of organization.

- McClland, Masol, Herzberg

The studies under this grouping found that too little motivation leads to sluggishness and too much motivation leads to disruption and defence against anxiety. These studies established that factors which motivate people vary with the level of employees, their competence, individual personality and work environment. Herzberg's study further suggested a two factor theory which separates those factors which reduce dissatisfaction in the work situation i.e. hygiene or maintenance from those which seem to provide high satisfaction in the work i.e. motivators.

- Allport and Murray

The studies under this grouping found that the human subject, being essentially rational, will perform better on a task if his (or her) ego is involved in it. It was further observed that the desire to maintain or establish a positive self evaluation (or self esteem) operates as a powerful motivating force due to the fact that the self esteem in the eyes of others makes people concerned about symbols of social standing such as prestige, recognition, status, etc.

- Vroom, Atianson

The studies under this grouping attempted to identify the various interacting variables and their relationship in the process of motivation. The studies suggested that an individual's motivation towards an action at any time would be determined by his anticipated values of all the outcomes of various actions multiplied by the strength of that individual's expectancy that the resultant outcome would yield the desired goal.

- Prescott Leacky

The study proclaimed that motives, such as exploration and curiosity whilst helping us in understanding comfort, affection, love, etc. act as an important and powerful source of human motivation.

- March & Simon

This study suggested that through the intermediate effect of rewards, the performance increases satisfaction. However, since a worker may not perceive that productivity will satisfy his needs, performance may result from a state of dissatisfaction. According to this study, motivation is a function of perceived consequences of evoked alternatives and individual goals, in terms of which alternatives are evaluated.

SOME POPULAR THEORIES & MODELS OF MOTIVATION

To understand the 'why' of human behavior it is important to examine various theories of motivation. The prevailing theories of motivation can be loosely classified into McGregor's theory "X" and theory "Y" (the thoughts of management philosophy) and two broad categories, namely: Content (or need) theories and Process theories - as suggested by Karen R. Hardic.

However, there are other useful motivation models which also have applicability.

Content theories are concerned with what causes people to act. These involve identification of needs, incentives, and perceptions. The most popular theories under this category include: (i) Maslow's Hierarchy of needs theory, (ii) McClland's need-for-achievement theory, and (iii) Herzberg's motivation-maintenance theory.

Process theories are concerned with the process by which human behavior is energized, directed and related to performance and satisfaction. The currently accepted theories under this category include: (i) *Expectancy theory* and (ii) *Reinforced theory.*

Other useful motivation models include (i) *March & Simon model approach* (ii) *Traditional social action model* (iii) *Effort reward approach* (iv) *New strategies for motivating employees* (e.g. Job satisfaction, Job enrichment, team building, promotional policies etc.).

MCGREGOR'S THEORY "X" & THEORY "Y" (thoughts of management philosophy)

In order to provide direction to the proper modification of management style and organizational environment, an understand of Douglas M. McGregor's Theory "X" and Theory "Y" has been proved a helpful guide. Douglas M. McGregor has divided the thoughts of management philosophy into two parts namely: (i) Traditional (or "X") theory and (ii) Modern (or "Y") theory.

(i) Theory "X": This theory is based on a traditional view which holds that management does not trust the labor and use restraining policies so that labor will be unable to act against the authority of the management, and that work could be extracted from the labor through strict discipline, fear, rebukes and without the co-operation of the labor in the management affairs. McGregor has identified that in this traditional approach to management i.e. Theory "X", management withholds creativity and actually reduces effectiveness resulting from human nature to resist this type of control, instead of increasing motivation and productivity. Theory "X" is based on certain assumptions such as the following:

* A worker is inherently lazy (or disinclined to work) and will take advantage of the management by doing little work unless he is closely supervised i.e. he always shirks from work.

* To get work from an employee he is to be rebuked and frightened so that through fear he becomes ready to do the work.

* Employees care more for their job security, hence work slowly.

* Employees are less ambitious, therefore, do not try to do (or improve) work through interest but wait for directions and instructions.

* Employees try to shirk from responsibility and put off the work till the work is not urgent.

* Employees act on the basis of greed (financial) and if they are paid more, they will take more interest in the work.

* Management acts right or wrong, labor cannot say anything and thus mentally it is dependent on the management and is not given any opportunity to show work ability or to develop it.

This theory presents a pessimistic view with the above assumptions as labor is thought to be a part of the machine and is not given a chance to use its own intellect. The management does the thinking, the employees obey the orders because labor apart from financial greed also care for human values. Therefore, McGregor himself has said that this approach does not represent the modern views on motivation and do not portray the correct nature of human beings.

(ii) Theory "Y": According to McGregor the application of theory "X" insults the employee's intelligence much more than managers are willing to accept. McGregor proposes that the management creates a freer environment that enables employees to utilize their intrinsic abilities to their full potential and postulates theory "Y". Theory "Y" is quite opposite to theory "X" as it assumes labor to be a partner in the management and work is conducted with the co-operation of labor. Theory "Y" is also based on certain assumptions such as the following:

* Employees are not instigated to work by fear, strict restriction or outer restraint, but they feel responsible for their work assignments.

* Opportunities are based on democratic principles, where everybody has equal chances.

* Every work is not uninteresting and like a game (playing again and again) gives satisfaction.

* Recognition of work is a great prize as for the execution of work it is necessary that it should be recognized.

* By and large, employees are not instigated to do work by financial greed but non financial greed also instigates to work.

* Management thinks personnel on an equal footing for advice, seek their co-operation to solve the problems of the enterprise and established co-ordination between basic individual objectives and the collective objectives of the organization.

* Among the employees, tendency to escape from the responsibility is not natural but the reason is lack of ambition and more stress on job security. This theory has many distinct advantages, the principal of which is that through the application of theory "Y" a new work environment is created which trusts the employees willingness to work, provides for greater amounts of employees' responsibility and consequently minimizes the need for close supervision and also creates jobs that are more interesting and challenging. According to McGregor theory "Y" is a more valid concept of human nature. Although assumptions of theory "Y" are not fully accepted by employees in every work environment, but considerable evidence is available in many organizations characterizing themselves as managing by theory "Y", particularly in the engineering and scientific work environment. According to McGregor, the concepts of participation and consultative management, management by objectives (MBO), job employments etc. are quite consistent with theory "Y".

CONTENT THEORIES OF MOTIVATION

The content theories identify needs as important motivating forces and in so doing adopts a stimulus-organism-response (SO)R model of behavior in which the correct stimulus must first be applied and then a desired behavioral response is to be obtained. However, to organize this model within a work setting, it has been found necessary to make certain assumptions about human nature and expressing them in the form of individual wants, needs, desires and expectations. The desired human behavioral response is achieved by designing the job or organization so as to satisfy the identified needs.

- Maslow's Hierarchy of Needs

This theory is based on the assumption that behavior is a function of needs satisfaction. This theory is considered an important theory of motivation because it highlights the needs of the people.

Maslow's hierarchy of needs concept has been based on two principles, namely: (a) human needs may be arranged in a hierarchy of importance progressing from lower to a higher order of needs, and (b) a satisfied need no longer serves as a primary motivation of behavior.

Maslow proposed that human needs can be arranged in a particular order from the lower to the higher order as shown in Fig. 11.3.

Maslow points out that needs arise in a certain order of preference and not randomly and ranked in a hierarchy having a definite sequence of domination i.e. once first level need is reasonably satisfied, the next higher one becomes predominant. Once a need or a certain order of needs is satisfied, it ceases to be a motivating factor. From Maslow's theory two important points are emerged namely: (a) It is pointless trying to motivate employees by considering lower rank needs if these are already satisfied, and (b) it is not worth trying means to satisfy employees self-actuation needs, if the lower end needs are not met.

However, Maslow's hierarchy of needs theory should not be regarded as an absolute explanation of human behavior but should be considered only a general guide to managers. There are many exceptions and criticisms of the need priority model and theory, it may not be applicable at all times in all places due to the following explanation.

* There are creative people in whom the drive for creativeness seems to be more important. For example, a starving artist who makes sacrifices in his personal comfort while trying to achieve self-actualization through creating his work.

* A survey conducted in European countries and Japan have revealed that Maslow's hierarchy of needs model does not apply very well to their managers as their degree of satisfaction in needs does not vary according to the need priority model. For example in Belgium and Spain managers

felt that their esteem needs are better satisfied than their safety needs and even if safety needs are not satisfied the social needs may emerge. Therefore, the proposition that one need is satisfied at one time has been proved of doubtful validity.

* Some people are much less achievement-oriented or security-oriented than others and their needs satisfaction may not follow the sequence postulated by Maslow.

* According to Maslow, when the lower level needs are relatively well satisfied, they cease to be important motivators of behavior, but when these needs are threatened, they suddenly become important again.

* Another criticism of the hierarchy of needs theory is that when a need has been satisfied for a long time, this may be under evaluated.

* Due to many new challenges and opportunities for growth, achievements and recognitions, the two highest levels of Maslow's hierarchy of needs can hardly ever be fully satisfied.

- McClelland's need-for-achievement theory

McClelland in his book "The Achieving Society: concluded that a country's economic development depends on the extent to which its citizens have a need for achievement and a high positive correlation exists between effective performance, executive/enterpreneurial success, and the need for achievement. McClelland further postulated that, since an individual's motives and desires are not fixed as a result of childhood experience, the need for achievement can be developed more in matured people. This theory helps in developing certain characteristics in achievement-oriented people such as (a) a skill in long-range planning and organizational ability, (b) an urge for feedback about their performance, (c) an aptitude for setting moderate achievement goals and taking calculated risks i.e. supporting MBO management technique having positive correlation between goal setting and performance levels, (d) an interest in moderate risk taking (as a function of skill not chance), accepting personal responsibility for outcome, and also accepting challenge.

McClelland, through further research, identified the needs people have for affiliation (essentially the same as Maslow's social need) and power and discovered that male managers with higher need for power had more productive results than those with high needs for affiliation.

In this context the word power should not be taken as having a negative connotation (i.e. self-aggrandizement), but should be considered as that power which is closely related to leadership resulting in influencing decisions (including people and events) within the organizations through positive reinforcement for achievements (including participation and support of the subordinates).

- Herzberg's Motivation Maintenance (Hygiene) Theory

Resulting from a research by Herzberg and his associates in the mid 1950's based on the interview of 200 engineering and accounting personnel from eleven different industries in Pittsberge area in the USA, a significant development in motivation was distinguished between motivational factors and maintenance (hygiene) factors in a job situation.

The findings of the research were that the good feelings in the group under test were more related to specific tasks or assignments that the people performed rather than background factors (i.e. money, security, working conditions etc.) and the bad feelings in the group under test were more related to when some disturbance occurred in these background factors which caused them to believe that they were being treated unfairly.

From this Herzberg drew a distinction between motivators (satisfiers) and hygiene (dissatisfiers) factors i.e. factors primarily preventing dissatisfaction like hygiene preventing sickness, and postulated that work environment could be divided into these two sets of factors. Herzberg maintained that job satisfaction and job dissatisfaction are two mutually exclusive factors in the organizational environment. This implies that the opposite of job satisfaction is 'not job satisfaction' and not 'job dissatisfaction' and vice versa.

The research findings concluded that the real motivators in the group under test were opportunities to become more expert and to handle more demanding/ challenging assignments; and the absence of the hygiene factors served as dissatisfiers (resulting in loss of money and efficiency). When the hygiene factors are inadequate, then these will significantly have a negative effect on the workers' attitude, but do not have any positive effect when all the factors are available. Herzberg's model of maintenance and motivational factors is shown in Fig. 12.4.

Herzberg further pointed out that the underlying reason that why managers

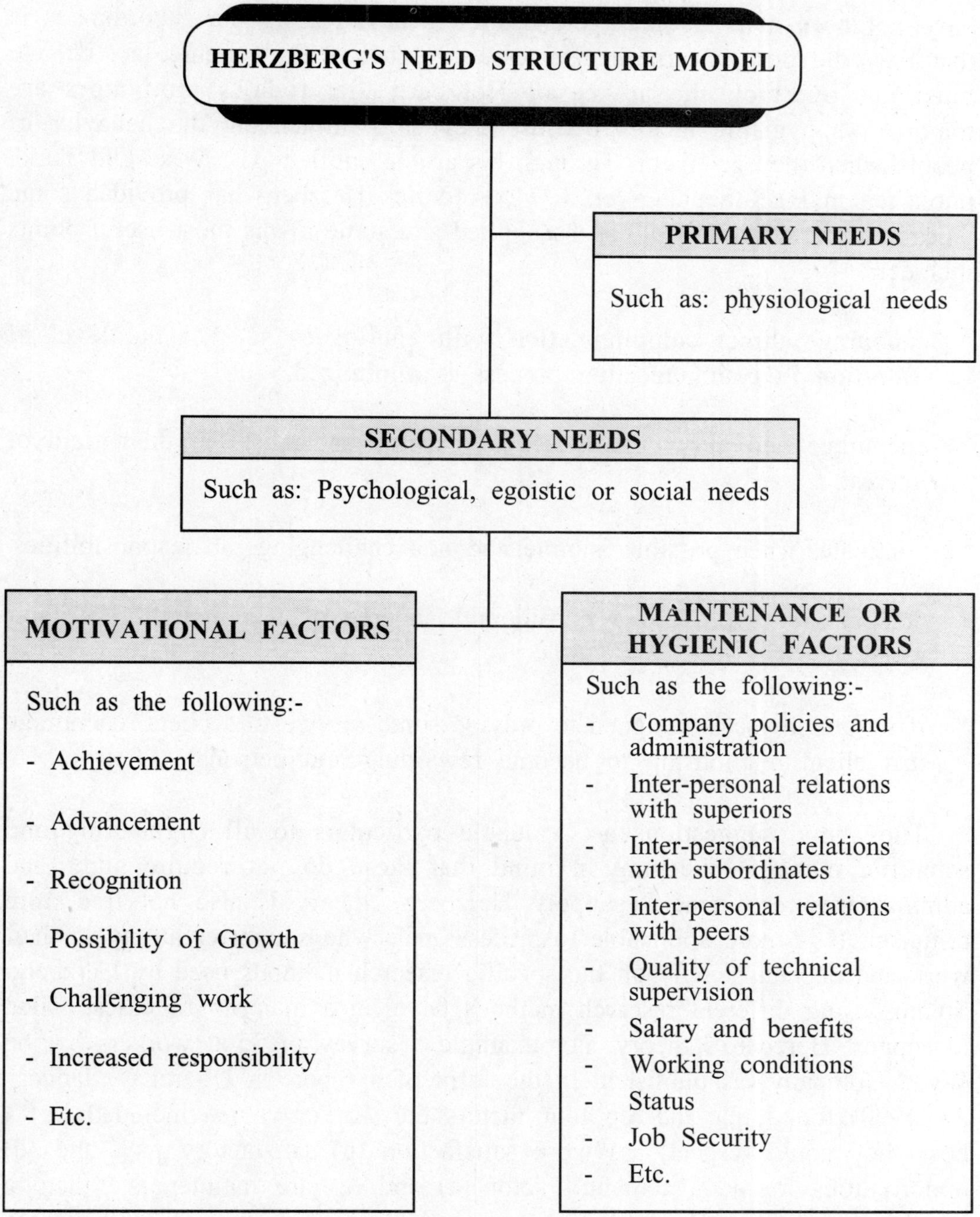

FIG. 12.4: HERZBERG'S NEED STRUCTURE MODEL

have not been able to obtain the desired behavior from the subordinates is that they did not concern themselves very much with hygienic factors. We must not overlook the advice of Herzberg that today's motivators are tomorrow's hygienic factors because they stop influencing the behavior of people when they get them. Through his article entitled 'The Wise Old Turk', published in HBR Sept. - Oct. 1974, Frederick Herzberg has provided some clues as to how this model can be applied and some of his most useful points include:

* encourage direct communication with employees so that the level of distortion in communication process is minimized.

* encourage and allow employees to become specialists in their field of interest.

* eliminate, when possible, simple and non challenging job responsibilities.

* delegate to employees a considerable degree of responsibility of their work.

* If the employee is assigned to provide some service to a client, encourage that client relationship to become rewarding and personal.

The above suggestions are valuable particulars to all engineering and scientific managers keeping in mind that these do not require additional administrative or financial support. Herzberg's theory is also not free from criticism. It is more applicable to professionals who sought creativity in their work and depend heavily on the specific research methods used by Herzberg. Studies using different research methods have, in a majority of cases, failed to support Herzberg's theory. For example a survey of 3500 workers by the Wyatt Company (as published in the form of a report in US today, January 24, 1990) found that the top four factors the worker valued included: (a) a boss they could respect, (b) work satisfaction (c) satisfactory pay, and (d) opportunities for advancement. Factor (a) and (c) are maintenance factors, which according to Herzberg are not motivators. However, in spite of the weakness, Herzberg's theory is a valuable guide to understand motivation at work.

COMPARISON OF MASLOW, HERZBERG & MCGRAGOR THEORIES

Some researchers have compared these theories as illustrated in Fig. 12.5. Herzbergs two sets of factors parallel Maslow's concept of hierarchy of needs and also with McGregor's Theory "X" & Theory "Y".

PROCESS THEORIES OF MOTIVATION

These theories concentrate on the mental processes involved in motivation and contain a degree of intuitive logic. These theories have made no significant impact on practicing managers, being notoriously difficult, if not impossible to operationalize.

Expectancy Theory

It suggests that motivation is the product of the valancy of the outcome of a certain action and expectancy that outcome will result from that action. Victor Vroom has developed this theory which is one of the most recent models of motivation. It views motivation as a process of governing choice. This theory has been refined by Lawler and Porter in their paper entitled 'Antecedent Attitude of Effective Managerial Performance' published in organizational behavior and Human Performance, Vol. 21967. This theory is based on the assumption that motivation is a product of the needs a worker seeks to fulfil, and an estimate by that individual that certain acts will lead to the fulfilment of those needs. In other words expectancy is the belief that a particular act will yield a particular outcome. This theory is generally termed as 'Expectancy Theory'.

By following this theory, individuals are predicted to be high performers when they see a high possibility that their efforts will lead to high performance, a high probability that high performance will lead to favorable outcome, and that these outcomes will be, (on balance) attractive to them. Accordingly if an individual has a particular goal, some behavior must be performed in order to achieve the goal, and the individual weighs the likelihood that behavior will achieve the desired goals. Also if certain behavior is expected to be more successful than others that type of behavior is likely to be chosen by that individual.

An important contribution of this theory is that it explains how the goals

	Maslow's Theory	Herzberg's Theory	McGregore's Theory 'X' & Theory 'Y'
MOTIVATIONAL FACTORS	HIGH STRATA NEEDS - Self fulfilment/self actualization - Esteem/ego	MOTIVATIONAL FACTORS - Achievement - Creativity & challenging work - Recognition - Advancement - Increased responsibility - Possibility of growth	THEORY 'Y' - Satisfaction of esteem - Self actualization needs - Increased responsibility - Self direction & self control - Imagination and creativity

MAINTENANCE FACTORS	LOW STRATA NEEDS
	- Social/belonging
	- Safety/security
	- Physiological/ biological
		HYGIENE FACTORS
		- Status
		- Supervision
		- Inter-personal relations
		  - With supervisors
		  - With subordinates
		  - With peers
		- Company policy and administration
		- Salary & benefits
		- Working conditions
		- Job security
			THEORY 'X'
			- Job security above all
			- Direction & supervision preferable
			- Threat and punishment needed

FIG. 12.5: COMPARISON OF THREE CATEGORIES OF MOTIVATIONAL THEORIES

of individuals influence their efforts and that the behavior selection to individuals is dependent upon their assessment of the probability that the selected behavior will successfully lead to the goal.

People in organization do not always place the same value to such job factors as promotion, job security, high salary and improved working conditions, but rank them differently. Under this situation if one individual places high value to increase in pay and perceive a superior performance as instrumental in reaching the goal, he will strive towards a superior performance to achieve his goal. But if another individual places a high value to get promotion and perceive behavior as instrumental to achieve it, he is not likely to strive for a superior performance in reaching his goal. Thus, as Vroom has pointed out, the important motivation factor is the perception and value the individual places upon certain goals i.e. individual goals influence individual effort. Therefore like Maslow's and Herzberg's theories, Vroom's expectancy model reveals that behavior is goal oriented.

In organizational terms Victor Vroom postulates that people are motivated to work if they expect increased efforts leading to increased rewards, and value the rewards resulting from their efforts. Vroom's value expectancy theory yields the following results[40].

Motivation = (Expectancy that increased effort will lead to increased rewards)
X (Value of rewards to the individual resulting from his effort)

Research findings of this theory have produced two different results on the intensity of motivation. One research has found that there is a likelihood of successfully completing the job (or assignment) and receiving a reward. In this situation an individual is more likely to be motivated to perform the job well through influence of his manager who understand his needs and abilities by way of setting challenging but attainable goals and providing suitable awards.

Another research has found that if a person is internally motivated, the motivation tends to be more powerful. In this case the individual's motivation is based on his belief that he will be adequately rewarded if he works hard.

Reinforcement Theory

This theory is based primarily on the understanding of Edward Thorndike's Law of Effect, which postulates that behavior followed by satisfying consequences tends to be repeated and behavior followed by dissatisfying consequences tends not to be repeated[38]. This theory is further developed by the work of B.I. Skinner who makes a distinction between *reinforcement* i.e. the presentation of an attractive reward following a response, and the removal of an unpleasant or negative condition following a response and *punishment* i.e. providing unpleasant consequence for undesirable behavior. The reinforced theory advocates a method of motivation in which favorable behavior is *reinforced* by satisfying consequences and unfavorable behavior is *eliminated* by dissatisfying consequences.

In organizations, this theory can work in two ways, namely: (a) Through reward or praise, you can reinforce the employee's favorable behavior thus encouraging him to repeat it and (b) through disciplinary warning or scolding, you can discourage the employee's unfavorable behavior thus encouraging him not to repeat it. Through positive reinforcement i.e. focusing behavior response on what should be done, training, development, and growth of human resources occur. This principle provides a basis for MBO. However, this principle has some limitations. It does seem to operate when standards are clearly set and an assumption is made that, in anticipation of the desired awards of positive reinforcement and recognition, the employees will be motivated to perform satisfactorily. In this context it is important to highlight that when properly the applied positive reinforcement includes praise, it must be sincere, otherwise it cannot be effective in influencing motivation because business flattering can backfire. However, some researchers believe that praise even poorly given may have a positive effect on an individual's behavior.

OTHER USEFUL MOTIVATION MODELS

- March and Simon Model

March and Simon have established a positive correlation between productivity and motivation by means of a theoretical model based on the assumption that motivation is a function of perceived consequences of *evoked alternatives* and *individual goals,* in terms of which alternatives are evaluated.

The main generalization in this model include:

* Higher level of aspiration leads to lower satisfaction.

* Lower individual satisfaction leads to greater search for better ways of

improving the performance.

* More search for alternatives leads to greater expected rewards.

* Greater expected rewards lead to a higher satisfaction and level of aspiration.

From the above generalization we may deduce that levels of aspiration and satisfaction are negatively correlated. However, if the level of aspiration rises at the same rate as the expected reward, the individual will continue to be motivated even by resulting in mild dissatisfaction. But if the level of aspiration is too high i.e. beyond the reach of the individual, the individual will get frustrated. On the other hand if the level of aspiration does not rise with the rise of rewards, the individual becomes complacent and his search of alternatives declines.

From the above analysis, March and Simon postulate that high satisfaction does not necessarily stimulate productivity rather it is the dissatisfaction that stimulates productivity.

- Traditional Social Action Model

Before we proceed to explain this model, it is important to understand work place behavior found in the social action perspective of organizations. We must try to find the answers to two questions with respect to work namely: (i) why do people work at all? and (ii) why do people work hard and with a sense of commitment? The answer to the first question is a concern of *motivation to work,* whilst the answer to the second question is a concern of *motivation at work.* Goldthorpe suggested that the meaning a situation had for an individual would be reflected in his *orientation* to that situation which in turn provides a starting place for understanding work place behavior and also a useful starting point for the study of organizational behavior. However, this concept of orientation has two major criticisms, namely: (a) whether an individual's orientation is fixed by forces external to the work situation and (b) whether the orientation remains constant over a period of time.

The crucial arguments of both the above noted criticisms are likely to be represented by the traditional social action model shown in Fig. 12.6.

However, if we consider behavior at work i.e. motivation to work and

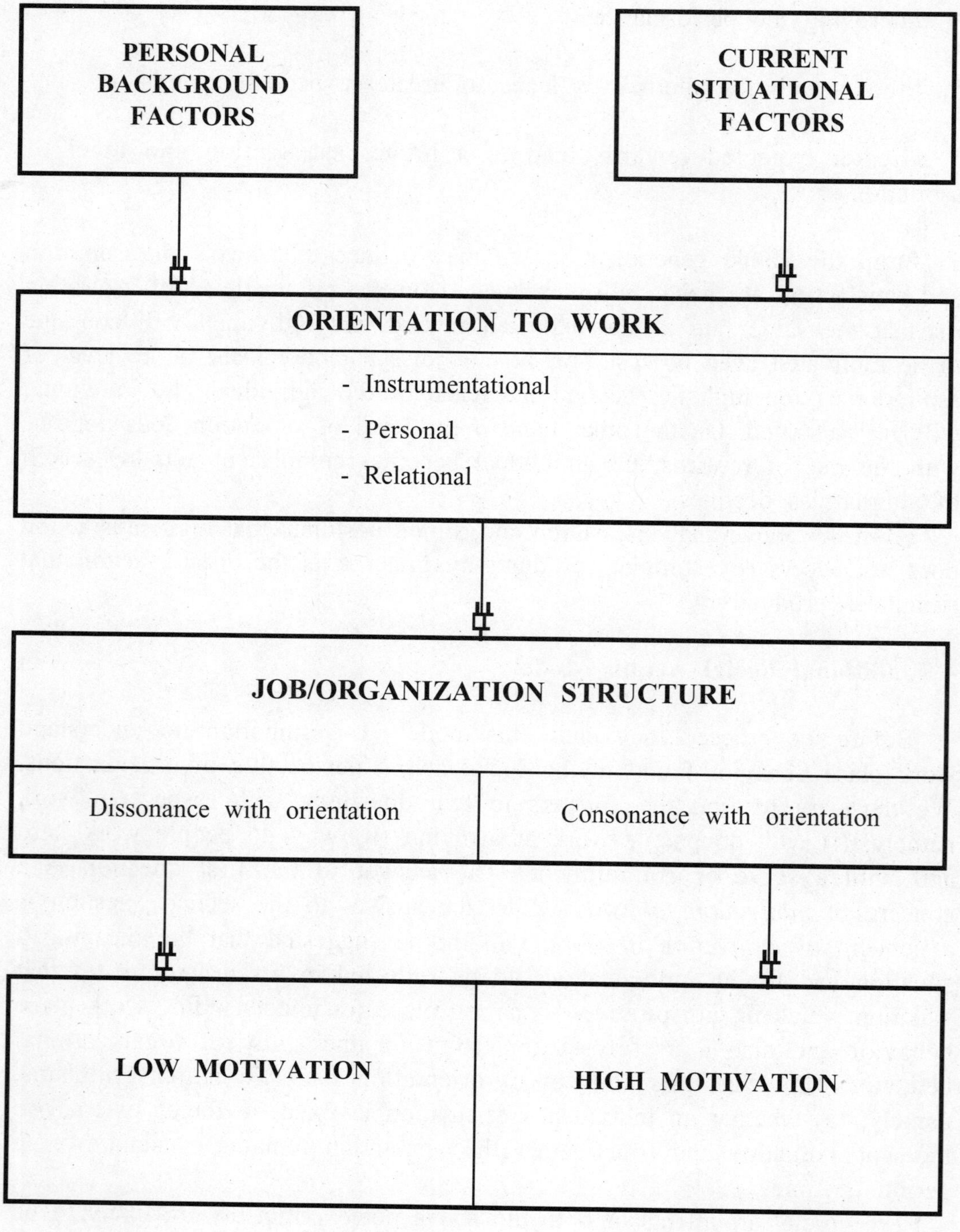

FIG. 12.6: THE TRADITIONAL SOCIAL ACTION MODEL

motivation at work as a dominant influencing force on the orientation to work then we need to modify the tradition action model by replacing the concept of orientation by the twin concepts of motivation to work and attachment to work, as shown in Fig. 12.7.

- Effort Reward Approach

This approach has its origin in the scientific management of F.W. Taylor and has its manifestation in providing incentives i.e. Salary, Promotion & benefits etc. on the basis of accomplishment. Rewards in this approach are considered to be a function of effort put in, to reach the standard set by the management. To operationalise this approach, managers are required to set up standards of performance, monitor the behavior of the employee to observe the level to which these standards are adhered to (or attained), and allocate rewards and penalties based on the performance so observed. This approach states that more efforts carry more pay. This approach can be described in a simple model as: 'Effort-Reward-Effort Model', which illustrates that greater effort not only leads to greater pay but also rewards of greater pay stimulates, greater effort. This approach has only a very limited application only where performance and results can be directly and quantitatively measured. This approach is not considered adequate because it addresses only a single course (or aspect) of behavior and assumes that people work in an organization with the only incentive of making money without any necessity of providing on-the-job satisfaction to the employees.

- New Strategies of Motivating Employees

Under new strategies, unlike traditional management and organizational practices, motivation is an internalized force (i.e. Self generating, self rewarding and self controlling) and not subject to external control. In modern industry due to economic pressures and a need to utilize man power more effectively, it has become crucial to find ways of realizing the full potential of human resources.

Motivation is not a simple or fixed human quality that can be switched 'on' or 'off' with a push of a button but is a complex and dynamic phenomenon requiring various techniques and approaches such as the following:

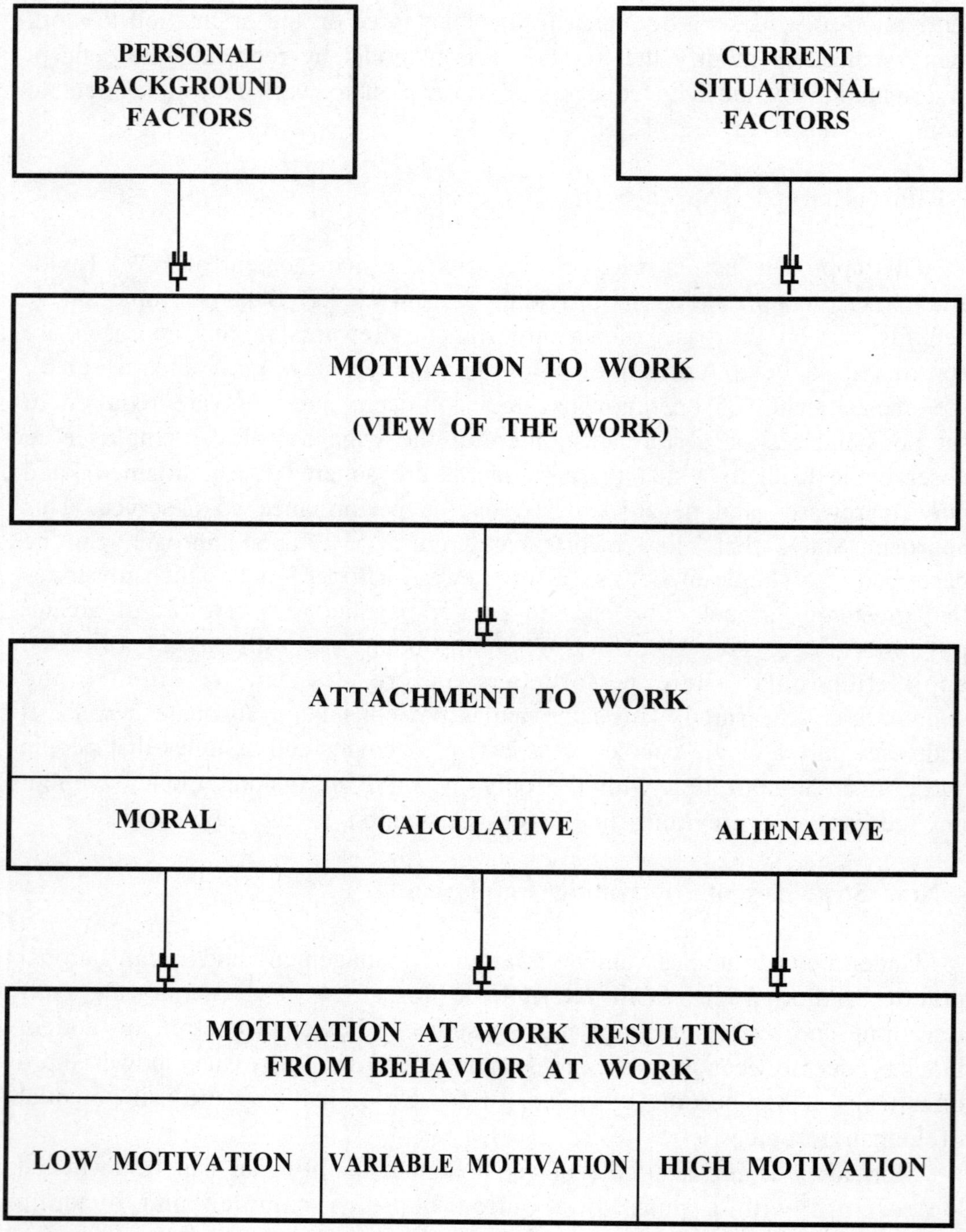

FIG. 12.7 : THE TRADITIONAL SOCIAL ACTION MODEL

- Job Satisfaction: Factors that must be taken into consideration for intrinsically motivating work/job satisfaction include: (a) a work or job should contain full module and meaningful activities with clear functions; (b) an employee should be able to take decisions and exercise some discretion and (c) an employee should receive some feed-back preferably from the work. Although terms, job satisfaction, industrial morale and attitude, are often used synonymously, but an attitude may contribute to job satisfaction which in turn may contribute to morale. One of the simplest and widely used approaches of identifying the job satisfaction of an employee is the ranking of job factors in order of their relative importance by the interview or questionnaire method. The other approaches include direct observation and projective techniques.

The job satisfaction factors may be divided into two types namely: The characteristic of the individual i.e. money, security, working conditions, etc. and the characteristic of the job i.e. interesting and challenging assignments providing opportunities for advanced recognitions etc. However, the satisfaction and dissatisfaction employees derive from various sources in their job environment depends to a large extent on the organizational structure and the production technology of the organization. Researchers have found that there is a relationship between job satisfaction and the age of the job holder. By and large, the studies indicate that job satisfaction follows a certain pattern. It is high for younger people immediately after the employment but drops sharply after a few years and then it begins to increase and becomes high near to retirement age.

According to the study conducted by Herzberg, in almost all cases, the factors that caused job satisfaction were found all intrinsic to the job content thus having a stimulating effect on feeling, morale and performance. Whereas, the factors that caused job dissatisfaction were found all extrinsic thus having a negative effect on feeling, morale and performance.

- Job Enrichment: In industry many employees perform the same jobs every day and the jobs remain essentially unchanged thus causing the workers to become bore, stagnant and disenchanted with their jobs (which initially may have been viewed as interesting and challenging). To overcome such situations and increase the motivational level of particularly mature employees, a strong argument has been made for taking the simple jobs and making them more interesting and challenging by applying various techniques. Such a process is generally termed as 'job enrichment' or 'work enrichment'. The strategy of job enrichment is applied as a motivational tool to bring satisfaction of higher order needs of the workers i.e. self esteem satisfaction which according to

Abraham Maslow leads to "feelings of self-confidence, worth, strength, capability, and adequacy of being useful and necessary in the world"[21].

Some of the key ingredients of job enrichment include: a well defined job, job variety, more responsibility, opportunity to utilize skills and abilities, control of employees over decision making, opportunity to see job completion i.e. concrete results of work namely: achievement, contribution, shortcoming on the job etc. The core dimensions that provide job enrichment include: task variety, task identity, task significance, autonomy and feedback.

John Heinrichs through his work 'The Motivational crisis' published in 1974 by the Americcan Management Association, has identified certain assumptions underlying the notion of work enrichment. These include: (a) sizeable number of people are working in jobs that do not fully utilize their abilities and skills, (b) people are not inherently lazy; they need to have their abilities and skills more fully utilized, (c) given an opportunity, people will put more effort into their work, and (d) when this occurs, their productivity will increase, as well as the satisfaction they derive from their work.

Currently various techniques are being used for job enrichment such as: job redesign, job rotation, job enlargement, job stylizing, the use of temporary task forces, job training, job-man measurement, task progression, etc.

Effective managers should always be alert to the rich possibilities of using work enrichment as a means of promoting job satisfaction, job growth, and self-esteem for their subordinates.

Herzberg after conducting several successful experiments in industry suggests the following steps to job enrichment:

I Select those jobs in which (a) the investment in industrial process does not make changes too costly, (b) attitudes are poor, hygiene is becoming very costly, and motivation will make a difference of performance.

II Approach these jobs with a conviction that they can be changed.

III Brainstrom a list of changes that may enrich the jobs, without concerning practicality.

IV Screen the list to eliminate suggestions that involve hygiene, rather than actual motivation.

V Screen the list for generalities, such as: 'giving them more responsibilities'.

VI Screen the list to eliminate any horizontal loading suggestions (reducing the personal contribution of employees rather than giving them opportunities for growth in their accustomed job).

VII Avoid direct participation by the employees whose jobs are to be enriched.

VIII Set up a controlled experiment in the initial attempts at job enrichment.

IX Be prepared for a drop in performance during changeover.

X Expect some anxiety and hostility over the changes from first-line supervisors.

- **Team Building:** This technique seeks to increase a group motivation through *acquisition* of a capacity for self diagnosis, self evaluation and self correction and by *sharing* responsibility, decision making, risk taking and *seeking* growth and recognition through members' own work and through their organization.

Promotional Policies: In the modern industries there is a dire need to lay down sufficient promotional policies to generate continued motivation of the employees reinforced with the creation of such a climate in which promotion is not only based on seniority but also on merit rating and performance reports. However there are certain disadvantages for which the management must be aware of. For example in promotion by seniority, people will be less inclined to acquire better qualifications or make extra efforts for self improvement, whereas in a merit rating system, long serving workers may be demotivated knowing that their seniority has no meaning for the organization and their initiatives may be killed.

GENERAL GUIDELINE TO MOTIVATION

General guidelines in the performance of steps of motivation include, but by no means limited, to the following:

1. Always remember William Faulkner's advice: "always dream and shoot higher than you know you can do. Don't bother just to be better than your contemporaries or predecessors. Try to be better than yourself".

2. Draw up a motivational plan by addressing various organizational aspects such as sizing up the situation; preparing a set of motivating tools; selecting and providing motivational policies; formulating follow up procedures; and taking into consideration appropriate applications of various motivational theories discussed above.

3. Consider self interests, attainability, proportioning rewards, human element, and individual group relation to their optimum limit. For example, self interest is not an undesirable foundation provided it does not tend towards greediness.

4. Always be alert to the current and future trends and development concerning motivation keeping in mind that in modern industrial environment workers do not always run after money but also seek status, recognition, job satisfaction, job enrichment, self esteem and satisfaction of other egoistic needs. Therefore, non-financial incentives such as those listed below are becoming more and more important and should adequately be implemented in organizations.

* Workers participation.
* Healthy competition among the individuals and groups.
* Safe and secure working conditions.
* Suggestion system to encourage creativity, discovery and innovation.
* Praise and recognition for good performance.
* Feedback of the resultant outcomes.
* Group incentives.

IMPACT OF SOCIALIZATION ON ORGANIZATIONAL EFFECTIVENESS

WHAT IS ORGANIZATIONAL SOCIALIZATION?

Each organization is a part of the broader social structure of a given culture on the basis of which the culture of the organization emerges. There is usually a little understanding, by either organizations or incoming employees, of the need to learn about this corporate culture. It is important to know that an organization is not merely a collection of roles positioned on an organization chart, but it has also a personality i.e. organization culture. Therefore, in organizations, as in societies at large, culture conveys important norms and assumptions, governing aims, membership activities and values.

PERSPECTIVES ON ORGANIZATIONAL SOCIALIZATION

The discussion of organizational socialization is organized around some major themes such as: (i) the general characteristics of organizational socialization, (ii) stages of socialization, (iii) and the content of socialization. Organization socialization is the process by which a new incumbent comes to appreciate the abilities, values, expected behaviors and social knowledge essential to function as a member of the organization.

According to Meston (1957), the process of organizational socialization begins in a stage called 'anticipatory socialization'. New incumbents anticipate (being still outsiders) their experience in the organization they are about to enter and develop expectations about their life in the organization and on the job (including the unrealistic expectations as identified by Wanous: 1977). Accordingly, each position in the organization carries with it certain realistic expectations with regards to status, performance and privileges that accrue to the incumbent, which in turn become a defined role for him. Therefore, each time when a major passage or role change takes places, it involves socialization into the new role and setting.

During the encounter period (3 to 4 months on the job) experiences are critical in shaping the individuals long term orientation to the organization. During this period new incumbents anticipations are tested against the reality of their new work experiences and if a resultant difference between anticipation and real experience becomes apparent it contributes to 'reality shock' (the phrase that Huges: 1958 used to characterize what new incumbents often experience in entering an unfamiliar setting). In taking a new role, the incumbent is typically given some time in which to gain momentum to master the basic of the job to reach performance above the minimum expected level and also to 'learn the ropes' which is necessary in each new organization culture.

Completion of the socialization stage is reached when the incumbent assumes an insider role and is given responsibility and autonomy, entrusted with 'privileged information', encouraged to represent the organization, included in informal network, and above all sought out for counsel/advice by others.

Content of socialization involves role-related learning and a more general appreciation of the organizational culture. In order to perform adequately in a new role, an incumbent needs ability, skill, motivation, and an understanding of what others expect of his role. The new incumbent must also understand critical organizational values to identify and appreciate essentials of pivot role behaviors in shaping up his performance to avoid the risk of an early termination.

PERSPECTIVES ON SOCIAL RESPONSIBILITY

In organizational terms social responsibility is, by and large, considered as 'management's' obligation to set policies, make corporate decisions and follow courses of action (beyond the requirements of law) that are desirable in terms of the norms, values and general objectives of the society to which the organization is a part. There are numerous perspectives on the extent of practicing social responsibility as views on it vary from the limited (or restricted) to unlimited (or extensive).

The proponents of the limited view of social responsibility argue that since managers are employees of the owner (not the public), therefore, they should act for the owner i.e. minimise the cost of social responsibility which would otherwise be at the expense of higher prices to consumers. On the other hand the proponents of the unlimited view of social responsibility argue that, since business is a major segment of society and exerts a significant impact on the way society functions, it is imperative to provide all the possible help to maintain and improve the overall welfare of society.

Some authorities hold the view that since profitability and growth go hand in hand with responsible treatment of groups such as employees, customers/clients and the community, therefore, business should perform socially responsible activities and earn greater organizational goodwill and credibility. Many reputable organizations have been undertaking specific action programs such as: employees relations, environmental protection, urban renewal, public and community service, consumerism, culture/art and recreation, and eduction/medical assistance, etc. and are receiving national acclaim. Likewise employees who have been making substantial contribution in this respect are being respected and recognized by their respective management. However, to strike a balance between social responsibility and corporate profits remain a matter of great concern for organizational theorists.

HUMAN RELATIONS

To achieve organizational objectives and goals, managers need a network of contacts and human relations by using the efforts of other people. Therefore, good human relations are the best guarantee any organization can have of continued success in any field of endeavor. It is a widely held belief among senior executives that there is a dire need for better human relations particular in employees as the achievement of good employees relations means the attainment of that intangible known as 'morale'.

In management of enterprises managers need to possess many different skills including behavioral and analytical skills to work with people. Therefore, the important skills that effective managers generally use include: human relations skills in addition to conceptual, technical and administrative skills. It is necessary to keep in mind that one can buy person's time and physical presence at a particular place but his (or her) enthusiasm, loyalty, initiative and devotion cannot be bought. These can only be assured through the good employer-employees relations. Oliver-Sheldon (1894-1951) with his statement made in the year 1923 emphasized that management has social responsibilities "as a major partner in the community, alongside capital and labor"[26]. Accordingly, ever since it has been recognized that the approach to management must also include the process of motivating individual in a given situation to achieve a balance of objective between human satisfaction and attainment of organizational goals.

Industrial research has shown that when the worker's economic, physical and social wants are fulfilled he will work hard with his full physical and mental aptitude and enthusiasm resulting in improvement of production and co-operation. This implies that an effective human relations program is the key to maximum productivity and efficiency for the benefits of both the employer and employee.

Some important factors responsible for human relations include: physical needs, safety needs, social needs and self-realization needs. (See Fig. 12.8).

Organizations must develop a suitable climate which will motivate the employees to produce more and also to achieve better human relations. Fig. 12.9 shows some suggestions for improvement in human relations which should be followed.

FACTORS RESPONSIBLE FOR HUMAN RELATIONS

PHYSIOLOGICAL NEEDS

These include: the necessity of food, clothing and shelter. These needs must be fulfilled so as to keep the worker worriless. Workers also want a guarantee that these needs will also be met in the future

SAFETY NEEDS

Security for job and protection against danger/threat are fundamental requirements of the workers.

SELF-REALISATION NEEDS

Man always desires that he should be put to such a job for which he is fit. A worker will not remain happy on the post which is lower than that for which he is suitable.

SOCIAL NEEDS

Main social human desires are reputation, which can be recognised by providing opportunities for employees to participate in the organization.

FIG. 12.8 : SOME MAJOR FACTORS RESPONSIBLE FOR HUMAN RELATIONS

SOME SUGGESTIONS FOR IMPROVEMENT IN HUMAN RELATIONS

PROPER WAGE/SALARY LEVEL

A worker should get sufficient wages, so as to fulfill his or her minimum needs. For better human relations and to benefit both the employer and employee (through increased productivity) decent wages should be paid to the worker.

SPECIAL INDUCEMENT/INCENTIVES

Fair wages satisfy only physiological needs of the worker. However, to get the optimum output some incentives in the form of bonus, upgrading, promotion, etc. are necessary.

OPEN COMMUNICATION

Exchange of informations, views, and feelings are very essential as a means of promoting communication among various sections. This in turn helps them to understand each other and in making decisions.

MUTUAL TRUSTEESHIP

Mutual trust and social responsibility on the part of both labor and management reduces the conflicts and enhances the sense of cooperation.

HUMAN DIGNITY

Human dignity is the moral basis for human relations, as it is the desire of every person that he or she should be treated with respect and dignity. Each individual should, therefore, be recognised as a separate personality.

PROGRAM FOR SUGGESTIONS

By this program, workers take keen interest in the affairs of the employer's organization, especially in the matter of production. In the absence of such a program, workers generally criticise management.

FIG. 12.9: SOME SUGGESTIONS FOR IMPROVEMENT IN HUMAN RELATIONS

MORALE BUILDING

In management, the right type of attitude and willingness to work and people to achieve the organizational goals are the keys to the success of any enterprise and the pre-requisites of building morale.

MORALE DEFINED

For managerial purposes morale has been defined in many ways but each definition revolves around the attitude and willingness to work to achieve the organizational goals.

The generic definition expressed in the Webster's New Collegiate Dictionary is "the mental and emotional condition (as of enthusiasm, confidence or loyalty) of an individual or group with regard to functions or tasks at hand" or "a sense of common purpose with aspect to a group: ESPRIT DE CORPS". Morale has also been defined as: "the attitude of the employee towards his work environment and more specifically towards the employer as represented by high supervision."

In military terminology Beishline, in his book Military Management for National Defense, defined high morale as: "the state of mind which makes a soldier concerned with his surroundings; confident of himself, his comrades and his leaders, and determined to execute all of his missions with effectiveness and efficiency. It relates to the condition of an individual or group with regard to courage, confidence and enthusiasm in the performance of duty".

Morale has been recognized as one of the most important factors in winning or losing a war. According to Napolean, "In war, morale conditions make up three-quarters of the game; the relative balance of man-power accounts for the remaining quarter".

Leighton in his book "Human Relations in a Changing World", describes morale as "the capacity of a group of people to pull together persistently in pursuit of a common purpose".

In general terms we may define morale as 'the attitudes and capacities of individuals and groups towards their assigned tasks and towards voluntary co-operation in pursuit of organizational objectives and goals'.

On analysing the above definitions, we come to the conclusion that morale is the degree of willingness and enthusiasm with which the members of a group set out to perform the work assignments. Accordingly if willingness and enthusiasm is low, morale is low and if willignness and enthusiasm is high morale is high.

IMPORTANCE OF MORALE BUILDING

Modern organizations have more and more interests in employees' attitudes and morale due to a general trend towards greater recognition of social responsibilities of organizations. Morale is a much abused term and has resulted in many kinds of mistaken ventures. However, in organizations employer-employee relationship is the major factor that determine the importance of morale. Though high morale and good employee relations are not identical, but there is no doubt that the establishment of good employee relations is the major contributing factor in building high employee morale. Morale is a relative concept as there is no absolute state of morale but only the degree or satisfaction of high morale or low morale. Morale is likely to be high if the worker is convinced of the following factors:

* Work is important and of significance.
* There exist a fair opportunity of advancement.
* Outstanding work performance is recognized.
* Job continuity is ensured as long as the worker continues to do satisfactory work.
* Image of the employer in the community is well thought out.
* Workers are treated fairly by the employer and an adequate opportunity for grievance exists, if not being treated fairly.

In this context it is important to highlight that merely good intentions or good policies alone cannot result in good employee relations and high employees' morale but these need to be effectively administered by sound management practices.

CONSEQUENCES OF HIGH & LOW MORALE

High morale results from job satisfaction and is indeed a manifestation of the employees' confidence, pride, devotion, strength and dependability. It makes for effective work by the employees. Employees with high morale like their jobs and provide voluntary contribution towards the achievement of goals of the organization. On the other hand, low morale indicates the presence of mental tension and unrest in the organization and leads to loss in productivity. The other consequences of low morale include as follows:

* Friction and frustration among the workers.
* Antagonism towards corporate policies and management.
* High rate of labor turnover and absenteeism.
* Excessive complaints and grievances.

Whatever may be the consequences of low morale, one thing is clear that it will cause suffering to both the quantity and quality of productions. It is therefore imperative that approrpiate steps should be taken by the management to maintain the high morale of the employees.

It will not be an exaggeration to say that all other things remaining the same, high morale certainly leads to success and low morale brings defeat in its wake.

In order to appraise the morale of the employees, the implore must consider those factors which determine morale such as shown in Fig. 12.10.

In order to improve the degree of morale, the management should take measures such as shown in Fig. 12.11.

CONCLUDING REMARKS

If we raise a question that can a person, a manager or an executive do anything to prevent loss of meaning and distortion in conveying messages. The answer to this question is definitively yes, because communication depends on skill that can be learned.

Communication is a most important part of managing as it is linked very closely to the managerial functions of planning, organizing, leading and controlling/evaluating. Therefore, every organization should take all possible steps to promote effective communication and provide necessary skills to managers which will help them to reduce communication errors and remove

MORALE DETERMINATIONS

JOB-RELATED FACTORS

Such as the following:-

- Types of job

(Nature of the job, fatigue associated with the job and skill required to do the job)

- Job satisfaction

(Enthusiasm to work will be higher due to opportunity for growth and advancement).

- Compatability with fellow employees

(confidence in fellow employees and feeling of togetherness generate high morale)

- Working conditions

(With the provisions of better conditions to the workers, morale will be high)

- Nature of supervision

(Supervision which is social fairminded and helpful often creates confidence among its subordinates and this in turn increase their morale)

PERSONAL FACTORS

Such as the following:-

- Age
- Training as less training generally results in low morale
- Intelligence of employees
- Time span by workers on the job
- Interest in work taken by the workers

OTHER FACTORS

Such as the following:-

- Goals and objectives of the organization

(Commoness of the purpose which leads the workers to work enthusiastically)

- Reward/inducement

(Good systems of remuneration and other incentives, e.g. promotion/advancement, always have a stimulating effect on the workers and help to increase their morale)

- Physical and mental factors (If job is below the workers' expectation, it can give rise to mental worries)

FIG. 12.10 : SOME FACTORS DETERMINING MORALE

SOME MANAGEMENT GUIDELINES TO IMPROVE MORALE

- Monthly employees' meeting may be held to discuss with the employees the problems of the previous month and the program for the next month.
- Private discussions may be held by the managers with individual employees to know their views on the working of the organization and personnel policies.
- Employees should be kept informed about organizational policies and programs and they should be allowed to comment over these.
- After an employee is assigned a particular job, it is necessary to follow up his or her performance to ascertain whether a 'job to man' match exists. If the employee is suitable to the job, his or her morale will be high.
- Management should encourage group activities by the employees, outside work, such as: sports, or other social events, etc. to help them to develop in them high morale, since they consider themselves an integral part of the group.
- There should be a clear-cut policy about development/promotion through training and proper incentive schemes. These help to improve morale and ensure higher monetary rewards for exceptional work in terms of both quality and quantity.
- Management should provide for welfare measures and other aminities such as: housing allowance, credit facilities, loans educational allowance for children, etc.

FIG. 12.11 : MANAGEMENT MEASURES TO IMPROVE MORALE

communication barriers in their respective organizations. Remember that the golden rule of communication in an organizational setting is 'to communicate effectively, generously, and globally within the organization except those items of importance where, as a deliberate matter of policy it may be necessary to withhold information'. However, if the communication process encourages too much secret atmosphere it can create an attitude of cynicism down the line management and inner tensions within the organization which may in turn lead the organization to isolation and becoming inert in respect of fresh creative ideas and innovation.

In the context of understanding the process of motivation it should be remembered that merely providing satisfaction of needs of employees would not necessarily lead to better performance, but it would be equally necessary to provide situational factors and incentives in such a way that their personal needs are integrated with the goals of the organization. Motivation deals with human behavior in order to determine the factors that prompt an individual to do his best. It is therefore imperative for managers to know what are the motivational factors influencing the behavior of employees. In its most simplest form we may say that the strength of motivation depends upon the motive, expectancy and incentive. By and large, managers are now facing the difficult task of implementing and evaluating social behavior and finding more effective means to improve human relation and build high morale within their respective organization.

We may conclude this discussion by stating that effective communication, motivation, socialization, good human relations and high morale indeed are the most significant contributory factors for the effectiveness of the interaction of human elements and, without doubt, act as the lubricant that makes the organization function smoothly.

REFERENCES AND RECOMMENDED READING

1. Argyris, Chris. - *'Explorations in interpersonal competence'*/Applied Behavioral Science, Vol. 1, No. 3, 1965, pp. 255.
2. Argyris, Chris. - *'T-Group for Organization Effectiveness'*/HBR, March - April 1964, pp. 60.
3. Bell, Arther H. - 'Communication for Management and business'/Glenview, II.: Scott Foresman 1989, pp. R-43.
4. Black, R.R., L.S. Mouton, L.B. Barnes, and L.E. Greiner. - *'Breakthrough in Organization Development'*/HBR November - December, 1964, pp. 135.

5. Carlsen, Brown - 'Listening Comprehension Test'/Yonkers - on - Hudson World Book Company.

6. Couch, Lester and R.P. French Jr. - *'Overcoming Resistence to Change'*/Human Relations, Vol. 1, No. 4, 1948. pp. 512.

7. Davis, Keith and John W. Newstrom - 'Human Behavior at Work: Organization Behavior'/ New York: McGraw - Hill, 1985, pp. 425.

8. Gibson, George W. - *'The Filmed Case in Management Training'*/HBR, May - June 1957, pp. 123.

9. Green, David and Kathleen F.Hansell - *'Video Conferencing'*/Business Horizon, November - December 1984, pp. 57-61.

10. Hardie, Keren R. - *'Motivation in Business and Management: An Information Sourcebook'*/Greensboro, NC: Center of Creative Leadership, 1990.

11. Heilman, Arther W. - *'An investigation in Measuring and Improving Listening Ability of College Freshmen'*/Speech Monographs, November 1951, pp. 308.

12. Herzberg, Frederick - *'One More Time: How Do You Motivate Employees?'*/HBR 46, January - February 1968, pp. 53-62.

13. Johnson, Wendell - *'Fateful Process of Mr. A Talking to Mr. B'*/HBR, January - February 1953, pp. 49.

14. Johnson, Wendell - 'Your most Enchanted Listener'/New York: Harper and Brothers, 1956.

15. Katy, Rober L. - *'Skill of an Effective Administrator'*/HBR January - February 1955, pp. 33.

16. Koontz, Harold, Cyril O'Donnell and Heinz Weihrich. - 'Management'/New York: McGraw - Hill Book Company, 1980.

17. Kramar, E.J.J. and Thomas R. Lewis - *'Comparison of Visual and Nonvisual Listening'*/ Journal of Communication, November 1951, pp. 16.

18. Levenson, Harry - *'Management By Whose Objectives?'*/HBR, July - August 1970, pp. 125-134.

19. Marrow, Alfred - 'Behind the Executive Mask'/New York: American Management Association, 1965.

20. Marrow, Alfred - *'A Theory of Human Motivtion'*/Psychological Review, 1943, pp. 370.

21. Marrow, Alfred - 'Motivation and Personality'/New York: Harper & Row, 1954.

22. McClelland, David C. - 'The Achieving Society'/New York: Van Nostrand, 1961.

23. McClelland, David C. and David H. Burnham - 'Power is the Motivator'/HBR 54, March April 1976, pp. 100-110.

24. McGregor, Douglas - 'The Human Side of Enterprize'/New York: McGraw - Hill Book Company, 1960 -

25. Megginson, Leon C., Donald C. Mosley and Paul H. Pietri, Jr. - 'Management: Concepts and Application'/Harper Collins Publishers, 1992.

26. Peter, Tom and Nancy Austin - 'A Passion for Excellence'/New York: Random House, 1985.

27. Pincus, Marilyn - 'Mastering Business Etiquette and Protocol'/New York: National Institution of Business Management, 1989.

28. Roethlisberger, F.J. - 'Management and Morale'/Cambridge: Harvad University Press, 1950.

29. Rogers, C.R. and F.J. Roathlisberger - 'Barriers and Gateways to Communication'/HBR 1990, pp. 19.

30. Ronken, O. and Paul R. Lawrence - 'Administrative Change: A Case Study of Human Relation in a Factory'/Boston Division of Research, harvard Business School, 1952.

31. Schnake, Mel E., Michael Dumler, Donald Cochran and Timthy R. Barnett - *'Effects of differences in Superior and subordinate Perception of Superiors Communication Practices'*/Journal of Business Communication 27, Winter 1990, pp. 37-39.

32. Sheldon, Oliver - 'The Philosophy of Management'/New York: Pitman, 1939.

33. Sirota, David and Alan D. Wolfson - *'Job Enrichment: What are the obstacles'*/ Personnel, May - June 1972.

34. Sirota, David and Alan D. Wolfson - *'Job Enrichment: Surmounting the Obstacles'*/ Personnel, July - August 1973.

35. Skinner, B.F. - 'Beyond Freedom and Dignity'/New York: Knopf, 1971.

36. Skinner, B.F. - 'About Behaviorism'/New York: Knopf, 1974.

37. Stryker, Perrin - *'The Growing Pains of Executive Development'*/Advanced Management, August 1954, pp. 15.

38. Thorndike, Edward L. - 'Human Learning'/New York: Century, 1931.

39. Ticky, Noel and Ram Charan - *'Speed, Simlicity, Self-confidence: An Interview with Jack Welch'*/HBR September - October 1989, pp. 113.

40. Vroom, Victor H. - 'Work and Motivation'/New York: Wiely, 1964.

41. Winn, A. - *'Training in Administration and Human Relation'*/Personnel, September 1953, pp. 139.

TECHNICAL PRESENTATION SKILL: A KEY TO PROFESSIONAL GROWTH AND DEVELOPMENT

CHAPTER 13

INTRODUCTION

One of the dictionary definitions of presentation covers the specialized sense generally used in the industrial, governmental, professional and business world; namely: 'a presentation is a specialized form of communication generally supported with visual aid'. However, one of the generic definitions of presentation "something set forth for the attention of the mind'[5], may be closely related to the subject.

We all know that some of us can prepare high quality written material but are unable to cope with the requisites of the real-time personnel communication demanded by technical presentations. On the other hand some individuals may be able to communicate easily and effectively with a few people on a face-to-face basis but feel nervous when asked to speak in front of a large group. However, modern professionals including Scientists, Engineers, Teachers, Managers and others are often confronted with the task of presenting a technical proposal, describing a scientific innovation, outlining a management or financial plan etc. need mastering in not only written communication but also in effective communication with a large audience as H.I. Phillips puts it "oratory-the art of making deep noises from the chest sounds like important messages from the brain". In this era of advancing technology in computer graphics, video, electronic publishing, and telecommunication it has become relatively easy to prepare and give presentation in an effective manner as its execution has been, to a large extent, simplified and enhanced by evolving technology. However it must be kept in mind that inspite of availability of evolving technology, there are other considerations such as, planning, content integrity, audience consideration, delivery techniques, etc. that remain essential factors in achieving success.

In planning a technical presentation, the most important consideration is the audience to whom a particular message is to be communicated. The presenter needs to know about the peculiarity of the audience, their size and then should tailor the presentation accordingly.

The purpose of this chapter is to provide some guidelines for preparing and delivering a better technical presentation.

IMPORTANCE OF PRESENTATIONS

Presentations can be an effective tool for setting an idea, project, product, or service, or explaining a problem or proposing a solution etc. These are in fact the backbone of interdisciplinary communication among various technical professionals with the intent of aiding or influencing decision-making. There are two important features of presentation, namely:

* The presence of written material, graphic material, or other audio-visual aid; and

* The pervasive effort to secure a response (often predetermined) from the audience.

The other importance of presentations lies in the fact that these are the mark of a true professional and act as bench marks of all true professions. In a true profession i.e. accountant, physicist, engineer, technologist, medical, legal or teaching etc. the obligation to communicate in the form of a presentation is a chief common characteristic. In other words, what one knows and what one can do has to be implemented by one's ability to communicate by means of effective written or oral communication. He is also expected to know in advance all the steps he has to take to ensure excellence and improved response.

Successful presentations are an avenue for advancement for an individual or an enterprise. One excellent presentation may lead to a significant decision, increase company's business or help to win a promotion. Mastering of presentation is in fact a significant part of one's professional growth.

IMPORTANT PRE-REQUISITES OF PRESENTATION

Defining the Objective

Before making the presentation, the first step is to figure out why the presentation is being made i.e. it must have a clear objective. Without a clear objective, the message will be muddled and the opportunity will be lost. Therefore presentation should never be abused. The presenter must know before hand his objective to make his point. He should ask himself questions such as:

* What do I want to achieve from the presentation?
* Why I am making the presentation?
* How best I can achieve my objective(s)?

Remember, knowing the clear and unambiguous objective is the foundation for purpose, clarity, direction and depth of the presentation.

Defining the Audience

It is important to know as much as practically possible about the audience and get as much information as you can about them. The presenter should try to find the answers to questions such as:

* What do the audience want from the presentation?
* What are the audience interests and attitudes?
* What is their level of apprehensions about the subject?
* What are their specific characteristics i.e. likes & dislikes, etc.?

Defining the Approach

The presenter should consider having such an approach that makes it easy for the audience to get the message being presented. The approach should reflect what's on the audience's minds and it must be clear, understandable and satisfying to the audience. In defining the best approach, the answers to the questions such as the following should be secured.

* Are the needs, interests and doubts of the audience considered and how they relate to the objective of the presentation?

* Is the conceptual approach that best leads to the objective of the presentation?

* Has the message got a focus?

* Is the environment friendly and has the necessary comfort and rapport

between the presenter and audience been developed?

Developing the Presentation

Think and Plan of the presentation being made up of three major integral elements, the introduction, body and conclusion i.e. the opening, body and closing.

Opening needs to be developed to support the objective and the approach of the presentation, be most interesting, exciting and must be pointed towards grabbing the audience's attention. It should be brief (less than 30 seconds). In this context it is most appropriate to quote Milo Frank's text which was used by a doctor speaker as an opening of the speech on preventive medicine.

"How would you like to die young at a very old age? Preventive medicine is the answer. Do you know that a heart attack is just your heart getting angry with you? You can keep that from happening by treating your heart well and keeping it happy. All you have to do is exercise regularly, not smoke, avoid fatty foods, and give yourself a totally relaxed day at least once a week. Do these simple things and your heart won't get angry with you. I want you to stay healthy, so don't just come to me when you're sick."[6]

If the above text is read out loud, it will not take more than 30 seconds. Such an opening would not only grab the attention of the audience but also present to them the core of the message. The opening is a very important factor of a successful presentation, therefore, it requires a good deal of effort, but it definitely, pays dividends.

The body of the speech or presentation, likewise the opening, should be developed in such a manner that it keeps the audience's attention intact once caught by the opening. The body needs to persuade, inform, inspire and also in some events entertain to keep the audience's attention and interest in the presentation. The body does not have to be very long but must need to be accomplished in minimum time as to convey an important message you don't need a lot of words. However, in preparing a body, the presenter must be sure about his knowledge of the subject and that all facts are straight and the structure incorporates the approach and the objectives of the presentation. The body can be built on three pillars, namely: one that explains, the second that reinforces, and the third that proves the main point. The other method can be firstly start out with a compelling point, secondly explain it and thirdly convince the audience to act. Whatever the method used to develop the body, the vital factor is not to lose site of the objective and approach, identified earlier.

The closing is equally important as it can reinforce what has already been said by summarizing the main points in few short memorable sentences. A key to a closing session is to know exactly what you want from the audience and to inspire them by leaving them with a strong statement of your message. In this context Lord Mancroft's words may be appropriate to quote: "A speech is like a love affair; any fool can start one, but to end it requires considerable skill".

DELIVERING THE PRESENTATION

All real professionals such as Teachers, Engineers, Scientists, Doctors etc. need to give a presentation in some form or another which requires careful planning, organization, construction and methodology. Almost everyone amongst these can carry on a conversation, technical discussion in a one-on-one situation or with a small information group, but when this discussion is changed to technical presentation to say 20-30 people only very few can effectively stand up and take up the challenge to give a presentation. The reason for this is not due to lack of expertise, but simply fear of public speaking. According to Butrand Russel, most people would rather die than deliver a speech. But as Elbert Hubbard puts it: "The greatest mistake you can make in life is to be continually fearing you will make one". A key to diminish this fear is a thorough preparation as Dale Carneige puts it: "When you are afraid, keep your mind on what you have to do. And if you have been thoroughly prepared, you will not be afraid".

Whilst delivering the presentation remember that your movements, gestures, posture, and voice etc. should attract your audience to your message rather than distract them. Use the most appropriate words, a variety of facial expressions, and vary your vocal tones. Unfortunately we develop vocal habits which are often injected into the speech or presentation without we being aware. Many speakers puntuate their presentation with "OK", "right", "you know", "uh", etc. but later if you point out, they will not believe that they were using the vocal faults during presentations. As a result of the vocal tones, the audience's ability to concentrate on the real message is lost. Every effort should be made to let such vocal additives disappear from the delivery of the presentation.

Voice plays a dominating role in the delivering of a presentation. By changing pace, intensity and pitch, the speaker can show points of emphasis on the audience. The length of a pause can be effective, if the speaker wishes to indicate the importance of the topic covered or alert the audience to the information that is about to be given. However, if pauses are continually used, effectiveness will be dulled or lost and the interest of the audience will be diminished. Gestures can also be effective in a presentation but only if these fit the presentation. It should be used to reinforce the point being made and the speaker must need to be conscious of inappropriate gestures which will result in the loss of attention of the audience who may be wondering what the speaker meant. Some of the gestures are unconscious signs of nervousness which are irritating mannerisms and must be avoided.

Research has shown that multiple sensory inputs aid to remember things best. There is also an old saying: "What I hear, I forget, what I see, I may remember, what I do, I understand". However there are certain ground rules that need to be followed such as:

* The aid must be pertinent.

* The aid must be meant to assist both the audience and the speaker.

* The visual aid material must have characteristics such as pertinence, simplicity, and clarity.

* The visual aids must be related to the point.

* The visual aids must be compatible in numbers with the time available.

* The visual aids must help the speaker in making his point, and not to be used as a replacement for the speaker nor a reiteration of his words.

The organization and structure of the presentation i.e. the opening, the body and the closing should be systematically delivered. Remember that 'the opening' must provide a bridge for the audience, the body must make the audience understand what the speaker is looking for and that he is willing to accept criticism; whilst the closing provides the speaker with a bridge from the body of talk to the concluding remarks focusing on the attention of the audience. (See Fig. 13.1 for Presentation Fundamentals).

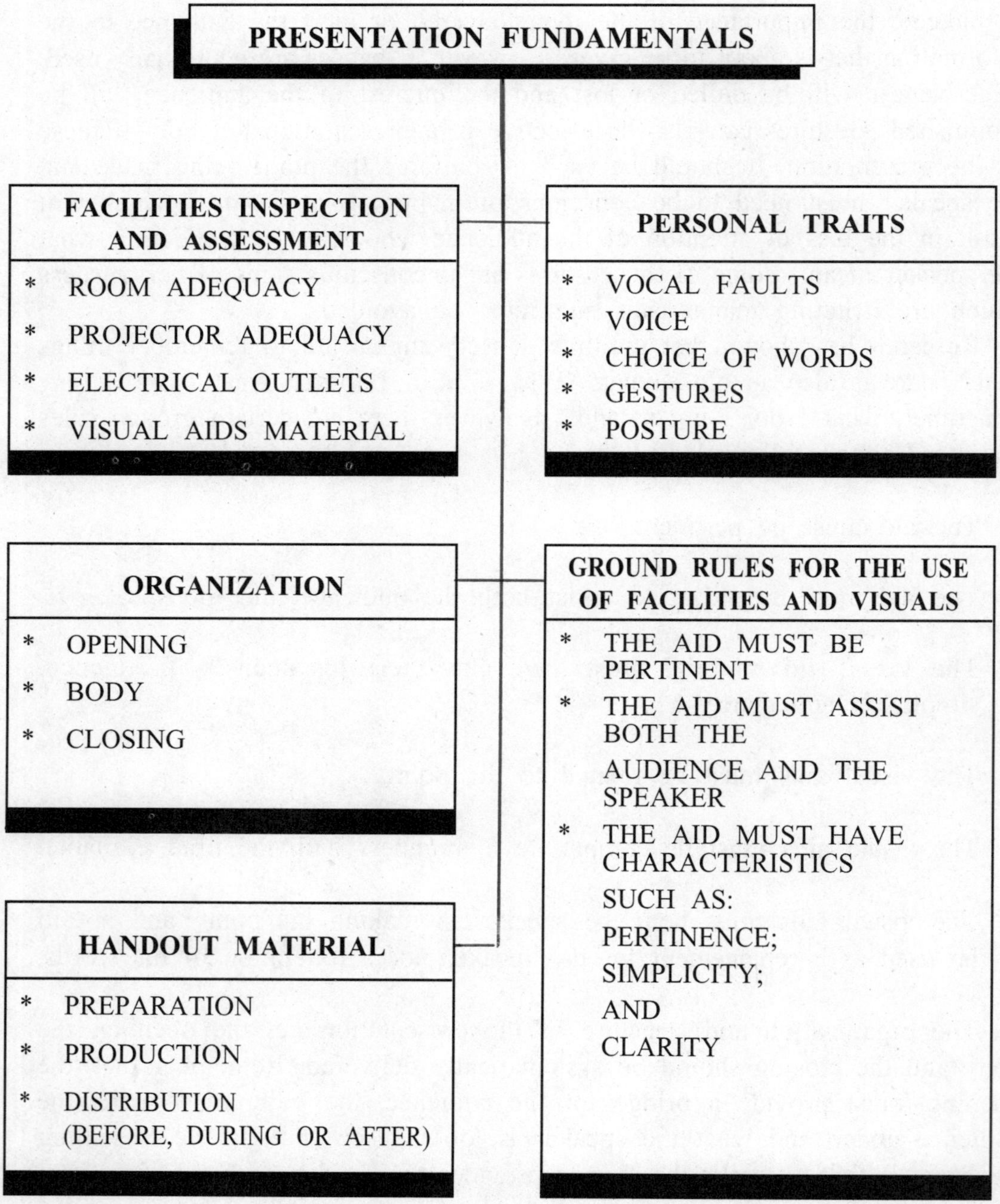

FIG. 13.1 : SOME PRESENTATION FUNDAMENTALS

PRESENTATION AND SPEECH DISTINGUISHED

A speaker may address an audience in the form of a speech, a lecture, or a presentation. A speech, by and large, is made for the purpose of expressing ones opening, or attempting to sway the opinions of others. The important features of an effective speech include: Succintness, Voice modulation and personal appeal. A presentation is a speech supported by visual aids. An oral presentation is usually identified as information presented by one or more individuals by way of a combination of speeches, visual aids or other support. We may say, that a speech becomes a presentation if visual aid is used to explain particular aspects of the speech. A lecture usually is concerned with education and training when the audience, by and large, respond to the discipline established by the speaker i.e., Note taking and/or reference to handouts etc.

For the speaker to be effective it is vital that he makes a clear distinction between a lecture, a speech, and a presentation. This importance is highlighted by Calvin R. Gould in his paper on "Anatomy of a Presentation" published in IEEE Trans. Eng. Writing Speech, Vol. EWS-13, PP 17-24 (May 1970) in these words:

"The distinction is important to make because a presentation requires so much more support than a speech. Perhaps a major reason for some poor presentations is that the presenter thought of his presentation as a speech and he planned it independent of any outside support; then when he realized he needed help it was too late for that help to be effective."

Calvin R. Gould Further states:

"Another important reason for the distinction is the trauma caused by the term "speech". Many good presentations have been made by nontrained speakers. The value of a presentation is measured by its content more than by its showmanship, and its content is related to the knowledge and experience of the presenter on the subject he is presenting. If he looks upon his task as a conversation between him and his associates on the subject of his speciality, he will have a higher confidence level than if he thought of it as a speech before a large and strange audience."

In a presentation, two or more members of a team may speak in sequence on specific topics related to the presentation subject. A well delivered presentation is a smooth interplay between presenter and audience and can be an enjoyable magic moment in which information and ideas are communicated and uplifting experience for both is gained.

SOME BASIC PRESCRIPTIONS FOR A SPEECH

A good speech is well worth the effort and it takes a lot of practice. Anyone who is able and willing to put forth that effort can master the art and can become a good speaker. Some of the basic recipes for a speech include: 'Planning ahead'; 'logic of a speech'; and 'organizing a speech'.

Planning Ahead

Planning ahead and being prepared is a key which breeds confidence and opens the door for the speaker to poise for guide response when asked to speak on a very short notice. To plan ahead, the following guidelines should be followed.

— Highlight the key points of the speech that needs to be made to the audience.

— By using the careful logic, plan your talk as if you are planning a technical project.

— Brainstorm yourself and ask all the relevant questions you may think of and seek answers. Fit the questions and answers together in an orderly sequence for an effective delivery.

— Consider all the possible questions you may think that the audience may ask and formulate the best responses you can to satisfy them.

— Prepare diagrams, handouts or other support material as work tools or report elements.

— Discuss the speech substance whenever possible with colleagues or peers and make notes of any beneficial feedback.

— Review and simplify support material so that it can best serve as visual aids to a speech.

— Try out your rationale on an interested colleague and readjust your strategy and tactics based on his feedback.

Logic of a Speech

By and large, the purpose for a speech is threefold, i.e. to interest, to inform, and to steer to action. The talks can be of three types, i.e. the self contained speech; the technical society talk; and the technical presentation. However these types of talks differ a great deal in their emphasis on data and interpretation.

Regardless of types of talk or the occasion, your first task as a speaker should be to orient your audience before driving them into the nitty-grity of the speciality of the subject. In this respect questions such as the following should be posed and appropriate answers secured.

— Why should we make this product? or why do we do this work?
— Where does it fit into the overall activity?
— How does it affect the audience?
— Why this (speech) is preferable to other alternatives?

Organizing a Speech

A speech should be organized by using guidelines for developing the presentation as discussed earlier. However speakers differ in their methods of organizing a speech. Some prefer a speech which is written out in full, whilst other simply prefer outlined details i.e. on note cards.

HOW TO IMPROVE YOUR SPEECH OR TECHNICAL PRESENTATION SKILL

The formal speech training of the person presenting the information has a great bearing on the delivery of a technical presentation (which can be either dry or dramatically dynamic). Some of us may have a natural flare for public speaking, whilst others may be timid in such situations. However, the experience has shown that in either case, with training, you can be a more effective speaker.

Some Keys for Improving your Speech

Many witnesses on the subject of effective speaking have suggested many traits such as:

— Persuasiveness, forcefulness, directness and pleasantness.
— Making the data and information as clear and interesting as possible.
— Developing a keen mental attitude and speech outline.
— Knowing and understanding on the audience as much as possible.
— Enunciating speech words clearly.
— Developing the subject matter as close to perfection as possible.

How of Improving a Speech

It is not sufficient for the speaker to motivate himself but he must also motivate his audience. He must develop in himself the clinical approach to creative speech which will contribute considerably in improving his speech skills. It will make him a sought-after speaker, enable him to enjoy delivering a presentation, improve his poise and self confidence, and give him a new stature with his colleagues and peers.

Some researchers have proved that the probability of effectively delivering a creative and interesting presentation will be greatly enhanced if the following five steps are followed by the speaker:-

i. The speaker must show a desire to inform and interest his audience.

ii. The speaker should be consciously aware of himself but not self-conscious.

iii. The speaker should develop the clinical approach to creative speech, and must motivate himself and his audience.

iv. The speaker should project his personality and must allow his audience to be aware of his interest for the subject.

v. The speaker must desire to be of a service and value to his employer and his audience.

Public Speaking Panic and How to Cure It

Fear of public speaking and nervousness is a natural phenomenon but it can also be a blessing as with the rush of adrenaline, you could be a passionate speaker. It's up to an individual speaker to harness that energy by turning panic into power so that it works for him and not against him. There could be numerous causes for public speaking panic and some of these include:-

— Testing your fear against reality: 'What if' scenarios only stemmed from imaginary fear and not out of reality. If a speaker knows that he can live with "What if I make a mistake", he would feel more positive about public speaking.

— Reassuring yourself: Always think positively and anticipate a happy outcome as negative thought could sabotage your efforts and sap your energy.

— Watching your poise and body language: Research has shown that a speaker's body language can carry more weight than his words. Gestures, mannerisms and tone of voices play an important role to secure responses from an audience.

— Asking for feedback: Seek feedback by asking colleagues whom you trust to criticize your speech/presentation and learn lessons to improve the next presentation.

Role of Visual Aids in a Presentation

Illustrations by pictures, charts and line graphs play a great role as a communication tools. The simple equation often cited is:

"1 Picture = 1000 words" (or one picture is worth a thousand words)

Research psychologists have proved that over 80% impressions comes through the eyes and around 10% through the ears and the remaining through other senses. Therefore, the showing of a visual is important as the human mind, through preconception and preattention perception, comprehends a visual representation much faster than words and also retains it far longer.

The type of visuals may include: Boards, Overhead projector, Slides, flip charts, cards, computer display, posters, picture/photographs, film slides, film strips, video, motion pictures, and multi-media etc. Currently numerous alternative technologies are available to display computer generated graphics which can be used to stimulate interest and faster understanding in technical presentation and public speaking.

The selection of a particular type of visuals depends on several factors such as: nature of the subject and desired quality level, audience type and size, production/presentation flexibility and cost, etc.

HUMOR AND ELOQUENCE CAN IMPROVE A TECHNICAL PRESENTATION

In a technical presentation, by and large, information exchanged is dry, tedious or loving but it is important to communicate for effective results. Humor certainly helps in attracting the attention of the intended audience and keeping their interest intact with the presentation. Furthermore humor can make technical information more memorable by offering an audience a psychological advantage and making them more receptive to the presented information. Humor can lighten the tone of a presentation by applying wit to less essential areas while having preserved the integrity of transmitting the technical information. Therefore, humor must be used judiciously to maintain the professionalism and must not be applied to important areas to avoid observing necessary data.

Some people are humorous without any great effort, whilst others have to study and practice to learn the art of using humor effectively.

Eloquence likewise can improve a presentation. However, before we proceed further to explain how, it is important to understand 'what is eloquence?'. The generic definition of eloquence is "speech that steers the feelings" - "a flow of speech with grace and force" - "discourse marked by force and persuasiveness; also: the art or power of using such discourse". The above definition presents three factors i.e. speaker's feelings, speaker's words and audience's feelings.

The speaker can show his feelings by using such phrases: "I am enthusiastic", "I am concerned". Also by using the confession and stressing the achievement themes, using the appeal, and bringing testimony the speaker can transmit his feeling to the audience. The speaker should also consider the wants and discuss them with the audience by recognizing a build up of their self-esteem. Facility with words, shapes eloquence a great deal and show strong feelings. The use of three word combinations, three phrase combinations, and words of opposite meaning can enhance eloquence. For example pushing, eager, selfish; confusing, meaningless, bewildering; stingy, cheap, niggardly are series of three words which can add emphasis. Likewise a combination of three phrases add rhythm, i.e. to cultivate wisdom one has to 'recognize it' - 'study it' - and 'put what he has learnt to practice'.

Edward J Hegarty makes a suggestion to use eloquence to the best advantage of the speaker in the following words:

"Start your speech with an eloquent unit that indicates you are serious about this cause. Lift listeners up on your cloud. Then bring them back to reality with facts and figures. Now take them for the second ride into the wild, blue yonder. Next soothe them with your factual material. When you have them relaxed, lift them again, hold them up a short time, then bring them down. Try to finish with your most eloquent unit. Make it the ask for action. This outline gives you a pattern that is sure fire"[12].

From the outset it is evident that eloquence can improve a technical presentation (or a speech) as it attracts attention, arouses interest, and also triggers action.

Both Humor and Eloquence assures a good impression which is a prime objective of a speaker. It gives a good start which in turn builds anticipation and rapport, it inspires confidence in the speaker in the handling of material, and also gives a good ending which in turn gives the impression that the listeners take with them.

CONCLUDING REMARKS

Effective oral and written presentations are not only the mark of a true professional but also an avenue of advancement. One principal characteristic that is common with members of teaching, medical, legal, engineering, and other professions is the obligation to communicate in this special way. We all know that technical presentations are a vital part of almost every phase of the governmental, academic, and industrial sectors.

The importance of technical presentations is further enhanced due to advancing technology in the fields of video, multi-media telecommunication, electronic publishing and computer graphics. Furthermore, due to changing audience interests, socio cultural composition and technological background, adoption of a more global perspective has been necessitated. However, an effective technical presentation must need to be tailored to the condition and requirements of a particular application, by considering variables such as: Nature and size of the audience; facilitates and location; types and quality of visuals; amount of time available; amount of money available to execute the presentation; types and quality of information and data available to be collated, etc.

For making presentations that command attention you need confidence which you will get only by being fully prepared. This implies that logical planning and adequate preparations are absolute requisites for effective presentations. Planning is the cornerstone of preparation and it demands tasks such as: determining the purpose, analyzing the audience, collating and analysing the information and data; and formulating an outline of the presentation. Remember the arch enemy of a good presentation is lack of adequate preparation.

A good delivery is also an absolute requisite for the effective presentations. If delivery is poor, a good presentation may be killed or not be effectively received even if it consists of the best conceived idea and the most profound work. Good delivery demands repeated rehearsal and thorough practice, subtle changes in expression and pace could be developed that can make a presentation dynamic.

Analyzing feedback and dealing with it properly is another important requisite of the effective presentation. By and large, questions from the audience do prompt, which the presenter should think out in advance and try to secure appropriate answers to avoid any awkward moments. Explanation should be provided for the benefit of the audience and to help reinforce and sustain interest.

We may conclude this discussion by emphasizing that the presenter's success as a professional may depend not only on his creative and intricate abilities but also on his capabilities of expressing his ideas in a most creative manner.

REFERENCES AND RECOMMENDED READINGS

1. Berger, Peter L., and Thomas Luckman. - 'The Social Communication of Reality'/Garden City, N.Y. Doubliding, 1966.

2. Bettinghous, Ervin P. - 'Persuasive Communication'/New York: Holt, Rinchart and Winston, 1966.

3. Coulter, C. - 'Winning Words: A New Approach to Developing Effective Speaking skills'/ Boston,, MA: CPI, 1982.
4. Demer, L.J. and L.H. Fentnor - *'Multiple image presentation of technical papers - the concept'*/IEEE Transactions Vol. EWS-13, May 1970 pp. 2-8.
5. Fearing, B.E., and F.M. Sawer - *'Speech for technical communication: A bibliography'/* IEEE Transactions,' Vol. pc-23, No. 1, March 1980 pp. 53-60.
6. Frank, M.O. - 'How to get your point across in 30 seconds, or less'/New York: Simon and Schuster, 1986.
7. Gagne, R.M. - 'Condition of Learning'/New York: Holt, Reinchard, and Winston, 2nd ed. 1970.
8. Garn, Roy - 'The Magic Power of Emotional Appea'/New Jersey: Englewood Cliffs, Prentice - Hall, 1960.
9. Hall Edward T. - 'The Hidden Dimension'/New York: Douhliday, 1966.
10. Hall Edward T. - 'The Silent Language'/New York: Douhliday, 1959.
11. Haney, William V. - 'Communication and Interpersonal Relations'/Homawood, IL: R.D. Irwin, 1979.
12. Hegarty, E.J. - 'Humor and Eloquence in Public Speaking'/Wellingborough: A Thomas Co., UK, 1976.
13. Holcombe, M. and J. Csiein - 'Presentation for Decision Makers'/Belmont, CA: Lifetime Learning, 1983.
14. Hollingsworth, H.L. - 'The Psychology of the Audience'/New York: MacMillan, 1935.
15. Howell, W - 'Presentation speaking for business and the professions'/New York: Harper and Row, 1971.
16. Humes, James - 'Roles Speakers Play'/New York: Harper and Row; 1976.
17. Kemp, J. and D. Dayton - *'Planning and Producing Instructional Media'/*San Francisco: Harper & Row, 1985, pp. 122-123.
18. Lang Kurt, and Cladys E. Lang - 'Collective Dynamics'/New York: Crowell, 1961.
19. Linton, Ralph - 'The Study of Men' - New York: Appleton Century, 1936.
20. Lockheed Missiles and Space Co. - 'Effective Chart and Slide Presentation'/California: Sunnyvale, 1963.
21. Lovey, G.M. - 'Briefing and Conference Techniques'/New York: McGraw Hill Book Co., 1959.
22. Martin, James G. - 'The Tolerant Personality'/Detroit: Wayne State University Press, 1964.
23. Membert, W.A. - 'Presenting Technical Ideas'/New York: John Wiley and Sons, 1968.

24. Membert, W.A. - 'Effective Presentation - A short course for professionals'/New York: John Wiley and Sons, 1976.

25. Morrisey, G. - 'Effective Business and Technical Presentation'/Reading, MA: Addison-Wesley, 1975.

26. Olbricht, Thomas H. - 'Informative Speaking'/IL: Scott Foreman, 1968.

27. Prasad, S. - *'Effective Presentation A Bibliography'*/IEEE Transactions on Professional Communication 30, 1, 1987, pp. 39-40.

28. Ross, R. - 'Speech Communication'/Englewood Cliffs, NJ: Prentice Hall, 1977, pp. 287.

29. Sandfold, W.P. and W.H. Yeager - 'Effective Business Speech'/New York: McGraw-Hill Book Co. Inc, 1960.

30. Skopec, Eric W. - 'Business and Professional Speaking'/Englewood Cliffs, N.J.: Prentice-Hall, 1983.

31. Smith T. - 'Making Successful Presentations'/New York: John Wiley and Sons, 1984.

32. Stuwmueller, E.K. - 'Address by International President'/Palo Alto, CA: Conference, Distinct Four Toastmasters, Nov. 1979.

33. Tucker, Charles O. - *'An Applications of Programmed Learning to Informative Speech'*/ Speech Monographs 1964: 31 pp. 142-152.

34. Weaver, Carl H. - 'Human Listening'/Indianapolis, IN: Bobbs-Merrill, 1972.

35. Weiss, H. and J.B. McGrath - Jr. 'Technically Speaking'/New York: McGraw-Hill Book Co., Inc., 1963.

36. Wilcox, Roger P. - 'Oral Reporting in Business and Industry'/Englewood Cliffs, NJ: Prentice Hall, 1967.

A CONCEPTUAL APPROACH TO JOB EVALUATION

CHAPTER 14

INTRODUCTION

Job is a regular assignment to an individual employee to discharge his or her duties and responsibilities by the utilization of knowledge and skills, etc.. The process of job evaluation starts from job analysis and ends with the classification of the job according to its worth.

Money is one of the most important prequisites to sound industrial relations. Therefore, the primary objective of a pay administration program is that each employee should be equitably compensated, for the services rendered by him to the enterprise because of the type and nature of the job and its effectiveness. These factors are very closely related to 'Job evaluation' and the performance appraisal.

Job evaluation is a systematic procedure of determining the relative worth of jobs having aims at measuring the value of job description (what a job actually is) and job specification (what a job should be).

A clear distinction between job evaluation and performance appraisal must need to be clearly understood. 'Job evaluation' is concerned with the determination of worth of different jobs, whereas 'performance appraisal' refers to the task of rating or assessing the individual performance and abilities at work.

JOB EVALUATION DEFINED

Job evaluation is the process of comparing jobs with a job in terms of pay that a worker should receive for performing the given task. In other words it is a technique which aids in establishing a base rate of jobs. Most common definitions of this term are as follows:

"The procedure to determine the relative values of the job in a plant and to determine the basic wages for that job."

"A method which helps to establish a justified rank order of jobs as a whole, being a foundation for the setting of wages."

"The process of analysis and assessment of jobs to ascertain reliably their relative worth using the assumptions as a basis for a balanced wage/salary structure."

"An attempt to determine and compare the demands which the normal performance of particular jobs make on normal workers, without taking into account the individual abilities of performance of the workers concerned. It rates the job and not the rank".

"A measurement technique which helps to support the organization with payment by time and is a rational device to establish and control pay, differential and hierarchy."

The present view of job evaluation is that it is used to deal with problems of comparative equity in wage/salary determination mainly, though not exclusively, at the level of individual plant or firm and does not contribute much for hierarchy or differentials.

OBJECTIVES OF JOB EVALUATION

There are numerous objectives of job evaluation. Some major ones include as follows:

* To estimate the correct wages for the work performed and to provide a base from which individual performance may be measured, if so desired.

* To provide a means to reduce wages imbalance by establishing correct wage differentials for all jobs within the production unit which will also have parity with other competitive ones.

* To help in the standardization and classification of authority, responsibility and promotion.

* To resolve wage disputes by placing wage negotiation on a sounder and impersonal basis.

* to bring a new job in line with the job previously established.

* To help determine job specifications for a job for new employment, and also make sure employees occupying various jobs, satisfy the specification.

BRIEF HISTORY OF JOB EVALUATION

Job evaluation has been in existence informally in the industries since the middle ages. However the first formal attempt of job evaluation was made by the US civil service commission in the year 1871. In the modern concept the origin of formal job evaluation originated in the years 1909 & 1910. In 1909, the civil service commission of Chicago developed a pioneering plan for governmental employees. In 1909-10, Common Walth Edison Company, under the direction of Griffinghan, developed a Job evaluation Program for an industrial situation. In 1924, Merrill R. Lott introduced a method of formal job evaluation which is the fore-runner of the point system used today. During the thirties wage negotiations were made in many industrialized countries through collective bargaining, and forced wage level upwards thus impeding establishment of a defensible system of wage determination which could serve as a basis for collective bargaining.

During the Second World War, the need for job evaluation was greatly felt, partly because as a means to justifying wage increase under the statute and partly because many new occupations were originated as a result of changes in or introduction of new production methods.

During the 1940s and the beginning of the 1950s, in the USA, the pressure for development of job evaluation was mounted to meet the legislation i.e. the wage and salary stabilization law of 1942 and the Defense Production Act of 1950. Accordingly, under an approved job evaluation plan, adjustment of inequalities of wage or salary and the granting of normal seniority and merit increases were permitted.

PROCESS OF JOB EVALUATION

In the modern industries the primary objective of a wage and salary administration program is that each employee should be equitably compensated for the services rendered by him (or her) to the enterprise according to the nature of the job, type of the job and effectiveness of the job. These factors being closely related to the job evaluations and performance appraisal have given rise to their importance. Some why's of job evaluation are shown in Fig. 14.1. The principles on which job evaluation is based are shown in Fig. 14.2, Fig. 14.3 shows the process of job evaluation as a flow of sequential events starting from a fact finding survey and progressing through job analysis, job description, job specification, job rating, structuring of wage and

SOME MERITS OF JOB EVALUATION

Job evaluation is a valuable technique by which a consistent and rational wage and salary structure can be evolved	Job evaluation helps in bringing or maintaining harmonious relations between labor and management, since it tends to eliminate wage inequalities
Because of increasing automation it has become unrealistic to pay workers on the basis of their output, so job evaluation will be of much use in fixing the realistic wage structure	Job evaluation provides a rating for the job and not for the rank. Many workers work together on same, similar or technically independent jobs. Job evaluation helps to define the job and fix wages accordingly.
Since job differentials should not be based on skill differences alone, job evaluation takes into account various other factors (e.g. working conditions, risks) in determining the worth of jobs	Job evaluation helps in keeping down the costs of recruitment and selection of workers. Job evaluation involves job analysis and appraisal which help in objective selection by matching the qualifications with job requirements.
Through job evaluation the process of determining the wage deferentials for dirrerent jobs becomes standardised	In a modern dynamic economy it is necessary to arrange for continuous job evaluation for translating needs into fiscal terms thus, facilitating budget preparation
Job evaluation provides a basis for orientation and in-service training programs	Job evaluation provides a systematic method of picturing the policies and opportunities relationship which is essential for orderly staff development, promotion and placement procedure

FIG. 14.1 : SOME WHY'S OF JOB EVALUATION

SOME PRINCIPLES OF JOB EVALUATION

Rate the job, not the person as job requirements are definite and fixed. The person selected may have some plus or minus points as regards to job, therefore, wages/salaries should be fixed accordingly

The success of job rating is dependant totally upon the uniformity of understanding with the definition assigned to each element, and also on the consistency in the selection process of the degrees of those elements

While doing rating the elements selected should cover the requirements of jobs, and the elements should be kept to a minimum

The job rating plan should be simple and unambiguous so that it could be easily understood by supervisors or workers

Supervisors must be asked to participate in the formulation of the rating plan

Job rating plan should be free from any bias or favoritism

While discussing with supervisors and workers consider the job related points only and not the monetary aspects of the rating plan

Too many occupational wage rates should not be established

FIG. 14.2 : SOME PRINCIPLES OF JOB EVALUATION

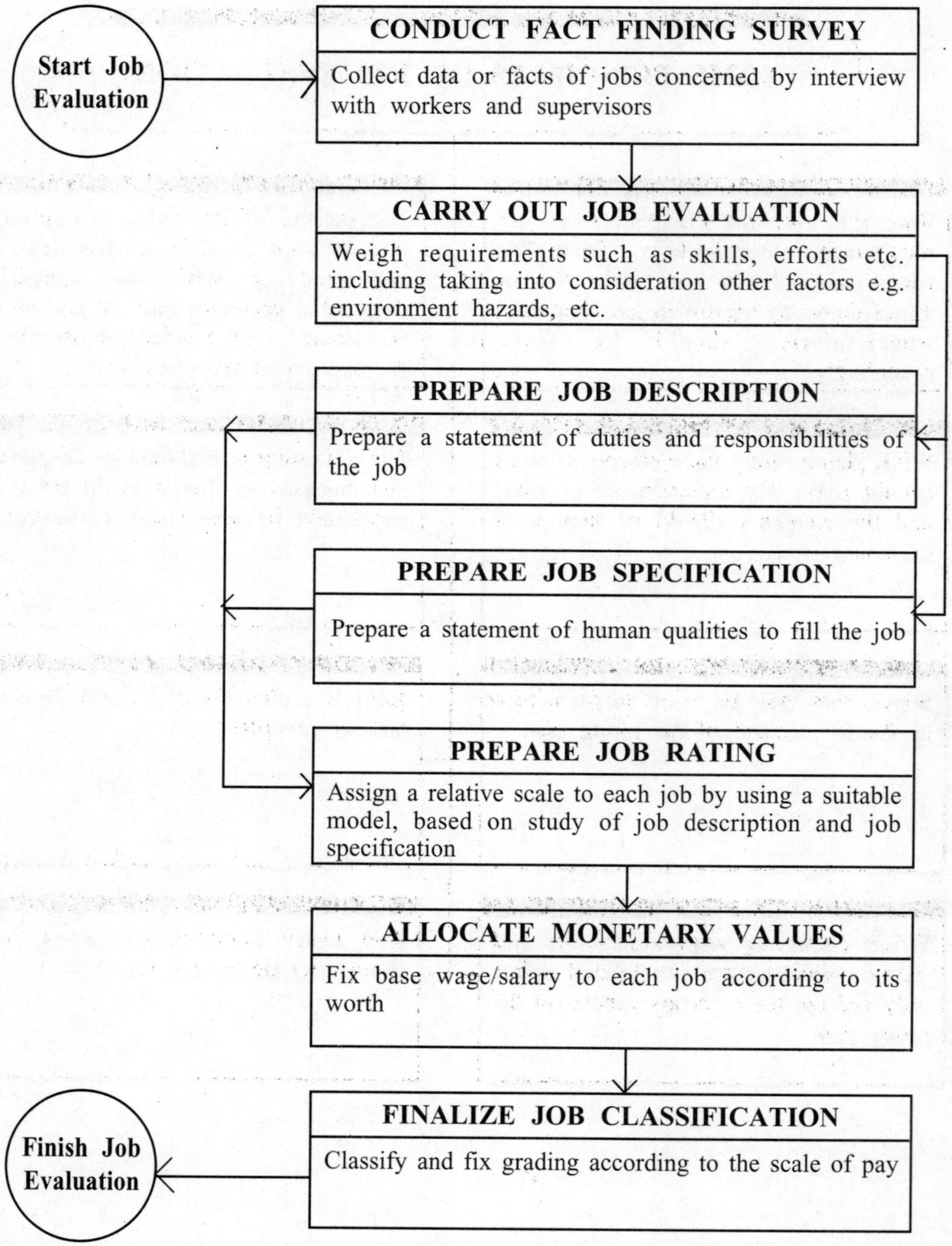

FIG. 14.3 : JOB EVALUATION PROCESS

salary and finally terminating at the fixation of job classification and wage/salary payments to individuals.

The detailed steps required for job evaluation are shown in Fig. 14.4. However, for success of job evaluation there are many pre-requisites such as the following:

* Co-operation of employees.
* Manager involvement, support and commitment.
* Intellectual honesty at all levels.
* Technical ability of specialist and his acceptability by employees (in line functions).
* Dissemination of knowledge of job evaluation to all parties involved in the process.
* Good administration and follow up.

DEFINITIONS OF TERMS RELATED TO JOB EVALUATION PROCESS

Job Analysis

It is a process of gathering information and carefully studying the activities of an employee on a particular job to obtain different operations and other elements involved, which are helpful for job description, and job specification. It also includes presenting the results in a written report by setting procedures to discover the facts about each job requirement, personal qualities for satisfactory working, and determination of existing hazards which are helpful for avoiding accidents. Job analysis is the term used to describe a process which involves the analysis of a job into its component tasks (or part) to provide the data required for various purposes, such as: recruitment, establishing training needs of the incumbent, pay structuring, improving job methods and safety, management development and, of course, developing organizations. By and large, job analysis is applicable for employees excluding management and professional expertise. The reason for this common belief

* STEPS REQUIRED FOR JOB EVALUATION

STEP 01	Most suitable method or technique must be selected
STEP 02	First select the major characteristics, then minor ones etc.
STEP 03	Proper information should be given to all concerned, i.e. workers, formen, etc.
STEP 04	Build definitions and their measuring scale, for comparison purposes
STEP 05	Prepare job rating questionnaires, and collect initial description
STEP 06	Sort out initial descriptions and establish grades or classes
STEP 07	Identify and evaluate the key jobs selected
STEP 08	Evaluate the remaining jobs and award the job titles to them
STEP 09	What jobs? Make sure that representation of workers is considered
STEP 10	For key jobs only, make inter company survey, but try to find at least one per grade
STEP 11	Transfer the rating value in money values temporarily
STEP 12	Plot a scatter diagram, for the more key jobs and end job
STEP 13	Bargain on wage level
STEP 14	Decide the range limits and line of reference
STEP 15	Readjust all rates relative to the reference, put into working forms and finally fix all operational procedures

* Adapted from the suggestions made by Lytle, a renowned figure in job evaluation

FIG. 14.4 : STEPS REQUIRED FOR JOB EVALUATION

is that non managerial/non professional jobs generally involve a process which is more easily definable and suitable for the use of analytical methods. However, for managerial and professional staff, job analysis can pay dividends, among other things optimizing managerial performance through improved time management.

Job Description

It is an abstract of data received from the job analysis report. It outlines the information regarding the skills (or training requirements), knowledge, responsibility, authority, working conditions i.e. environment and inter-relationship involved in each job. It may also include, the type of persons which should be employed.

Under the framework described above, it is advisable that the job holder, with his (or her) benefit, of experience, write a job description setting out precisely what it entails by covering areas including but not limited to the following:

* The purpose/objectives of the job and its scope.

* The work activities performed in the job i.e. details duties/tasks/functions and whether operational, supervisory or managerial etc.

* The responsibilities for resources and policy decisions.

* The organization relationship i.e. position in the hierarchy & cross functional interfaces etc.

* The education, knowledge, skills, experience and training needed for the job.

Job Specification

It is the written statements about each job and qualifications of the person to perform the job successfully. On the basis of details of a job stated in the job specification, the capabilities and qualification necessary for performing the job are determined. It develops from information contained in job analysis and job description reports. It can be compared with the material specification. Material specification helps in the purchasing and procurement of material and likewise, job specification helps in the recruitment/selection of employees. Accordingly, job specification must provide a statement of the minimum acceptable standards that the potential employee should meet in performing the job satisfactorily.

METHODS OF JOB EVALUATION

Job evaluation involves the evaluation of various jobs in terms of certain factors such as: skill; effort and initiative; experience; working environments; supervision needs, and responsibility to be undertaken etc. To measure these factors, the clear and accurate job descriptions and specifications must be available to provide the necessary data for this purpose. In fact, there are no standard classification of factors to be considered under job evaluation, but in general some factors hold for most jobs and serve as indicators of what pay should be. These factors include as follows:-

* The more difficult the job, the more it is worth in fiscal terms.
* The more skill, education and responsibility required in a job, the more it is worth.
* The more scarce the labour or expertise supply and higher the demand, the more a job is worth.

Over the years several systems of job evaluation have been developed which take into account, directly or indirectly, the above mentioned factors. There are four main job evaluation schemes based on four different methods which are divided into two categories as follows:

(A) Non-Quantitative Methods

i. The Ranking or Job Comparison Method
ii. The Grading or Job Classification Method

N.B. This category covers the simple methods which apparently make no use of detailed job factors, but however they do affect the results. Under this category the job is treated as a whole and job descriptions rather than job specifications are often utilized.

(B) Quantitative Methods (or Analytical Methods)

iii. The Point Rating Method
iv. The Factor Comparison Method

Ranking Method

This is the simplest method as no effort is needed to break a job down into its, elements. The aim is to judge the job as a whole. In this method job descriptions are arranged in order of rank and according to the report of job analysis, by a committee of several executives which is to be constituted for this very purpose. Job descriptions are arranged in ascending order of importance beginning with the least important job (minimum requirements) to the most important job (maximum requirements). No specific factors are selected for consideration. However, whilst ranking the following facts should be kept in mind by each member of the committee.

* Knowledge, skill and experience needed.
* Responsibility required for the job.
* Level of supervision needed.
* complexity/difficulty in the work.
* Working conditions.
* Monotony of work.
* Any other special constraints imposed.

Each member of the committee prepares an estimate for each occasion when jobs are ranked. For example if committee members are four persons and the jobs are ranked on four occasions, the final ranking would be calculated on the basis of 16 different estimates.

This method is particularly suitable for use in small organizations to establish the relative worth of jobs. Ranking method is simple, inexpensive and expeditious and it is easily understood and easily administered. However, this method is not free from disadvantages and it has serious limitations, one of which is that it limits objective judgement in jobs ranking.

In addition, jobs may be ranked on the basis of incomplete information and without the benefit of well defined standards, serious error in ranking can occur. Arbitrary ranking resulting from this method may create differences in similar jobs which may be resented by the employer. Appraising each job as a whole (based on judgement only) does not allow any analysis or statistical interpolation and cannot be expected to give accurate measure of the worth.

The Grading or Job Classification Method

This method consists of the sorting of all jobs being evaluated into grades or classes which have been predetermined and arranged in order of importance. After grading the different jobs are fitted into the particular classification and the relative position can be determined. This method is considered to be an improvement over ranking method as in it a predetermined scale of values i.e. functions etc. is provided. These grade definitions are prepared by the evaluation committee who, having a clear picture of all jobs in the organization, goes through each job description and carefully weighs it in the light of certain factors, such as: skill required, experience, mental requirement, physical requirement, responsibility, and working conditions, etc. In this way the evaluation committee assigns each job to a particular grade or class for which different rate of a wage or salary is already fixed. Simple classification used in light industry is threefold i.e. unskilled, semi-skilled and skilled.

This method may be used in industries which have a relatively small range of jobs (typical of these are shown in Fig. 14.5) for which standard rates of remuneration can be fixed. This method has many merits such as the following:

* It is simple, inexpensive and can be used for calculating the worth of unlike jobs.

* It is very flexible and can be applied to a combination of clerical, manual and supervisory staff.

* It is easy to apply and not difficult to understand, even by workmen.

However, this method too is not free from disadvantages such as the following:

GRADE OF JOBS

GRADE 1	**POLICY MAKING**	The positions under this classification are those of the policy makers, i.e. President, Managing Director, Chief Executive, General Manager, etc.
GRADE 2	**ADMINISTRATION**	The positions under this group involve responsibilities of a large magnitude, i.e. Vice Presidents, Senior Managers Directors, etc.
GRADE 3	**EXECUTIVE**	The positions under this classification are those of departmental managers, i.e. Engineering Manager, Production Manager, O&M Manager, etc.
GRADE 4	**CREATIVE**	The positions under this classification are those of a creative character, i.e. Specialists, Advisors, etc.
GRADE 5	**ROUTINE**	The positions under this group call for ability to classify work and apply established procedure to its accomplishment, i.e. Supervisors, Foremen, etc.
GRADE 6	**SKILLED**	The positions under this classification call for acquisition of some skill of hands or mind through training or practice, i.e. Technicians, Draughtsmen, Secretaries etc.
GRADE 7	**UNSKILLED**	The positions under this group call for accuracy and dependability, i.e. Clerks, General Workers, etc.

FIG. 14.5: GRADING OF JOBS OF A TYPICAL MEDIUM INDUSTRIAL ENTERPRIZE

* It requires multiple system, for different types of jobs e.g. description of production jobs differs widely from those of office jobs.

* Its installation is not appropriate for big organizations.

* It requires job evaluation staff which must be highly competent and qualified.

* Plaçing of jobs in grades may be influenced by prevailing wage or salary rates.

* Due to an overlap in job specification, difficulties may arise in locating a job into a correct grade or class.

* Difficulties encountered whilst using this method of job evaluation may result in the development of other plans which are based upon the breaking of jobs into their components and evaluating them in terms of those components.

The Point Rating Method

This is the most widely used method of job evaluation used in most of the modern large scale industries. This method makes a comparison of the characteristics of a job with a set of standards or definitions and then assigns point values to a particular occupation, having common characteristics, in proportion to the degree of presence of the requirements and conditions measuring the worth of the job. For example, supposing that a job is given 100 point values, then other jobs will be compared with it in all aspects and they are given point values, which becomes the basis of job evaluation and fixation of the wage level appropriate for each job.

The point system is more analytical in approach. It deals with various job factors where a job factor is a specific requirement levied upon the job holder which he must contribute, assess or endure (e.g. skill, efforts, responsibility and working conditions). In a point system, four major job factors namely: skills, efforts, responsibility and job conditions are taken as a basis of point values and in some cases these factors are further sub-divided to arrive at more accurate results. These factors or points are then converted into money values.

A good deal of thought has to be given in choosing or designing the plan for point rating method. In designing the plan the following procedure should be adopted:

i. Make a study of all the jobs in the business and then determine, only those factors or characteristics that need to be used in measuring job worth, and define them properly.

ii. Determine the type of job to be evaluated.

iii. Determine the number of degrees or levels to be allocated to each factors and work out a suitable definition of each in a simple and unambiguous language.

iv. Assign weights or points to factors and degrees in proportion to their relative importance in a particular firm. In order to determine the number of points to be allocated to succeeding degrees of each factors it is necessary to extend the points assigned to the first degree in an arithmetic progression.

v. Select a certain number of key jobs (say 5-10), and by applying the previous step, evaluate each of them. Based on these key jobs, a review can be made to ascertain whether the factors and degrees taken are sufficient to reflect all jobs and also to arrive at a equitable base for fixing of an acceptable wage or salary structure.

The table explaining the point method job evaluation developed by the US National Metal Traders Associations is shown in Fig. 14.6. Based on the bench marks established in the key job, all other jobs will be evaluated. This method of job evaluation is more effective because the major factors are sub-divided which ensures accuracy of job evaluation. Furthermore, compensable factors are not limited to any particular number and only those factors, which the parties decide as important, can be used.

However, this method too is not free from disadvantages. Developing a point rating scheme is not easy and a considerable amount of skill is needed in defining factors and their degrees in such a way that all rates will have the same meaning. The point system is difficult to explain and its working cannot be easily interpreted to employees.

* TABLE : ALLOCATION OF POINTS OF DEGREE

Characteristic	First Degree	Second Degree	Third Degree	Fourth Degree	Fifth Degree
1. Skill (a) Education	14	28	42	56	70
(b) Experience	22	44	66	88	110
(c) Initiative & Ingenuity	14	28	42	56	70
2. Effort (a) Physical Demand	10	20	30	40	50
(b) Mental Demand	5	10	15	20	25
3. Responsibility (a) Equipment or Process	5	10	15	20	25
(b) Material or Product	5	10	15	20	25
(c) Safety of others	5	10	15	20	25
(d) Work others	5	10	15	20	25
4. Job Conditions (a) Working conditions	10	20	30	40	50
(b) Unavoidable Hazards	5	10	15	20	25
Total	100	200	300	400	500

* Developed by the US National Metal Company Trade Association

FIG. 14.6: THE POINT METHOD OF JOB EVALUATION

The Factor Comparison Method

This method of job evaluation determines the relative rank of the jobs to be evaluated in relation to monetary scale. This method is, by and large, used for evaluating supervisory, professional and managerial positions, though it is equally suitable for grading others as well. However in evaluating jobs of supervisory, professional and managerial positions, it must be noted that characteristics may differ as they depend upon the nature of jobs and their importance. For example major characteristics of supervisory positions are as shown in Fig. 14.7 whilst for professional and managerial positions, as shown in Fig. 14.8. This method is essentially a combination of the ranking and point systems as it rates job by comparing one job with another (like the rank order method), and it is more analytical in the sense of subdividing jobs into comparable factors (like the point system). The process of evaluation of jobs under this method is shown in Fig. 14.9.

It should be remembered that first of all key jobs are noted (followed by others) by considering each of the five factors separately and then a salary level or wage rate is fixed. The advocaters of this method believe that it, by and large, results in more accurate job evaluation being more objective, logical, simple, flexible and it utilizes a few factors (less likelihood to overlap).

However, the factors comparison method suffers from serious limitations such as: (a) it is difficult to explain to the employer, (b) it is a very expensive system of job evaluation because experts are needed particularly in selecting weights which are based on actual analysis, (c) in using only the universal factors, there is a danger that some of the important factors may be omitted, as compensable factors for every organization may not be the same; and (d) since money values are used, the rates may unconsciously assign higher levels of the factors to a higher paid job even if such assignment is not justified.

ESTABLISHING PAY STRUCTURES FOR BASE WAGES (OR SALARIES)

Regardless of the method of job evaluation used, the ultimate objective is to establish pay structure by ascertaining the proper rate of pay for all jobs. There are three major steps in achieving the final pay structures for base wages (or salaries), namely: (a) Decision about range i.e., maximum and minimum wages for each grade. (b) Decision about the number of grades for

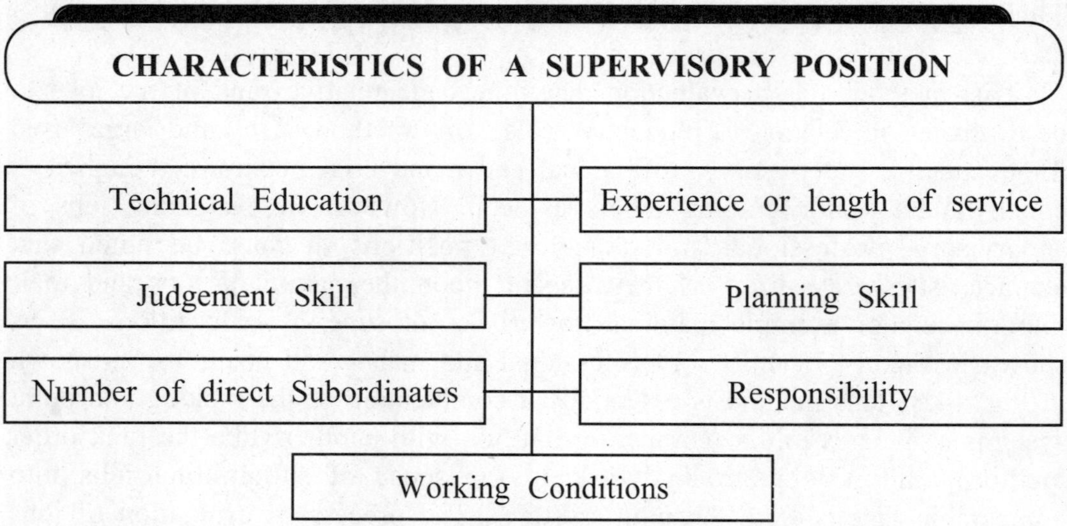

FIG. 14.7: SOME MAJOR CHARACTERISTICS OF A SUPERVISORY POSITION

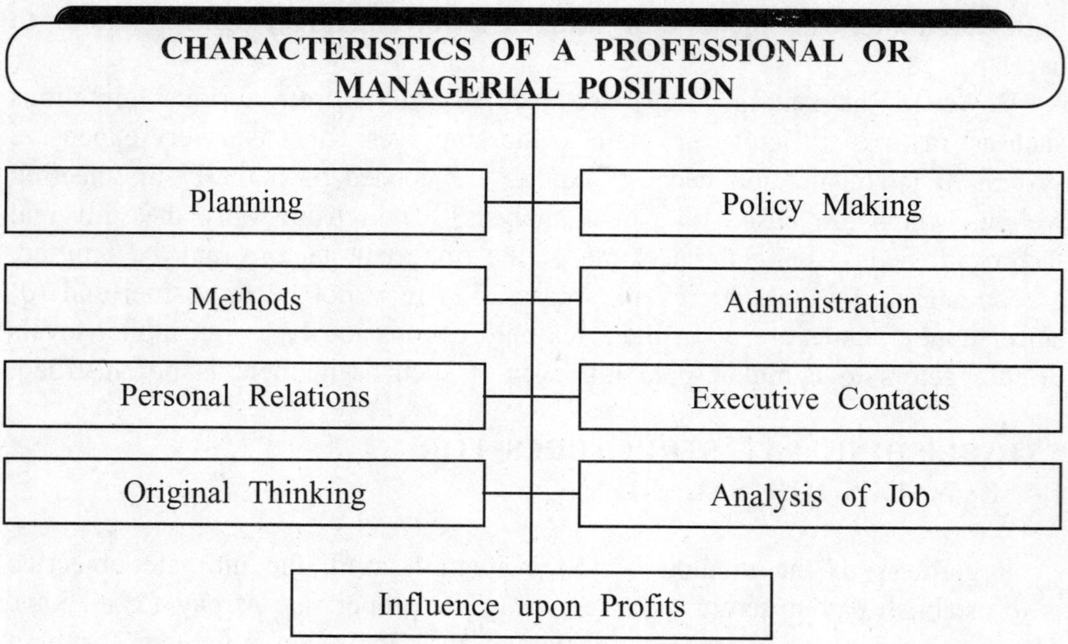

FIG. 14.8 : SOME MAJOR CHARACTERISTICS OF A PROFESSIONAL OR MANAGERIAL POSITION

JOB EVALUATION PROCESS UNDER FACTOR COMPARISON METHOD

- Select the factors and prepare a clear and unambiguous definition of each
- Select the key jobs i.e. a job whose content has become stabilized
- Allocate salary/wage for each job to different factors
- Develop a job comparison scale and insert key jobs in them. When all of the key jobs have been evaluated and salary allocation is completed in this manner, a job comparison can be constructed.
- Evaluate the job in question, factor by factor, in relation to key jobs on the job comparison scale. Then each job is to be evaluated and compared with other jobs in terms of each factor
- Design, adjust and operate the pay structure

FIG. 14.9 : STEPS IN EVALUATION OF JOBS BY USING FACTOR COMPARISON METHOD

employees. (c) Decision about overlap between different grades. The above steps are not mutually exclusive, but are closely related to each other i.e., if one's affected by a change, it will cause some change in others and so on.

For points (a) and (b) there are so many theories about the decision but for point (c) a pay graph may be prepared by plotting difficulty points i.e. points, rank or grade level etc. (obtained by using suitable evaluation methods) on the horizontal axis (abscissa), and existing rate (prevailing) on the vertical axis (ordinate), and then a best filling graph is drawn.

If the prevailing rates are reasonably fair and if rating of the jobs have been done carefully, then the plotted point can be expected to fall along a trend line with very little depression. But if data used is loaded with inequalities and errors, then considerable dispersion will be faced from the trend line.

Fig. 14.10 presents an example of a pay curve showing an average pay curve, range +/- 10% and an overlap between the grades. The overlap can be reduced by increasing the slope of the pay line, or by reducing the number of grades, or by reducing the wage range.

Though overlapping should be avoided any way, it is in fact intentionally designed to give flexibility for management in transferring an employee from a job in an adjacent grade without changing his (or her) pay or in paying more on excellent performance to a lower grade employee than to an employee working under high grade having poor performance.

CONCLUDING REMARKS

Job evaluation can rarely be once-all-time operation. Following its installation it requires a constant check of the job description and review with a view to bring the description and evaluation up-to-date. While undertaking job evaluation it is imperative that regional and environmental factors are taken into consideration and also to see that it is properly introduced, administered and followed up. Job evaluation, though not a scientific process, is a systematic method aimed at yielding accurate and equitable results while serving as a tested technique or as an aid in determining the relative worth of jobs or wage rates. It is pertinent to point out that from the industrial experience it has been found that this area is the largest from where unsuitable differences arise.

Therefore, there is a great need to win a large measure of acceptance and

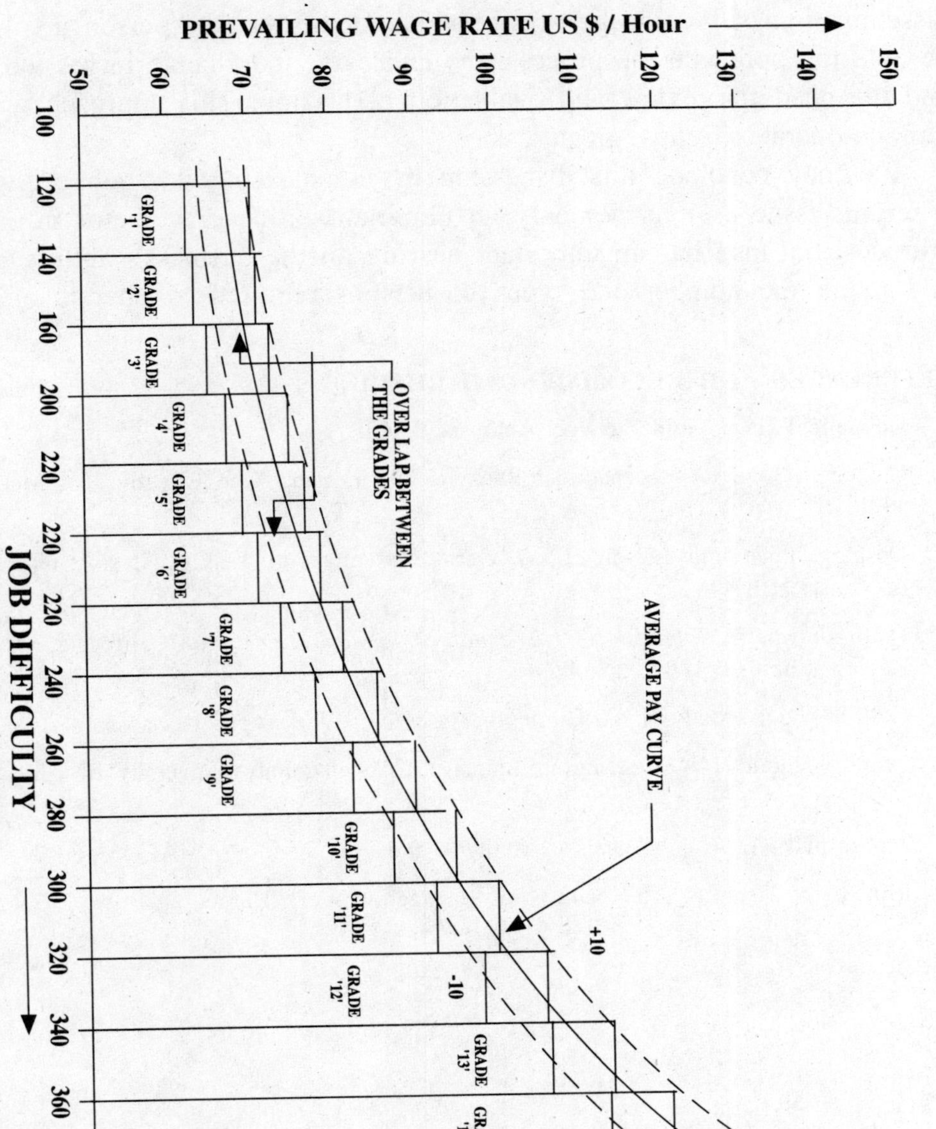

Fig. 14.10 : PAY CURVE

understanding of job evaluation at all levels of the organization. In this respect it is essential that procedure is introduced to provide employees the dissemination of knowledge of job evaluation so that the person involved will be able to appreciate the process, the endeavor, the change in his job content and the need for review and evaluation of his job. This approach will make him co-operate in this great task.

We may conclude this discussion by emphasizing that job evaluation is a serious issue as it is not only an important influencing factor in employee attitudes, but also has an important bearing on the business's ability to obtain and retain the number and types of persons required to operate efficiently.

REFERENCES AND RECOMMENDED READING

1. Boydell, T.H. - 'Guide to Job Analysis'/BACIE.
2. Campbell, John P. - 'Managerial Behavior, Performance and Effectiveness'/McGraw-Hill, 1970.
3. Desberg, Peter and Judson H. Taylor - 'Essentials of Task Analysis'/University Press of America, 1987.
4. Dyal, Ishwar - *'Role Analysis Techniques in Job Description'*/California Management Review Summer 1969, pp. 47.
5. Gall S - 'Job Analysis: A Guide to Assessing Work Activities'/Jossey-Bass, 1983.
6. Leanitt, Herald J. - 'Reading in Managerial Psychgology'/University of Chicago Press, 1980.
7. McCormick, E. - 'Job Analsis: Methods and Applications'/AMACOM, 1979.
8. Mintzberg, Henry - 'The Nature of Managerial Work'/Harper & Row, 1973.

A PRACTICAL APPROACH TO PERFORMANCE APPRAISAL IN ORGANIZATIONS

CHAPTER 15

INTRODUCTION

'Performance appraisal' (also termed 'merit rating', employee appraisal, performance evaluation and efficiency rating) is one of the most important functions of human resources management. It is a process an employer uses to make an assessment of an employee's performance. By and large, the factors such as; attendance, judgement, honesty, creativeness, co-operation, initiative, intelligence, safety consciousness, etc. play an important role in the performance appraisal process.

Fundamentally the performance appraisal process involves three stages. The first stage starts at the assessment of the employee's personal traits, i.e. knowledge, skills, aptitudes, attitude, abilities, motives, values, interests etc. responses, actions, functions, motions and conduct etc. and terminate at the assessment of achievements/output/productivity i.e. work performance. The second stage involves the manager's appraisal of the employee's qualities and behaviors identified during stage '1' which is used as a basis of taking actions. The third stage involves personnel actions taken by the management in the form of pay increases, rewarding employees, promotions, training, career progression, placement, transfer, termination etc.

The performance appraisal concept is central to management. According to Harry Levison; "Performance appraisal has three basic functions: (1) to provide adequate feedback to each person on his or her performance (2) to serve as a basis for modifying or changing behavior toward more effective working habits; and (3) to provide data to managers with which they may judge future job assignments and compensation"[8]. However, the research has indicated that none of the present methods of performance appraisal serve any of these functions well.

PERFORMANCE APPRAISAL SYSTEM

According to Dale Yodder, the term performance appraisal refers to all formal procedures used in the organization to evaluate personalities contributions and potentials of its members. We may deduce from this that the satisfactory performance is only a part of the performance appraisal process as a whole. The other aspects include evaluation of employee's potentials for the development and determination of the differences among the employees working in the organization.

Performance appraisal is, by and large, done by the individual's immediate supervisor in an organization, who is also subjected to be rated by his supervisor and so on. Performance appraisal, therefore, can be regarded as a formal program in an organization which is concerned not only with the contribution of employees who are a part of the organization, but also with the identification of potential.

Although, performance appraisal is a fundamental human act, nevertheless, it focuses not so much on 'behavior'. Its main focus is on 'outcomes of behavior' which contributes to the main sources of trouble with performance appraisal system. However, adequacy of the system is acceptable to a level which can meet the management requirements to achieve organizational goals and objectives. In other words it should act as a control mechanism for the individual organization in regard to personal action.

PERFORMANCE APPRAISAL DEFINED

Performance appraisal can be defined as the systematic evaluation of an employee's performance on the job in terms of requirements of the job and his potential for development. Performance appraisal employs rating techniques for making a comparison between individuals in a work group, in terms of requirements of their respective jobs and personal deficiencies or qualities. It is important, however, to understand the clear distinction between job evaluation and performance appraisal. Job evaluation is concerned with the determination of the worth of different jobs, whereas performance appraisal refers to the tasks of merit rating or making an assessment of the individual performance at work.

WHY PERFORMANCE APPRAISAL IS NEEDED

For any organization to function, it is important that the information regarding the capacity and performance of its members is available. Since people differ in their abilities and aptitude and these differences are natural (to a great extent) and cannot be eliminated completely even by giving them the same type of basic education and training. Therefore, there is bound to be some differences in the quality and quantity of work done by different employees even on the same job. It is important for the management as well as the individual to know these differences so that the employees having better potentials may be rewarded by additional remuneration, whilst the individual may improve his performance in comparison to his fellow employees. Performance appraisal has many benefits, some important ones are shown in Fig. 15.1.

OBJECTS OF PERFORMANCE APPRAISAL

The objects of performance appraisal fall into two broad categories, namely: (i) administrative and (ii) self-improvement.

Administrative Objects: These include: wages/salaries administration, training and development, personnel research, and other personnel actions, etc. (See Fig. 15.2 for detail).

Self-improvement: Performance appraisal helps to identify the individual's abilities, qualities and traits. It also helps the organization to solve its problems by highlighting a sort of total managerial action e.g. planning, organizing, directing/leading, controlling etc. including financial knowledge. It aims at making an assessment of the record of the manager's success (not the managers personality), acts as a control mechanism for the individual organization with respect to personnel actions, and restricts the management from making arbitrary decisions. Fig. 15.3 shows the cases where merit rating serves to guide the management in its action.

METHODS OF PERFORMANCE APPRAISAL

Ideally, merit rating aims at objectively assessing the individual performance of personnel, but in reality subjectivity cannot be eliminated completely even if the most systematic method is used. Fig. 15.4 shows a battery of traditional methods of performance appraisal. In the text to follow, a brief review of each method is carried out.

Unstructured Appraisal

Under this system, the appraiser is required to write down his impression of appraisal in an unstructured manner.

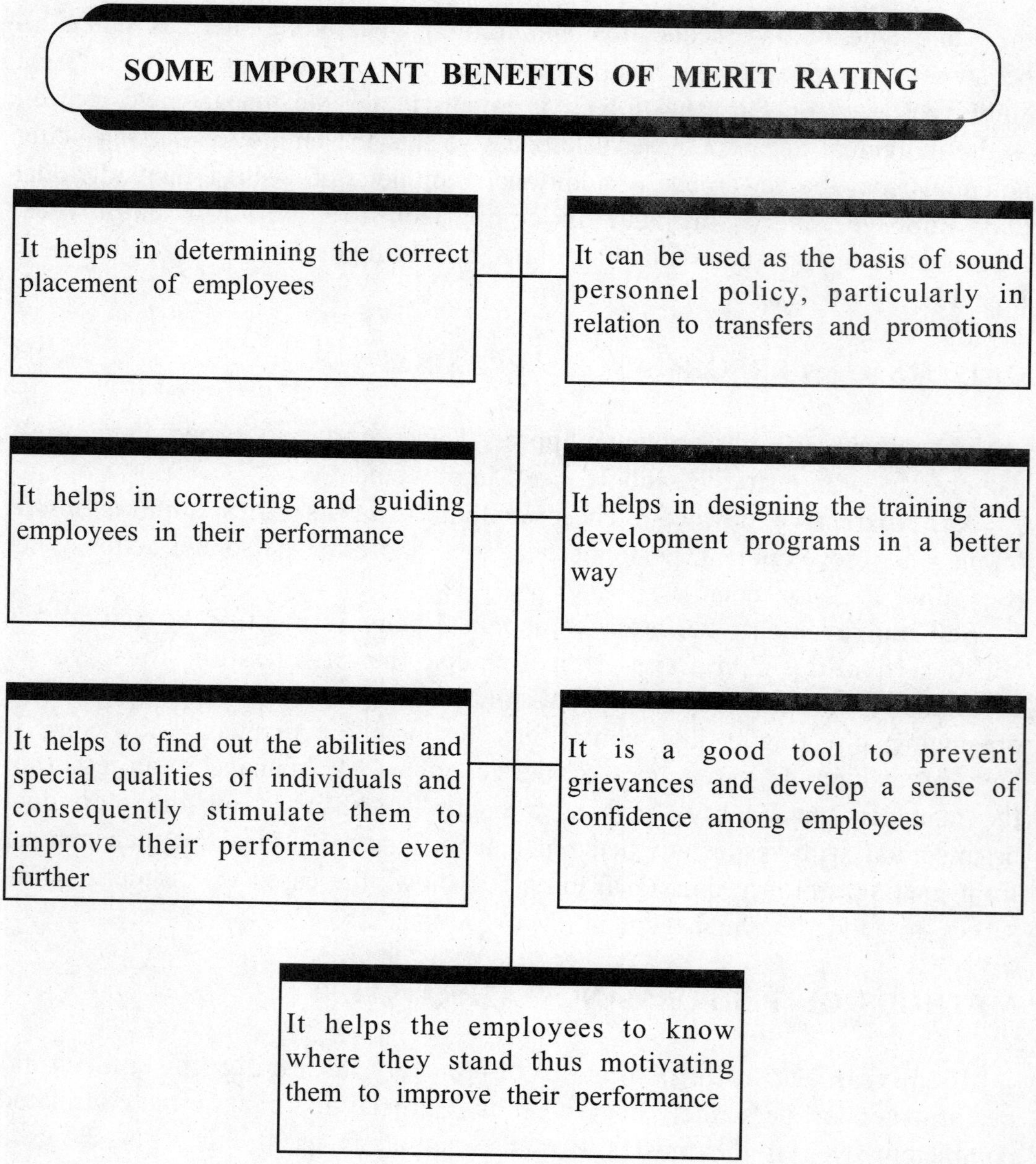

FIG. 15.1 : BENEFITS OF PERFORMANCE APPRAISAL

MAIN ADMINISTRATIVE OBJECTS OF MERIT RATING

WAGES/SALARIES ADMINISTRATIONS

In many industrial organizations, increases in wages/salaries are based on the performance appraisal

PROMOTION/ADVANCEMENT

Promotion/advancement is perhaps the most important administrative use of performance appraisal. It aids the decision making process to determine promotion/advancement

PERSONNEL RESEARCH

It helps in research, especially in the fields of personnel management and human relations. Research efforts to find out the causes and effects, and the relationship between the personnel and performance, have resulted in emergence of various theories in human relations

TRAINING & DEVELOPMENT

It helps to identify the areas of knowledge and skills in which employees are not upto the desired standards, and to take corrective actions

OTHER PERSONNEL ACTION

These include lay-offs, demotions, terminations, transfers, etc., resulting from unsatisfactory performance or due to economic conditions or changes in the production process

FIG. 15.2 : MAIN ADMINISTRATIVE OBJECTS OF PERFORMANCE APPRAISAL

SALIENT CASES WHERE PERFORMANCE APPRAISAL AIDS MANAGEMENT ACTION

When promotions are recommended, the employees so chosen should generally be those who have received high ratings, unless other factors influence the decision

Performance appraisal helps in pointing out outstanding individuals in the organization so as to maintain inventory of talents

Performance appraisal influences management decisions in laying off the employees and tells the management whether it is losing its best persons or is improving the organization by shunting out the inefficient ones

In taking people from other organizations, merit rating helps in ascertaining that they have the sufficient merit to join the organization

Performance appraisal motivates the management to give proper weightage to merit when considering pay increases

In re-hiring, the management should give preference to those workers whom it had previously considered most effective

FIG. 15.3 : SALIENT CASES WHERE MERIT RATING AIDS MANAGEMENT ACTION

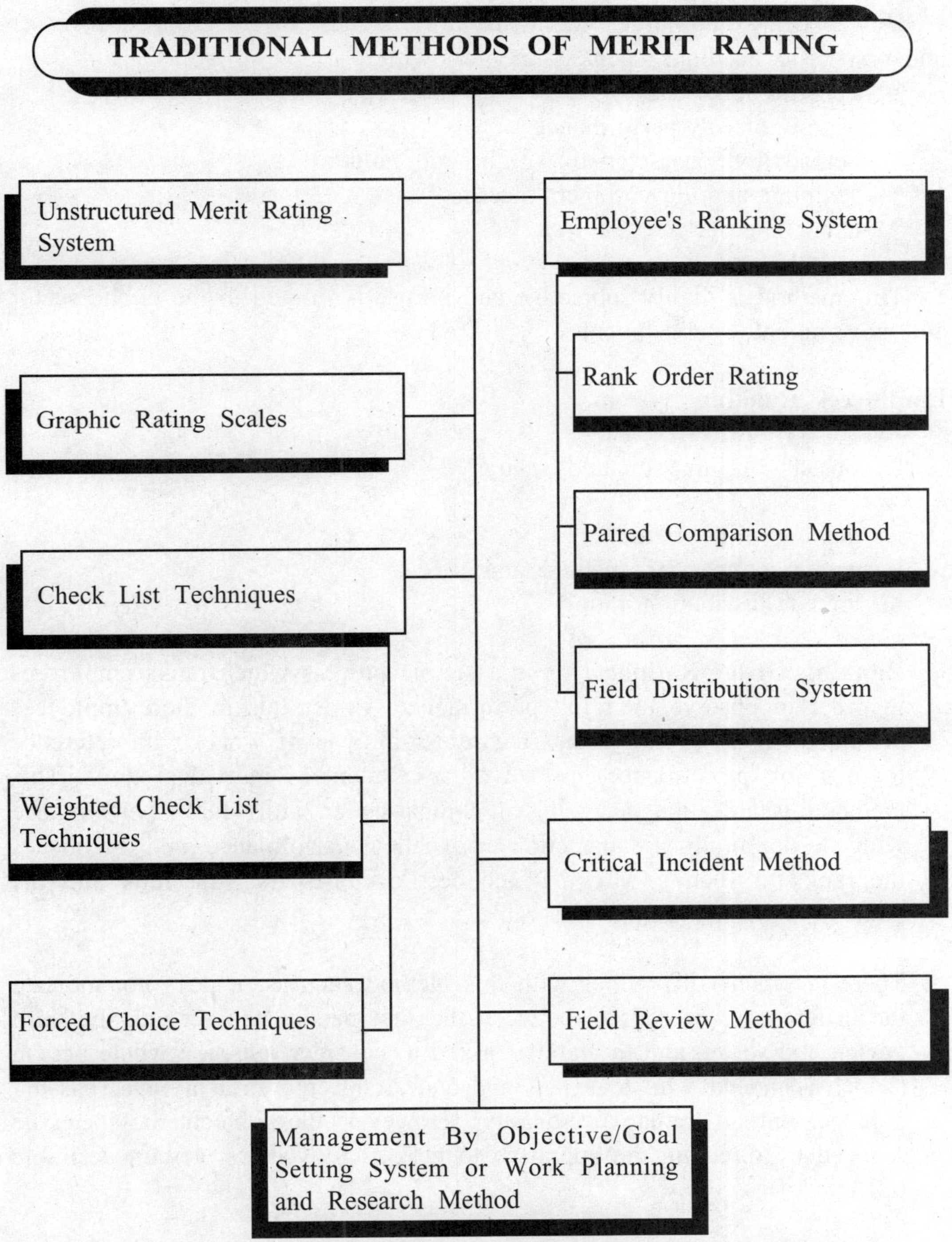

FIG. 15.4: A BATTERY OF TRADITIONAL METHODS OF PERFORMANCE APPRAISAL

However, by and large, comments are required to be grouped together under specific headings such as the following:

* Specific job behavior.
* Nature of job performance.
* Personality, characteristic of the job holder.
* Training and development needs.
* Other aspects.

This method is highly subjective and its use is limited to the public sector and government establishment.

Employees Ranking System

It consists of three methods namely:

i. ranking order rating,
ii. paired comparison method and
iii. forced distribution rating.

I. **Ranking Order Rating:** This is a simple process which ranks employees in order to observe their job performance. Under this method employees are rated on an overall basis (regardless of type of work) with reference to their job performance, instead of assessment of individual traits. This method discards, the necessity of comparing an individual's performance with the definition of satisfaction or excellent performance, and establishes the ranks in such a way that the best occupies the first rank and the poorest is placed in the last rank.

There are many difficulties with this method such as: it does not indicate the differences (or degree) between the first person, the second, the third person and so on; and the rater is asked to consider rate as a whole person (which is indeed a difficult task and undesirable too as it involves passing a judgement on human personality). However, the subjectiveness can be reduced by directing the appraisee to rank employees on certain desirable traits.

II. **Paired Comparison Method:** In this method the whole organization is considered as a job family whose every member is compared with every other member to determine who is better at work. The rater, by and large, uses a little booklet containing two names on each page and in this way each employee is compared with every other employee in the same job family.

This method gives a more reliable rating than the rank order rating, but is more tedious to construct and implement. This method is not suitable for merit rating of employees whose performance needs to be appraised periodically as it is difficult to make an evaluation of improvements made by the appraisee over a period of time.

III **Forced Distribution Method:** There is a tendency amongst certain appraisers to either rate all worker as average, excellent or poor. They fail to evaluate the excellent, average or poor employees clearly and cluster them around a particular point in the rating scale. To eliminate this tendency, the forced distribution method is used to force the appraiser to fit the employees being rated into a predetermined range of scale. An illustration of this method is shown in Fig. 15.5. This method has an obvious advantage over the paired comparison system as it is simple to administer, two or more employees can be given an equal rating and also the scope for subjective judgement on the part of the appraiser is minimized.

The objective of this technique is to spread out rating in the form of a normal distribution (See Fig. 15.5).

Graphic Rating Scales

Under this method scales are established for a number of specific factors i.e. qualities and characteristic to be rated. However, extreme care is needed in selecting the factors as this is an important point under this system. These factors are of two types namely: (a) Characteristics e.g. initiative, integrity, dependability, relation with superiors, relation with colleagues & peers, relation with subordinates, reliability, attendance/punctuality and (b) Contribution (e.g. efficiency, safety, accuracy, coordination, responsibility, care for the tool and equipment, general quality of work according to the nature of the job, etc.). In this system, scores in numerical values are given (generally '1' for the poorest and '12' for the best worker.

Fig. 15.6 shows an illustration of this method. Graphic rating imposes a heavy burden upon the rater in evaluating the performance on a scale

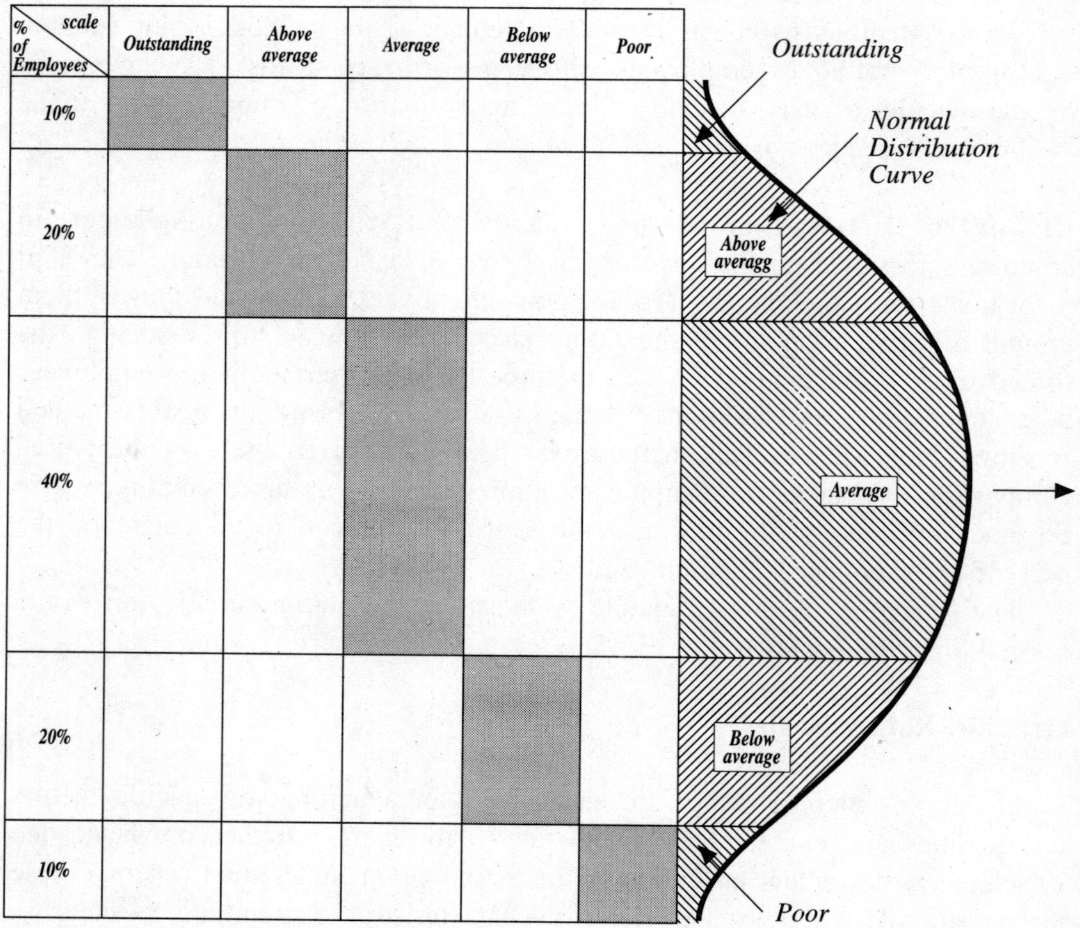

Note: Distribution of employees is shown thus

Fig. 15.5 : FORCED DISTRIBUTION METHOD RATING SCALE

FACTORS		RATING SCALE												REASON FOR RATING
		1	2	3	4	5	6	7	8	9	10	11	12	
CHARACTERISTICS	Initiative													
	Effort													
	Integrity													
	Attendance/ Punctuality													
	Relation with Supervisors													
	Relation with Peers													
	Relation with Subordinates													
	Reliability													
	Special Qualities													
CONTRIBUTION	Care for the tools/equipment/ material													
	Safety													
	Accuracy of work													
	Coordination													
	Efficiency/ Speed													
	Responsibility													
	Quantity of Work-general													
	Quality of Work-general													

Note: Total of these rated scores are used to compare the workers

General Remarks	

FIG. 15.6 : GRAPHIC RATING SCALE

involving as many as fifteen or so different factors; some of which being highly subjective.

The main weakness of this system is that the rates may be biased. To overcome this drawback the rater should be asked to explain the reason by giving specific examples of the ratee's behavior that justifies his rating, under the remarks box provided at the bottom of the form, in addition to giving a brief reason under each factor.

Other drawbacks include: (a) a high score on one factor can compensate for a low score on another, (b) low scores for contribution may be balanced by high scores for characteristics and (c) In practice, ratings tend to cluster on the high side. This method is one of the oldest and most widely used for performance appraisal.

Check List Techniques

I Weight Check List Techniques: This method specifies the following techniques.

* Preparation is carried out of various statements in such a manner that they describe various types and levels of behavior for a particular job.

* A scale value is attached with each statement.

* Collection and checking of all the statements at the time of rating of the employees is carried out and weights of values to the individual traits attached.

* The weights are then averaged and applied to the evaluation of each employee.

* The rating is then placed on separate cards and sorted out by a rater who has actually observed the accomplishment of the work.

* Employees are then ranked from poor to excellent (outstanding).

* Finally weights are assigned to the statement in accordance with the way they are ranked by the raters.

This method is relatively costlier and involves a lengthy procedure for evaluating employees.

II Forced Choice Techniques: In this method greater objectivity is created by removing bias and avoiding room for personal prejudices. Under this method the following techniques are used.

* The rater is forced to choose between descriptive statements, seemingly equal worth, describing the person to be rated.

* Statements are chosen from both the aspects i.e. favorable and unfavorable of the qualities and characteristics.

* The rater may feel that either of the two statements in a pair is applicable, but must eliminate the one that is less descriptive and select the one which is more descriptive.

* Only one of the statements in each pair (represented by the supervisor) is correct in identifying the better performance and this score key must be kept a secret from the raters.

* In this way bias is removed from the appraisal process. This method offers greater objectivity than most of the other methods. However, this method too has drawbacks. It is very expensive to install and the procedure involved is very lengthy and hence more time consuming. Also rating cannot be discussed freely with the employees.

Critical Incident Method

The critical incident method is not new but has been in use as a method for first-level supervisors to evaluate line employees. This technique requires every supervisor to record all significant negative incidents of each employee's work activities which indicate ineffective or poor behavior and all significant positive incidents which indicate effective or successful behavior.

The examples of such incidents are:

i. An employee refused to help a fellow worker (negative).

ii. An employee became upset over work (negative).

iii. An employee suggested an improvement in the work process (positive).

iv. An employee tried to convince a fellow worker to accept the management decision (positive).

These are recorded in a specifically designed notebook which carry pre-recorded categories or characteristics under which the various behavior can be recorded (preferably on a daily basis to avoid forgetfulness). Examples of such characteristics are productivity, judgement, dependability, learning ability, accuracy, initiative and responsibility. This process (collection of data) then helps the management to perform the basic functions of performance appraisal i.e. providing feedback, determining training needs and providing advancement and promotion data etc.

Some people argue that this technique provides an objective basis for the appraisal of performance of an employee, but in practice it is not a rating method as it requires the supervisor to pay close attention to what the employee is doing. Furthermore, because behavior is too complex to be measured along the few dimension and then rated, therefore, this method has not worked well in practice.

It has been observed that most of the time the employees have neither positive nor negative incidents and the critical event did not occur thus making it difficult to rate an employee. This method has also other drawbacks such as: it may be difficult for a supervisor to decide what is the exceptional incident or critical, and human bias may occur. To overcome this drawback Gerald Whitelock has designed a specimen checklist, by collecting behavior incidents from a sample of experts in this field (ranging from 80 to 150 incidents) equally divided between effective and ineffective job behavior. A few typical incidents from such checklist are:

* An employee remained punctual at work.

* An employee remained consistently missing from work.

* An employee displayed an unpleasant behavior to an interested party.

* An employee displayed a courteous behavior to an interested party.

* An employee refused to work over-time when asked for.
* An employee showed willingness to work over-time when asked for.
* An employee talked abruptly and rudely on the telephone or created a disturbance with a loud talk.
* An employee failed to follow the chain of command.
* An employee helped fellow employees to solve their problems at work.
* An employee rejected a bid that was unreasonably priced.
* An employee suggested a new method of work.
* An employee developed a new procedure that reduced paperwork.
* An employee accepted inferior quality goods from a supplier.

If such a checklist is used, it would ensure greater objectivity.

Field Review Method

Under this technique an expert belonging to the personnel department does all the necessary work i.e. filling up forms etc. and conducts interviews of the line department supervisor of employees to be rated. The expert, questions the respective supervisor to obtain all the pertinent information regarding each employee and takes notes. Subsequently these notes are converted in a formal report and sent to the supervisor for his comments or modification or approval. The scope of these questions covers 'how' and 'why' of the requirements of each job, the respective organization unit, and the performance of each worker. The workers are, by and large, placed under three categories, namely: (A) outstanding i.e. above program requirements, (B) satisfactory i.e. meets program requirements and (C) unsatisfactory i.e. below program requirements. A typical 'staff appraisal standard form' is placed in Appendix. This method relieves the line supervisor of tedious work of filling out forms etc. as the personnel or development department largely controls the process.

Management by Objective Approach of Performance Appraisal

The traditional methods described above have faced a general criticism being too subjective in nature because all of them are based on a personal judgement of the supervisor or rater resulting in bias or prejudice or pressure from certain other areas from the rater's part and antagonistic response from the ratee's part. To overcome these limitations, the 'Management By Objective' (MBO) approach is designed. This approach is result-oriented and its use has become popular in a number of organizations. This approach is also known as 'Goal Setting System' or 'Work Planning and Technique' or 'Work Planning and Research Method'. This method is different from the traditional method on various aspects such as (a) more frequent discussions, (b) more emphasis on goal setting and (c) more emphasis on employees participation. This method is based on clear and time bound objectives from all levels i.e. corporate to department to individual. In addition this method encompasses self appraisal and post appraisal interviews. In devising the procedure the following techniques should be adopted.

* Both superior and subordinates jointly agree on the quantitative measurable performance goals.
* Each subordinate is requested to set for himself short term goals by which he may improve his department efficiency and also that of his own.
* The senior executive/superior will help his subordinates to set goals for themselves.
* The senior executive/Supervisor will discuss with his subordinates what is required to meet these goals.
* The senior executive/supervisor will make necessary adjustment to the goals in consistence with the organizational goals.
* The subordinate writes his own accomplishment report and thus participates in self-assessment.
* Both superior and subordinates will meet to evaluate how well these goals

have been met and discuss what could be done better to make improvement and also to set goals for the next period.

* Subordinate appraises himself and then becomes eager to know how he might improve his own methods, attitude or behavior and accordingly adjusts his target.

This method is a two way process when not only the subordinate performance is appraised but also the relationship between superior and subordinates improves. However, it is important that goals set by MBO techniques must be made consistent with organisational long range plans and budgets. The MBO process is shown in Fig. 15.7 and MBO in action is shown in Fig. 15.8.

MBO techniques has many advantages over conventional appraisal such as the following.

* In the MBO techniques the individual knows the standards on which he will be judged.

* MBO method creates for each individual, a standard of evaluation based on the special characteristics of his job.

* This method emphasises the future (which can be changed) rather than the past (which cannot be changed).

* Subordinate-supervisor mutual respect and co-ordination improves as superior helps to improve records of the subordinates rather than curiosities of the subordinates.

* This method facilitates internalized motivation as it allows subordinates to set their own goals.

* This method helps subordinates to discuss where they stand (due to feedback) and thus enhances learning.

* This method is consistent with the psychological principle that people work better when they have definite goals and targets.

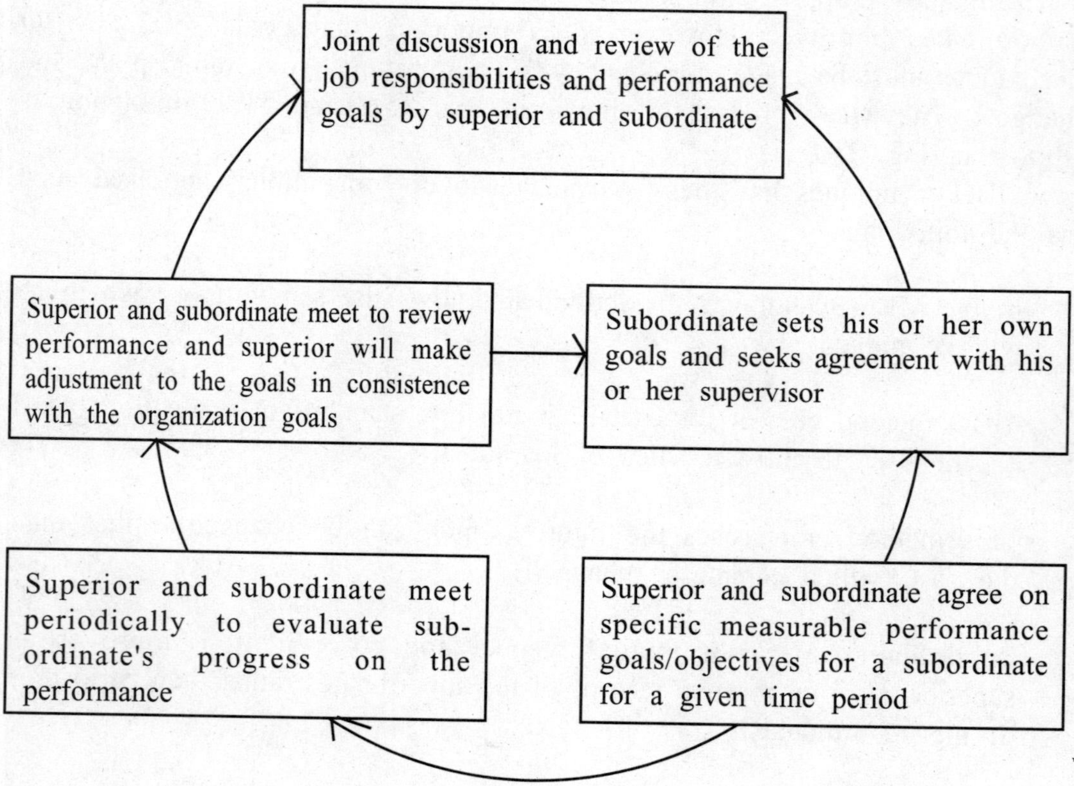

FIG. 15.7 : KEY ASPECTS OF 'MBO' PROCESS

MANAGEMENT BY OBJECTIVE STATEMENTS **Sheet 1 of 3**

Name: ________________ Position: ________

Objective Number: __________

Objective Statement (s) (What):

____

____

Action Plan (How)

____

____

____

PERFORMANCE EVALUATION **Sheet 1 of 3**

____

____

____

____

____

____

____

FINAL PERFORMANCE RATING **Sheet 1 of 3**

UNSATISFACTORY: ☐ **SATISFACTORY:** ☐ **COMPETENT:** ☐

COMMENDABLE: ☐ **DISTINGUISHED:** ☐

Employee's comments:

Signature: ______________________

Supervisor's comments: ______________________

Signature: ______________________

FIG. 15.8 : PERFORMANCE APPRAISAL THROUGH 'MBO'

* This method emphasises more on specific performance, rather than personal traits and characteristics.

* This method emphasises more on forward planning and helps to clarify duties and responsibilities, organize the job resolve and problems or difficulties in advance.

* If universally applied, this method becomes a style of management, rather than just a method of appraisal.

* This method facilitates effective interdepartmental coordination and communication.

However in spite of the extensive advantages listed above and despite the initial enthusiastic reception, experience has shown that MBO method too has drawbacks and limitations such as (a) goals setting by subordinates for themselves could be illusory, (b) subordinates may set their target too low, (c) the superior who regularly consults his subordinates find this approach to appraisal quite easy, but not so for the superior who is decisive and directive, (d) a careful planning and implementation is required as without it success will not be achieved, (e) it takes time especially during the first cycle, (f) it increases paperwork, (g) it may overlook qualitative objectives, (h) it may have poor or inadequate top-management support, (i) it may be poorly communicated and understood, and (j) it may be inconsistent with managerial philosophies.

INADEQUACY OF APPRAISAL SYSTEMS

The general criticism of appraisal systems is that almost all of them are based on personal judgment of the rater or the supervisor resulting in many errors, weaknesses and obvious drawbacks such as the following:

* The rating scale techniques of performance appraisal is particularly susceptible to the halo effect which occurs when the rater allows one aspect of an individual's characteristic (or performance) to influence his entire evaluation. In many supervisors/raters this tendency exists as they get influenced by one characteristic and base their appraisal on single characteristic rather than on all subsequent characteristics or give an

employee approximately the same rating on all factors. One way to minimize the effect of such a halo error is to instruct the rater/supervisor to judge all of his subordinates on a single factor or trait before preceding to the next.

* Judgments on performance are, by and large, impressionistic and subjective even if the dimensions for rating on quantitative goals are well defined. Also because of the availability of inadequate information to compare employees for merit rating, the rater has often to make arbitrary judgment.

* It has been observed that rating by different supervisors/raters, particularly in different departments are usually incomparable i.e. excellent work in one may be just satisfactory in the other in the same organization.

  This tendency is due to miscellaneous biases. For example, the rater may tend to give higher ratings because he thinks that it would look bad on him if employees in other departments receive better rewards i.e. salary increases etc., than his unit due to better merit rating results, or he may rate their subordinates on an average rating scale i.e. middle of the spectrum, and follow the path of least resistance. The example of the other basis could be that some raters/supervisors may show bias against caste, religion, nationality, or members of the opposite sex. Also they may give a higher rating to those holding senior positions i.e. influenced by organizational positions, or to senior employees i.e. because they do not accept that no improvement under their leadership has occurred.

* There is a tendency among some raters to be harsh in their rating whilst among others to be lenient. Both these trends can arise from varying standards of performance among supervisors/raters and from different interpretations of the rating of employee performance. The ratings of a lenient rater follow a trend of a curve of nominal distribution which in turn is based on a rating of results rather than on behavior. This is a very serious weakness of the appraisal system that competent employees may become demotivated.

* The systems are not fool proof with respect to feedback as delays in feedback creates both frustration (when good performance is not readily recognized) and anger (when judgment rendered for inadequacies is long

past). Appraisal and feedback are equally important for both the organizational view-point as well as for employees as it assists effective learning so that tasks are completed and stimulated efforts towards specific goals is maintained, and it can satisfy the personal needs of employees for information on progress.

Improvements to Tradition Appraisal Methods

In all the traditional methods of merit rating, it is best hoped to obtain an impartial, factual, objective, and acceptable measurement scores. However, the reliability and validity of traditional systems remain questionable due to the judgment role of the supervisor/rater and the antagonistic response of the employee/rater. A study of the appraisal system in General Electric is a typical example in this respect. The main source of trouble for this inadequacy is, as Harry Levinson puts it, "that the outcome of behavior rather than behavior itself is evaluated"[8]. Therefore, to overcome inadequacy introduction of behavioral approach in the appraisal process is of a paramount importance. Research has indicated that with the behavioral approach more favorable attitude of employees are observed on factors such as respectfulness of their supervisors, amount of help received, ability of the supervisors to plan and the extent to which their abilities were utilized. One way of introduction of behavioral approach (suggested by Harry Levinson) is to upgrade a 'static job description' (descriptions in terms that are only quantitatively measurable) to a 'dynamic job description' (that "amplifies statements of job responsibility and desired outcome by describing the emotional and behavioral topography of a task to be done by the individual in the job") and then evolve a contemporary performance appraisal system that will provide feedback on verifiable behavior i.e. critical incident process. Harry Levinson also suggests some support mechanism for: (a) managing the guilt, (a) group appraisal, and (c) upward appraisal. The other way is to introduce Management By Objective approach which is already discussed.

POST APPRAISAL INTERVIEW

The post appraisal interview is the most difficult part of the entire appraisal process as the actual face-to-face situation with the job holder causes anxiety. Some managers do not feel easy and comfortable while telling their subordinates that an improvement is needed. An employee will not feel happy to be told that he or she is doing a bad job and thus a negative attitude against the manager may emerge. The common fault with such situations is that these cases are based upon the traditionally held view of appraisal, which regards appraisal as a one way method of control and communication and the interview is used for the purpose of informing the job holder exactly where he stands in the eyes of his superiors, in addition to justify decisions, attempting to stimulate improved performance followed by criticism and encouragement to improve. However, such interviews contribute very little towards effective performance appraisal, unless an interchange of views geared to the problem solving and planning process by way of a two-way communication.

Need for Post Appraisal Interview

Post appraisal interview is necessary for reasons such as the following:

* To help the manager in understanding his subordinates' aim, abilities, strengths, weaknesses, likes and dislikes etc.

* To develop mutual understanding of what is expected, what subordinates are aiming for as to their personal goals, and how they feel about their work.

* To provide counselling which can prevent industrial disputes by creating a better understanding between the management and the workers.

* To let the employees know where they stand thus identifying the training needs and to avoid cases of unnecessary worry, unjustified self confidence, and insecurity.

Objectives of Post Appraisal Interview

Under the traditional approach objectives have been two-fold. Firstly to justify recommended salary action i.e. salary increase/promotion or no salary increase and secondly to present an opportunity for the manager to review his subordinate's performance and discuss face-to-face with the subordinate the true causes of problems (if exist) which are affecting the job performance and promote discussions on needed improvement to minimize the effect on the job results and remove any causes if so identified. However, in practice it has been found that the first part (i.e. salary action) had been dominating and the post performance appraisal interview that plans for improvement remained a passive issue. To overcome this problem, many organizations split up the post appraisal interview in two sessions. In one session the discussion is centered around performance appraisal and salary action whilst the performance improvement action plan is discussed in the other session (sometime later). This traditional approach tends to display the rater's various characteristics such as: superiority, a lack of concern, a judgemental attitude, intentions to control and an attitude of finality on the part of the interviewer etc.

Under the behavioral approach, an interview tends to concentrate upon reviewing the subordinate's progress towards goals which have earlier been mutually agreed. The objective of the post appraisal interview under this approach (task oriented and problem solving rather than person oriented or 'tell & sell') is improvement and development rather than scolding, criticizing and praising. Behavioral approach tends to be characterized by factors such as: empathy respect, atmosphere of quality, shared definition of problems/ solutions and an attitude of provisional rather than final conclusions on the part of the interviewer etc. However, behavioral approach does not tell the subordinates where he stands (in the eyes of the management) in relation to others and also he has to trust that forthcoming decisions concerning salary increase/advancement/promotion/other rewards will be generally consistent with his expectation of the resultant post appraisal interview.

Preparation for a Post Appraisal Interview

First of all the interviewer i.e. manager or supervisor should collect his thoughts and notes of performance appraisal highlighting any significant differences which he wants to communicate with the subordinate. He should then select the right place (having privacy) and the right time (both in relax moods) and with sufficient available time (should not start if unlikely to be finished in one session). The time and date for the interview must be firm and should be set far enough in advance. Preparation also includes a thorough analysis of the differences between desired and actual performance so that verification can be done easily. The following checklist will prove a good guide for preparation.

* Make a comparison of actual performance with the standards previously agreed.

* Make a list of significant differences between desired and actual performance.

* Carry out a thorough analysis of differences for possible causes.

* Work out an action plan by considering possible solutions.

* Arrange a firm time and date for interview.

* Ensure that sufficient time is set aside for the interview.

* Arrange a suitable place with privacy and no interruptions.

* Arrange your thoughts and performance appraisal information into a logical and understandable framework and anticipated sequence.

* Make an agenda with notes for use in the interview.

* Advise the subordinate to review his or her own performance against the previously agreed standard, prior to the past appraisal interview.

It is important to make every effort to ensure that each subordinate knows that the interview is going to be an objective exchange of views with an express purpose of improving performance.

Preparation for the subordinate is equally important and accordingly, he (or she) should make an agenda with notes to be used in the interview, including salient points of self appraisal. Self-appraisal can overcome many problems traditionally associated with performance feedback in the post appraisal interview.

Conducting Post Appraisal Interview

It is important that the interviewer (the manager or supervisor) should be flexible in his approach while conducting the interview with different kinds of people. A prerequisite of proper conducting is the recognition and acceptance of the fact that stress can have ill effects on a well prepared interview and therefore it must be minimized if not eliminated.

Adequate skill and experience in conducting post appraisal interviews reinforced with good preparation is a secret of success. Accordingly a conscious effort to improve is essential and the managers should look for improvement through training, short courses and practice at interviewing and receiving sufficient feedback from the subordinates (which would not be easily forthcoming) and develop a positive attitude towards appraisal.

There are also a number of factors which may contribute to the subordinate's feeling of stress during the interview, such as (a) the relationship that exists between the manager and the employee, which if closer and more open will contribute less to any stress, (b) power difference i.e. the power the manager has over the subordinate, which the manager should reduce to facilitate a good objective exchange of views.

To achieve the real objective it is important for the interviewer to ask questions in a manner or form that can bring best results. Researcher have found that the following type of questions will prove effective for the success of the post appraisal interview.

Type (a): Open Questions

This type of questions necessitate, the subordinate (interviewee) to think and to talk openly without feeling under pressure, and stems, by and large, from the fact that the response to the question will take longer to communicate than the question itself, thus enabling the interviewer to concentrate on listening carefully to what is being said. Here more emphasis is for the interviewer to understand what is being 'felt' instead of what is being 'said'.

The emphasis of open questions are:-

* Would you please explain to me how ---------------------------------------?

* Would you please tell me about ---?

* Would you please describe to me how you have arrived at ------------?

* Would you please explain to what extent does this cover ---------------?

Type (b): Close Questions

This type of questions are those which can be answered by a 'yes' or 'no' response. A limited use of such qeustions can be appropriate but, by and large, such questions should be avoided during the interview. The instances most appropriate for the usage of such questions are: (a) at the beginning of the interview (to collect some primary facts), (b) at the end of the interview (to summarize the interview), and (c) during the interview only when the interviewer wishes to interrupt and when the interviewer does not seem to want to stop talking.

The examples of closed questions are:

* Did you review your performance against the standards as we agreed?

* Are you feeling comfortable for the interview?

* Would you agree that --?

* Do you think that --?

* Is it true that --?

* Do we agree that --?

Type (c): Probe & Link Questions

To ensure that the interview is not drifted from the right track, it is useful to identify something said by the subordinate (interviewee) which will allow the manager (interviewer) to link up with the topic to be pursued. Under this type sometimes silence is used to collect more information. The examples of probe questions are:

* Why do you think that your approach is correct?

* You said this is better but explain in what way?

* You mentioned your dislike for ------------------------, how you will improve the way ---?

* You said that you are facing difficulties in finding time, explain what are your ways on delegation.

However, this technique, like any other, will have inhibiting effects on the interviewee, if it is over-used.

The above types of questions are useful techniques to aid the successful appraisal interviews. However, in practice, people have a tendency to use other types, which seldom work favorably such as: leading questions (indicate the answer required or expected), evaluating questions (manager's opinion with regard to the subordinate statement) and limited choice questions (to be answered only within the preset, limits).

In appraisal interviews the importance of being an effective listener should not be underestimated. The interviewer needs to be adequately trained in communication skills including effective listening as listening is the means by which the interviewer learns about the interviewes. In this context, it should be understood that effective listening is not merely hearing with ears, but it is listening with understanding which includes listening with eyes, which can cause improved relationships.

Post appraisal interview should be closed with an agreed plan of action for implementation which should be based up on an examination of all aspects of the appraisal process and be realistic and specific.

Checklist for Conducting Post Performance Appraisal Interviews

The following checklist is proposed:

* Interviewer should be a good listener and encourage the subordinates to do most of the talking.

* The interviewer should concentrate on ways and means to minimize stress at all times.

* Questions and replies should be carefully chosen as signposts to remind both, the manager and the subordinate where they are going.

* The interviewer should avoid the use of leading, evaluating, and limited choice questions as far as practically possible.

* The interviewer should develop the skills and use it in selecting and phrasing the questions which encourage the interviewee to talk openly.

* The interviewer should practice the skills of an effective communicator including 'listening with understanding'.

* The manager (interviewer) must agree on a realistic plan of action and to provide subsequent follow up of all action agreed.

* The interviewer should add the lesson learnt to his experience and the appraisal of his (or her) own and how well he (or she) has conducted the interview.

Some Words of Advice to the Interviewer

* Effective feedback should emphasise the performance of the individual rather than his (or her) personal characteristics.

* Restrict the criticism to not more than two aspects of the subordinate in one session as there is a clear limit to what an individual can take without putting up the barricade.

* Do not fall into the trap of unsuccessful interviewing. A study (conducted by Alban Metcalf) found that managers in unsuccessful appraisal interviewing spent an average of a quarter of their time either disagreeing with, personally attacking or criticizing the subordinates whom they were appraising. Beware of such practices.

* Be convinced that a balanced view of performance, i.e. covering strength as well as weaknesses not only seems desirable but also consistent with the research findings.

* Be mindful of the fact that, to handle the interview and in particular to encourage the extent of subordinate participation, is a very crucial issue.

* The research evidence is consistent with the fact that those interviews have been proved to be most productive which were conducted by managers who give good feedback to their subordinates throughout the appraisal

period and who have been in most frequent communication with their subordinates.

* Remember appraisal based on an individual's own self assessment is not only a more flex and robust appraoch i.e. that has ample evidence of effectiveness but also it can overcome many of the problems traditionally associated with performance feedback in the appraisal interview.

CONCLUDING REMARKS

Performance appraisal i.e. performance evaluation or merit rating is one of the most important functions of management of people i.e. the most important assets). It is highly complex in nature because of the fact that it is related with human beings and their behavior. In an industrial environment it is important to maintain the desired behavior, therefore it is necessary to assess the performance of an individual after a regular interval. Furthermore, performance appraisal helps the organization to satisfy the aspirations and the needs of the individual by providing him or her with more facilities, improved working conditions and career advancement.

We should be conscious of the fact that the principal objective of performance appraisal is to derive the point to the appraisee without inviting his resentment of drawing back into taking a defensive attitude. The underlying purpose is to give him an insight in such a manner that he takes suitable steps, by a constructive motivation, to improve upon his job performance. In other words performance appraisal helps to spot out an individual's ability to see an organizational problem, devise ways of addressing them, translate his ideas into actions, incorporate new information and carry out his plans through the final results.

REFERENCES AND RECOMMENDED READING

1. Armstrong, Michael. - 'A handbook of Human Resources Management'/Kogan Page, 1987.
2. Dyal, Ishwar. - *'Role Analysis Techniques in Job Descriptions'*/California Management Review Summer 1969, pp. 47.
3. Flanagan, John C. - *'The Critical Incident Technique'*/Psychological Bulletin 51: pp. 327, 1954.
4. Flanagan, John C. and Robert K. Burns. - *'The Employee Performance Record: A New Appraisal and Development Tool'*/HBR Sept. - Oct. 1955, pp. 95.

5. Johnson, Robert G. - 'The Appraisal interview Guide'/AMACOM, 1980.

6. Lasagna John B. - *'Make Your MBO Pragmatic'*/HBR November - December 1971, pp. 64.

7. Lawson Lan. - 'Appraisal and Appraisal Interviewing: Notes for Managers Series'/ Industrial Society, 1981.

8. Levinson, Harry. - *'Management By Whose Objectives'*/HBR July - August 1970, pp. 125.

9. Levinson, Harry. - 'The Exceptional Executive'/Cambridge: Harvard University Press, 1968.

10. Long, Phil - 'Performance Appraisal Revisited'/IMP, 1980.

11. Meyer, Herbert H., Emanual Kay, and John R.P. French, Jr. - *'Split Roles in Performance Appraisal'*/HBR, Jan. - Feb. 1965, pp. 123.

12. Meyer, Herbert H. - 'The Pay for Performance Dilemma'/Organizational Dynamics, Winter 1979, P. 39.

13. Robinson, Kenneth R. - 'Effective Performance Review Interviews', IMP, 1983.

14. Stewart, Valeria, and Andrew, Stewart. - 'Practical Performance Appraisal'/Gower Publishing, 1978.

15. Thompson, Paul H., and Gene W. Dalton. - *'Performance Appraisal: Managers Beware'*/ HBR, Jan - Feb. 1970, pp. 149.

APPENDIX TO

'A PRACTICAL APPROACH TO PERFORMANCE APPRAISAL'

PERFORMANCE APPRAISAL

Name: ______________________________ Appraisal Date. ....

Post: ______________________________

Period under review From .... To ....

Date of last appraisal ....

In Attendance	Review	Interview
1. _______________	__________	________
2. _______________	__________	________
3. _______________	__________	________
4. _______________	__________	________

Remarks arising from review: ______________________________
____
____
____
____
____

Comments ____
____
____
____
____

Department	Development	Employee
....	....	....

PERFORMANCE APPRAISAL

TASK COMPLETED FOR PERIOD UNDER REVIEW

TASKS FOR NEXT APPRAISAL PERIOD

PERFORMANCE APPRAISAL SHEET

	Remarks
1. Job Knowledge.	
2. Quality of Work	
3. Quantity of Work	
4. Administration	
5. Supervisory Performance	
6. Written & Spoken Communications	
7. Decision Making & Accepting Responsibilities	
8. Motivation & Initiative	
9. Work Relationships	
10. Time Keeping/Attendance	

PERFORMANCE APPRAISAL SHEET

	Remarks
11. Overall Performance to Date	
12. Special Task (if any) completed during this phase	
13. Others	

A- Above Program Requirements

B- Meets Program Requirements

C- Below Program Requirements

Program		Rating
A	B	C

DYNAMICS OF TRAINING AND LEARNING IN AN INDUSTRIAL SETTING

CHAPTER 16

INTRODUCTION

Training is a systematic development of knowledge, skill, attitude and behavior pattern required by an individual to perform a given task or job or assignment adequately. In the past, training has been a part of Personnel Management but more emphasis has been placed upon training and development in industry some 25 years ago and by and large most of the industrial organizations have established independent training departments with an express purpose to promote training. In this context training to be considered as the platform where organizational and personnel growth can occur simultaneously.

Learning may be defined as the sum total of behavioral changes resulting from experience at training and is said to have occurred if a change in the individual behavior is effected. However, training cannot be a substitute for individual responsibility of self development as management can only provide facility and a climate where an individual should be able to develop himself according to his own desires and needs.

TRAINING DEFINED

Training is a term which has a wide variety of connotations depending on one's background and experience. It is often integrated or associated with further education. It is also often equated with courses of instruction which may either be inside or outside the organization. The use of learning experience to integrate the concept of education and training is common. For the purpose of our discussion here, we may define training as receiving learning by any instructional or experimental means to develop an individual's behavioral pattern in the areas of knowledge, skill and attitude in order to achieve a desired level (or standard) of performance.

LEARNING AND BEHAVIOR

Learning may be defined as the sum total of behavioral changes from experience at training. It is said to have occurred if there is a change in the individual behavior. Although learning may happen without any instruction, but since instruction is a human understanding whose purpose is to help people learn, the effects of learning are often beneficial and usually easy to observe. Instruction is a set of events which affect learners in such a way that learning is facilitated. The entire process of learning is based on understanding and remembering. This process has been investigated by the methods of science (mainly by Psychologists) for many years. Researchers have observed that many sensory channels are functioning at the time of learning, such as: Seeing, hearing, smelling, testing, and touching. During general education, a major sensory channel under function is 'seeing' whilst 'on the job' training it is 'hearing' Fig. 16.1, shows utilization of sensory channels during a general education and Fig. 16.2 shows utilization of sensory channels during 'on the job' training. Learning investigators are basically interested in the explanation of how learning takes place. They usually construct theories about structures and events, conceived as occurring in the nervous system, that could operate to bring about the remarkable behavior that can be directly observed as 'AN ACT OF LEARNING'. They then decide certain consequences which can be tested out by a set of controlled observations. For learning to occur efficiently, only those clients of the learning theory should be selected which pertain to the events that are controllable. A model of simplified learning theory is shown in Fig. 16.3.

There are several varieties of learning capabilities i.e. information, intellectual skills, cognitive strategies, motor skills and attitude etc. Concentrating instruction on any one type of capability alone, or any two in combination is not sufficient as human learners needs to attain several varieties of learning capabilities. Therefore, multiple aims for instructions must be recognized.

ACTION LEARNING DEFINED

Action learning is that mode of learning which stems from responsible experience and is reinforced when the experience is shared with others. Reginald Revans, a renowned researcher, has advocated methods of improving managerial group effectiveness by the use of action learning. He has explained

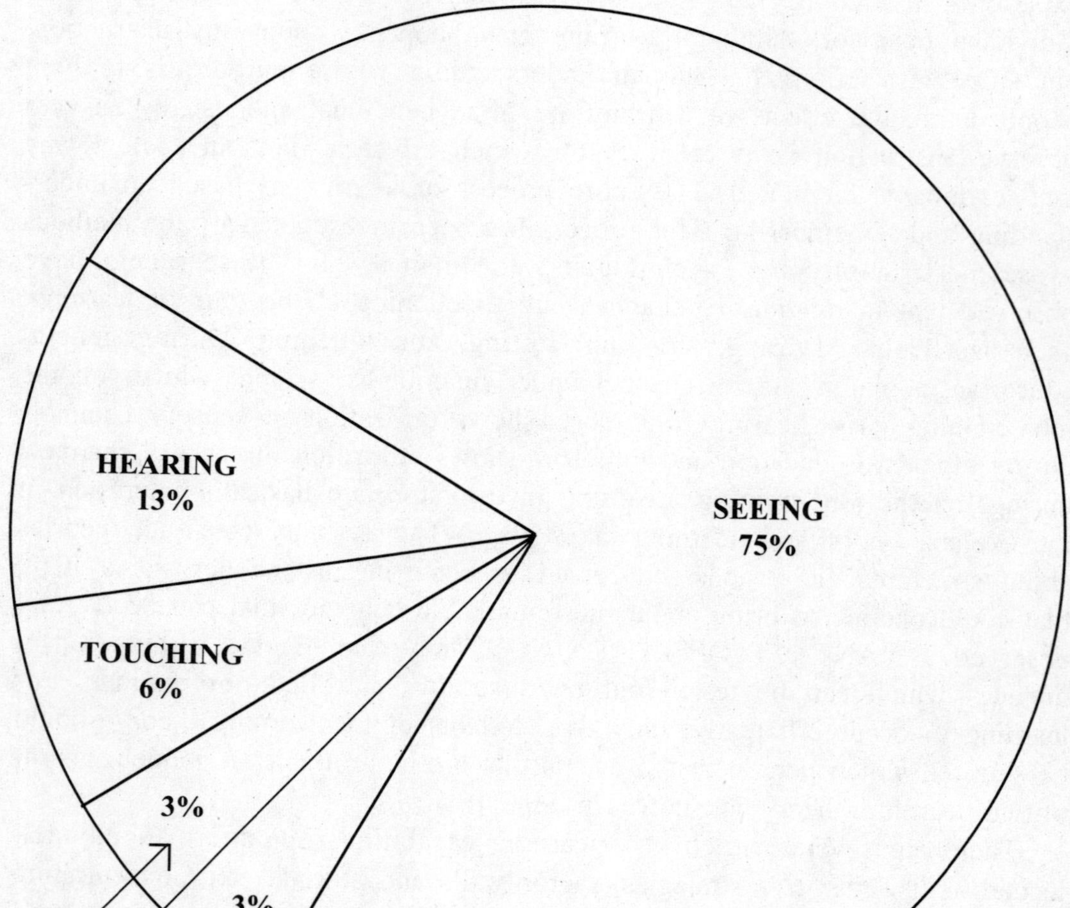

FIG. 16.1 : UTILIZATION OF SENSORY CHANNELS DURING THE GENERAL EDUCATION

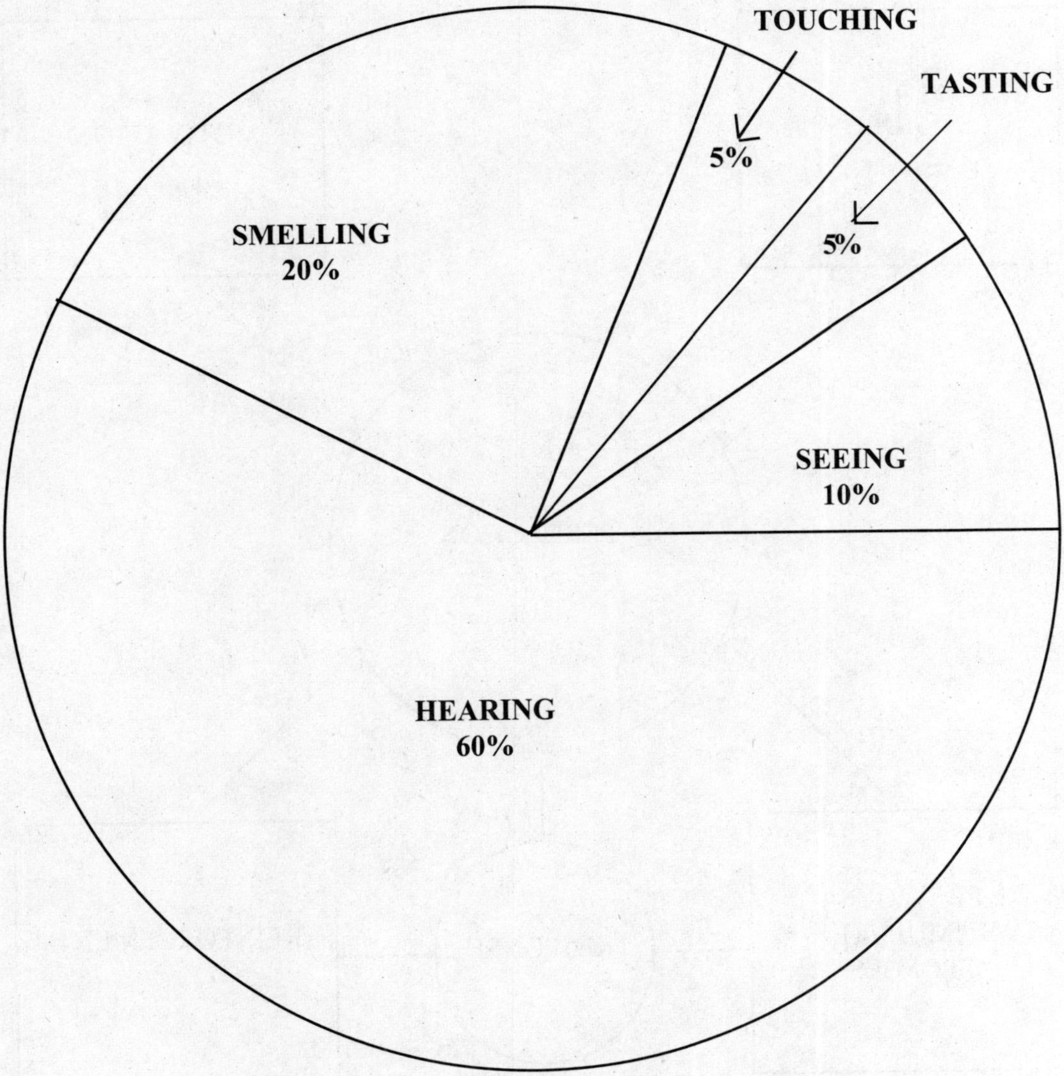

FIG. 16.2 : UTILIZATION OF SENSORY CHANNELS DURING 'ON-THE-JOB' TRAINING

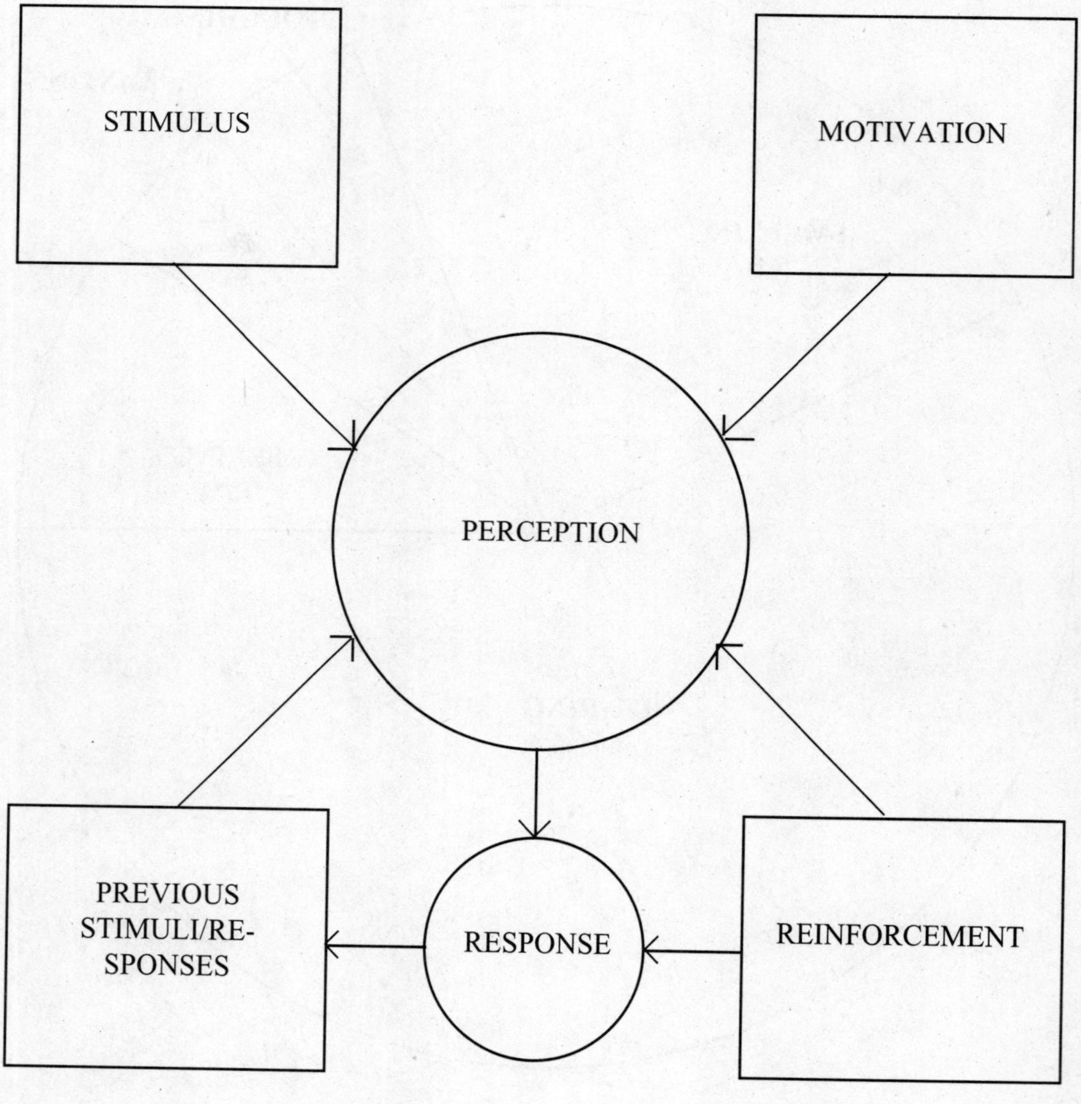

FIG. 16.3 : A MODEL OF SIMPLIFIED LEARNING THEORY

an important aspect of this proposition in these words: "Action learning distills from that comradeship in adversity which seeks responsibility through action rather than avoids it through discussion"[1&2]. According to Mike Pedler, Harry Barrington and Alan Mumford, effective task-oriented groups engaged on work-based projects use an action learning approach[3,12,4].

LEARNING PROFICIENCY

It is important for the management to know and understand the pattern in which new skills are learnt by the trainees. A typical learning curve is shown in Fig. 16.4. This learning curve shows that when the trainee first begins to learn a new skill, the trainee/learner needs the trainer's encouragement. During the next stage the rate of learning is rapid due to a rest in the trainee's confidence and satisfaction. This is the stage of increasing returns, in which a small amount of patience by the trainee produces substantial increases in job proficiency. The next stage is called plateau during which very little or no improvement takes place (due to loss of motivation as the trainee begins to feel that there is nothing further to learn or further progress becomes more difficult). The plateau in the learning curve can be eliminated by improved methods of instruction thus making further progress possible. To break away the plateau and to establish a high level of proficiency some form of motivation inducement in the form of financial and non-financial incentives is required. The next stage is known as overlearning and involves continuously repeating the training so that overlearning takes place which diminishes the likelihood of forgetting the skill.

PRINCIPLES OF LEARNING

The major learning principles that need to be taken into consideration whilst designing a training program are summarized and shown in Fig. 16.5.

ROLE OF LEARNING IN AN INDUSTRIAL SETTING

Learning is and has always been at the centre of our existence. We all have to learn about the organization of which we form a part. We need to learn about work-based activities in which we are involved, or for which we may be responsible. Also we need to learn about other people with whom

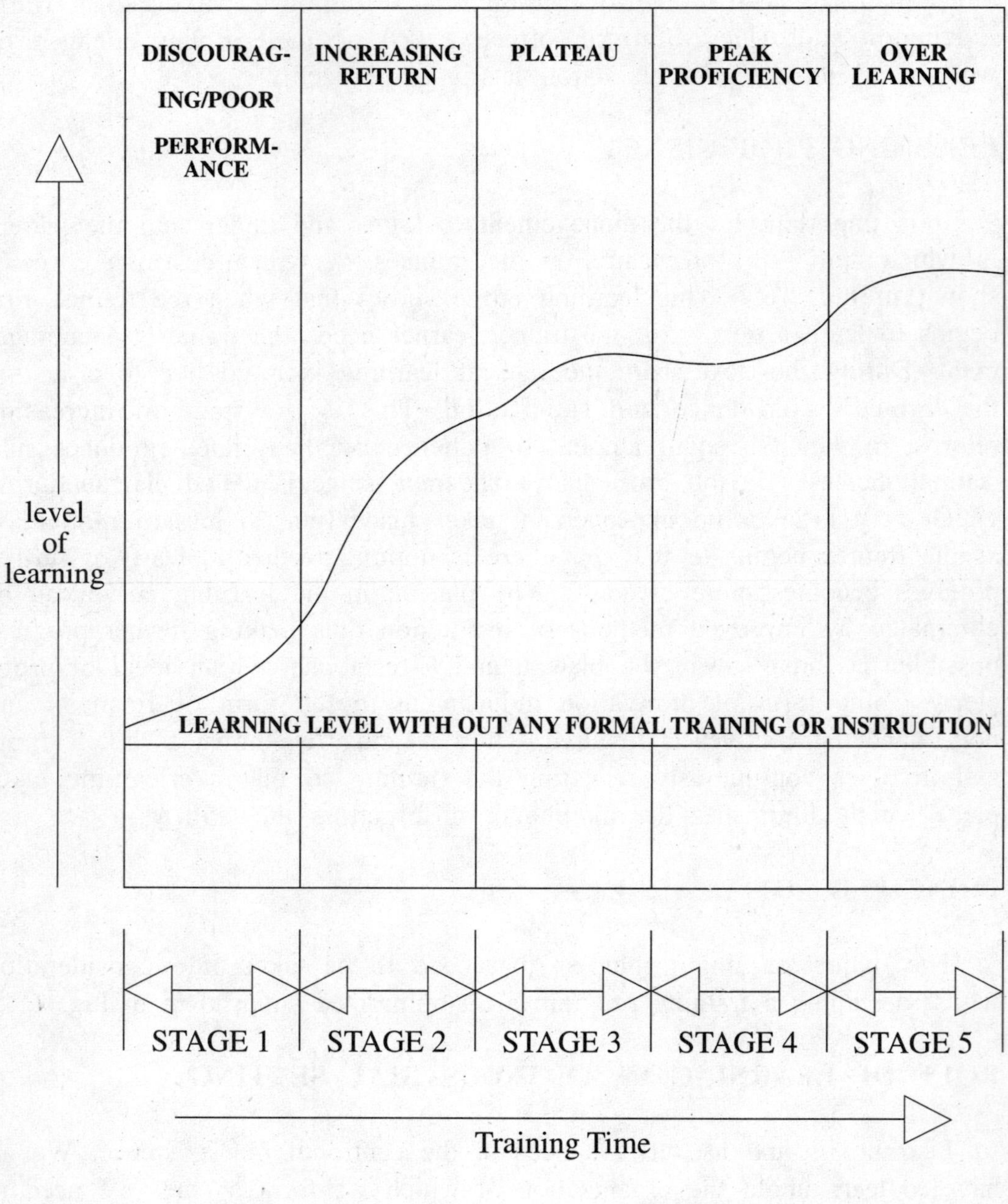

Fig. 16.4 : LEARNING PATTERN (CURVE) SHOWING PROFICIENCY

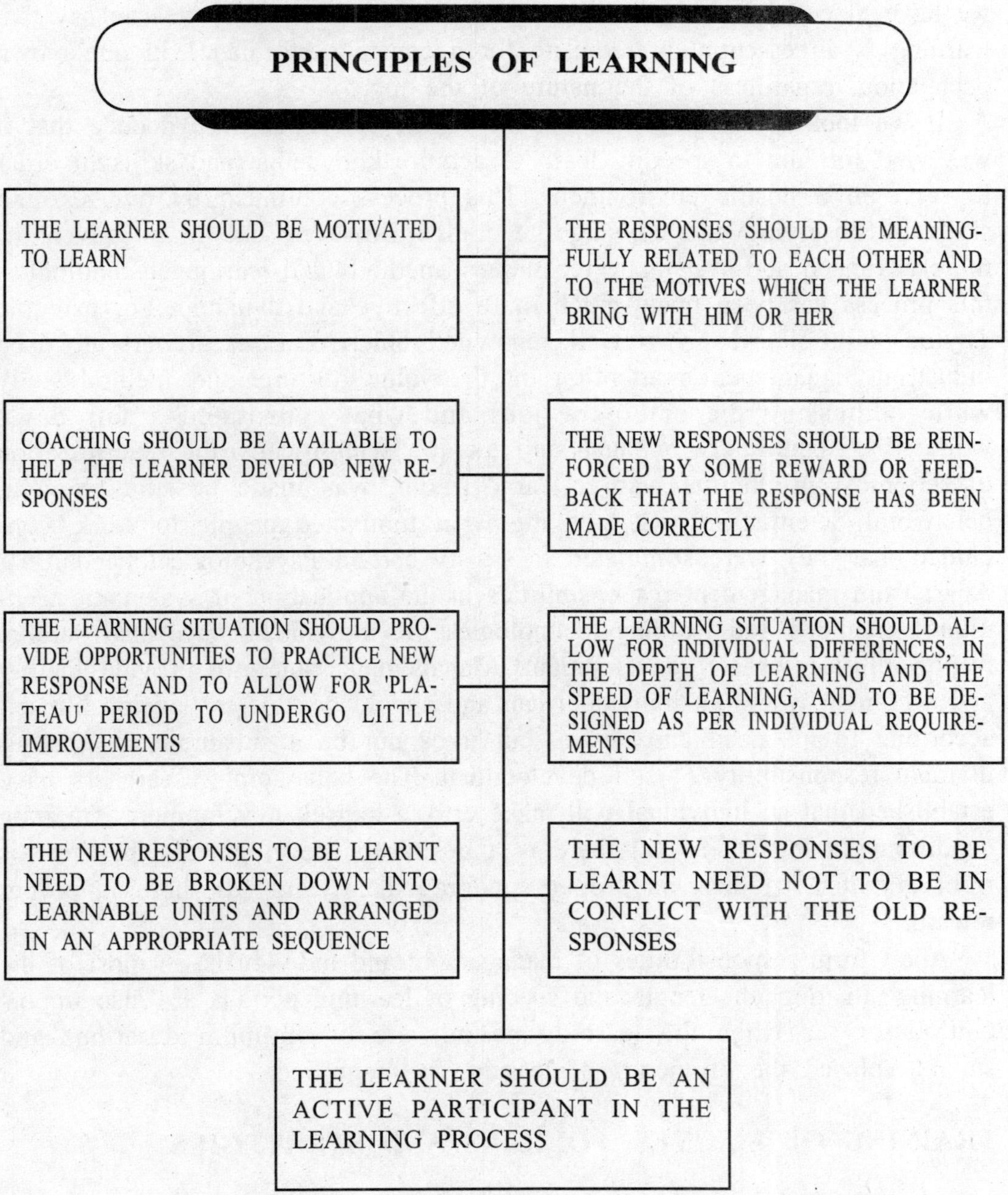

FIG. 16.5 : SOME MAJOR PRINCIPLES OF LEARNING

we have to come into contact, and so forth. In other words we can say that learning is an essential prerequisite for adequate performance in one's own occupation, regardless of the nature of the job.

If we look at the pages of history of the early man, we deduce that it was vital for him to speedily learn to acquire knowledge and skills in order to serve in a hostile environment. This process continued by our learning skills by observing and copying the adults. However, due to an advent of more advanced and systematic techniques, methods and learning technologies, this process has been made much more effective and dynamic. For example Taylor and Gilberths, two well renowned behavioral researchers, focused industrial management's attention on the value of time and method study while addressing the nature of jobs and what constituted a fair day's work.[13&14] Accordingly by analysing the job scientifically the determination of the most productive way to carry it out, was made possible. Several behavioral Scientists, whilst studying what motivated people to work, concluded that they were stimulated to satisfy certain Psychological needs.[15&16] Apart from management responsibilities in the application of systematic techniques, methods and learning technologies the individuals have also parallel responsibilities for self development. Management can only provide facility and a climate where an individual can and should be able to develop himself according to his need and desire, but it cannot be a substitute for the individual responsibility of self development. The behavioral researchers have established that an individual will make efforts for self development if certain conditions exist such as (a) there is a desire for development; (b) there is right climate; (c) there is proper encouragement; and (d) there is proper reward.

Apart from responsibilities of management and individuals, in most of the learning situation, the length and spacing of learning periods are also important factors as when the learning periods are of optimum durations and suitably placed the efficiency of learning is magnified.

TRAINING OBJECTIVES, POLICIES AND STRATEGIES

Training Objectives

The principal object of training is to maintain and improve the performance at work; whilst training relates to specific skills associated to job performance. Since the manager/supervisor is accountable to the top management for the performance of his staff, therefore, the responsibility for training his subordinates has to rest very firmly on his shoulders.

For training, education is the most important prerequisite as it is extremely difficult to train an uneducated person. However, Human Resources Development (a modern term often used for training) consists of developing the attitude and personality in addition to the skills needed for job performance, and therefore include both training and education. This important relationship i.e. training, education and development is shown in Fig. 16.6.

The objectives of training should also include an effective training program. Important requisites of an effective training program in an industrial setting is shown in Fig. 16.7.

Training objectives should also include management development. Many major organizations of today promote Management Development Program/ Scheme due to many inherent benefits such as career progressions of individuals, improvement and maintenance of standards of managerial performance, assurance of a continuing supply of suitably trained managers to meet the organization's future needs.[17,23]

It has been recognized that likewise organizations, individuals have objectives, outside interests, home background and beliefs, etc. These objectives may create problems for management as whilst quite being logical and realistic in relation to the individual could often be in conflict with those of the organization. Training objectives should address this issue and provide valuable support in exploring such difficulties in training programs.

Training Policies

In this modern industrialized world, every organization needs to have a declared training policy. It is not enough as Blake and Mouton put it, that it is the policy of the organization to ensure that, in the interest of the corporate excellence, everyone is developed to the limit of his or her ability. Training Policy must be tangible, simple and unambiguous. It should be understood at levels of the organization, supported by all employees, and everyone should be clear about its implementation.[24&25]

Employees must see training not as a penalty but as an opportunity for them to acquire further skills, expertise and knowledge for their own interests as well as the interests of their organization. However, the management must create a climate in which employees should be able to eagerly seize such opportunities to further their individual objectives. In this context the impor-

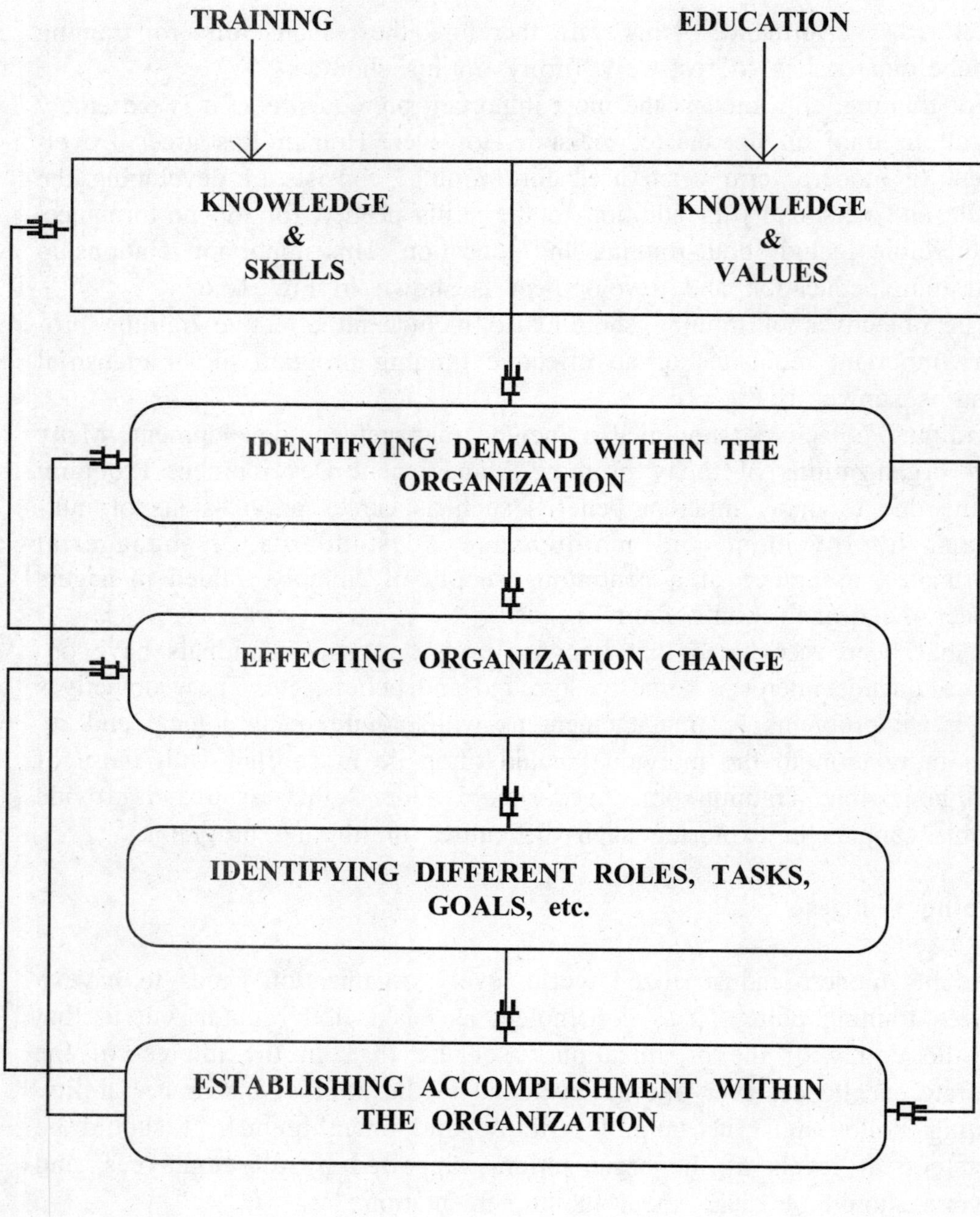

FIG. 16.6 : RELATIONSHIP OF TRAINING, EDUCATION AND DEVELOPMENT

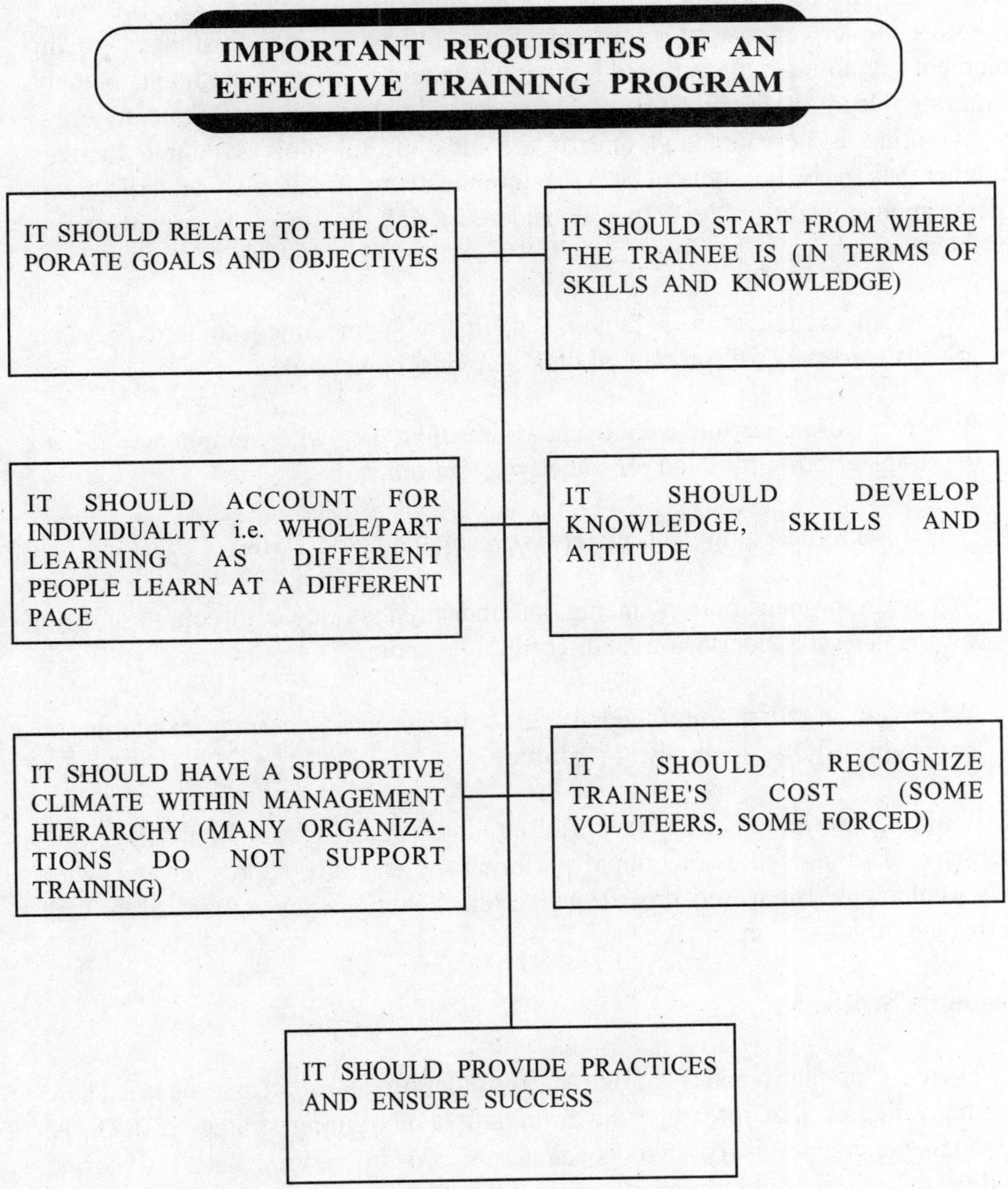

FIG. 16.7 : SOME IMPORTANT REQUISITES OF AN EFFECTIVE TRAINING PROGRAM

tance of self-development should not be underestimated.[26-29]

In a modern industrial environment, by and large, it is customary to implement a training policy through an independent service department, namely: Training Department or Human Resources Development Department.

Training is potential and one of the most useful tools available to management as it is not only a service to management but also an adjustment of the management process. It is considered a solution to many organizational problems such as:

* When an organization is facing a difficulty in meeting standards because of insufficiency of present skills, methods or attitudes.

* When an organization is buoyant or resilient i.e. when employees are to be transferred, promoted or otherwise retired.

* When facilities/equipment dictate new methods or skills.

* When an organization is facing an undesired strategic direction in spite of managerial supervision and corrective action.

* When an organization is easily able to surpass existing standards by improving skills, methods, or attitude.

Training policy should be formulated in such a way that all major premises of organization functional performance are fully addressed and when it is implemented it would provide maximum benefit to the individual as well as to the organization.

Training Strategies

There is no hard and fast rule in formulating a training strategy. There are many factors that influence the formulation of training strategies, such as: a management/supervisory style, local community influences, nature of work, quality of working environment, organizational climate, and so forth. Since these factors, by and large, differ from one establishment to another, therefore, the strategies called for may vary from one organization to another. Furthermore, it may be difficult to arrive at a consensus of training strategy for the following reasons:

(a) Some of the organizations may induct professionally qualified people from the work places (the open market) while others may engage fresh university graduates and put them under training in their own training institutes. Therefore, the training may manifest itself in quite different ways.

(b) Since changing in the structure and organization policy might effect the progress faster than training, therefore, training is not always the best or most reasonable means to adopt to solve local problems.

However, certain guidelines may be adopted in arriving at the best strategy for training in an industrial organization such as the following:

* Training is to be seen as the area where organization and individual development can match and where personal and organizational growth can occur simultaneously.

* Training is seen as a systematic development of knowledge, skills, attitude and behavioral pattern required by an individual in order to perform adequately a given task or job.

* Training is seen as an organizational procedure for increasing the knowledge and skills of people for a definite purpose. Any good training program should lay down the procedure by which people gain knowledge and skills to perform their job efficiently and effectively.

* The use of learning experience to integrate the concept of education and training is an increasingly common phenomenon and consequently training as a process is seen to rest upon the application of a system model.

* Training is often associated and integrated with further education.

* Training strategy should revolve around a total training doctrine and it should satisfy not only organizational requirements but also meet the psychological needs of the employees whilst not conflicting with the

management philosophy.

The organizational unit responsible for training should adopt a doctrine which will encompass its overall approach to learning i.e. overall sense of directions, training intervention, strategies, tactics, flexibility, objectivity, comprehensiveness, co-ordination, planning, commitment to a set of principles and methodology important for fulfilment of training objectives, ways and means to gain acceptance of training styles i.e. participating styles as against traditional teaching styles, delivery, monitoring and control procedures, modification etc. Training strategy needs to be well co-ordinated with a total organizational strategy, geared to the solution of real problems which affect performance of the business as a whole, and is sufficiently effective in ensuring that the training is reaching to the root of the organization needs.

In order to identify the organizational problems and determine whether training might help to resolve or reduce them, the answers to questions such as the following should be sought.

* What is the current kind, nature and level of performance?

* How does the current performance compare with the desired kind and level?

* What changes are desirable?

* Can changes be identified?

* Where are changes desired i.e. in structure, procedural practice, policy or behavior ?

* Can the desired changes be affected by training requirements?

* Is there a room for training in an overall change process.

TRAINING PROCESS

Training Process Defined

Training process involves learning about the job by the employee. This process is cyclic in nature. It starts with the identification of job difficulties and travels through problem recognition, defining learning needs, organization of formal training, follow up and back to the starting point. This procedure is shown in Fig. 16.8 & Fig. 16.9.

Establishing Training Needs

On making of that training needs analysis, with a view to improve the learning process it is possible to identify the gap between the current results (present capacities of incumbent) and the desirable results (the requirements of a given job). If this gap is substantial which could be economically and effectively reduced by training then training needs are to be determined. Therefore, in the training process, one of the most important steps is to establish the training needs[31,32]. The responsibility for determining training needs belong, by and large, to the line managers. In discovering training needs, a four stepped approach shown in Fig. 16.10 is recommended. The Research Commitee of the American Society of Training Directors have proposed eleven techniques for determining training needs which are shown in Fig. 16.11.

ELEMENTS OF TRAINING SYSTEM

Every training system includes four elements namely:

Trainees, Trainers, a Training Program, and Training Material (Fig. 16.12 refers).

The following guideline should be adopted in formulating a training system.

For Trainees

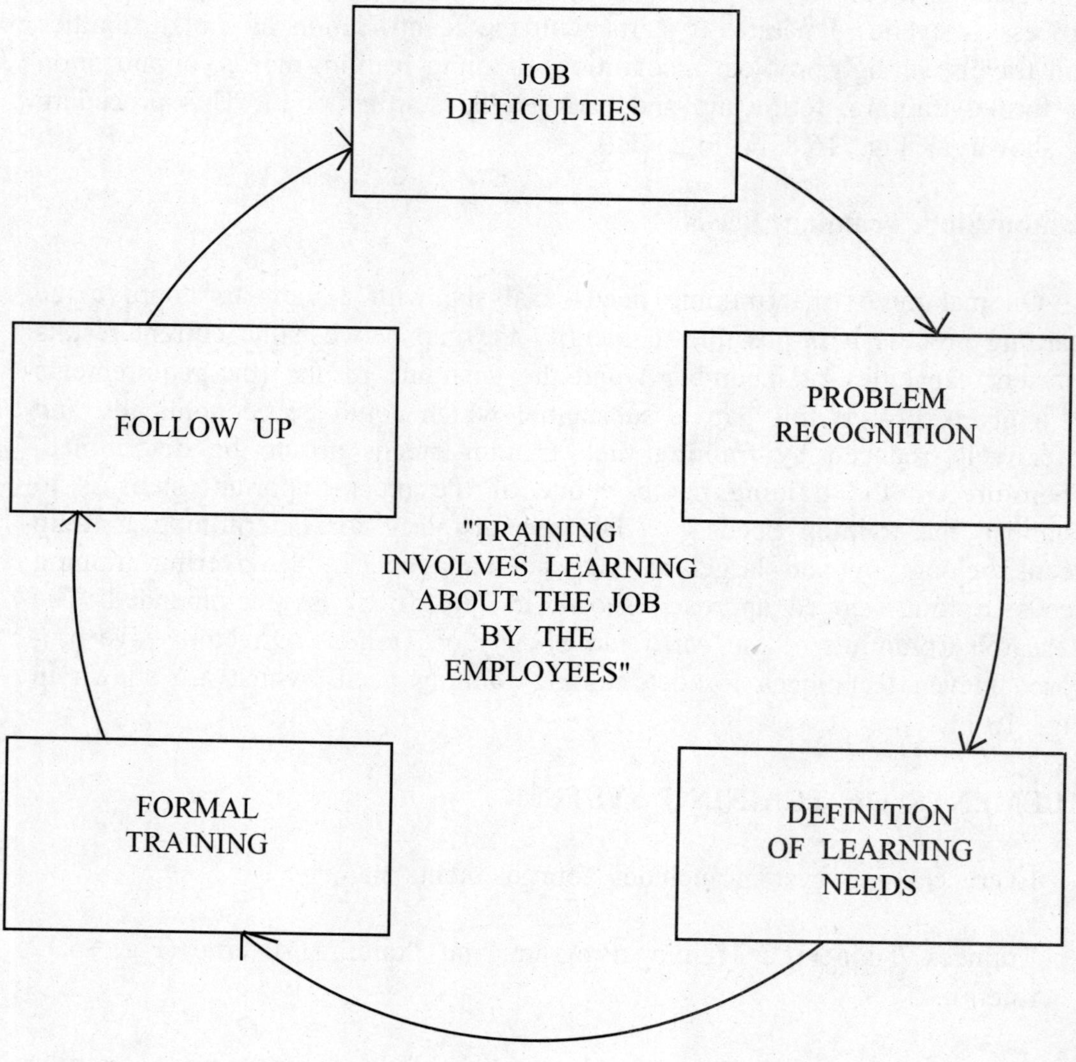

FIG. 16.8 : A SIMPLE MODEL OF TRAINING PROCESS

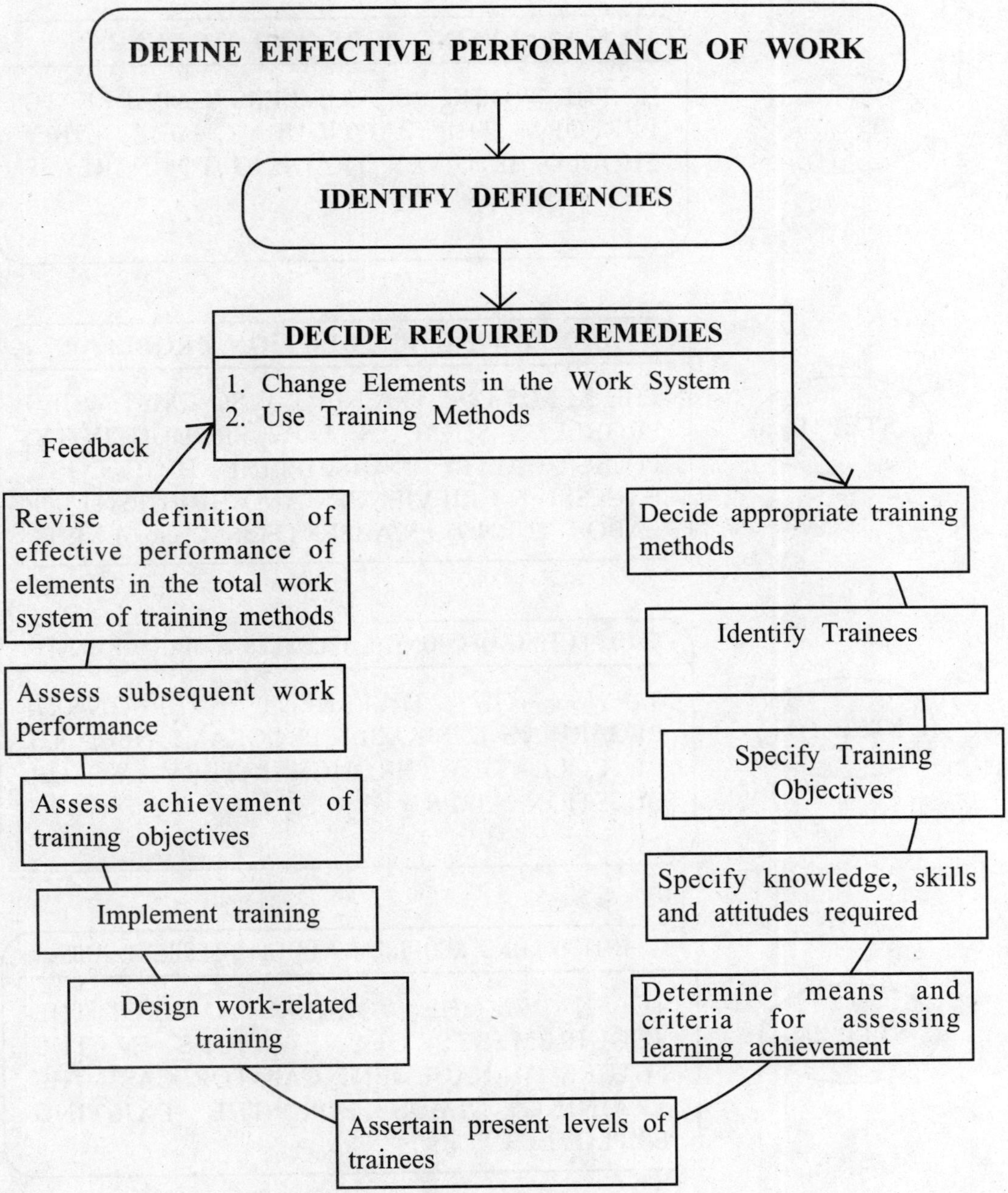

FIG. 16.9 : A CYCLIC PROCESS OF A TRAINING SYSTEM

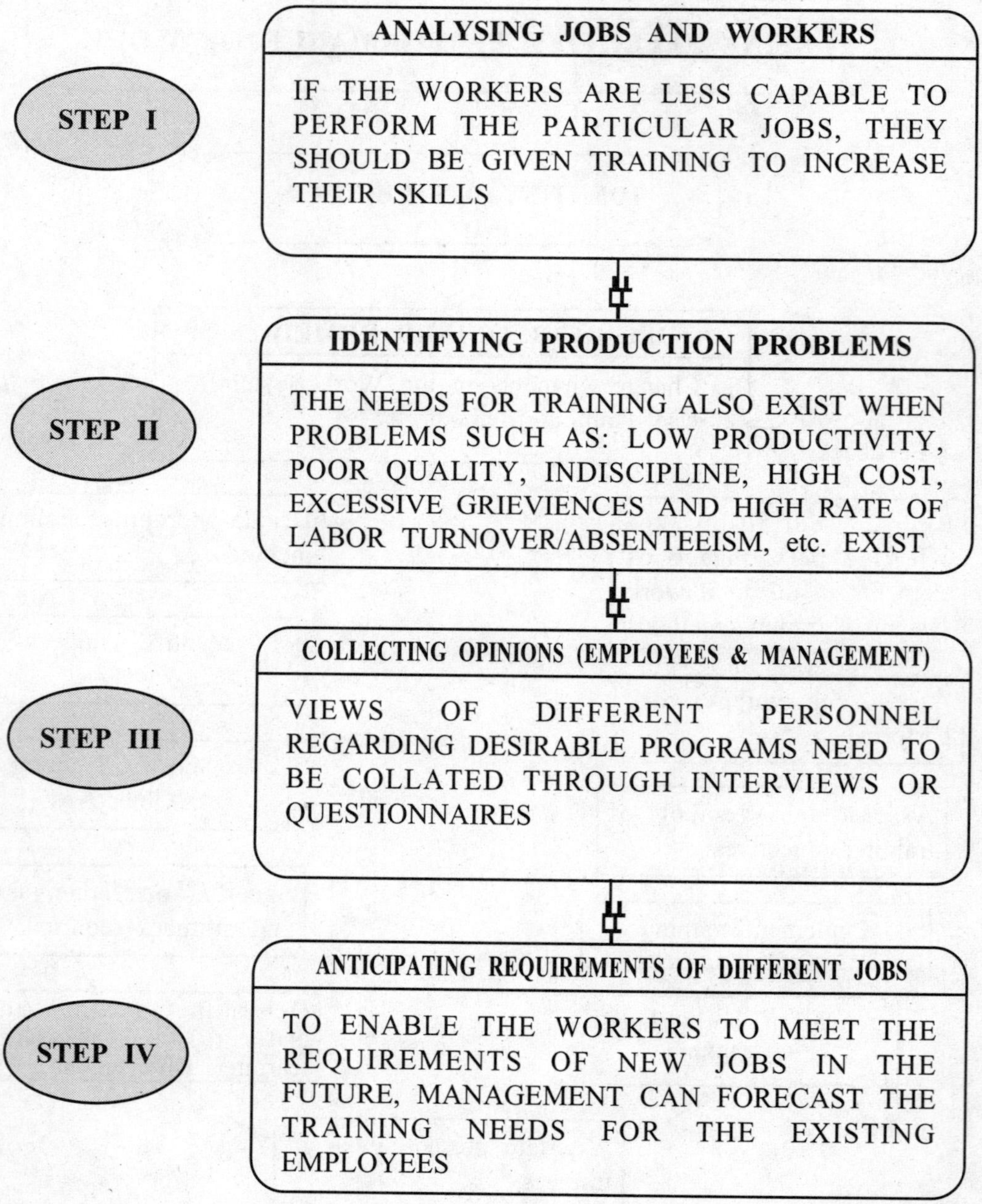

FIG. 16.10 : STEPS FOR DETERMINING TRAINING NEEDS

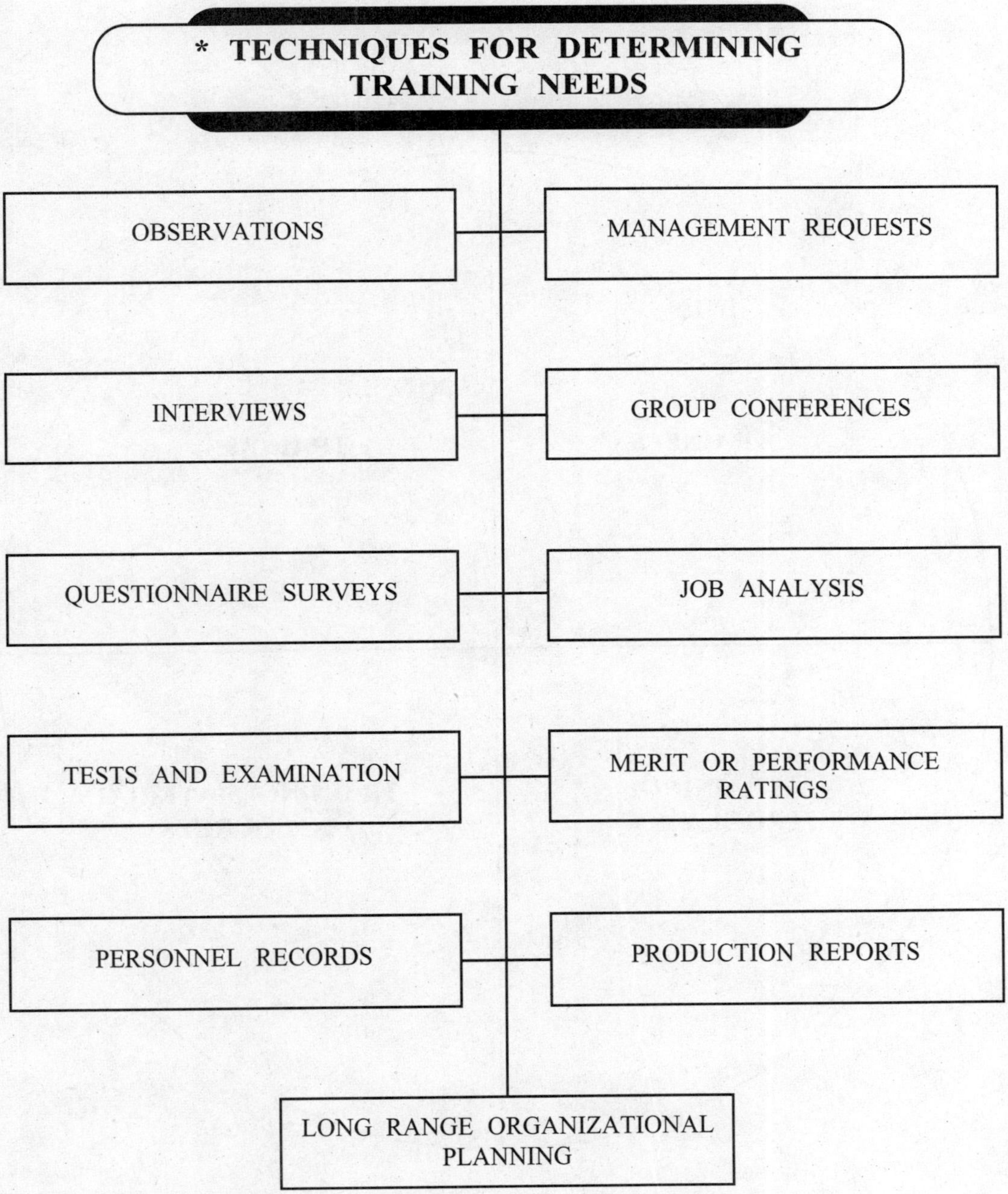

*Adapted from the listing of the research committee of American Soeiety of Training Directors

FIG. 16.11 : TECHNIQUES FOR DETERMINING TRAINING NEEDS

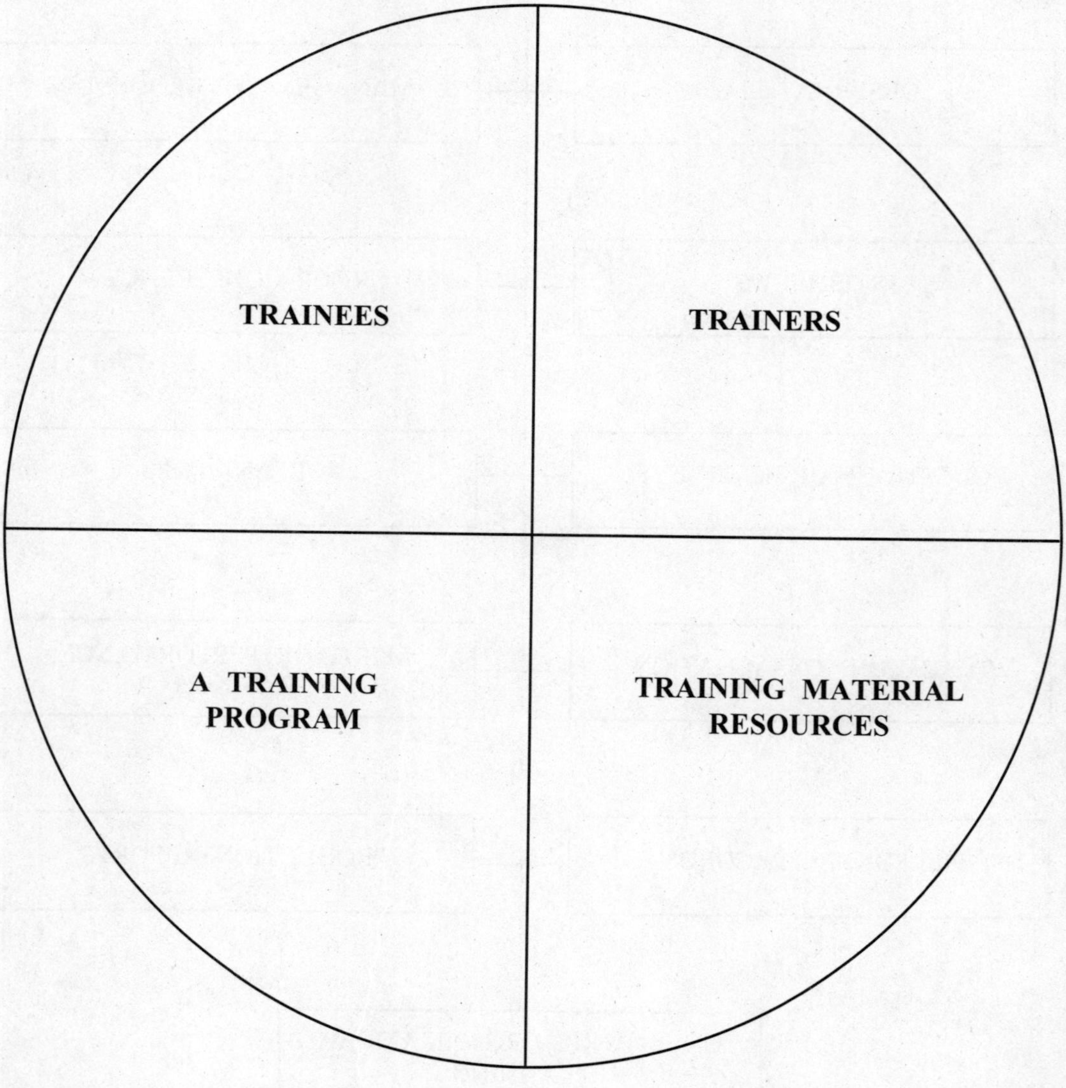

FIG. 16.12 : ELEMENTS OF A TRAINING SYSTEM

* If permanent and gainful results are to be obtained, the proper selection of trainees is of paramount importance. Careful screening of candidates for training enhances the effectiveness of the training activities.

* For employees/workers training, an incumbent should be placed at ease and must be given the proper background information before he or she starts learning the new job skills and knowledge.

* For supervisory staff, each incumbent should be given a fair opportunity for promotion and advancement and some should not be excluded from receiving training on the ground that they are already performing satisfactorily.

For Trainers

* Careful selection should be made as the trainer is a key figure in an effective training program. In this respect the following qualities and characteristics should be sought:

- The trainer should be well qualified having professional expertise in order to fulfil his responsibility.

- The trainer must be able to divide the job into logical parts and should be able to teach one part at a time without losing sight of the perspective of the whole.

- The trainer must have sufficient knowledge and skills to instruct, and he must be tolerant and patient.

- The trainer must have an understanding of what employees are in order to import the knowledge, skills or attitude for which the program is desired for.

- The trainer must be able to appreciate the value of training work in relation to the enterprise's overall goals and objectives and must have a clear cut idea about the requirements of organization.

- The trainer must need to have atleast a minimum knowledge about the job which he is going to instruct to the trainees.

- The trainer should be a good presenter and be able to deliver an effective presentation or demonstration.

For Training Program

- Follow the basic logic of a training program as shown in Fig. 16.13.

- Keep in mind the principal values of training such as shown in Fig. 16.14, whilst formulating a training program.

- Consider the benefits of staff training such as shown in Fig. 16.15 whilst formulating a training program.

- Design carefully the training period keeping in mind the skills to be acquired, the learning capacities of trainees, the training capacity, and the training media to be used. In this context it is important to note that the use of effective visual material usually helps to reduce the training time. (Remember "a picture is worth more than a thousand words").

- Choose appropriate training methods or techniques for imparting trainees, keeping in mind cost, time available, depth of knowledge, skills required, number of persons to be trained, trainees background, etc. The principal methods commonly in use include: 'On-The-Job' training and 'Off-the-job' training. 'Off-the-job training in turn includes (a) classroom method and (b) vestibule training. Other methods include: apprentices training, relations training, programmed learning, prescribed reading, distance learning, induction training, procedure training, participative methods (e.g. conferences, seminars, discussions, team training, case studies, simulation/business groups, brainstorming, workshops, sensitivity training, transactional analysis, training within industries, visual presentation, field trips, job rotation, coaching, transactional meditation etc.).

- Reinforce a training program with self development, executive development and organizational development programs with a view to improve the effective performance or managers, who make all the crucial decisions affecting the whole organization.

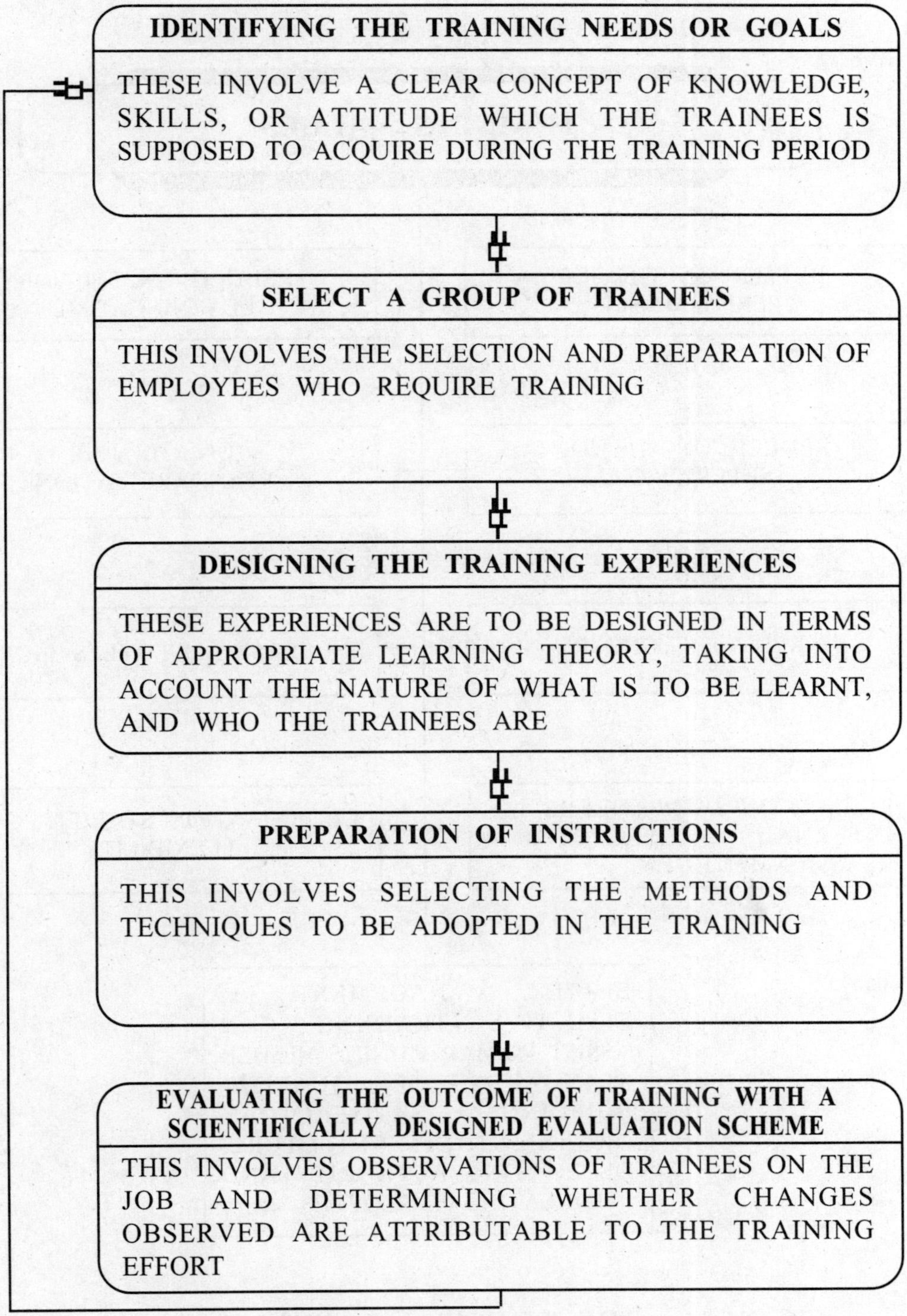

FIG. 16.13 : THE BASIC LOGIC OF A TRAINING PROGRAM

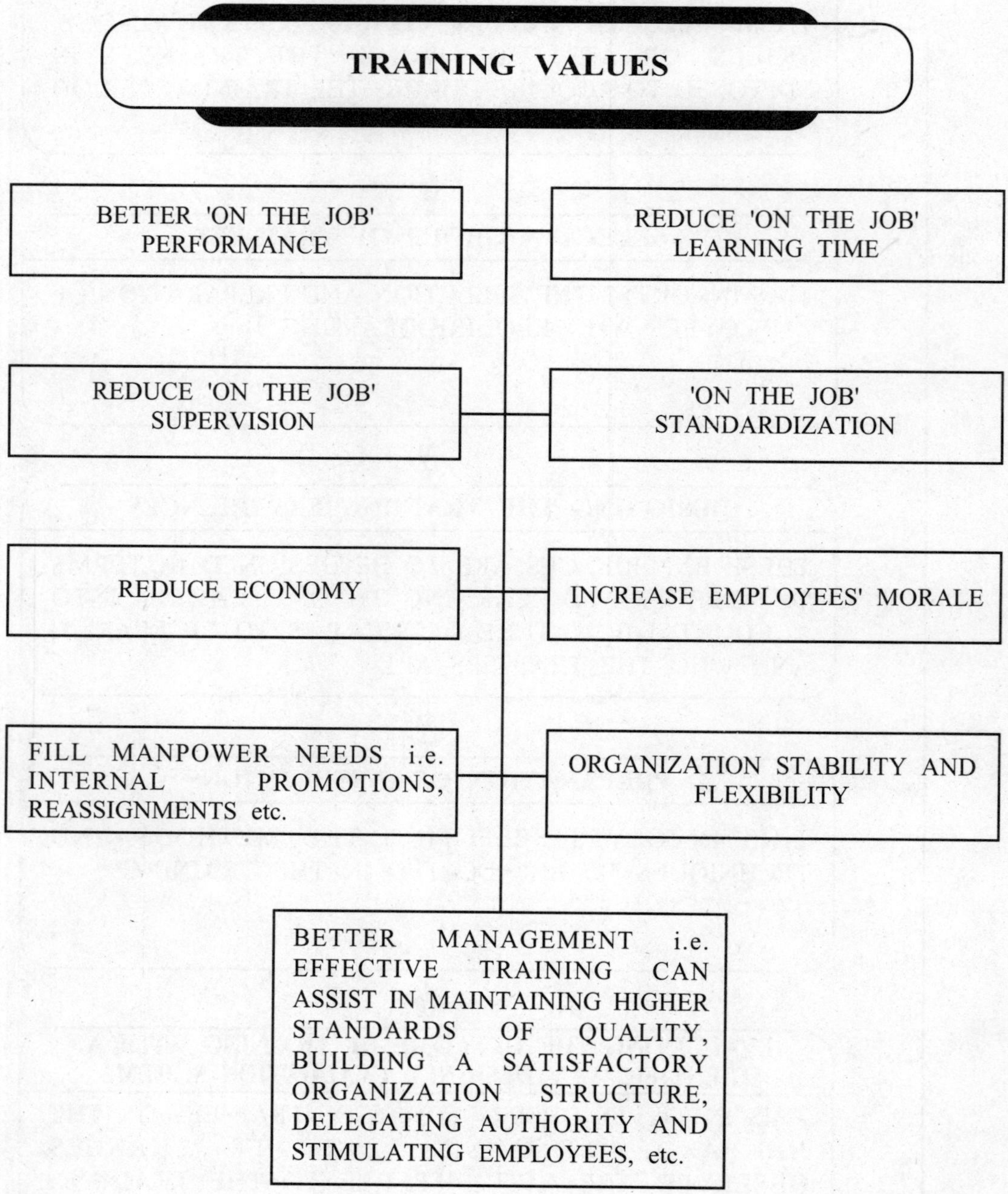

FIG. 16.14 : THE PRINCIPAL VALUES OF TRAINING

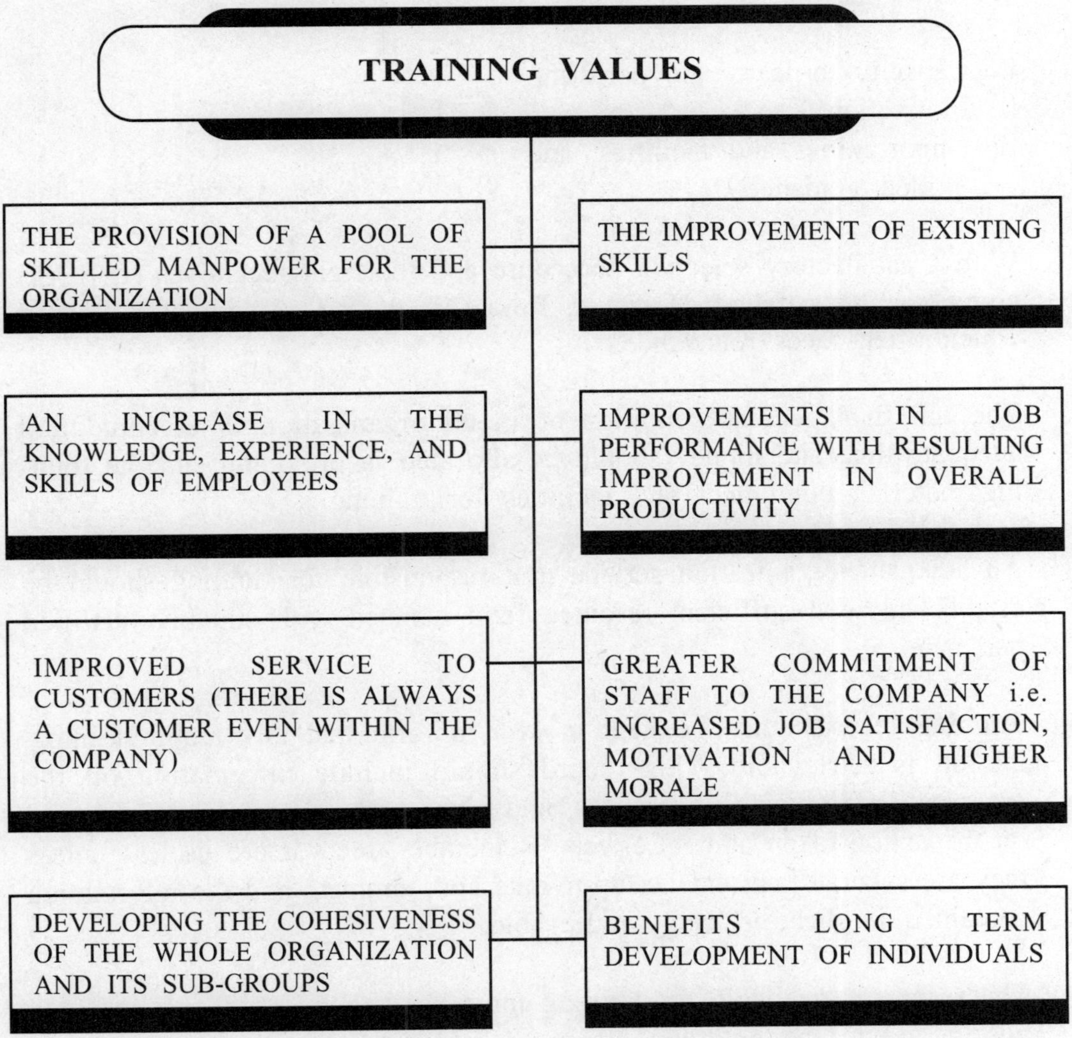

FIG. 16.15 : SOME BENEFIT OF SYSTEMATIC TRAINING

For Training Material/Resources

- Remember in order to be able to acquire skills and knowledge, the employee has to have:

  i. Capacity to learn and perform;
  ii. Motivation;
  iii. Opportunities and facilities; and
  iv. Skilled guidance.

  With a satisfactory selection procedure and the right incentives (i) & (ii) above can be satisfied. However, from (iii) & (iv) investment is needed which often faces reluctance.

- The top management commitment in an organization is essential and adequate time and money should be allocated in providing suitable training material, equipment and facilities for training.

- An adequate organization service unit responsible for training should be established with sufficient resources and manned with suitably qualified personnel.

- Training records must be kept in such a form that any required information is retrievable. This record should include information on the organization's objectives, policies, and plans with respect to training and on the action taken and its effects. Remember, records are useless unless they are accurate, current i.e. up-to-date and complete and the information contained in them is easily retrievable.

- The resources available for training must need to be used and managed wisely and to the optimum effect.

PLANNING A TRAINING PROGRAM

During World War II Training approach was developed consisting of four steps as shown in Fig. 16.16 which is suitable for planning small training programs. However, for planning major training programs, the training cycle

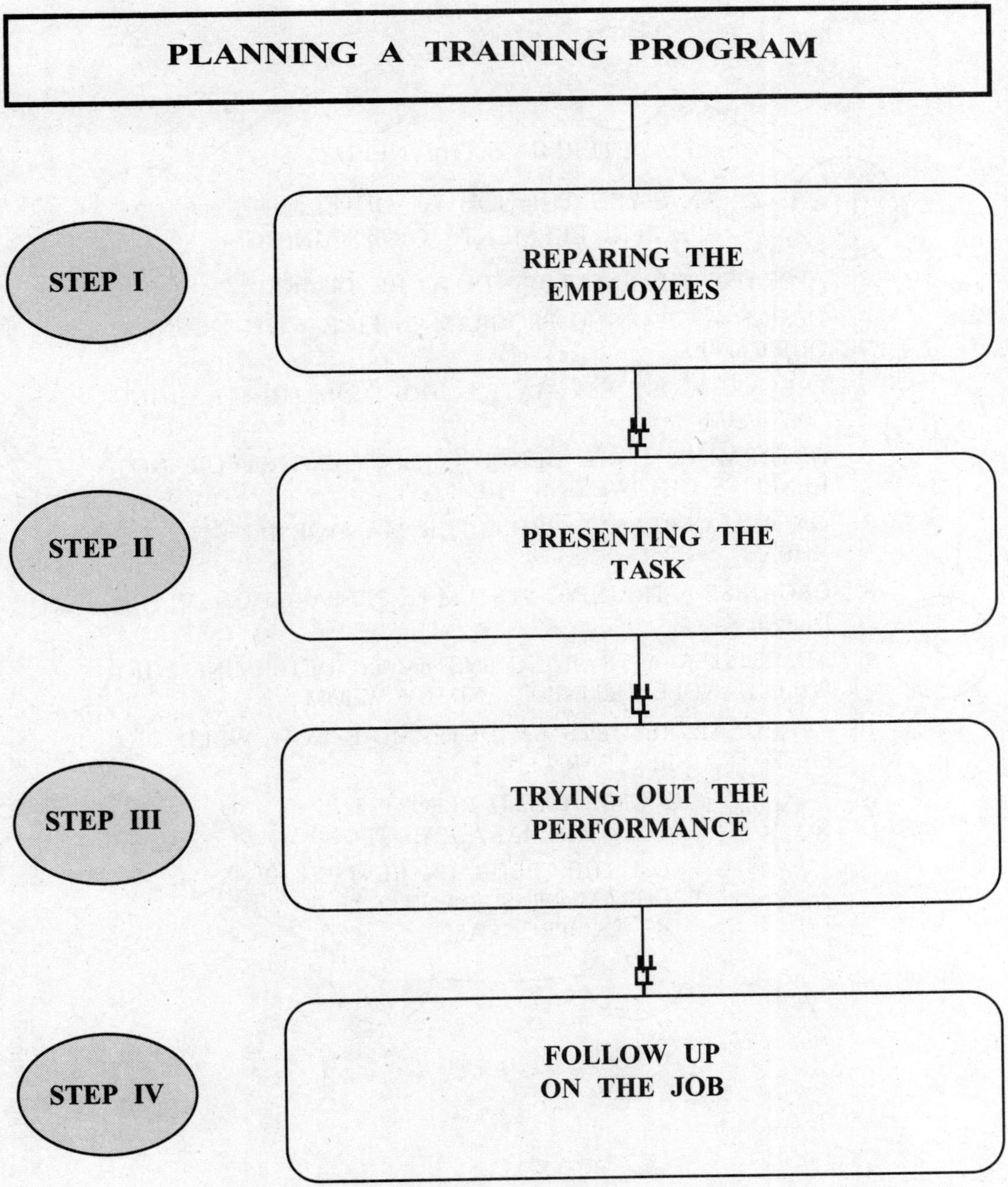

FIG. 16.16 : A SIMPLE FOUR STEPPED TRAINING APPROACH

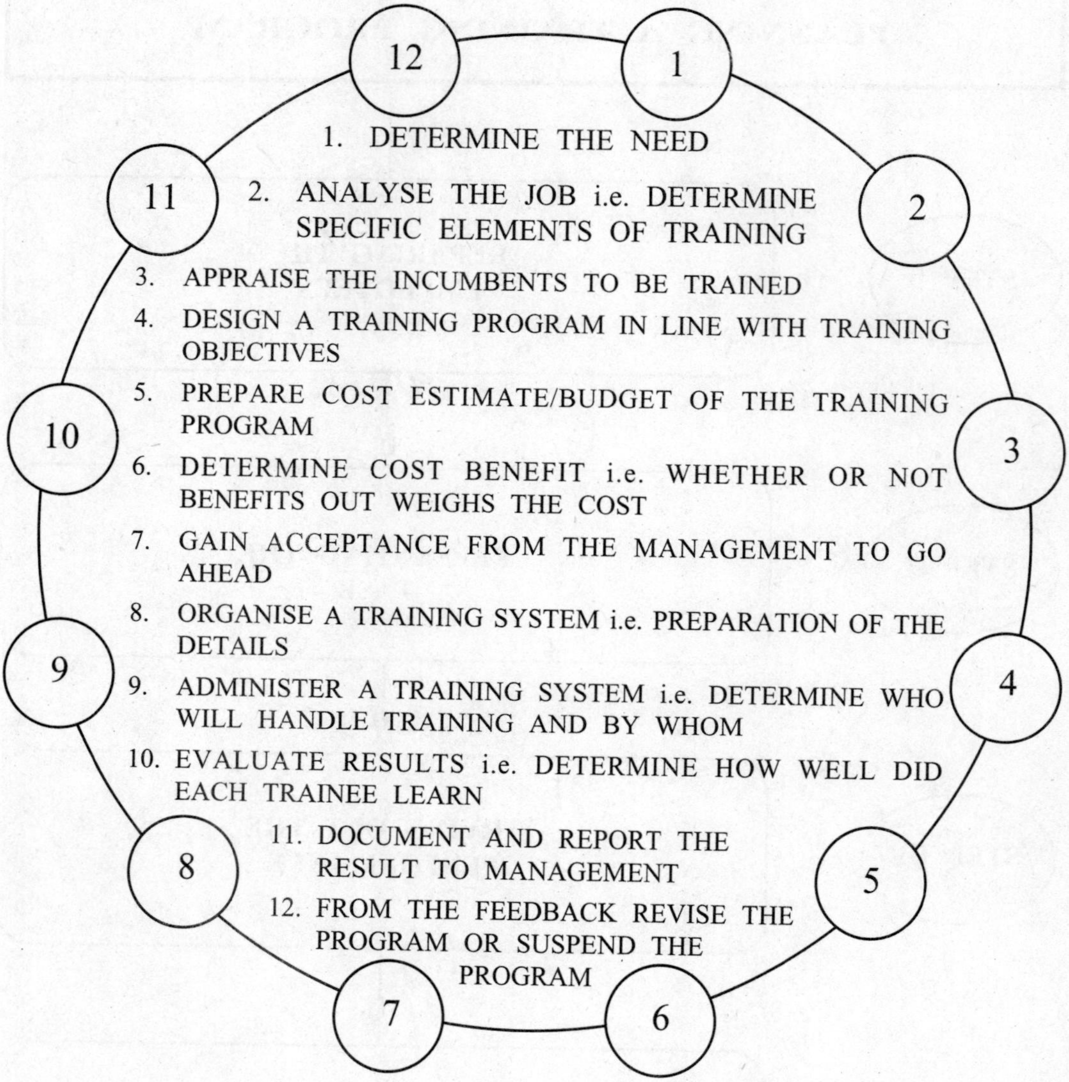

FIG. 16.17 : TRAINING CYCLE FOR PLANNING MAJOR TRAINING PROGRAMS

is somewhat complex requiring many steps as shown in Fig. 16.17.

Essentials of Training

The first essential of training is that every person should be adequately educated as it would not be easy to train an uneducated person. Other essentials include: knowledge, attitudes, conformity with objectives, continuous participation, fulfilling certain needs of employees, stimuli, responses, motivation, reward and incentives, and management attitude and commitment (see Fig. 16.18).

TRAINING PROCEDURES

The various steps involved in the training procedure are shown in Fig. 16.19. By following this procedural model, any training program systematically developed and introduced is bound to bring a desirable change in behavior of incumbents. Formal training should be imparted only when the request for training comes from the concerned department and training objectives are clearly specified by the training analyst who should test and obtain an object measure by matching with the proper performance of the given task (job).

Fig. 16.20 shows a model of training analysis which is concerned with identifying the causes of performance deficiencies and also shows an equation to measure performance deficiency. A decision whether to train or not to train can be based on the extent to which performance deficiency results from either execution or acquisition. Fig. 16.21 shows two essential elements in training program, namely: (i) determination of training objectives and (ii) continuation of performance measures.

In this respects certain aspects require some special considerations such as the following:

* For strategies and Techniques grouping should be made to match the technique with the training strategy.

  For example: For 'Self Training Strategy" i.e. individual learn by themselves, suitable techniques to be used may include self instruction on the job or program learning.

  For 'Tutorial Training Strategy' i.e. individuals, get the guidance in one

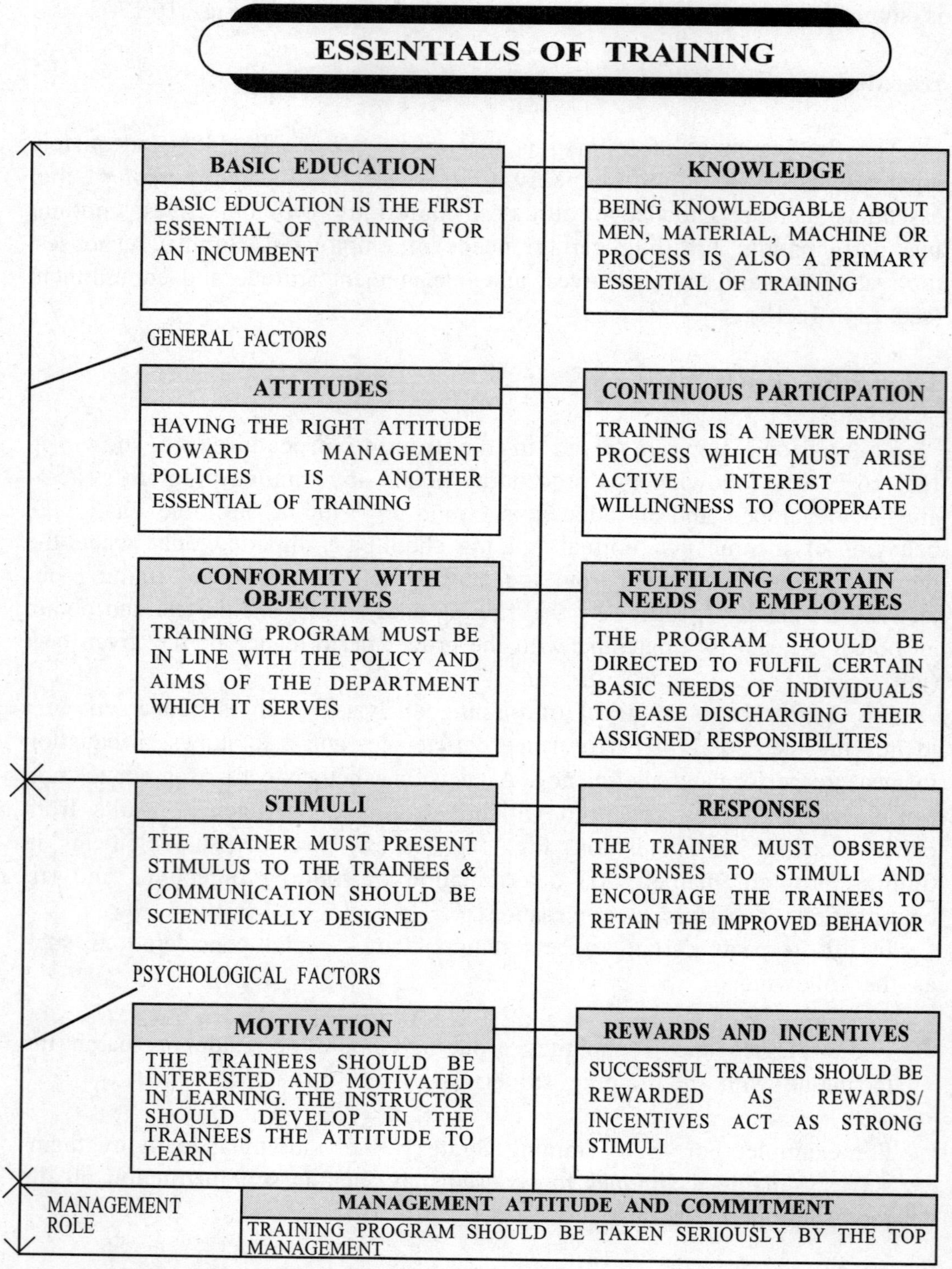

FIG. 16.18: SOME ESSENTIALS OF TRAINING

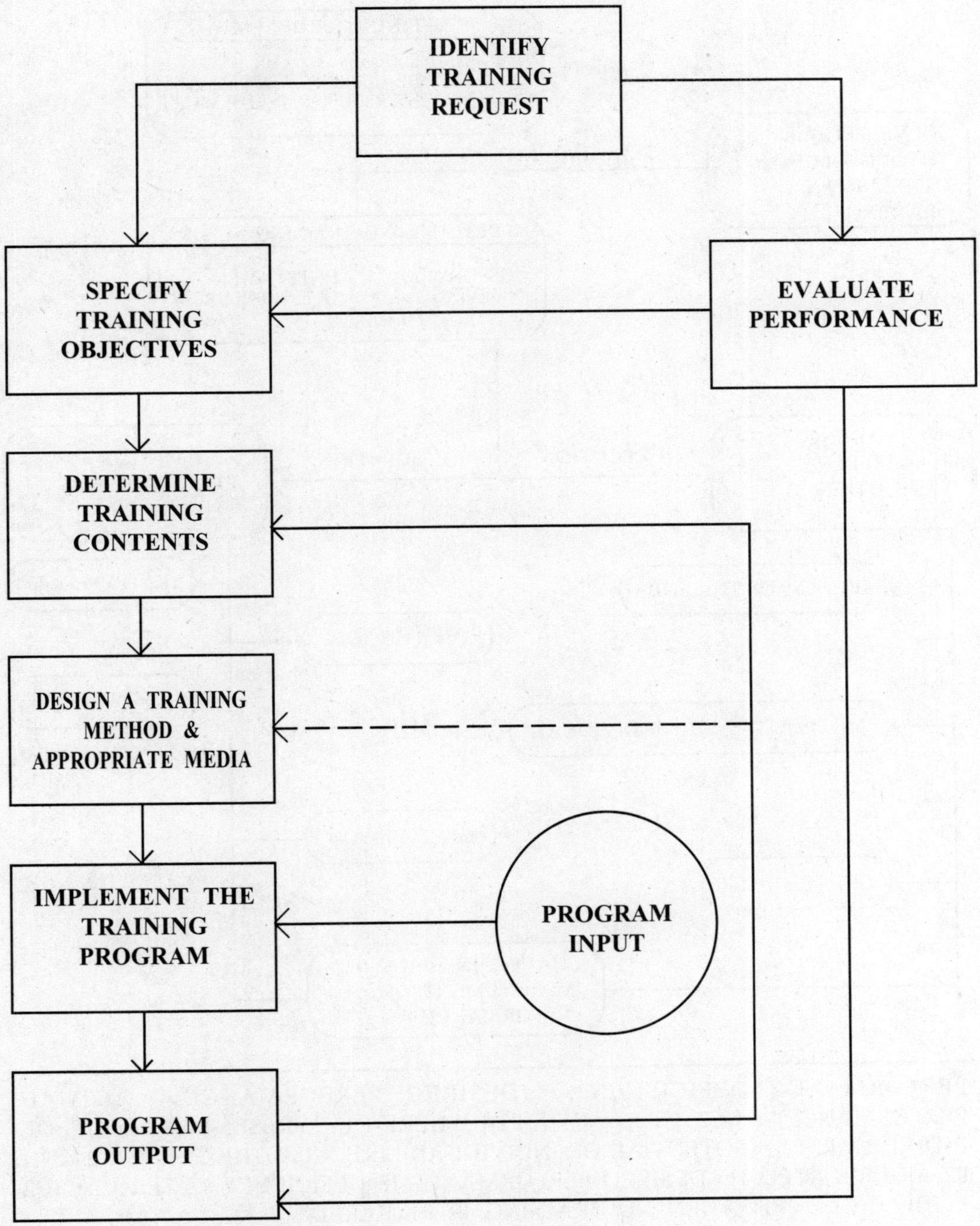

FIG. 16.19 : A MODEL OF TRAINING PROCEDURES

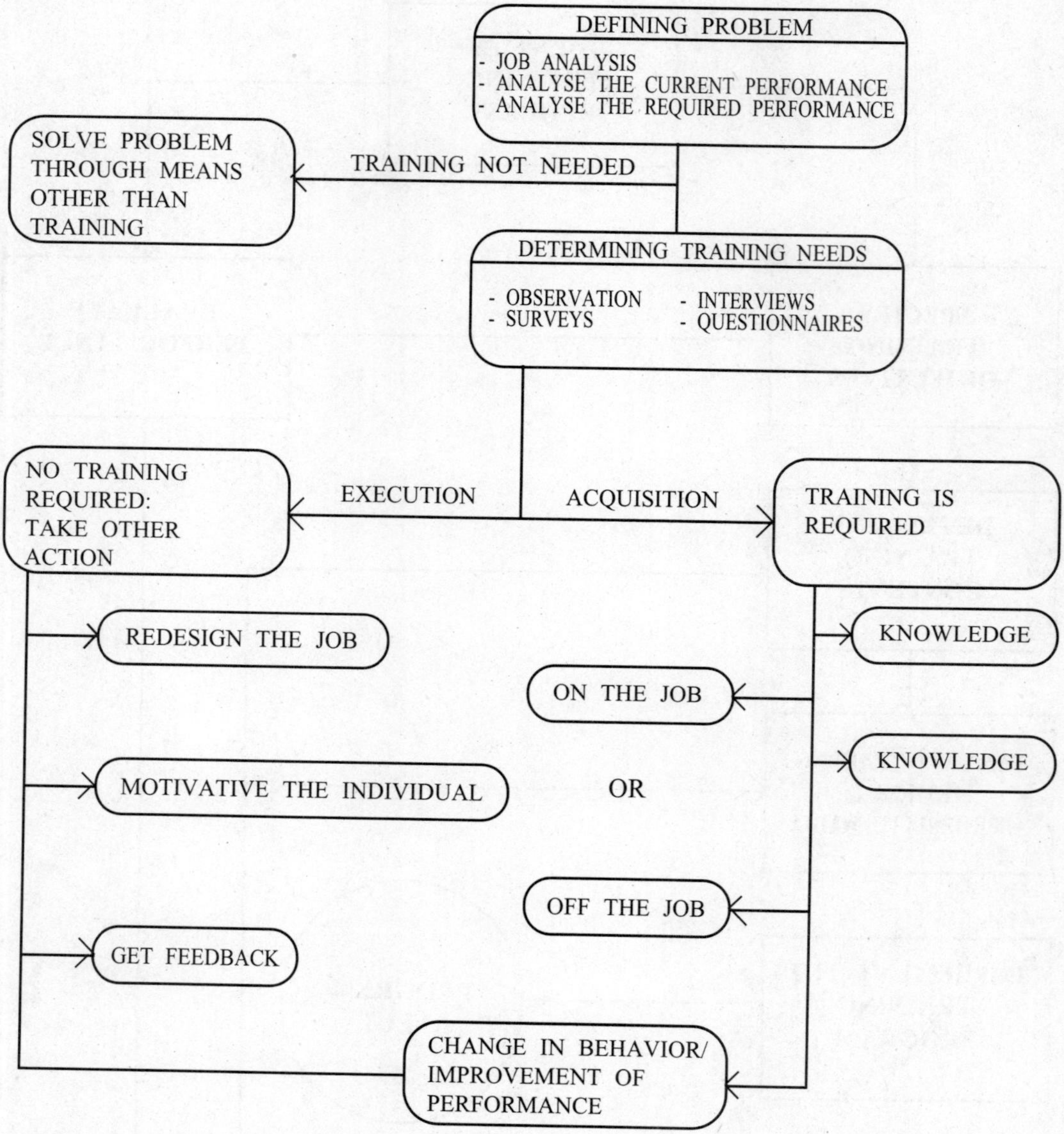

PERFORMANCE DEFICIENCY = (DESIRED PERFORMANCE - ACTUAL PERFORMANCE) = [(C2 + P2) - (C1 + P1)] WHERE C1 = PRESENT CAPACITY OF INDIVIDUAL, P1 = POTENTIAL OF INDIVIDUAL LIKE WISE THE TERMS C2 AND P2 ARE RELATED TO DESIRED PERFORMANCE IF DEFICIENCY IS ZERO i.e. (C2 + P2) = (C1 + P1), THEN NO TRAINING IS REQUIRED

FIG. 16.20 : A MODEL OF TRAINING ANALYSIS

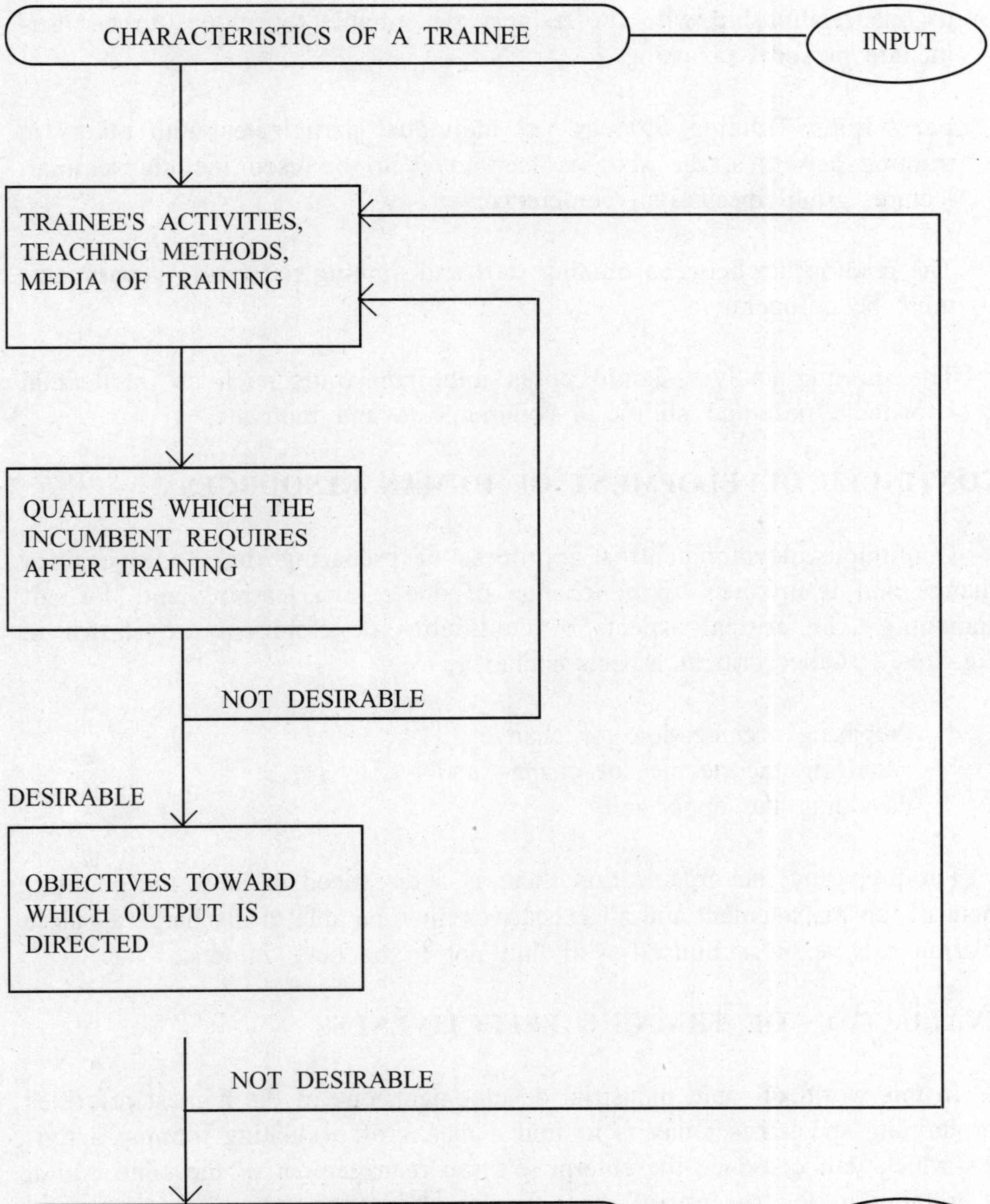

FIG. 16.21 : A MODEL OF ESSENTIAL ELEMENTS IN A TRAINING PROGRAM

to one relationship with the trainer, the suitable techniques to be used include personal coaching.

For 'Group Training Strategy i.e. individual participates with others in training activities, the suitable techniques to be used include seminar, lecture, group discussion, conference, etc.

* The relationship between training staff and training requesting departments must be co-operative.

* The training analyst should poses important traits such as intellectual knowledge/skill and ability to communicate and motivate.

CONTINUED DEVELOPMENT OF HUMAN RESOURCES

Continuous development is a process of preparing the employees for change and it involves taking change of one's own learning and the self managing. The critical aspects of continuous development are shown in Fig. 16.22. Other critical aspects include:

* Preparing organization for change
* Preparing the people for change and
* Providing the opportunity

For preparing the organization there is a dire need to have the commitment of top management and all executives must be able to discharge a public relation role, express himself well, but not to be best trainers.

EVALUATION OF TRAINING EFFECTIVENESS

In this world of rapid industrial development, one of the highest priorities for training specialists today is to find a means of evaluating training activities which will convince the enterprise's top management of the contribution of training to the success of the enterprise[33,34,35].

Evaluation is a concept which is most commonly interpreted in determining the effectiveness of a program in relation to its objectives i.e. management expectation of tangible benefit derived therefrom. However, this concept becomes operational only when there is a real or tangible product to measure

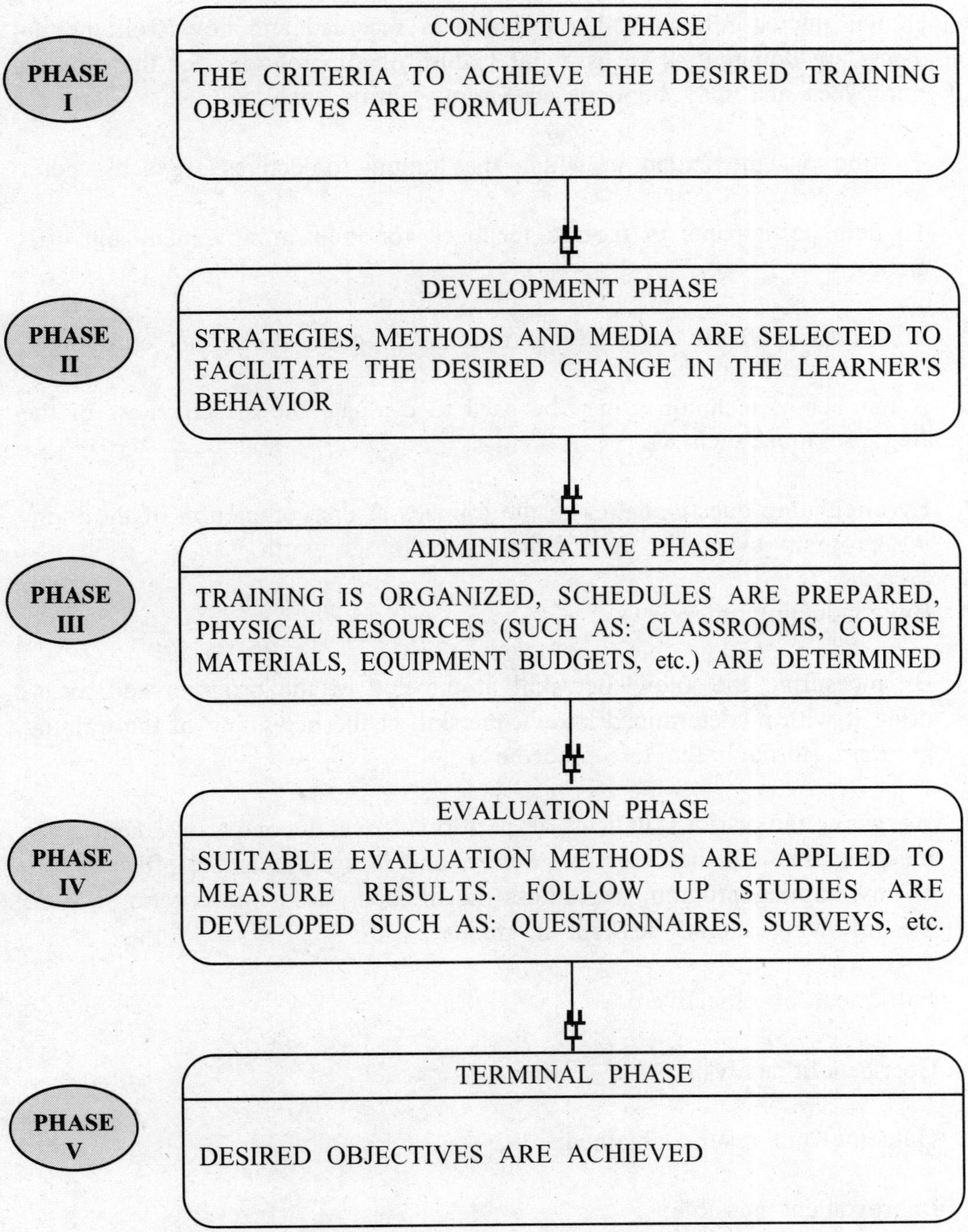

FIG. 16.22 : PHASES OF A TRAINING DESIGN PROCESS

which will increase how well a program is received and how well the incumbents are doing. It is an essential feature of all programs for the training of employees and may be done in various forms such as:

* To find out the extent to which the training objectives are achieved.

* To help participants to receive feedback for their improvement and efficiency.

* To increase effectiveness of the training program during its execution.

A number of techniques may be used to evaluate the effectiveness of the training program; such as:

* By circulating questionnaires to the trainees at the completion of the training program to obtain their opinions as to its worth.

* By conducting interviews.

* By measuring the knowledge/skill at the end of the program and measuring it with predetermined knowledge/skill at the beginning of the training program (through the test procedure).

* By using the various indices of performance and comparing them after the program with the objectives below, and in evaluating the effectiveness of any training program, regardless the methods used, the criteria such as the following should be kept in mind:

* Fulfilment of objectives;

* Cost-benefit analysis;

* Outcome and results obtained;

* Improvement possible;

* Staff required.

Effective evaluation of training performance is of itself one of the criteria for success due to the following reasons:

* It reveals a weakness in the training carried out.

* It provides the means for remedial action which will bring the activity back on course.

* It provides the confirmation that the training is adequate to satisfy the needs and thereby gives the department confidence in its ability to meet its target.

* It provides the employee (who has been trained) with the confidence and stimulation to put effort into his work and to seek promotion and advancement.

From the outset we may conclude that: Effective evaluation of training, effectiveness without doubt is a profitable pursuit from everyone's point of view.

CONCLUDING REMARKS

Training is an organized procedure for increasing the knowledge and skills of people for a definite purpose with an aim to achieve a change in the behavior of those being trained. Training should not be confused with education though to make a clear distinction is not easy as the two overlap each other and in many cases both occur simultaneously. Training, by and large, concerns with increasing knowledge and skill needed to do a particular job and it has a more immediate purpose than education.

For any training program to be successful, the selection of the trainer is of prime importance. The needs of training should be based on the organization's needs and also be influenced by the employees needs. An other important factor is the importance of human relations.

Training is a vital tool of management and is one of the most important activities. Industrial growth cannot be achieved without trained manpower. To keep abreast with the technological advancement as knowledge and skills required by an individual is becoming absolute at a much faster rate; systematic training is now felt in almost all organizations to fully utilize employees talents. Furthermore the need for systematic training has increased because of the rapid technological changes which create new jobs which in turn require some sort of special skills which may be developed in the existing work force only by giving them necessary training.

Training is an important contributor to the goals of organization, is a never ending process, and an integral part of the business system. It aims at bringing about a change in behavior of people at their work places. The effectiveness of a training program depends upon the extent to which an organization is committed to support it, and the use of suitable systems of evaluation i.e. measuring and follow up results. Furthermore, top management must provide a climate which is conducive to continuously learning and growth.

We may conclude this discussion by stressing that line managers have a great responsibility for the training of their employees. They need to co-operate with the training service organization and specialists in determining the training needs, devising suitable training programs, helping in conducting and evaluating the training activities, and above all encouraging and helping the subordinates in applying to their job what they have learnt from training.

REFERENCES AND RECOMMENDED READING

1. Revins, reginald W. - 'Action Learning - New Techniques for Management'/Boland & Briggs, 1980.
2. Revens, Reginald W. - 'The Origin And Growth of Action Learning'/Chartwell Bratt Ltd. 1982.
3. Pedler, Mike. (ed.) - 'Action Learning in Public'/Gower Publishing, 1983.
4. Mumford, Alan. (ed.) - 'Action Learning'/MCB University Press 1987.
5. Farnworth, Terry. - 'Developing Executive Talent'/McGRAW-HILL, 1976.
6. Hall, N. - 'Cast-Benefit Analysis in Industrial Training'/Manchester: University of Manchester, 1976.
7. Kearsly, Gere. - 'Casts Benefits And Productivity In Training Systems'/Addison-Wesley 1982.
8. Kearsley, Gug. 'Training and Technology', Addison-Wesley, 1984.
9. Philips, Jack, J. - 'Handbook of Training Evaluation And Measurement Methods'/Gulf Publishing, 1983.

10. Kearsley, Greg - 'Computer-Based Training - A Guide To Selection And Implementation'/ Addison-Wesley, 1983.
11. Jenkin, J.M. - 'Computer-Based Training - A Guide For Trainers And Managers'/MSC 1983.
12. Harry Barrington A. - 'Learning about Management'/McGRAW-HILL, 1984.
13. Roberts, C.R. Wynne, 'Introduction to Work Study'/International Labor Organization (ILO), 1979.
14. Currie, R.M. - 'Work Study'/British Institute of Management, 1977.
15. Maslow, Abraham H. - *'A Theory of Human Motivation'*/Psychological Review Vol. 50, 1943, pp. 370-396.
16. Maslow, Abraham H. 'Motivation and Personality'/Harper and Row, 1987.
17. Burgoyne, John and Roger Stuart. 'Management Development: Context and Strategies'/ Gower Publishing, 1978.
18. Watsoin, Charles E. - 'Management Development Through Training'/Addison-Wesley, 1979.
19. Woodcock, Mike and John E. Jones. - 'Manual of Management Development'/Gower Publishing, 1985.
20. Huezyorski, Andrzej. - 'Encyclopedia of Management Development Methods'/Gower Publishing, 1983.
21. Taylor, Bernard, and Gordon Lippitt. (eds) - 'Management Development and Training Handbook'/McGrraw-Hill, 1983.
22. Munford, Alan. - 'Handbook of Management Development'/Gower Publishing 1986.
23. Molander C. - 'Management Development: Key Concepts for Managers and Trainers'/ Chartwell-Bratt Ltd., 1986.
24. Blake, Robert R. and Janu S. Mouton. - 'Corporate, Excellence through Gid Organization Development'/Gulf Publishing Company, 1968.
25. Blake, Robert R., and Janu S. Mouton. - 'Consultation: a Handbook for individual and Organization Development'/Addison-Wesley, 1983.
26. Hague, Hawdon. - 'Executive Self Development: Real Learning in Real Situation'/ MacMillan, 1974.
27. Hague, Hawdon. - 'Helping Managers to Help Themselves'/Context, 1979.
28. Woodcock, Mike. - 'Fifty Activities for Self Development'/Gower Publishing, 1982.
29. Jaap, T. and Sheila ampshire. - 'How to Realise Your Potential'/PM, 1981.
30. Jones J.A.G. - 'Training Intervention Strategies'/Industrial Training Services Ltd., 1981.

31. Turrell, M. - 'Training Analysis'/Philadelphia: Trans-Atlantic, 1980.

32. Boydell, T.H. - 'A Guide to the Identification of Training Needs'/BACIE, 1976.

33. Easterly-Smith, Mark. - 'Evaluation of Management Education Training and Development'/ Gower Publishing 1986.

34. Bramley, Peter. - 'Evaluation of Training: A Practical Guide'/BACIE, 1986.

35. Rae, Leslic. - 'How to Measure Training Effectiveness'/Gower Publishing, 1986.

SOME CURRENT SUCCESSFUL PRACTICES AND FUTURE TRENDS IN HUMAN RESOURCES MANAGEMENT

CHAPTER 17

INTRODUCTION

People in organizations from top to bottom have been widely recognized as the key ingredients for the success of their respective enterprises. The chance of such a success can be further enhanced if people are adequately developed. It is, in fact true that Human Resources Development though is one of the most talked about topics, yet is a least productive process in many organizations. Such organizations should be aware of the experience that, has shown that people can perform to their highest level of knowledge and skills if adequately developed, motivated and committed to their performance objectives.

However, in some of the major successful organizations various approaches have been used to achieve optimum results such as the following:

i. open door policy, team work and consensus whilst managing people,

ii. shared responsibility and joint problem solving,

iii. freedom from self-imposed crisis and encouraging creativity,

iv. superior leadership and

v. removal of excessive bureaucracy, etc.

To illustrate the above approaches, some case studies are cited hereunder.

OPEN DOOR POLICY, TEAM WORK AND CONSENSUS IN THE DEVELOPMENT OF HUMAN RESOURCES

Case Study: Case # '1' Delta Airlines Inc.

Delta Airlines Inc. is operating as one of the most effective airlines in the USA. The principle reasons behind this success have been its open communication policy and emphasis on team work and consensus in managing human resources. The Delta's top management did not hesitate to shift the burdens of management to the nucleus of top officers and impressed upon them the value of Delta's employees to its success.

Delta's top management maintains an open door policy and works diligently to keep the line of communication open at all times. Top management of Delta Airlines has adopted the following practice.

Top management meets with all employees at least once in every 18 months in groups of around 30. The management, after giving a formal briefing on the current company activities and their results, opens the meeting to the floor for suggestions, questions or complaints. This practice helps the top management to be updated on all important activities and also to define responsibilities for an effective and cohesive management team. Delta's policy of promoting within is an excellent demonstration of human resources development. For example, Ronald W. Allen joined Delta Airlines Inc. In 1963 as a part-time intern and through development, became the youngest 'Chief Executive Officer (CEO)' in 1987 having received continuous growth as administrative assistant, director, vice-president, senior Vice-President and president before becoming CEO.

Another excellent demonstration of human resources development is to keep high morale and motivation of its employees. For example in early 1990, following a 16 percent increase in passengers during 1989-1990, Delta's management gave substantial corporation-wide raises and cash bonuses.

Delta has a warm, family approach to management that has resulted in staunch, conscientious and a loyal workforce. Employees are paid better salaries and benefits. Employees are encouraged to air their difficulties and problems directly with the senior management. Employees are also encouraged to point out problems and make suggestions. Delta has adopted a policy of full employment and refused to lay any of their employees off inspite of its biggest ever quarterly loss of $18 million. But instead, Delta gave employees an unexpected 8% raise. Such policies are serving as the backbone of the Delta success story. For example during loss making period, as a token of appreciation, the employees of Delta pledged 2.5% of their annual salary and purchased a Boeing 767 jet and presented it to the company as a gift. This is an excellent example of workers loyalty with their employer. Delta also believes in entrusting employees with some decisions, on matters affecting them, which would normally be made by the management. For example mechanics choose their own immediate supervisor.

Delta's practical approach on the above aspects has been proved as the backbone of the Delta success story which has earned Delta the title of 'favorite' (source: references, 1, 2, 3, 5, 6, 8, 15, 16, 17).

SHARED RESPONSIBILITY AND JOINT PROBLEM SOLVING APPROACH IN GROUP DEVELOPMENT

Case Study: Case # 2: Small Parts Manufacturing Plant

In USA alone over 300 manufacturing plants use some form of self-managing work groups having shared responsibility and joint problems solving approach. To illustrate this aspect, a case of a small Southern Plant which manufactures small parts is cited here. This small parts plant is owned by a large corporation and employs around 320 workers. The organization is structured in such a way that various work groups are set up each consisting of between 8 and 12 members with its own leader selected by its members, under the direction of a coordinator who is responsible for a number of work teams and reports to the support team at an upper management level. The coordinators encourage the teams to be self-managing and do things themselves and thereby act as development leaders. This approach has resulted in over 20 percent productivity gains (Source: reference No. 9).

Case Study: Case # 3 (Eastman Kodack Company)

Eastman Kodak Company allowed their divisional manager Ralph Olney to act as a developmental leader with tasks of building a shared-responsibility team, continuous development of individual skills and to determine and build a common department visions Ralph Olney eliminated five tiers of management and 95 employees engaged on the shop floor manufacturing professional films (including Kodachrome and 75 mm movie film) and put hourly workers incharge of "Kodak's 13 Room" operation. Some of these workers were given decision making powers such as: the authority to design equipment to suit their needs, to start or stop the assembly line and even to make purchasing decisions.

This developmental leadership approach and putting the workers in charge of the "13 Room" operation, Kodak instead of $1 Million over its $30 Million annual budget in 1988 turned, in 1989, $ 1.5 million under budget.

Furthermore, zero defect finished films increased from 75% to 99%. However, transition to those operations and departure from the traditional approach of management was not free from difficulties (source: reference No. 7).

FREEDOM FROM SELF-IMPOSED CRISIS AND ENCOURAGING CREATIVITY

Case Study: Case # 4 (Rockwell International)

In one of his recent speeches, Donald R. Baall, President and Chief Executive Officer of Rockwell International emphasised that "student should be encouraged to develop an insatiable appetite for understanding everything they can about their business .... its history, product, customers, and competitors". Fortune magazine has characterized Baall as a strong ambitious leader having deep roots in all aspects of defense and aerospace industries. Baall joined Rockwell International in 1968, but in 1974 he made his mark as the divisional manager of Collins Radio division when after having slashed overhead, guided the flounding company to the road to success and becoming one of the leading communications companies of the USA. In 1979 Baall was installed as the President of the Rockwell International. Between 1974 and 1989, Baall essentially ran the company with CEO Robert Anderson's serving as his mentor. During this period of his presidency he had stressed his main objectives as a manager to eliminate as many layers of middle management as possible and encourage creativity. In 1989 he took over the position of the Chief Executive Officer in addition to the Presidency of Rockwell International. In this capacity, he has been emphasising that American business has become "over organized, overstaffed, short-term and myopic", and business practice of 1950s, 1960s, 1970s and 1980s will definitely not hold water in the 1990s, year 2000 and beyond. He has identified various components of a self-imposed crisis, such as: lack of internal communication and cooperation, lethargy in research and development antiquated manufacturing strategies, neglect of human resources development, lack of focus on long-term viability and antipathy between industry and government. As a remedy to these problems at Rockwell, he believed in creating a new corporate culture which encourages increased individual participation in the way of personal ownership in the company and generation of an entrepreneurial spirit in the managerial ranks. He says, "employees participation and team building are - and will continue to be - two of the biggest drivers of this new revolution in American management" (source: references 10, 13 & 18).

SUPERIOR LEADERSHIP: DEVELOPING A STRATEGIC VISION

Case Study: Case # 5: (AMR, The Parent Company of American Airlines)

In the development of human resources, the role and vision of leadership is of paramount importance. According to Sir William Slim "Leadership is of the spirit, compounded of personality and vision, its practice is an art ... that combination of persuasion, compulsion and example - that make other people do what you want them to do".

Robert Crandall, Chairman of AMR Corporation, the parent company of American Airlines, has exhibited the traits of a superior leader as envisaged by Sir William Slim. He developed a strategic vision and strived hard by putting his entire energy into achieving it. Even in the face of a recession, an industry slump and an annual operating loss, Crandall kept himself charging ahead and managing for the long term. In 1990, Crandall was selected as "USA TODAY/FNN CEO of the year". According to USA Today and Financial News Network (FNN), Robert Crandall was successful "because he developed a strategic vision and put his entire energy into achieving it" (Source: reference No. 4).

REMOVAL OF EXCESSIVE BUREAUCRACY AND REDTAPISM

Case Study: Case # 6: General Electric (GE)

Jack Welch took over as the Chairman of General Electric (GE) in 1981 at the age of 45, from Reginold H. Jones, the popular and well thought-of Chairman and CEO of GE. Jones earned high regard due to his hard effort and professionalism in removing GE from a state of critical cash shortage to a state of high financial strength. On the other hand Jones created many tiers of management causing decisions to be reviewed at many levels thereby leading the organization to an excessive bureaucracy.

Jack Welch immediately identified the problem of excess bureaucracy which he inherited from Jones tenure and went to war to remove it. He streamlined the company from 100 business units down to 14. Although due to Welch's tough and ruthless approach over 100,000 jobs were eliminated through sales of businesses attrition, or layoffs, but nevertheless his strategy proved successful as 12 of GE's units are considered as market leaders, and the world's tenth largest industrial corporation was elevated to first or second globally in the market it serves. Financially speaking Welch's strategy also paid dividends as stockholders earning per share rose almost 50% from 4.9% under Jones to 7.6% under Welch.

Welch adopted an open forum approach in the form of a series of regularly scheduled town meetings to remove more troublesome aspects of bureaucracy namely: unnecessary paperwork, rituals, routines, multiple approval, excessive report work, etc. Although, ideas and opinions were at first voiced hesitantly by people, but soon after those began to flow especially when people could see action taken on the ones already advanced. From "one of the most ruthless, unfeeling CEO's in America" to "a statesman and one of the most visionary of all America's CEOs". To satisfy both view points, he himself provides the answer in the following words:

"We have the ultimate chance at GE during the 1990s to create a corporate atmosphere where it is culturally acceptable to speak out - where telling the truth is rewarded and where bosses who yell at people for speaking up are not".

The secret of successful management approach of Welch lies in his style of leadership who released him from bureaucratic impediments and distraction and instead through 'work out' sessions to concentrate more in focusing on more challenging tasks. Such tasks include examining the myriad processes of the business in order to identify the crucial ones, to discard the rest and to find a simple, better and faster way of doing things. In 1989, Welch was elected as CEO of the year by the Financial World (Source: references 12, 14).

Case Study: Case # 7: Toyota Motor Company

Toyota in August, 1989 abruptly eliminated two tiers of middle management consisting of around 1000 middle managerial positions and people reassigned, primarily to lower level jobs. This was one of the most dramatic efforts to depart from the traditional seniority system in which middle-aged white-collar workers were receiving automatic seniority promotions. Surprisingly instead of expecting resentment and discouragement due to less chances of ascending to higher level positions, some lower level managers were over delighted. Mr. Heroshi Hashimoto, one of the lower level managers reporting to a section chief remarked: 'Before, the Kacho (Section Chief) just gave instructions. From now on, we can ask him to move the pencil too. Now, I feel we are people working together".

This move was probably due to the belief held by many professionals in Japan who felt the need to flatten out some vertical management structure to reduce bureaucratic levels involved in strategic planning and key business decisions. Mr. Yoshihisa Murasawa, a Vice-President of Boonz-Allen & Hamilton (Japan) has been cited as saying:" "By eliminating titles, the organization becomes more flexible. Business is becoming much more complex, and it was too easy for decisions to fall between different sections in the same company". At the time of Toyota's reorganization in 1984, the company's officials thought that quick decision making was important, especially in their efforts to get new car models into production and out into

REFERENCES AND RECOMMENDED READING

1. Banks, Howard - *'Is Delta too nice for its own good'*/Forbes, November 28, 1988.
2. Carrol, Doug- *'Airlines' Big Three Positioned to Dominate skies*/USA Today, June 6, 1990, pp. 9B.
3. *'United Delta Get Eastern Asset Nod'*/USA Today, February 6, 1991, pp. 1B.
4. Carrall, Doug and Mindy Fetterman - *'Robert Crandall: Piloting American Airlines through Turbulent Skies'*/USA Today, Dec. 10, 1990, pp. 1B and 2B.
5. Dumaine, Braine - *'How to Manage in a Recession'*/Fortune, November 5, 1990, pp. 58-72.
6. Graham, Paul A. - *'Air Transport Industry'*/Value lines, December 29, 1989, pp. 261.
7. Hillkerk - *'Kodak Develop New Ways of Managing'*/USA Today, August 8, 1990 pp. 4B.
8. Janet, Guyou - *'Family Feeling' at Delta creates loyal workers'*/The Wall Street Journal, July 7, 1989, pp. 13.
9. Manz, Charles C. and Henry P. Sims - *'Super Leadership'*/Englewood Cliffs, NJ Prentice - Hall, 1989.
10. National Honorec - *'Baall Call for Changes in Corporate Management Practice*/Beta Gama Sigma Hewletter, Summer 1990, pp. 1.
11. Ono, Yumico and Marcus W. Brouchli - *'Japan cuts the Middle-Management Fat'*/Wall Street Journal, August 8, 1989, pp. 1B.

12. Quickel, Stephen W - *'CEO of the year: General Electric's Jack Welch!*Financial world, April 3, 1990, pp. 62.

13. Rowan Roy - *'America's Most Wanted Managers'*/Fortune, February 3, 1986, pp. 18-19.

14. Sherman, Stratford P. - *'Inside the Mind of Jack Welch'*/Fortune, March 27, 1989, pp. 39.

15. Smith, Sarah - *'American's Most Admired Corporations!*Fortune, January 29, 1990. pp. 58 & 92.

16. Ticir, Scott - *'Why the Folks of Delta are walking on Air!*Business Week, August 1, 1988, pp. 92-93.

17. Woods, Wilton - *'Taking Off overseas'*/Fortune, September 24, 1990, pp. 52-53.

18. Wrubel, Robert - *'Cliff Function: Don Baall is proving Rockwell's critics wrong, There is life after the B-1B Bumber'*/Financial World, August 8, 1989, pp. 30-33.

SECTION: 4

DIRECTORY OF LEADING ORGANIZATIONS OFFERING SERVICES IN TRAINING AND DEVELOPMENT OF HUMAN RESOURCES

This section lists several leading organizations that provides services for training and development of human resources. This listing is not comprehensive or official in status and is subject to addition or deletion at the time of each edition of this publication.

Please be advised that this listing is provided for information purposes only as a ready reckoner for the readers who may wish to seek further professional help in their endeavour towards the development of capabilities & potentialities of human resources including themselves.

Accordingly, in no way it is intended to be an endorsement of any particular organization's services and neither the author nor the publisher accepts any responsibility for error or ommission.

* ORGANIZATIONS IN EUROPE

Academic Services, Tavistock Clinic
120 Belsize Lane, London, NW3 5BA
ENGLAND, UNITED KINGDOM

ACEA Educational Trust
141-149 Fonthill Road, London N4 3HF
ENGLAND, UNITED KINGDOM
Fax: 0044 171 281 5723

Action Based Leadership Limited
The Old Church House, Chapel Road
Rotherwas, hereford, HR2 6SX
ENGLAND, UNITED KINGDOM

Alexander Consultancy Associates
37 Cowbridge Road, Pontyclun
Mid Glamorgan CF7 9EV
ENGLAND, UNITED KINGDOM
Fax: 0044 1443 728 048

ARAMARK PLC
Aramark House, Honey End Lane
Tilehurst, Reading, Berks RG3 4QL
ENGLAND, UNITED KINGDOM

ASE
Darville House, 2 Oxford Road East
Windsor, Berks SL4 1DF
ENGLAND, UNITED KINGDOM

Aspey Associates Limited
Lincoln House, 296/302 High Holborn
London WCIV 7JH
ENGLAND, UNITED KINGDOM
Fax: 0044 171 405 5541

Ashton penney Partnership Limited
(Interim), Suite 201, Albany House, 324-326 Regent Street, London WIR 5AA
ENGLAND, UNITED KINGDOM
Fax: 0044 171 580 8376

ASR Computers Limited
Ashton Lodge, Ashton Road
Dunstable, Beds. LU6 1NP
ENGLAND, UNITED KINGDOM
Fax: 0044 1582 667346

Association of Financial Controllers and Administrator,
141-49 Fonthill Road (Second Floor)
London N4 3HF,
ENGLAND, UNITED KINGDOM
Fax: 0044 171281 5723

Aston Business School
Aston University, Birmingham B4 7ET
ENGLAND, UNITED KINGDOM
Fax: 0044 121 332 4731

Audio Book Direct
P.O. Box 4066, London W9 1ZP
ENGLAND, UNITED KINGDOM

Belbin Associates
The Burleigh Business Center
52 Burleigh Sreet
Cambridgeshire CB1 1DT
ENGLAND, UNITED KINGDOM
Fax: 0044 1223 68746

British Olivetti
Olivetti House, P.O. Box 89
86/88 Upper Richmond Road
London SW15 2UR
ENGLAND, UNITED KINGDOM
Fax: 0044 181 874 3014

Burston Distribution Services
Freepost (BS 8911)
Briston BS4 4BR
ENGLAND, UNITED KINGDOM
Fax: 0044 117 971056

Center-File Limited
75 Leman Street, London E1 8EX
ENGLAND, UNITED KINGDOM

CEPEC
Prince House, 36 Jermyn Street
London SW1Y 6DN
ENGLAND, UNITED KINGDOM

Chromasonic Computer Center
48/50 Junction Road, Archway
London N19 5RD
ENGLAND, UNITED KINGDOM
Fax: 0044 171 272 55046

City College
Manchester Fielden Center
Barlow Moor Road, West Didsbury
Manchester M20 2PQ
ENGLAND, UNITED KINGDOM

Cityside Training & Conference Center Limited
Black Lion House, 45 Whitechapel Road
London E1 1DU
ENGLAND, UNITED KINGDOM
Fax 0044 171 247 2145

Coopers & Lybrand
Plum Tree Court, London EC4A 4HT
ENGLAND, UNITED KINGDOM
Fax: 0044 171 822 4652

COPE
255 Ashchurch Drive, Wallaton
Nottingham NG8 2RB
ENGLAN, UNTED KINGDOM
Fax: 0044 115 928 9172

Corporate Health Limited
30 Bradford Road, Slough SL1 4PG
ENGLAND, UNITED KINGDOM
Fax: 004 1753 517889

Cottrills Presentations
The Old Stables, Brook Street
Macclesfield, Cheshire SK11 7AA
ENGLAND, UNITED KINGDOM
Fax: 0044 1625 611724

Cranfield Institute of Technology
Cranfield, Bedford MK43 OAL
ENGLAND, UNITED KINGDOM
Fax: 0044 1234 751806

Cyberaid Limited
Broadlands Hall, Hoverhill
Suffolk CB9 7UA
ENGLAND, UNITED KINGDOM

Data General Limited
Data General Tower, Great West Road
Brenthford, Middlesex TW8 9 AN
ENGLAND, UNITED KINGDOM
Fax: 0044 181 758 6758

Dunchurch EAC
The GEC Management College
Dunchurch, Rugby
Warwickhire CV22 6QW
ENGLAND, UNITED KINGDOM

Economic Conferences
55 Regent Street, London SW1Y 4LR
ENGLAND, UNITED KINGDOM
Fax: 0044 171 409 3296

Education Magazine Seminars
FREEPOST, 128 Long Acre
London WC2E 9BR
ENGLAND, UNITED KINGDOM
Fax: 0044 171 240 8018

Erskine Data Systems
Erskine House, School Lane
Chandlers Ford, Hamshire SO5 3YY
ENGLAND, UNITED KINGDOM
Fax: 0044 1703 262253

Executive Business Channel Ltd.
Dept. PP, Shaw House
18 Shaw Road, Stockport
Cheshire SK4 4AE
ENGLAND, UNITED KINGDOM

Faculty of Business
London Guildhall University
84 Moorgate, London EC2M 6SQ
ENGLAND, UNITED KINGDOM
Fax: 0044 171 320 1422

Fairfax University, UK
Representative Office, EES Offices (M)
14a Stamford Walk, Stamford PE9 2 JE
ENGLAND, UNITED KINGDOM

Filax Limited
65 Tredegar Square, London E3 5AE
ENGLAND, UNITED KINGDOM

Foxx Associates Limited
14 Rocks Lane, Barnes,
London SW13 0DB
ENGLAND, UNITED KINGDOM

GN. Companies
FREEPOST, Amor Way, Letchworth
Herts SG6 1UG
ENGLAND, UNITED KINGDOM

Henley Management College
Greenlands, Henley-On Thames
Oxfordshire RG9 3AU
ENGLAND, UNITED KINGDOM

Hewitt Associates
Romeland House, Romeland Hill
St. Albans, Herts AL3 4EZ
ENGLAND, UNITED KINGDOM
Fax: 0044 1727 830122

Hotel & Catering Traning Company
International House, High Street
Ealing, London W5 5DB
ENGLAND, UNITED KINGDOM
Fax: 0044 181 8406217

IBC UK Conferences Limited
Gilmoora House, 56-61 Mortimer Street,
London W1N 8JX
ENGLAND, UNITED KINGDOM
Fax: 0044 171 631 3214

Inn-Ventory Computers Limited
Westwod House, 88 Warwick Street
Leamington Spa, Warwicks, CV32 4QG
ENGLAND, UNITED KINGDOM
Fax: 0044 1926 30311

Insight Consultants Limited
Sheerspeed House, Healthpark Way
Hamilton EX14 8BB
ENGLAND, UNITED KINGDOM
Fax: 0044 1404 46879

Intellect Business Consultants
28-30 Rivington Street
London EC2A 3DU
ENGLAND, UNITED KINGDOM
Fax: 0044 171 613 3132

Interactive Skills Limited
Cygnet House, Market Place
Henley-On-Thames
Oxfordshire RG9 2AH
ENGLAND, UNITED KINGDOM
Fax: 0044 1491 410262

Interactive Learning Systems
ICL Beaumount, Old Windsor
Windsor, Berkshire SL4 2JP
ENGLAND, UNITED KINGDOM

International Graduate Center
Boston University
30 Kensington Church Street
London W8 4HA
ENGLAND, UNITED KINGDOM
Fax: 0044 171 937 8970

Jasbro Limited
97 Kingsley Road
Hounslow, Midlesex TW3 4AH
ENGLAND, UNITED KINGDOM
Fax: 0044 181 577 0967

J.M. Solutions
8 Corney Road, Chiswick
London W4 2RA
ENGLAND, UNITED KINGDOM
Fax: 0044 181 995 8170

John Matchett Limited
Linden House, 55 South Bar
Banbury, Oxon OX16 9AB
ENGLAND, UNITED KINGDOM
Fax: 0044 1295 272108

John Stamford + Associates
34 The Bury, Pavenham
Bedsford MK43 7PY
ENGLAND, UNITED KINGDOM
Fax: 0044 1234 823041

Junior Woolf Consulting Partners Ltd.
180 Bermondsey Street,
London SE1 3TQ
ENGLAN, UNITED KINGDOM

Kaigen Institute of Europe
4 Tavistock Place, London WC1H 9RA
ENGLAND, UNITED KINGDOM
Fax: 0044 1222 874434

Knightsbridge University
Department International
Stefansgade 22, 2200, Copenhagen,
DENMARK: Fax: 0045 3181 5814

Kogan Page
120 Pentonville Road, Lindon N1 9JN
ENGLAND, UNITED KINGDOM
Fax: 0044 171 278 6348

Kudos, UWCC School of Education
42045 Park Place, Cardiff CF1 3BB
ENGLAND, UNITED KINGDOM

Lesley Harris, School of Management
Thames Valley University (TVU)
Wellington Sreet, Slough
Berkshire SL1 1YG
ENGLAN, UNITED KINGDOM

Lexicon P.DS.
FREEPOST SY 10 05,
Oswestry SY11 2BR
ENGLAN, UNITED KINGDOM

Link Group Consultants Limited
Chestnut Farm, Tarvin Road
Frodsham, Cheshire WA6 6XN
ENGLAN, UNITED KINGDOM
Fax: 0044 1928 735839

Loxton Consulting Group
The Old Barn, 226 The Fairway
Ruislip, Middlesex HA4 0SL
ENGLAN, UNITED KINGDOM
Fax: 0044 181 422 1107

Malpas Flexible Learning Limited
Woodland, 79 High Street
Greenehill, Kent DA9 9NL
ENGLAN, UNITED KINGDOM
Fax: 0044 1322 381335

Management School
Lancaster University,
Lancashire LA1 4YX
ENGLAN, UNITED KINGDOM
Fax: 0044 1524 844262

Management & Profesional Development Department
London Guildhall University
84 Moogate, London EC2M 6SQ
ENGLAN, UNITED KINGDOM
Fax: 0044 171 320 1585

Maritek Limited
Unit D2 Block 5,
Templeton Business Center
Glasgow, Lanarkshire G40 IDW
ENGLAN, UNITED KINGDOM
Fax: 0044 141 554 4240

Marlow Software
Salehurdt, Marlow Road, Bourne End
Bucks SL8 5NL
ENGLAN, UNITED KINGDOM

MBA (SPM) CPRU
The University of Birmingham
Edgbaston, Birmingham B15 2TT
ENGLAN, UNITED KINGDOM
Fax: 0044 121 414 3217

MCP Consulting Group
11 John Street, London WC1N 2EB
ENGLAND, UNITED KINGDOM

MCTS Business Center
Chappel Building, High Street
Winsford, Cheshire CW7 2AY
ENGLAND, UNITED KINGDOM
Fax: 0044 1606 552462

Microgold Unicom House
182 Royal College Street
London NW1 9NN
ENGLAND, UNITED KINGDOM

MRA International
The Clock House, Grove Street
Wantage, Oxfordshire OX12 7AA
ENGLAND, UNITED KINGDOM
Fas: 0044 1235 771167

NCR Limited
206 Marylebone Road, London NW1 6LY
ENGLAND, UNITED KINGDOM
Fax: 0044 171 402 8249

NFHA Training & Conference Services
175 Gray's Inn Road, London WC1X 8UP
ENGLAND, UNITED KINGDOM

Negotiation Limited
Broom House, Chestnut Grove
Great Stukeley, Huntingdon
Cambs. PE17 5AT
ENGLAND, UNITED KINGDOM
Fax: 0044 1480 431 529

Newport University, UK Campus
67-83 Seven Sister Road, London N7 6BU
ENGLAND, UNITED KINGDOM
Fax: 0044 171 281 9298

Nolan Norton & Co.
70 Fleet Street, London EC4Y 1EU
ENGLAND, UNITED KINGDOM
Fax: 0044 171 583 3539

ODL Consultancy Partnership
2 Eton Court, Eton Winds
Berkshire SL4 6BY
ENGLAND, UNITED KINGDOM

OSC (UK) Limited
Dragon Court, Backlin Street
Covent Garden, London WC2B 5LX
ENGLAND, UNITED KINGDOM
Fax: 0044 171 242 0568

Paul Twynam Associates
The Garth, Redacre, Redhill
Bristol BS18 7SJ
ENGLAND, UNITED KINGDOM

Pan Controls Limited
Drummore Doune, Perthshire FK16 6AX
ENGLAND, UNITED KINGDOM
Fax: 0044 1786 85387

Peak Partnership
Donkey Field, Tichborne
Alresford, Hants. SO24 0NA
ENGLAND, UNITED KINGDOM

Personnel Presentation
The Business Management Center
147 High Street, Barkway
Royston, Hets SG8 8ED
ENGLAND, UNITED KINGDOM

Personnel Publications Limited
17 Britton Street, London EC1M 5NQ
ENGLAND, UNITED KINGDOM

Peterborough Software (UK) Limited
Thorpe Park, Peterborough PE3 6JY
ENGLAND, UNITED KINGDOM
Fax: 0044 1733 312147

Philip Lynch Associates
69 The Mount, Yorks YO2 2AX
ENGLAND, UNITED KINGDOM
Fax: 0044 1904 627538

Phoenix Limited
95 Fetter Lane, London EC4
ENGLAND, UNITED KINGDOM
Fax: 0044 171 404 2945

Picture Tel (UK) Limited
258 Bath Road,
Slough, Berkshire SL1 4DX
ENGLAND, UNITED KINGDOM
Fax: 0044 1753 733014

Psychological Corporation
24-28 Oval Road, London NW1 7DX
ENGLAND, UNITED KINGDOM
Fax: 0044 171 482 2293

Psytch International
Icknield House, Eastcheap
Letchworth, Herts SG6 3DA
ENGLAND, UNITED KINGDOM

Rapid Recall Limited
Rapid House, Oxford Road
High Wycombe, Bucks HP11 2EE
ENGLAND, UNITED KINGDOM
Fax: 0044 149 421860

RCS Management Systems PLC
Whitecliff House, 252 Brighton Road
Parley Surrey CR8 2BH
ENGLAND, UNITED KINGDOM
Fax: 0044 181 668 8196

Richmond College
The American International University
in London, 16 Young Street
London W8 5EH,
ENGLAND, UNITED KINGDOM

R. Watson & Sons
Watson House, London Road
Reigate, Surrey RH2 9PQ
ENGLAND, UNITED KINGDOM

Saville & Holdsworth Limited (SHL)
Client Support Center
3 AC Court, High Street
Thames Ditton, Surrey KT7 0SR
ENGLAND, UNITED KINGDOM

SIA Limited
Ebury Gate, 23 Lower Belgrave Street
London SW1W 0NW
ENGLAND, UNITED KINGDOM
Fax: 0044 171 730 6762

S L Electrotech Limited
Loomer Road, Industrial Estate
Chesterton, Newcastle, Staffs ST55 7QT
ENGLAND, UNITED KINGDOM
Fax: 0044 1782 563398

South Bank Business School
South Bank University
103 Borough Road, London SE1 0AA
ENGLAND, UNITED KINGDOM
Fax: 0044 171 815 8280

Spiders Sysrems Limited
Spider House, Peach Street
Wokingham, Berkshire RG11 1XH
ENGLAND, UNITED KINGDOM
Fax: 0044 1734 771214

Speakers International Limited
London House, 19 Old Court Place
London W8 4PL,
ENGLAND, UNITED KINGDOM

Stormage Limited
2 Fleets Bridge Business Center
Upton Road, Poole, Dorset BH17 7AA
ENGLAND, UNITED KINGDOM
Fax: 0044 1202 666413

Stoy Hayward Consulting
8 Baker Street, London W1M 1DA
ENGLAND, UNITED KINGDOM
Fax: 0044 171 487 3686

Strathclyde Graduate Business School
The University of Strathclyde in Glasgow
Glasgow
SCOTLAND, UNITED KINGDOM

Suffolk Management Development Center (SMDC), St. Matthew's Street
Ipswick, Suffolk P13EW
ENGLAND, UNITED KINGDOM

Survey Solutions Limited
7 Mount Mews, High Street
Hampton - Upon - Thames TW12 2SH
ENGLAND, UNITED KINGDOM
Fax: 0044 181 941 8089

Tandon PLC
Dunlop Road, Hunt End
Rettitch, Worcestershire B97 5XP
ENGLAND, UNITED KINGDOM
Fax: 0044 1527 550770

Technology Training Center
21-25 East Street
London EC2A 2AL
ENGLAND, UNITED KINGDOM

Trainers Resources Limited
Business Center West, Avenue One
Letchworth, Herts SG6 2HB
ENGLAND, UNITED KINGDOM
Fax: 0044 146 248310

Trinity College
Ctra de, Mijas, KM5, 29650
Mijas, Malaga, **SPAIN**

Touche Ross Management Consultants
Hill House, 1 Little New Street
London EC4A 3TR
ENGLAND, UNITED KINGDOM
Fax: 0044 171 583 85517

Trafalgar House Construction Management Limited
Mitcham House, 681 Mitcham Road
Croydon, Surey CR9 3AP
ENGLAND, UNITED KINGDOM
Fax: 0044 181 689 6362

University Business School
The University of Durham
Mill Hill Lane, Durham City DH1 3LB
ENGLAND, UNITED KINGDOM

Vertical Systems Intercede Limited
Dennis House, Hawley Road
Hinkley, Leics LE10 0PR
ENGLAND, UNITED KINGDOM
Fax: 0044 1455 890821

Video Arts Limited
Dumbarton House, 68 Oxford Street
London W1N 9AL
ENGLAND, UNITED KINGDOM
Fax: 0044 171 880 8103

Video Production
First Field, Unit 3, 321 Essex Road
London N1 3PS
ENGLAND, UNITED KINGDOM

Walpole Corporate Psychologists
61-63 St. John Street
London EC1M 4AN
ENGLAND, UNITED KINGDOM
Fax: 0044 171 490 2941

West Associates
11 Berkeley Street, London W1X 6BU
ENGLAND, UNITED KINGDOM

Widening Horizon
Phoenix Lodge, 86 Highfield Lane
ST. Albans AL4 0RL
ENGLAND, UNITED KINGDOM

*Data is collated from the advertising data published in various professional journals.

* ORGANIZATIONS IN NORTH AMERICA

ABS Consulting Services, Inc.
16855 Northchase Drive
Houston, TX 77060-6008, **USA**
Fax: 001 713 874 5991

Advanced Consulting International Ltd.
751 Oaknoll Drive, Springboro
OH 455066, **USA**
Fax: 001 513 885 4319

Advancement Strategies
205 South Walnut, Suite 20
Bloomington, Indiana 47404, **USA**

Advent Management Associates Ltd.
P.O. Box 3203, West Chester
PA 19381-3203, **USA**
Fax: 001 215 431 2641

AME Conferences
110 Hartwell Avenue
Lexington, MA 02173, **USA**

API Ambrose Publication, Inc.
Inn Shore Ctr., Suite 210,
Pittsburgh, PA 15212-9812, **USA**

Applied Quality Systems
2845 Hamline Avenue N
St. Paul MA55113, **USA**
Fax: 001 612 633 7903

ARC Professional Group Inc.
134 Ashton Road, Suite E
Hanover MD 21076, **USA**
Fax: 001 301 6211930

Arch Associates
15770 Robinhood Drive
Northville MI 48167-2041, **USA**
Fax: 001 313 420 0122

Arther Anderson & Co
Center for Professional Education
HR Box TD02955, 1405 N Fifth Avenue,
St. Charles IL6017, **USA**

Associated Business Consultants, Inc.
201 E Kennedy Boulevard, Suite 715
Tampa, FL 33602, **USA**
Fax: 001 813 223 5406

Benewal Net
7990 SW 117 Avenue, Suite 100
Miami, Florida 33283, **USA**
Fax: 001 305 270 0627

Blanchard Training & Development Inc.
125 State Place
Escondido, CA 92029, **USA**

Booz Allen & Hamiton, Inc.
4330 East West Highway, Betherda
MD 20814, **USA**
Fax: 001 301 951 2255

BQS, Inc.
110 Summit Ave., Montvale, NJ07645,
USA
Fax: 001 201 1778

Brewer Education Services
2505 Locksley Drive
Grand Praive, TX 75050, **USA**
Tax: 001 214 641 1327

BTI services, Inc
1815 Ironstone Manor, Suite 16B
Pickering, Ontario L1W 3W9,
Canada
Fax: 001 416 939 0752

Bywater
Two Stamford Landing 68 Southfield
Avenue, Stamford CT06902,
USA
Fax: 001 203 973 0345

3C Technologies, Inc
122 Shaffer Blvd., Bryan OH 43506, **USA**
Fax: 001 419 636 72483

CEEM Information Services
10521 Bradock Road, Fairfax
VA 22032-2236, **USA**
Fax: 001 703 2505313

Center for Creative Leadership
P.O. Box 26300
Greensboro, NC 27438-6300, **USA**

Chase Development Center
33 Maiden Lane
New York, NY 10081, **USA**
Fax: 001 212 968 3835

Clark Wilson Group Inc.
1320 Fenwick Lane, Suite 708
Silver Spring, Maryland 20910, **USA**
Fax: 001 301 495 5842

Columbia Quality, Inc.
P.O. Box 506, Oxfield, PA 18069
USA
Fax: 001 610 391 9497

Compliance Quality International
No. 5 Hidden Trail, Lancaster
NY 14086-9685, **USA**
Fax: 001 716 685 0048

Computer Dynamics
1905 Denton, Texas 76205, **USA**
Fax: 001 817 382 5089

Conceptual Systems Inc.
1010 Wayne Avenue, Suite 1420
Silver Spring, MD, 20910, **USA**

Conway Quality, Inc.
Trafalgar Square
Nashua, NH0363-1968, **USA**
Fax: 001 603 889 0033

CTSC
14115, Farington Road
Livnia, M1 48154, **USA**
Fax: 001 313525 1681

de Candia International
120 Village Square, Suite 102
Orinda, California 94563-2502, **USA**

Delaware County Community College
901 S Media Line Road
Media, PA 19063-1094, **USA**
Fax: 001 215 359 7384

Development Dimensions Int.
1225 Washington Pike
Bridgeville, PA 15017-2838, **USA**
Tel: 001 412 257 3223

DK Systems Inc.
444 North Michigan Avenue
Chicago, Illinois 60611, **USA**
Fax: 001 312 644 2703

Donald W Marquardt and Associates
1415 Athens Road, Wilmington
DE 19803, **USA**
Fax: 001 302 478 9329

Douglas M. Sewell Associates, Inc.
288 Towson Drive, Warren
OH 44483, **USA**
Fax: 001 216 847 0988

Dow Leadership Development Center
Hillsdale College, Hillsdale M1 49242, **USA**
Fax: 001 313 481 0509

Excel Partnerhip Inc.
75 Glen Road, Sandy Hook
CT 06482, **USA**
Fax: 001 203 426 7811

Fair Measures
P.O. Box 2146
Santa Cruz, CA 95063, **USA**

Fed-Pro Inc.
5615 Jensen Drive
Rockford IL 61111, **USA**
Fax: 001 815 282 4304

Gilbert Europe
US Operations, P.O. Box 1498
Reading, PA 19603, **USA**
Fax: 001 215 775 9736

Grammer Group
Represented by Salam Associates
Cleveland Ohio, **USA**
Fax: 001 216 321 0444

Hall, Research Technologies
1506 Brookhollow Drive
Santa Ana, CA 92705, **USA**
Fax: 001 669 81506

Hewitt Associates LLC
100 Half Day Road
Lincolnshire, Il 60069, **USA**

Illinois Benedictine College
5700 College Road
Lisle Illinois 605532-0900, **USA**

Interpharm Software Systems
1358 Busch Parkway
Buffalo Grove, Ill 60089, **USA**

Intertek Technical Services
9900 Main Street, Fairfax, VA 22031, **USA**
Fax: 001 707 273 4124

IWCC, Training in Communications
30 East Beaver Creek Road,
Street 209, Richmond Hill Ontario,
Canada L4B IJ2.
Fax: 001 704 547 9178

J-E-T-S, Inc.
2843 Edwin Jones Drive
Charlotte NC 28269, **USA**
Fax: 001 609 924 1078

John A Kean & Associates
575 Edwing Street, Princeton NJ08540, **USA**
Fax: 001 609 924 1078

Joseph Titratlo & Associates, Inc.
5N Longview Road
Howell, NJ 07731-1701, **USA**
Fax: 001 908 367 8898

Kevin Drayton Associates
190 Fox Road, Dalton MA01226, **USA**
Fax: 001 413 684 4648

Kolka & Associates
2193 Spear Point Drive
Marietta, GA 30062, **USA**
Fax: 001 404 6519185

KPMG Peat Marwick
150 John F Kennedy Parkway
Short Hills, NJ 07078, **USA**
Fax: 001 201 912 6158

L.A. Seder & Associates
803 Massachusett Avenue
Lexington, Mass. 02173, **USA**

L. Marvin Johnson & Associates, Inc.
822, Montzuma Way
West Ovina, CA 91791, **USA**
Fax: 001 818 919 7128

Lexington Books
Publishing for Professionals
866 Third Avenue
New York NY10022, **USA**

Lowe & Associates
P.O. Box 130, Middlebury
CT 06762-0130, **USA**

Louisville Water Company
531 Stevens Avenue
Solana Beach, CA 92075, **USA**

Mallow & Associates, Inc.
321 Regatta Way
Seal Beach, CA 90740, **USA**
Fax: 001 310 493 5272

Mcdermott Associates
12212N Paradise Village Parway S
Suite 209C, Phoenix, AZ 85032, **USA**
Fax: 001 602 494 9500

Miller Consulting Group
750 Hammond Drive
Building twelve Suite 200,
Atlanta, Georgia 30328, **USA**

Moorhill International Group, Inc.
20155 Dobson Road, Suite 4-B56
Chandler, AZ 85224, **USA**
Fax: 001 602 732 9089

Moye Company Limited
59 Breadner Drive, Suite 102
Toronto, Ontario, M9R 3MS, **Canada**
Fax: 001 416 248 9187

Natonal Values Center
P.O. Box 797, Denton TX. 76202,
USA
Fax: 001817 382 4597

National Seminars Group
Rockhurst College
Continuing Education Center, Inc.
Kansas City, **USA**
Tel: 001 800 344 4613

N.C. Kirt & Associates, Inc.
900E Proter Avenue,
Naperville, IL 60540, **USA**
Fax: 001 708 357 3349

NLP University, DLC
Box 1112 Ben Lomond, CA 95005,
USA
Fax: 001 408 336 5854

Omni Tech International Limited
2715 Ashman Street, Suite 100
Midland, M1 48640, **USA**
Fax: 001 517 631 7360

Oxford Technologies, Inc.
1414 South Friendwood Drive
TX 77546, **USA**
Fax: 001 713 482 8088

Pachter & Associates
32 Whitley Road.
Cherry Hill, NJ 08003, **USA**
Fax: 001 609 751 6857

Pacific Bell
2600 Cannino Ramon Room 2N502
San Ramon, CA 94583, **USA**

Pacific Western University
600N, Suplveda Blvd, Dept 173
Los Angleas, CA 90049, **USA**
Fax: 001 310 471 6456

Paul E. Plsek
1005 Allenbrook Lane, Roswell
Georgia 300755, **USA**

P-E Handley-Walker, Inc.
17371 Irvine Boulevard, Suite 200
Tustin, CA 92680, **USA**
Fax: 001 714 730 0439

Penton Oversea, Inc.
The Global Language Specialist

2470 Impala Drive
Carlbaad CA 92008, **USA**

Pepiton Berksshire Piaget
3710 Rawlins, 11th Floor
Dallas, Texas 75219, **USA**

Perry Johnson, Inc.
3000 Town Center, Suite 2960
Southfield MI 48075, **USA**
Fax: 001 313 356 4230

Planto & Moran
27400 Northwestern Highway
P.O. Box 307, Southfield
MI 48037, 0307, **USA**
Fax: 001 313 362 0018

Process Management International
7801 E Bush Lake Road, Suite 360
Minneapolis, MN 55439-3115, **USA**
Fax: 001 612 893 0502

Productivity Improvement Center (PIC)
Durham College, P.O. Box 385
200 Simcoe Street, N, Oshawa
Ontario, L1H 7LH, **Canada**
Fax: 001 416 721 3339

Project Manager Mentors
2193 Fillmore
ST. Francisco, CA 94115, **USA**

Prodfoot Crosby
3260 University Boulevar, P.O. Box 6006
Winter Park, FL 32793-6006, **USA**

Fax: 001 407 677 3055

Qualified Specialist, Inc (QSI)
13231 Champion Forest Drive, Suite 104
Houston, TX 77069, **USA**
Fax: 001 713 444 6127

Quality Alert Institute
257 Park Avenue S, 12th Floor
New York 10010-7304, **USA**
Fax: 001 212 353 4526

Quality Management Consulting Services
62 Murrey Drive, Oceanside
NY 11572-7522, **USA**
Fax: 001 516 536 1859

Quality Management Services
P.O. Box 51, 503 4th Avenue
Fayetteville, TN 37334, **USA**
Fax: 001 615 433 6834

Quality Management Solutions
P.O. Box 349, Uncasville
CT 06382, **USA**
Fax: 001 203 442 3393

Quality Sciences Consultants, Inc. (QSCI)
22531 SE 42nd Court
Issaguah, WA 98027-7241, **USA**
Fax: 001 206 392 2621

Quality Works, Inc.
19 Out Town Square, Suite 238
Fort Collins, CO 80524, **USA**
Fax: 001 303 482 0251

Quartet
5700 Old Orchard Road
Skokie, Illinois 60077, **USA**

Richard Chang Associates
41 Corporate Park, Suite 230
Irvine, CA 92714, **USA**

R.P Cooney & Associate
240 S, Monaco Parkway, Suite 707
Denver, CO 80224, **USA**

Robert Leach & Associates
O.O. Box 28241, San Jose, CA 95159, **USA**
Fax: 001 408 267 65527

Rochester Institute of Technology, CQAS
High L. Carey Building, 98 Lamb Memorial
Drive, Rochester, NY 14623-604, **USA**

Robert Peach and Associates
200 W Cornwall Road, 126 Cary
NC 27511-3802, **USA**
Fax: 001 919 319 1984

Sanders & Associates
840 Gressner, Suite 940
Houston, TX 77024, **USA**
Fax: 001 713 465 9742

Scott Technical Services
34 Channey Street, Suit 400
Newton, MA 02158, **USA**
Fax: 001 617 527 0618

Service Process Consulting, Inc.
76 George Avenue,
Edison, NJ 08820, **USA**
Fax: 001 908 549 9117

Silton-Bookman Systems
20230 Stevens Creek, Blvd., Suite D
Cupertino, CA 95014, **USA**

Software Quality Associates
2725 Coliseum Street
Los Angeles, CA 90018, **USA**
Fax: 001 213 292 5288

Southern California University
1840 E, 17 St.# QP
Santa Ana, CA 92701, **USA**
Tel: 001 800 477 2254

Stat-A-Matrix Group
2124 Oak Tree Road
Edison, NJ 08820, **USA**
Fax: 001 908 548 0409

Stern Steward
40 West, 57th Street
New YUork NY 10019, **USA**
Fax: 001 212 581 6420

Thorhill USA
P.O. Box 3643, Wellington
DE 19807, **USA**
Fax: 001 215 444 1365

Time/Design
265 Main Sttreet, Agawam, MA
01001, **USA**

Total Quality Management Associates
11500 Olive Drive Boulevard, Suite
240, St. Lous, MO 63141, **USA**
Fax: 001 314 994 0035

Total Quality Resources Associates
411 Lakewood Circle, C205B
Colorado Spring, CO 80910, **USA**

Trading & Development
1640 King Street, Box 1443,
Alexandria
VA 22313-2043, **USA**
Fax: 001 703 683 9203

Training Media Association
198 Thomas Johnson Drive, Suite 206
Frederivk, Maryland 21702, **USA**

Trisys Software Solutions
9547 S. University Blnd., Suite 131
Highlands Ranch, CO 80126, **USA**
Fax: 001 303 791 8514

Union Institute for Advanced Studies
440E, McMillan Street
Cincinnati Ohio 45206, **USA**

Unique Solutions, Inc.
P.O. Box 1711, Royal Oak
MI 48068, **USA**
Fax: 001 810 435 6349

Verify Consulting Group, Inc.
12021 Wilshire Boulevard, Suite 825
Los Angeles, CA 90025, **USA**
Fax: 001 213 389 9701

Victoria Group Incorporated
10529 Braddock Road
Fairfax, VA 22030, **USA**
Fax: 001 800 845 0767

Video Productions
1105 East Superior Street
Duluth, Minnesota 55802, **USA**

Wickham International Management Services Limited
P.O. Box 86, Sugar Land, TX 77487, **USA**
Fax: 001 713 242 6462

Will Schuty Associates
P.O. Box 1339
Mill Valley, CA 94942, **USA**
Fax: 001 415 389 1630

Wilmington Quality Associates
303 Water Street, Box 9205
Wrightsville Beach, NC 28480, **USA**
Fax: 001 910 256 8149

Wright Quality/Reliability Planning
6 Susan Road, Marlborough
MA 01752-1535, **USA**
Fax: 001 508 481 2631

Xerox Document University
P.O. Box 2000,
Laesburg, VA 22075, **USA**
Fax: 001 703 729 2569

Zenger Miller
17355 Technology Drive
San Jose, CA 9555110-1313, **USA**
Fax: 001 800 566 0636

*Data is collated from the advertising data published in various professional journals.

Author Index

Subject Index